THE STEEL TIGERS:

77TH ARMOR

1940-1992

DONALD L. CUMMINGS

To All Steel Tigers

"I *WAS A* STEEL TIGER

I *AM A* STEEL TIGER

I *WILL ALWAYS BE A* STEEL TIGER"

Colonel Tom Miller (Retired)

Table of Contents

Preface

It has been 82 years since The United States entered World War II. Planning for the war began in earnest 84 years ago. Although the war clouds had been gathering over the Pacific and Europe before 1939, President Roosevelt declared the United States to be neutral in early September 1940, but, formal expansion of the armed forces did not begin until the Selective Training and Service Act of became law during the afternoon of September 16, 1940.[1]

Planning for post-WWI conflicts started during the interwar years with the establishment of the War Plans Division of the War Department (WPD) in 1921. Its portfolio included strategic planning for Army operations and interservice operations. The planners were challenged with estimating the numbers of the forces needed, and when they would be needed for the various scenarios, deployment plans, and operations in to-be-determined theaters. The last did not occur until the December 7-11, 1941 window opened with the Japanese attack at Pearl Harbor and Germany's declaration of war on the US. [2]

Thomas Schelling writes in his Foreword to Roberta Wohlstetter's *Pearl Harbor: Warning and Decision* that the US's analysis of the Japanese courses of action was wrong, and that surprise is caused by many widespread and disparate failures by people.[3]

Henry Kissinger joins Schelling in emphasizing that humans comprise all organizations. Success and failure are caused by the people at all levels of any entity. Kissinger focuses on leadership at the national level where political policy flowing from the commander-in chief's office to the national security community are set. He argues that leaders must first assess the realities of the state of the nation when leadership passes from one to another. This assessment is based on the current national political, economic, and social cultures which incorporate a nation's values, attitudes, and beliefs over time. Next, the new political leadership must determine what it desires to accomplish, and then, it must explain its goals to the population to gain domestic approval and support. Once the policies are in place, strategies flow from them across and through the lower levels of the government.[4]

The policies, strategies, and programs are implemented at the bottom level.

This study of the 77th Armor Regiment, nicknamed the Steel Tigers, begins with the 753rd Tank Battalion established as an independent unit supporting an infantry division during World War II, Reactivated in 1949, it became the 77th Tank Battalion. The battalion's parent unit was established as the 77th Armor Regiment in 1962 and has remained unchanged through the end of the Cold War in 1992 to the present. At least one of the 77th's five battalions has been active during nearly the entire Cold War years to the present. Steel Tigers deployed from West Germany to Eastern Europe, the Middle East, South Asia and Northeast Sub-Saharan Africa and the single remaining battalion is located now at Fort Bliss, Texas.

At this tier, Sir Arthur Conan Doyle best described how people contribute to their organizations by coining the term "brain attic" when Doctor Watson first met Sherlock Holmes in *A Study in Scarlet*.

Watson was dumbfounded by the depth and breadth of Holmes' knowledge about many subjects , but ignorant of many others which an educated person would be expected to know as the two men began taking each other's measure. Watson said something about the earth moving around the sun as presented by Copernicus three centuries earlier, and Holmes did not reply.

Holmes said,

> You appear to be astonished, he said smiling at my expression of surprise. Now that I do know it, I shall do my best to forget it.....
>
> You see, he explained, I consider a man's brain originally is like a little empty attic, and you have to stock it with such furniture as you choose. A fool takes in all the lumber of every sort that he comes across, so that the knowledge which might be useful to him gets crowded out, or at best is jumbled up with a lot of other things so that he has difficulty laying his hands on it, Now the skillful workman is very careful as to what he takes into his brain attic. He has nothing but the tools which may help him in doing his work, but of these he has a large assortment, and all in the most perfect order. It is a mistake to think that the little room has elastic walls and distend to any extent...It is of the highest importance, therefore, not to have useless facts elbowing out the useful ones.[5]

The Steel Tigers' history at the battalion, company, platoon, and section levels is not unlike other tank battalions or units in any other branch of the Army. Each is staffed with specified levels of commissioned and non-commissioned leaders, warrant officer and enlisted specialists, and enlisted soldiers at the junior ranks. The responsibilities of each are commensurate with their positions and experience. The brain attics of all have what they need to perform. The variable is human nature.

Samuel Huntington's 1957 *The Soldier and the State* is the seminal study of national militaries after World War II. In it, he argues that military institutions in all countries are influenced by their capability to respond to demands for national security and national political cultures by balancing their impact. The latter are the sum of national ideologies, values, attitudes, and beliefs. He stated that the function of an armed force is to be successful in combat. The officer corps organizes, equips, trains, plans, directs operations, and controls the human force. The enlisted corps specializes in applying violence with the tools with which they have been provided.[6]

The approach used to study the 77th Armor over time blends the following levels of analysis: national policy and strategy, military strategy, operational art, tactics, and the soldier's view nicknamed here as the "field ration" level.

    a. National Security Policy, National Defense Strategy and National Military Strategy:

    1) The National Security Policy: a document published by incoming administrations and delivered to the US Congress and others that gives its vision of the strategic issues to the Legislative Branch to address agendas and priorities and reconcile differences among entities within and between the Executive and Legislative Branches.[7]

    2) National Defense Strategy: produced by the Office of the Secretary of Defense is the US policy for its security by achieving Huntington's balance of domestic political, economic, and social values attitudes and beliefs, while maintaining the safety of the nation from external threats and projecting power. It focuses on force structure, modernization, infrastructure to support the armed forces, and business practices.[8]

    b. National Military Strategy: prepared by the Chairman of the Joint Chiefs and delivered to the Secretary of Defense specifying how the armed forces will contribute to achieving the goals of the Secretary's strategic goals.[9]

    c. Operational Art: a link between strategy and tactics. The Soviets introduced it. William Baxter describes it in his 1986 Soviet AirLand Battle Tactics as referring to theaters of operations, the branches of the military services, and preparing to engage in various types of military operations. The concept has been adopted by the US and other nations.[10]

    d. Tactics: direction to commanders about preparing for and conducting military operations for their units to achieve the military goals set at the operational level

    e. Field Ration Level: the situational awareness of soldiers, whether conscripts or volunteers in the tactical area of operations, and their reactions in response to their sense of support from their nation and leaders. The importance of this category in this study is the result of the US fighting wars of limited objectives including Korea, Vietnam, and subsequent conflicts elsewhere.

The soldier's perspectives during World War II are presented well in print by journalist and war correspondent Ernie Pyle and visually through the cartoons of Bill Mauldin. Their obituaries document the regard in which soldiers held them. All knew why they were fighting and for how long. Soldiers are introduced during the Korean and Vietnamese wars in the many detailed histories of specific operations. The author's research for this project and chance encounters with veterans of both conflicts resulted in similarities that further research can thread systematically.

Finally, there is the thread linking policy and strategy at the national levels with the men and women of US ground, naval, and air forces at the soldier's level. This link is the US political culture of values, attitudes, and beliefs that have been consistent since World War I that have been passed to them. Summarizing they include:

• General Ridgway's letter to the dispirited troops in the about what was at stake in Korea following the retreat from the Chosin Reservoir. He stated, " The real issues are whether the power of Western Civilization…shall defy and defeat Communism; whether the rule of man who shoot their prisoners, enslave their citizens, and deride the dignity of man shall displace the rule of those to whom the individual and his individual rights are sacred…."[11]

• Secretary of State retired General Colin Powell replied to a question raised at the January 2003 World Economic Forum in Davos, Switzerland about the US's use of military power. He stated, "The United States believes strongly in what you call soft power, the value of democracy, the value of the free economic system, the value of making sure each citizen is free to pursue their own God-given ambitions….There is nothing in American experience or in American political life that suggests we want to use hard power. But what we have found over the decades is that unless you do have hard power…you are forced into situations you can't deal with….We have gone forth from our shores repeatedly in the last 100 years…and put wonderful young men and women at risk, many of whom lost their lives and have asked nothing except enough ground to bury them…. "[12]

List of Figures.

List of Tables

Acknowledgements

Many contributed to this study of the 77th Armor Regiment.

Lieutenant Colonel James Gallivan, the commander and Command Sergeant Major Roger Yuraska of the 1st Battalion 77th Armor respectively invited a reunion of the Vietnam-era Steel Tigers to spend the day with the battalion at Fort Bliss, Texas in 2010. The professionalism and pride in their unit that the young noncommissioned officers and enlisted members of the battalion exhibited who talked with the reunion attendees were the inspiration to begin the project. They presented their briefings and demonstrations without more senior officers and noncommissioned officers in the backs of the rooms.

Robert Rushforth, the original historian of the Steel Tigers, 77 Armor Association passed his archives of email and typed exchanges between several Vietnam veterans including John M, Pickarts, Kevin Dunne and others that served as springboards for research conducted in original sources at The National Archives and Records Administration in College Park, Maryland. James McPhie donated his copy of Army armor and other regimental histories that was invaluable when identifying the lineage of Steel Tiger battalions between 1957 and 2011.

Unpublished personal memoirs, diaries, and recollections were donated by many. In particular, Richard Benson, Joseph Davis, Terry Fauver, Guy Holmes, Neil Howell, Orville Mefford, Carmelo Milia, Thomas Miller, Everett Nagel, Bill Rosevear, Lawrence Wills, and Kevin Zak

Jeremiah (Jerry) Brown and Robert Forman were close collaborators throughout this effort. They reviewed each of the chapters. Vik Khanna, Meredith Gurdak, and Richard Gurdak brought this manuscript together. Ben Andrews and Jack Wilson led the editorial team of Americas Book Writing whose recommendations resulted in invaluable improvements.

A special acknowledgement is due my wife Karolyn who encouraged and supported me during my commitment to tell the story of the Steel Tigers and stressed that I had to know when to end a chapter draft and proceed to the next.

I alone am responsible for any flaws.

Donald L. Cummings

Mesa, Arizona

March 2024

Chapter 1: Origins of 20th Century Armored Warfare

Introduction

September 1, 1939 witnessed two significant events. First, World War II (WW II) began in Europe on that day, and second, General George C. Marshall became the Army Chief of Staff. Between that day and December 7, 1941, when World War II engaged the US in Asia, the United States had to build an Army as well as other military services to assume worldwide responsibilities to begin a new international role for the United States continuing into the 21st Century. Reviews of Volume 3 of Forrest Pogue's four-volume biography, *George C. Marshall: Organizer of Victory: 1943-1945* pay tribute to Marshall for building the Army that defeated the Axis powers.[13]

The 77th Armor's history is caught up in US Army preparations, organization, and training prior to the United States entering WW II. It is important to note; however, that there were two new weapons that made their appearance during World War I that had a direct bearing on WW II: the airplane and the tank. Each expanded the Army's battlefield capabilities.

A 30-Years War: 1914 – 1945

World War I: 1914-1918

The proposal to build a land boat that would restore battlefield mobility was British. Its purpose was to overcome the stalemate along the western front's trench lines stretching from the Franco-Swiss border to the North Sea and the staggering numbers of casualties: 1,500,000 wounded and 500,000 deaths during August – December 1914 alone. The battles of the Somme, Verdun, Passchendaele, and the Marne, among others, were yet to come.

Construction of the initial prototype, the Lincoln 1 Machine, began in 1915. A modified follow-on prototype using a differently designed but improved tank track became the 18-ton Little Willie (Figure 1.1). The prototype's top speed was two miles per hour (mph) and could not traverse off of roads and trails. Little Willie was not ready to be placed into action.[14] The Willie follow-on weighed 30 tons The designers called it a landship because it would cross over trenches, and it was nicknamed a water tank that would carry water forward to the frontline troops to maintain the secrecy of the project. Naval terms including deck, bow, sponson, hatch, and hull stuck with the new weapon. A redesigned prototype, the Mark 1 was known informally as Big Willie, Mother, and the Centipede. Officially, its name was "His Majesty's Landship, Tank Mk1."[15]

The first tanks that entered combat a year later at the First Battle of the Somme when the completely redesigned 28-ton British Mark 1 tank with its crew of six appeared along the German lines between the towns of Flers and Courcelette on September 15, 1916 (Figure 1.2). There were 49 tanks sent to the assembly area; 32 crossed the Line of Departure (LD) ; and nine crossed into the German lines. Although they caught the Germans by surprise, the tanks advanced about two miles before artillery fire, breakdowns, getting mired in ditches stopped their progress. The best that can be stated for their performance is that the new weapon demonstrated potential.[16]

There were two follow-on models after Flers-Courcelette, but the next major commitment of tanks was the British Mark IV at a battle that began on November 10, 1917 at Cambrai about 81 miles southeast of Calais. Four hundred seventy-six tanks along with air, infantry, artillery, and cavalry were employed in a combined arms offensive during the next 17 days. Initially, the British attack was successful; however, the Germans counterattacked forcing the British to withdraw. There were 179 tanks lost. Casualties at Cambrai numbered 44, 000 British and 45,000 Germans.[17]

The French began building tanks shortly after the British. They developed three models: the six-man Schneider CA, in 1916 (Figure 1.3); The Saint-Chamond (Figure 1.4), and the Renault FT (Figure 1.5). The Schneider weighed 13.6 tons, had a crew of six, and a top speed of 5 mph. It mounted a 75mm main gun and had two 8mm machine guns.[18] The Model 1916 23-ton Saint-Chamond mounted a 75mm main gun and four 7-mm machineguns and carried an eight-man crew. This tank underwent a product improvement (Model 1918) and served in a support role as well as combat. There were 48 caisson carriers built in addition to 352 tanks.[19]

Louis Renault, owner of the Renault Automobile Company began designing a light tank entirely different from the Schneider and the Saint-Chamond. Its crew included only the driver and commander who had to stand. The Renault FT had a turret that revolved 360 degrees and contained either a 37-mm gun or a 7.92mm machinegun. It had a top speed of 4.3 miles per hour and weighed only 7.2 tons. Its engine was in the vehicle's rear. The FT also had a tail attached to the rear to assist in maintaining balance when crossing trench lines. This last feature has been a constant in tank designs worldwide since. [20]

The Germans reacted to the 1916 appearance of the British tanks by designing a competitor: the 34.7-ton AZ7 German tank (*Sturmpanzerwagen*) Figure 1.6). Its main gun was a 5.7mm Maxim-Nordenfelt fortress gun and its secondary weapons were six 7.9mm machineguns. A crew of 18-25 rode in the tank, and its top cross-country speed was four miles per hour. Between March and October 1918, 20 AZ7s were went into combat.[21]

The United States' American Expeditionary Force (AEF) commanded by General John J. Pershing landed in France at the St. Nazaire port on June 17, 1917. The AEF had no tanks and adopted the Renault FT. Pershing recognized the military importance of tanks and requested 600 heavy and 1200 light tanks be built in the US. The heavy tank was a joint Anglo-American designed vehicle based on the British Mark-series. It was to be the Mark VIII heavy tank and nicknamed the Liberty tank. The M1917 light tank was modeled on the Renault FT. It was accepted by the Army in October 1918 shortly before the November 11th Armistice. Sixty-four tanks had been completed by the end of WW I. Ten were sent to the AEF. All arrived after the shooting stopped. The US used French and British tanks during its fighting.[22]

Also, a tank command was in the process of organizing by October 1917. Initially, the US plan was to create 10 heavy tank battalions each with 45 British Mark VIs, and 20 Renault FT light tank battalions with 77 tanks each. Eight heavy battalions (301st-308th) and 21 light battalions (326th – 346th) were established, but only the 301st, 326th, and 327th went into combat. Captain George S. Patton, the headquarters company commander and adjutant of Pershing's headquarters, requested a transfer from the general's staff on October 3, 1917, to the new Tank Corps of the American Expeditionary Forces. Pershing approved the request and recommended him for promotion on October 20th. He was sent to Langres to establish the School for Light Tanks at the First American Tank Center on November 10th.[23]

The Army formed the United States Tank Corps in December 1917. Brigadier General Samuel D. Rockenbach was named Chief of the Tank Service. As such, he is the "Father of Armor." The Army ordered 4400 M1917s and about 950 were produced during the 1918-1919 period. The contract was cancelled in 1919. Most were scrapped as the Army reduced its manpower level following World War I. The tank corps that was created during the War was disestablished in the National Defense Act of 1920 and tank units using a new model tank designed during the War but rolled off the assembly line after hostilities were assigned to the infantry to the 67th Infantry (Tank) Regiment at Fort Meade, Maryland.[24]

The US 1st Army commanded by General Pershing initiated its first independent combat against the Germans in the Saint Mihiel Salient September 12-16, 1918 that was followed by the Meuse-Argonne Offensive (September 26-November 11, 1918. The German attacks in September 1914 established this bulge into the allied lines. Pershing's force included three US Corps and several French divisions. The effective and secret movement of troops and materiel from San Mihiel to begin the Meuse-Argonne offensive to support the operations and deceive the Germans was designed and managed by Major George C. Marshall. The tank brigade was commanded by now, Lieutenant Colonel Patton. His brigade had two tank battalions: 326th and 327th with 144 Renault light tanks and 45 French tanks. The attack began at 1 am on the 12th with an artillery preparation lasting until 5 am. Patton's two battalions were supporting the IV Corps' 42d Infantry Division commanded by Brigadier General Douglas MacArthur.[25] The Germans withdrew from the salient, and Patton received orders move off the battlefield at 9 pm on the 14th but only moving during the night. They occupied an assembly area during the night of September 18th.[26] The battle was successful, and the tanks proved their importance in the battle.

The Germans did not surrender at the end of World War I. The German Army was collapsing in western Europe in response to the French, British and American allies' attacks forcing the Germans to withdraw. The German Army's leadership told the government to end the fighting. The German Army requested a ceasefire while the terms of a peace agreement could be negotiated based on US President Wilson's Fourteen Points which were ignored when the final peace treaty at Versailles in 1919. The Germans were told that they had to sign the terms of the Armistice written by the Supreme Allied Commander, Marshall Ferdinand Foch within three days in Foch's personal railroad car at nearby Compiegne, France.

Interwar Years: 1919-1939

Following the November 11, 1918 Armistice, the US Army began to demobilize. The manpower of the Army in 1910 was 81,251. When Europe went to war in August 1914, the Army had 98,544. Four years later, there were 2,395,742 soldiers of which 20,000 officers and men were in the tank corps. This number shrunk to 204,292 in 1920 and 139,378 ten years later. The number reached 189,839 by 1939. Selective Service to increase the size of the Army began on September 16, 1940.[27]

The United States Tank Corps was removed as an independent combat branch of the Army in 1920, and was reestablished on July 10, 1940 as an independent branch of that would control all active and reserve tank units in the combat arms (Infantry, Cavalry, Field Artillery, Coast Artillery. Air Corps, Corps of Engineers, and Signal Corps) and wherever located in the service branches as they were created.[28]

Budgets, not lack of interest in the future role that armored and mechanized forces might play characterized year the interwar years. Much was published by the British and the Germans. Captain Basil Liddell Hart wrote about the indirect approach and the shock effect of rapid armored force maneuvering. Colonel J.F.C. Fuller whom Patton met when Major Fuller was the Chief of Staff of the British Tank Corps during November 1917 and discussed tanks at Cambrai.[29] Others including Ernst Volckheim's articles on armored and mechanized warfare after the Armistice influenced General Heinz Guderian in WW II who applied theory to operations in the fast-moving armored attacks into Poland and France. Volkheim a German junior officer joined its tank corps in April 1918 and was wounded in April 1918 at Villers-Bretonneux. He served in WW II as a colonel [30]

Preparations for US Entry to War,1939-1941

The strength of the U.S. Regular Army in July 1940 was 257,095 that included 14,000 regular officers. The National Guard had 226,837 enlisted soldiers who were trained by the states. Training standards were set by the War Department and the units participated in two-week field exercises annually. The Organized Reserve units existed in plans only but there was a manpower pool of reservists who had received military training between 1920 and July 1040. The Reserve Officer Training Corps (ROTC) graduated 99,228 second lieutenants and Citizens' Military Training Camp (CMTC) graduates produced 5,000 officers who had completed four summers of month-long training at Army bases across the country. There were 400,000 enlisted who completed at least one summer that was the basic training phase. None of the enlisted incurred an obligation to serve on active duty.[31]

It was at this point that General Marshall was assigned as the Assistant Commandant of the US Army Infantry School at Fort Benning (now Fort Moore), Georgia from 1927 until 1932 where he began preparing the US Army for what became second increment of another Thirty Years War (1914-1945) in the students' conceptualization of warfare and identifying future leaders of the Army. His methods of instruction included reducing class size from a lecture hall full of junior officers to a classroom groups and instructors talking informally with a class instead of reading prepared scripts and basing the subjects of the classes on real issues involving but not limited to the following: aircraft; mobile warfare with combat, combat support and combat service support equipment; bad weather;

outdated maps, and more. As a member of General Pershing's staff in France, he knew the emphasis was to foster creativity, innovation, and initiative in solving problems of a future battlefield. He selected his instructors from a pool of officers indicating high potential and giving them areas in which they were to develop expertise. His supervisory method was to release them to develop their classes, help when they missed deadlines, and relieve them if they did not meet his standards.[32]

Another assignment added to his experience in preparation for World War II. President Roosevelt created the Civilian Conservation Corps (CCC) in March 1933 shortly after he was inaugurated to place young men into conservation and natural resource development projects. His goal was to have 250,000 men in the program by July. Roosevelt knew that only the Army could organize, support, and administer the program in conjunction with his military assignments in different parts of the country. He had 19 camps in Georgia and Florida initially and then 11 in South Carolina, and finally 35 in Oregon and Washington State between 1933 and 1938. These assignments were his first major encounters with civilians. He emphasized the CCC member morale, camp-civilian community relations, and character development that camp members could apply in later life.[33]

Adolf Hitler was elected Germany's Chancellor on January 30,1933. In October, Germany withdrew from the League of Nations and the World Disarmament Conference. Conscription and open rearmament including displaying the presence of an air force began in 1935 thereby repudiating the Treaty of Versailles. The Germans occupied the Rhineland in March 1936 and annexed Austria two years later.

Marshall had a direct influence on the Steel Tigers. First was his placement of Major General Troy H Middleton as the commander of the Oklahoma, Colorado, and Arizona National Guard 45th Infantry Division. This division was the one that the 753rd deployed from Camp Patrick Henry on June 8, 1943, arrived in Algeria on June 22nd and invaded Sicily on July 10th. Middleton had a distinguished record becoming the Army's youngest regimental commander in France in World War I. His leadership made the 45th one of the few divisions to go directly into combat from deployment. The authors of the Center of the Army Military History study of World War II in the Mediterranean Theater, *Sicily and the Surrender of Italy*, Albert Garland, Howard McGaw Smyth, and Martin Blumenson, assert that Middleton's division was one of the best trained divisions in the Army when it deployed from the US in June 1943. Middleton, enlisted in the Army and retired in 1937 to join Louisiana State University (LSU), requested to return to active duty after Pearl Harbor, and began in a command training recruits.[34]

Middleton had the additional experience of supporting cartoonist Bill Mauldin, who was serving in the 45th Division's 180th Infantry in Sicily before Seventh Army Commander Lieutenant General George S. Patton who objected to his Willie and Joe cartoons. As an infantryman, Mauldin had been wounded for which he received a Purple Heart.[35]

During Fall of 1941, the Army conducted the Louisiana Maneuvers during August through September 1941 over 3400 square miles in Louisiana with 400,000 troops. The purpose was to assess the readiness and effectiveness of US troops to confront the mobile warfare executed by Germany across Europe. One of the divisions in the maneuvers was the 45th Infantry Division then commanded by Major General William Key, an Oklahoma National Guard Officer and veteran of the First World War. Following the exercises in Louisiana, the Regular Army Middleton replaced Key as the 45th Infantry Division Commander in June 1942.[36]

The Steel Tigers began its unit history of active duty on December 16, 1940 as the 73rd Tank Battalion (Medium) (M), GHQ Reserve. It was redesignated the 753d Tank Battalion (M), GHQ Reserve on May 8, 1941 with June 1, 1941 as its activation date at Fort Benning, Georgia. The initial cadre was three Regular Army Officers, 32 Reserve Officers, and 116 Enlisted men. [37]

Figure 1.1 Little Willie, The First Tank.
Source:By Andrew Skudder - Flickr, CC BY-SA 2.0, Retrieved from
https://commons.wikimedia.org/w/index.php?curid=3250684

Figure 1.2 First combat, British Mark 1 tank at Fers-Courcelette
Source: retrieved from <u>MLU - Dawn of the Tank (mapleleafup.ca)</u>

Figure 1.3 French Schneider CA 1 (M16)
Source: retrieved from <u>File:Schneider CA1 (M16) tank.jpg - Wikimedia Commons</u>

Figure 1.4 French Saint-Chamond tank
Source: the original uploader was Ericd at English Wikipedia. Later versions were uploaded
by RJHall at en.wikipedia. (Original text: *Halsey, Francis Whiting,*) - Transferred from en.wikipedia to
Commons. (Original text: *"The Literary Digest History of the World War", volume V, p. 288.*

Figure 1.5 French Renault FT
Source: <u>Renault FT - Wikipedia</u>

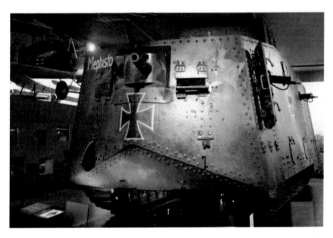

Figure 1.6 German AZ7 Heavy Tank WW I,
Source: By Skyring - Own work, CC BY-SA 4.0,
https://commons.wikimedia.org/w/index.php?curid=41938191 Retrieved from
<u>Mephisto_A7V_in_AWM_front_view.jpg (3503×2285) (wikimedia.org)</u>

Chapter 2: World War II

Introduction

Organization and US-Based Training 1940-1943

The 77th Armor Regiment traces its lineage to the 753d Medium Tank Battalion that was established on December 16, 1940, at Fort Benning Georgia, One of the Army's 72 separate tank battalions that were to be assigned to support infantry, airborne infantry, and armored divisions as dictated by the missions, it became part of the Regular Army on June 1, 1941 and it was redesignated as Company A, 753d Medium Tank Battalion.[38] with 32 officers and 116 enlisted men who came from the 2d Armored Division that was located at Fort Benning also. Lieutenant Colonel Robert B. Ennis was the first commander.[39]

Upon activation in June, the battalion moved from Fort Benning to Camp Polk, Louisiana. Initially, its equipment was a mixture of various tank models and other vehicles. These vehicles were upgraded to modern versions beginning in late 1941-1942 when M3 tanks arrived as well as 507 enlisted men from the Armored Force Replacement Training Center at Fort Knox, Kentucky (Figure 2.1).[40]

Figure 2.1 M3 Lee Medium Tank,
Source: retrieved from M3 Lee - American Medium Tank - Real History Online 02.19.2018

The 753d moved from Camp Polk to Camp Hood (now Fort Cavazos), Texas in April 1942 where it underwent tank training for the rest of the year. The battalion developed skills at the individual, platoon, and company levels, and the battalion formed an opposing force formation to participate in the training of tank destroyer and other tank units.[41] The 753rd organization included three medium tank companies that were equipped initially with the M3 Lee Medium Tank, and one light tank company with the M3 series Stuart light tank.

The M3 Stuart was replaced later by the M5A1 Stuart (Figure 2.3*)*. The M4A1 Sherman Medium Tank replaced the Lee.

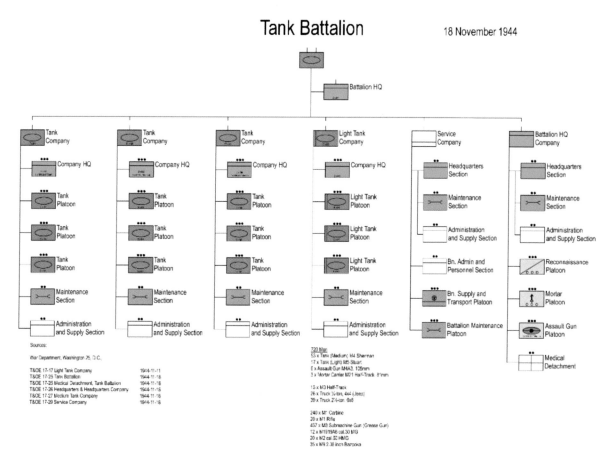

Figure 2.2 Organization of the Separate Tank Battalion 1944,
Source: retrieved from https://en.wikipedia.org/wiki/Separate_tank_battalion, October 2018, and *FM 17-32 Armored Force Field Manual the Tank Company Light and Medium*, War Department, Washington, DC, August 2, 1942 retrieved from <u>FM 17-32 Armored Force Field Manual, The Tank Company, Light and Medium 1942 : United States. War Department : Free Download, Borrow, and Streaming : Internet Archive</u>, November 5, 2022.

The light tank company used several tank models (Figure 2.3). The M2 carried a 37mm main gun and five Caliber .30 machineguns and was used for training only was used only for training by the Army, but the Marines used it at Guadalcanal. The M5 Stuart retained the 37mm main gun and had two Caliber .30 machineguns (one bow-mounted and one coaxially mounted). The M24 Chaffee mounted a 75mm main gun, a caliber .50 machinegun, and two .30 caliber machineguns. It was introduced into the European theater in late 1944.

Light Tank M2   Light Tank, M5 (Stuart)   Light Tank, M24 (Chaffee)

Figure 2.3 US Army Light Tanks M2, M5, and M24
Source: retrieved from M2 light tank - Wikipedia, Light Tank M5 Stuart - Tank Encyclopedia (tanks-encyclopedia.com), M5, Light Tank. M5 Stuart (Light Tank, M5) (Stuart VI) (militaryfactory.com)

The battalion was ordered December 1, 1942, to move to Camp Pickett (now Fort Barfoot) in Blackstone, Virginia. It left Texas and its M3 tanks in January 1943. It joined the 45th Infantry "Thunderbird" Division that was part of the Oklahoma Army National Guard when it arrived in Virginia. Here, M4A1 Sherman Medium Tanks were issued. The battalion employed its new vehicles undergoing tank gunnery and small unit tactical training (See Figure 2.4).[42]

Figure 2.4 M4A1 Sherman, Medium Tank
Source: retrieved from
https://www.bing.com/images/searchq=M4A1+Sherman+Tank&id=6403DE85B8486027A15F1D7A-4F93B1995E29DA89&FORM=IDBQDM 04.25.2018

While the 753rd Tank Battalion was moving to Virginia, the Soviets were on the verge of defeating the Germans at Stalingrad which occurred on February 2d. The Red Army continued on the offensive west toward Ukraine and Belarus. The next major battle occurred at Kursk. It began on July 5th the day after the 753d sailed for Sicily and ended on August 23rd. More than two million soldiers and 6,000 tanks took part. The Soviet victory ended German offensive operations in the east forcing them to shift to the defense.

US forces in the Pacific theater established control of the Solomon Island archipelago in February 1943 after the battles for Guadalcanal that included two USMC and two US

Army divisions. Two regiments from the 7th Infantry Division and units of the 10th Infantry Division were fighting Japanese forces who landed on the Aleutian Islands of Attu and Kiska.in June 1942. This campaign ended on August 14, 1943.

Planning for the next step in the Western European theater following the Axis defeat in North Africa began in November 1942 among the national-level policymakers President Roosevelt, Prime Minister Churchill, and the military strategy level planners, and then US-British combined chiefs of staff before the North African campaign Operation *TORCH* began. The story of why Sicily was chosen is told in great detail in Albert Garland and Howard Smyth's *Sicily and the Surrender of Italy: United States Army in World War II* (1993). It is enough to state here in the history of the 753rd Tank Battalion that the goal was to force Italy out of its partnership with Germany. The collapse of Italy would force Hitler to move troops into Italy to protect his southern flank and relieving some of the pressure on Stalin's to continue exploiting his successes on the eastern front.[43]

Garland and Smyth, again, detail the weakening of the Hitler-Mussolini alliance and the internal debates and planning within each country's national policymaking levels and their advisors and the German and Italian military strategy levels staffs examining options. The alliance remained firm until December 1941when Hitler sent the German Second Air Force under Field Marshal Albert Kesselring to Italy. The alliance continued deteriorating into Spring 1943 after the effects of the loss at Stalingrad weaved through Germany's manpower and industrial capabilities. Factions within the Italian military's senior ranks formed an anti-Mussolini coalition and were ready to act upon the King Victor Emmanuel III's approval by June[44].

Simultaneous with internal Italian intrigue, Hitler and his senior staff including Field Marshal Erwin Rommel conferred during May 20-22, 1943, over courses of action the Germans could initiate should Italy withdraw from the Axis. The result was Operation Plan *ALARICH*. The Germans would move up to 14 divisions into Italy under Rommel's command to take over Italian military installations if Italy left the war. Rommel was then reassigned to command German troops in Greece on July 21st. Plan *ALARICH* remained on a shelf until the Italian government removed Mussolini from office and arrested him on July 25th two weeks after US and British forces attacked Sicily.[45] This surprised the Germans and the US-British allies. Plan *ALARICH* came off of the shelf and adapted its framework to meet the current situation using it to prepare for the Allied invasion. Rommel returned from Greece to command the German units in northern Italy.[46]

Ground combat tank unit organization in World War II was symmetrical. Figure 2.2 above displays the organization of a separate US tank battalion assigned to an infantry division. Table 3.1 below presents an example of a German tank battalion. German and US infantry and armored divisions were comparable also

Battalion HHC Three tanks	Workshop Company	Three Panzer Companies Two tanks; 1 officer 1 senior NCO First Sergeant equivalent, 1 Noncommissioned officer, 14 crew and other enlisted
Communications Platoon	Two Workshop Platoons	Three platoons Four tanks 1 platoon leader, 19 crew
Armored Reconnaissance Platoon	Recovery Platoon	Medical
Area Reconnaissance Platoon	Armorer Detachment	Vehicle Repair detachment
Engineer Platoon	Communications Detachment	Two combat train vehicles
Antiaircraft Platoon	Spare Part Detachment	Baggage train
Replacement Crews: two NCOs, and 8 crew		

Table 2.1 German Tank Battalion
Source: adapted from German Heavy Tank Battalion retrieved from German heavy tank battalion - Wikipedia, and German Heavy Tank Company (1944-45) (battleorder.org). November 10, 2022

To Europe 1943

The 753d moved into Camp Patrick Henry in Warwick County, Virginia at the beginning of April 1943 to prepare for deployment with the division. Part of this pre-deployment preparation included training loading and unloading equipment onto Landing Ship Tanks (LSTs) at the Naval Amphibious Training Center, Little Creek located in Virginia Beach, Virginia. [47]

The 85th and 88th Infantry Divisions processed through Camp Patrick Henry in 1943 in addition to the 45th Infantry Division, and the 31st, 91st, and 92d Infantry Divisions as well as the 2d Cavalry Division left for the war in Europe in 1944.[48] Figure 2.5 below displays the base during World War II on the left and the same land today. In addition to the barracks and mess halls the camp had a movie theater, post office and a rail system to move the troops to the Port of Embarkation at Hampton Roads. A portion of Camp Patrick Henry became the initial Williamsburg-Newport International Airport (International Air Transport. Association Code PHF).[49].

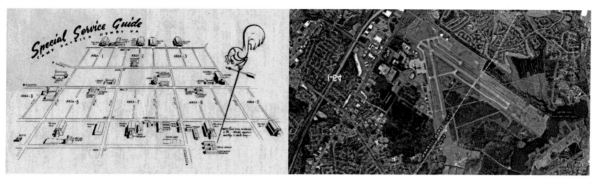

Figure 2.5 Camp Patrick Henry in WW II and Today,
Source: US Department of the Army - US Department of the Army Soldiers Welcome Home Guide,
Retrieved from Camp Patrick Henry - Wikipedia retrieved from Camp Patrick Henry | Military Wiki |
Fandom, and Williamsburg-Newport News International Airport, retrieved from Williamsburg Newport
News Airport 2022.png, October 5, 2022.

The 45th Infantry Division departed the United States on 13 attack transports five cargo attack vessels, and the combined headquarters and command ship USS *Ancon* (AGC-4) (Figure 2.6).[50]The division's ships joined Convoy UGF-9 on June 8,1943 and landed in Oran, Algeria on June 22nd.[51] From Oran, the division sailed for Sicily on July 4th, and the *Ancon* carried Lieutenant General Omar Bradley.[52]

Figure 2.6 USS *Ancon* (AGC 4)
Source: retrieved from USS Ancon (AGC-4) - Wikipedia October 7, 2022

Colonel Anthony F Daskevitch II, author of a 2008 Army War College study of separate tank battalions, *Insights in modularity: 753rd Tank Battalion in World War II* states that he could neither discover any records of tank-infantry combined arms training during the battalion's pre-deployment period in the United States nor while it was preparing for the Sicilian invasion with the 45th Infantry Division.[53] What did not occur before the deployment, happened whenever the 753rd and the infantry units to which its companies and platoons were attached were pulled away from the front lines for maintenance, tank crews proficiency training, servicing weapons, receiving replacements, and other activities throughout the battalion's service in World War II.

Major Joseph G. Felber, a member of the United States Military Academy's class of 1927, assumed command of the 753d on March 1, 1943.[54] The battalion was reorganized into a Headquarters Company, three tank companies, and a service company. The 753d left the United States for a 33-day trip on five LSTs in late April 1943 landing in Africa on May 26, 1943.[55]

Sicily 1943

A discrepancy in the information available exists about the date that the 753rd Tank Battalion left the US for Africa and with what major command. Daskevitch and others state that the 753rd was attached 45th Infantry Division departed the US and deployed to North Africa as stated immediately above. Histories of the 45th Infantry division state that the division left Hampton Roads, Virginia on June 8th on 18 ships. All sources agree that the 753rd landed in Sicily with the 45th Division on July 10th.[56] A 1946 history of the 45th division identifies the 753rd as a 45th Division unit. It states:

> July 16, 1943: Division began to move out to area east of Riesi. The 157th RCT and 189 FA battalion started at 0600B. 179th and 180th CTs held current positions until uncovered by passing British across front from east to west. 45th Rcn Tr and 753rd Tk Bn followed 157th. At 2130B orders were issued to CO 157th at 0400B 17 July. Seize the high ground north of Piertrapezia supported by 158th and 189th FA Bns and with Co 2nd Cml, one Plat, 45th Rcn Tr Co A 120th Engr Bn, and Co C 753rd Tn Bn attached.[57]

The same history of the 45th Infantry Division states the 191st and the 753rd Tank Battalions were both attached to the 45th 's landing and initial fighting in Italy that began on September 10th.[58] The 191st was a 5th US Army unit arrived at Bizerte, Tunisia in August 1943. It did not participate in the fight for Sicily.[59] Finally, "Appendix A, Composition of US Forces on D-Day 10 June, 1943" identifies the 753rd Medium Tank Battalion as a 45th Infantry Division unit in   Albert N. Garland and Howard McGaw Smyth, with Martin Blumenson, *Sicily and the Surrender of Italy: United States Army in World War II: The Mediterranean Theater of Operations*.[60]

The campaign for control of North Africa had ended successfully by the time the 753d arrived. Tunisia surrendered on May 13, 1943 with the capture of 250,000 prisoners of war. The 753d went to war on July 10, 1943 in Operation *HUSKY* as part of the 45th Infantry Division when Company C landed on a Sicilian beach near Santa Croce Camerina, southeast of Gela. The division was one of three US infantry divisions comprising US II Corps that was commanded by Lieutenant General Omar Bradley. Charlie Company was attached to the 3rd Battalion, 157th Infantry and defeated five Italian tanks beginning at 1400 hours on the 10th. Companies A, B, and the battalion headquarters debarked on July 11th.[61] Six weeks after it landed in Sicily, Company B's third platoon that was attached to the 2d Battalion of the 7th Infantry Regiment supported the entry of the 3rd Infantry Division into Messina on August 16, 1943.

Operations and Missions

Although formally a separate tank battalion subordinate to the 45th Infantry Division, platoons, and companies of the 753d supported various infantry units of II Corps including the 82d Airborne, 3rd Infantry, and the 1st Infantry Divisions during Operation HUSKYs drive to Messina throughout the 39-day campaign in Sicily. See Table 3.2 below.

753d Unit	Supported Unit	Dates	Location	Comment
C Company	3d Bn, 157th Inf Regt, 45th ID	July 10-11, 1943	Comiso	
B Company	Elements of 82d Abne Div	July 11, 1943	Vittoria	
B Company	180th Inf Rgt, 45th ID	July 11-13	Biscari	
A Company	179th Inf Regt, 45th ID	July 13-16	Caltigirone	
A Company	70th Tank Bn, and 16th, 18th, and 26th Inf Regts, 1st ID	July 16-22	Enna; Alimena; Bompietro; and Petralia	
C Company	157th Infantry Regt, 45th ID	July 23	Campofelice	
1 platoon (Not further identified)	3d ID battalion taskforce	August 8	Sant' Agata	Amphibious operation (battalion-size)
One platoon Company B	3d ID battalion task force	August 11	Brolo	Amphibious operation (battalion-size) received Presidential Unit Citation
3d Platoon, Company B	2d Battalion, 7th Inf Regt, 3d ID	August 16	Messina	

Table 2.2 753rd Tank Battalion in Sicily,
Source: Adapted from Colonel Anthony F. Daskevich II, Strategy Research Report: Insights into Modularity 753rd Tank Battalion in World War II, Carlisle, PA, US Army War College March 15, 2008, p.8-11.

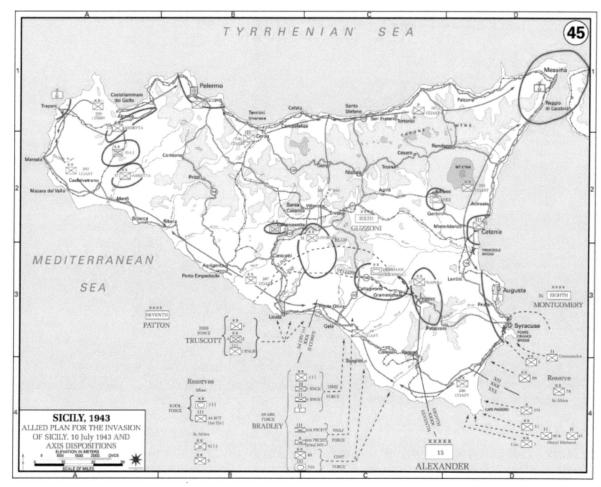

Figure 2.7 Allied Plan for Invading Sicily, July 1943,
Source: Sicily 1943, Invasion of Sicily 10 July 1943 and Axis Dispositions, retrieved from emersonkent
.com, June 1, 2023

Figure 2.8 displays the change in the invasion plan that occurred on July 13th. Despite successful attacks northward by General Patton's US Seventh Army, British General Alexander, commander of the 15th Army Group that included the missions of invading Sicily and Italy, grew concerned about protecting the British General Montgomery's Eighth Army's flank from a German counterattack using the existing west-east road network across central Sicily.[62] For the invasion of Italy, Lieutenant General Mark Clark's US Fifth Army replaced the Seventh.

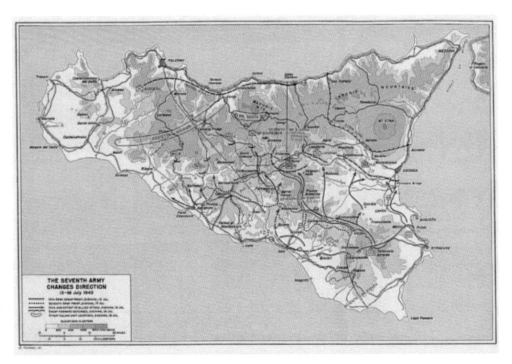

Figure 2.8, Seventh Army Alters its Sicilian Invasion Plan, Source: The Seventh Army Changes Direction, 13-18 July 1943, retrieved from <u>The War in Italy 1943-45 and Environs…: The Allied invasion of Sicily – Experience Part III</u> June 1, 2023

The Enemy

Italy: The defense of Sicily was the responsibility of the Italians There were 200,000 Italians troops in Sicily in July 1943. The Italian *Sixth Army,* present in Sicily since 1941*,* controlled *XII Corps* with its two subordinate infantry divisions: the *26th* and *28th*, and the *XVI Corps* that commanded the *4th* and *54th* infantry divisions. These four divisions (26th, 28th, 4th, and 54th) were combat (mobile) divisions. In addition, there were six coastal defense divisions, and two coastal brigades and one coastal regiment and under *Sixth Army* control. *Sixth Army* also known as *Armed Forces Command Sicily.*[63]

Germany: A troop list of German units to assist the Italians in the southern portion of Italy began to be identified beginning on May 6, 1943 when Kesselring offered Mussolini the *Hermann Goering Panzer Division* which included a regiment of airborne infantry to be sent to Italy which Mussolini accepted. The orders for the deployment occurred on May 10th and occurred on June 12th. The *15th Panzer Grenadier (motorized infantry) Division* was identified on May 23rd and the *16th Panzer Division*. The *XIV Panzer Corps* was in Italy but to be assigned once its reconstitution finished in June. The German high command responded to an Italian June 14th request for additional German reinforcements by ordering the *29th Panzer Grenadier* and *26th Panzer* divisions to southern Italy on June 17th. The 3rd *Panzer Grenadier Division* would be available to deploy to southern Italy.[64] The *15th Panzer Grenadie*r, *29th Panzer Grenadier, Hermann Goering* Divisions, and elements of *XIV*

Panzer Corps were the principal German defenders of Sicily, and they withdrew successfully across the Messina Strait to Italy during August 10 through August 16th along with the Italians.[65]

Italy 1943

Operations and Missions

The allies demanded that Italy surrender unconditionally before they invaded Italy. An armistice was signed on September 3 by Italian Brigadier General Giuseppe Castellano and General Eisenhower's Chief of Staff Major General Walter Bedell Smith This occurred the same day that British forces launched Operation *BAYTOWN* that was Phase 1 of the allied assault on the Italian mainland. The British moved from Sicily across the Strait of Messina and landed at Calabria. Italy's unconditional surrender occurred on September 8th.[66] Phases two and three began the next morning, September 9th: Operation *SLAPSTICK* with Montgomery's Eighth British Army's landings at Taranto, Italy, and Operation *AVALANCHE* in which Clark's US Fifth Army, landed in the vicinity of Salerno, Italy. Table 2.3 displays a summary of the Fifth Army's order of battle.

The German order of battle included the following: 2nd Parachute Division; 3rd Panzer-Grenadier Division; 24th Panzer Division; 26th Panzer-Grenadier Division; 44th Infantry Division; 65th Infantry Division; 71st Infantry Division; 76th Infantry Division; 94th Infantry Division; 305th Infantry Division; and SS Panzer Division Liebstandarte Adolf Hitler.[67]

US Fifth Army	Lieutenant General Mark Clark
US VI Corps	Major General Ernest Dawley
US 3rd Infantry Division	Major General Lucian Truscott
US 34th Infantry Division	Major General Charles Ryder
US 36th Infantry Division	Major General Fred Walker
US 45th Infantry Division	Major General Troy Middleton
British X Corps	Lieutenant General Richard McCreery
British 46th Infantry Division	Major General John Hawksworth
British 56th Infantry Division	Major General Douglas Graham
British 7th Armored Division	Major General George Erskine
Army Group Reserve	
US 82nd Airborne Division	Major General Matthew Ridgway
US 1st Armored Division	Major General Ernest Harmon

Table 2.3 Allied Invasion of Italy Order of Battle
Source: retrieved from Allied invasion of Italy order of battle - Wikipedia

The U.S. Fifth Army's attack north would follow along Italy's east coast. Salerno was the initial objective. The British Eighth Army would attack from the toe of Italy north along the Adriatic seacoast. The goal was to reach Rome as soon as possible. Company C of the

753rd tank battalion would operate separately from the battalion initially. It was attached to the 45th Infantry Division's 179th Regimental Combat Team (RCT) and this unit's mission was to support the Fifth Army's drive to Salerno by serving as the invading force's reserve. For this mission, the battalion commander reinforced the company with a mortar section and a section of assault guns. He added one-third of the 753d's medical and maintenance assets also. Table 2.4 Summarizes the 753d's missions, attachments, and detachments during the Italian campaign.

753d Unit	Supported Unit	Dates	Location	Comment
Company C	179th Regtl Combat Team	September 6. 1943	Termini Imerese	Reinforced with mortar and assault gun sections; one-third of bn medics and maintenance
Company C	179th RCT; 5th Army Reserve	September 10-18	Paestum	Landed near Paestum to reinforce 36th ID
Company C		September 19	Paestum	Returns to 753d Tank Bn. Bn released from 45th ID and assigned as VI Corps reserve
753d Tank Bn	36th Inf Div	Sep 21, 1943	Paestum	Stand down
		Early Nov		Move to assembly area near Capua
		Nov 17, 1943	Mignano	Began relieving 3d ID
	143d Inf Rgt	Dec 12-15	San Pietro	Battle of San Pietro
	6th Armored Inf Regt, 1st Armored Division	December 28 thru January 4-7, 1944	Monte Porchia	Joins Combat Command B, 1st Armored Division; Attacks Monte Porchia; *1st AD arrived in Nov*
	36th ID 12-16 Jan; then to 1st Tank Grp, Feb 12 to New Zealand Corps	Jan 12 – March 25	Cassino	Organized as a task force with infantry battalion, recon troop, Tank destroyer company and engineer company. 1st Tank Group renamed 1st Armored Group
	36th ID	March 25-May	Assembly area near Naples	Unit reorganized, received replacements, and trained
	88th Infantry Division and then French Expeditionary Corps 2d Moroccan Division and 3rd Algerian Division	May		Seized Ausonia, Esperia, Pico, and Utri
	VI US Corps with 36th ID	Late May – June 24		Assist Anzio beachhead breakout and move to Rome
		June 24	Assembly Area vicinity Salerno	Reorganization, maintenance, replacements, and training with amphibious tanks

Table 2.4 753rd Tank Battalion in Italy
Source: adapted from Colonel Anthony F. Daskevich II, Strategy Research Report: Insights into Modularity 753rd Tank Battalion in World War II, Carlisle, PA, US Army War College March 15, 2008, p.12-27

The C Company team joined the 179th on September 6th and sailed across the Tyrrhenian Sea for Italy on September 8th from Palermo, Sicily. The US Fifth Army began landing on September 9th, and the reserve 179th force landed on the morning of September 10[th.] It used the morning to organize for battle near the ancient Greek coastal town of Paestum in Italy's Campania province about 30 miles south of Salerno.[68] It moved to contact inland toward the city of Persano between the Sele and Calore rivers and met the enemy that afternoon. They encountered a determined defense for the next several days. The 753d's main body landed five days later with rear elements of the 45th Infantry Division.[69]

Figure 2.9 presents the allied command's progress from September 17, 1943 through the end of the war.

Figure 2.9 The Allied Campaign in Italy September 9 1943-May 7, 1945
Source: retrieved from Maps on the Web-The Italian front, WW2. (zoom-maps.com)., (100) Pinterest.

The battle to gain a foothold in Italy by capturing Salerno lasted until September 19, 1943, for Company C when it returned to its parent unit that was located near Paestum. The battalion was released from the 45th Infantry Division and went into the reserve of VI Corps.[70] The 753d was attached next to 36th Infantry Division on September 21st and began a six-week stand down while it received replacements, performed maintenance, and conducted training including exercises with divisional infantry units.[71]

The battalion moved with the 36th Infantry Division to an assembly area near Capua that is about 16 miles north of Salerno in November. The US Fifth Army's mission was to seize Rome that was 120 miles north. The German commander in the South, Air Force Field Marshall Albert Kesselring, ordered a belt of several defensive lines about 18 miles apart to defeat or delay the allied attack. The first belt of fortified defenses that the troops of the Fifth Army encountered was the Winter Line. It comprised the Gustav, Bernhardt (aka Reinhard Line), and the Hitler lines. Kesselring's defense had two consequences: first, the allies agreed to Fifth US Army's attempting to turn the German flank by conducting an amphibious landing at Anzio, Italy that was 39 miles from Rome; second, the allies did not reach Rome until June 4, 1944. The Germans continued fighting in Italy until May 2, 1945, the same day that Berlin fell to the Soviets.

The Gustav Line was the most heavily fortified. It crossed Italy from the Tyrrhenian to the Adriatic coasts and was centered on the town of Cassino along Highway 6 (now Route SS6). Cassino, about 90 miles south of Rome is the entry to the Liri Valley to Rome in the Rapido and Liri River valleys. To get to Cassino, the attacking force had to break through the Bernhardt Line about eight miles in front of the Gustav Line. This was known also as the Reinhard Line (Mignano Gap). This line was neither as heavily manned nor were its fortifications as developed as those along the Gustav barrier. Its purpose was to slow the allied advance toward the Gustav Line. The Mignano Gap was a mile-wide opening at 600 to 700 feet above sea level between Monte Lungo located on the right near the town of San Pietro and three mountains, Camino, la Difensa, and Maggiore, which formed the Camino-Difensa-Maggiore mass also containing Monte Rotondo on the left.[72] Figure 2.10 presents the area of operations from the gap at the Reinhard Line north to Monte Cassino and the Liri Valley.

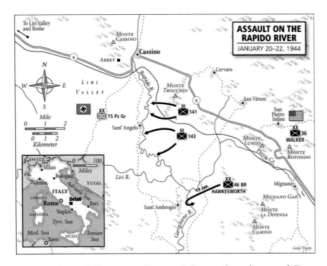

Figure 2.10 Mignano Gap to Monte Cassino and Beyond, Assault on the Rapido River January 20-22, 1944,
Source: Map by Gene Thorpe from Rick Atkinson, The Liberation Trilogy: The Epic Story of the Liberation of Europe in World War II, retrieved from Images of Maps From The Day of Battle - The Liberation Trilogy, by Rick Atkinson, The Liberation Trilogy, by Rick Atkinson

The attack on the Mignano Gap was named Operation *RAINCOA*T. US Fifth Army's US II Corps units began moving into position to begin the offensive on November 17th when the 36th Division with its attached 753d Tank Battalion began relieving the 3d Infantry Division which had been fighting since the September landings.[73] II Corps' role in the attack was to begin on December 3d.[74] Action for the 753d began on December 12 when it and the 143d Infantry Regiment received orders to attack San Pietro. The value of San Pietro was as an observation point for the highway leading to Cassino.

San Pietro was the first of three objectives that the Fifth Army had to seize in which the 753[rd]Tank Battalion participated (Figure 2.11). The town was at the base of Monte Summacro which rose to elevations of another 600 to 3,000 feet. The corridor through which Highway 6 passes north to the Italian capital begins at the Gap. Once through this terrain feature on the route to the Gustav Line, US forces would face two smaller mountains that were defended by the Germans: Lungo and Rotonda. The last obstacles on the route to Cassino were Mounts Trocchio and Porchia and the Rapido River.[75] The Hitler Line was established as a backup defense to the rear should the Gustav Line be penetrated.

Figure 2.11 753rd Tank Battalion at San Pietro December 1943
Source: retrieved from 1940s Battle San Pietro World War Stock Footage Video (100% Royalty-free) 4336865 Shutterstock and https://en.wikipeia.org/wiki/Battle_of_San_Pietro_Infine#:

The town was accessible only by narrow trails and a dirt road with animal-pulled wagon tracks leading to it.[76] The attack began at noon on December 15th with A Company's 17 tanks leading the 143d Infantry along the single trail capable of supporting tanks to the town and Companies B and C providing supporting fires. Mines, enemy artillery, antitank, and mortar fire, terrain. and thrown tracks caused the attack to fail. Four tanks returned. The tank-infantry attack failed as did an attack by the 143d a day earlier without armor support.[77] Subsequent attacks were launched. US troops entered San Pietro on December 17th.[78] Daskevitch describes this battle in detail.[79]

Subsequent objectives for the 753d were Monte Porchia and Cassino. The battle for Monte Porchia took place three miles west from San Pietro and began on January 4, 1944. The battalion received orders reassigning it from the 36th Division to Combat Command B, 1st Armored Division on December 28th. It was codenamed Task Force Allen. Its units included the 6th Armored Infantry Regiment, three tank battalions including the 753rd, a tank destroyer battalion, a combat engineer group, and artillery units from the 1st Armored Division Artillery. The objective was on the south side of Highway 6, and it is a mile long and rises to 900 feet.[80]

Task Force Allen confronted a determined enemy but forced the Germans to withdraw after three days of combat. Daskevitch summarizes the fight for Monte Porchia in detail as he does San Pietro.[81]

Preparations for seizing Cassino started by reattaching the battalion to the 36th Infantry on January 12th. To reach Cassino, it would be necessary to cross the Rapido River. This organization changed on January 16th when the 753d battalion was reassigned to the First Tank Group when the 36th Division failed to establish a crossing site on January 20th.[82]

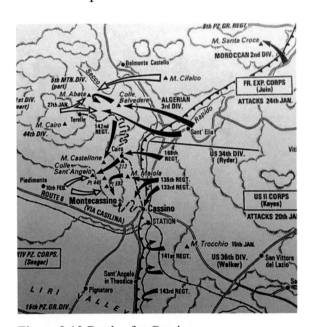

Figure 2.12 Battles for Cassino
NOTE: US II Corps activity during the First Battle of Cassino January 30 to February 13, 1944
Source: retrieved from (100) Pinterest, June 1, 2023

Concurrent with the allied attacks northward in Italy's center. The allied landing began at Anzio and Nettuno on January 22nd. The US VIth US Corps included the US Third Infantry Division, British 1st Infantry Division, Ranger battalions 1,3, and 4) and 504th and 509th Parachute infantry battalions, and combat service support units. began. The original plan was for the Anzio attack force to link with the center force moving through Cassino and the Liri Valley-Rapido River axis and beyond to reach the Gustav line quickly. Anzio settled into a deadlock until June 5, 1944, when the allies broke out and moved toward Rome - the day following the liberation of Rome.[83]

Breaking through to Cassino was also lengthy and a costly battle beginning in mid-January 1944 and ending in May. Initially, the 753rd and the 760th tank battalions were detached from their divisions and assigned in general support of the 34th Division with its organic 756th tank battalion. Multiple attempts to enter the city failed until March 15th. A New Zealand Corps with the 2d New Zealand and 4th Indian Infantry Divisions arrived to relieve US units. The 753rd was attached to the 2nd New Zealand Division. The 28th (Maori) New Zealand infantry battalion was attached to the 753d in mid-February and was given the mission to cross the Rapido and seize Cassino's railway station that began on February 17th. The 753d's mission was then to secure the route to Cassino once the crossing of the Rapido occurred. The 28th crossed the river but failed to hold the railway station. The Allied force was driven back by a German counterattack. A second attack supported by the 753rd occurred between March 15th through March 23rd Intensive air raids on Cassino forced the Germans to withdraw and enabled the New Zealanders to enter the town and fight in an urban combat environment. The New Zealand Corps withdrew in April. The Germans withdrew and the allies led by British and Polish troops seized Cassino in May and continued north to cross the Rapido and drive for Rome beginning May 25th.[84]

Meanwhile. the 753d was ordered to a rear area near Naples for rest and reorganization.[85] A fourth tank company of M3 light tanks was added, and its assault gun platoon received M-7 with 105-millimeter self-propelled howitzers to replace its older assault guns (See Figure 2.7).[86] The battalion used most of April training with the new organization and equipment and integrating replacements.

Figure 2.13 M-7 105mm Tank Destroyer,
Source: retrieved from https://en.wikipedia.org/wiki/M7_Priest#/media/File:M7_Priest_at_APG.jpg
04.24.2018.

Daskevitch II (15 March 2008) states that the battalion's records no longer exist for May and June; however, he was able to reconstruct operations in which the 753d participated during this period by examining other units' reports and studies of the Italian campaign.[87] Generally, the battalion moved from Cassino to Rome through the Liri Valley. It was attached to the 88th Infantry Division which joined US II Corps and the French Expeditionary Corps. It was next attached to US VI Corps as it moved from the Anzio beachhead. Finally, the unit was reunited with the 36th Infantry Division as the war passed through Rome and beyond.

France 1944

Operations and Missions

The 753d was ordered to the rear on June 24th after nearly one year of combat to prepare for Operation *DRAGOON*: the invasion of southern France.

It used the time to receive replacements, perform maintenance, and train with the M4A2 amphibious Sherman duplex drive (DD) tank. (See Figure 2.14). The battalion received one company of 16 DDs. [88]

Figure 2.14 M4A2 Sherman duplex-drive (DD) amphibious tank
Source: retrieved from https://en.wikipedia.org/wiki/DD_tank#/media/File:DD-Tank.jpg, By Photographer not identified. "Official photograph." Post-Work: User:W.wolny - This is photograph MH 3660 from the collections of the Imperial War Museums (collection no. 5207-04), Public Domain, https://commons.wikimedia.org/w/index.php?curid=320076 May 30, 2018.

Operation *DRAGOON* was the 753d 's final assault landing. Originally planned to be coincident with the June 6th invasion of Normandy and named Operation *ANVIL*, it was delayed for various reasons including the non-availability of landing craft, and the delays in achieving goals in the Italian campaign. *DRAGOON* had three objectives: establish the beachhead in southern France, capture the key ports of Marseilles and Toulon, and move north to link up with the allied forces that had broken out from the Normandy beachheads.[89] The 753rd Tank Battalion supporting the 36th Infantry Division that was part of US VI Corps and US Seventh Army, landed on Debarquement Beach in the La Dramont area that is about 3.5 miles southeast of Ste Raphael.[90] The landing site faces the L'ile D'Or. Ste. Raphael is located between Cannes and Toulon (Figure 2.15.[91]

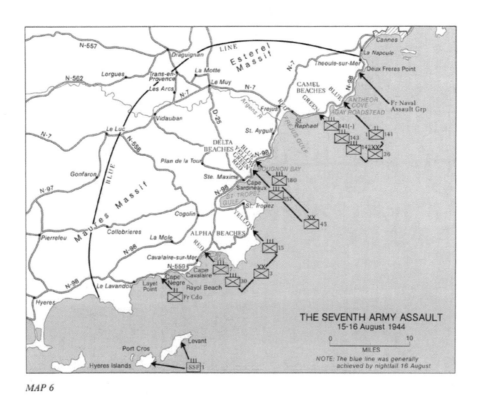

MAP 6

Figure 2.15 753rd Tank Battalion Lands with 36th Infantry Division in France August 15, 1944, The Seventh Army Assault 15-16 August 1944,
Source: FranceMap.png, retrieved from 1.bp.blogspot.com 06072023

The landings began following the preparatory aerial and naval bombardments on August 15th. The allies quickly gained control of the beachhead by the next day after facing an outnumbered defending force of two German infantry divisions.[92]

Task Force Butler, named after the Deputy US VI Corps Commander, Brigadier General Fred Butler, was a mobile task force that the Corps Commander Major General Lucien Truscott created during the pre-invasion planning. Its mission upon activation would be to exploit the landing by moving north to cut off retreating German forces. Composed of 36th Division units, it had a motorized infantry battalion from the 141st Infantry Regiment, and two tank companies from the 753d Tank Battalion, one light cavalry squadron, a self-propelled artillery battalion, and a tank destroyer company.[93] The 753d's commander and operations officer each prepared to command a tank company team in this strike force once the order was issued to implement the plans.[94]

Almost simultaneous with US VI Corps planning, Berlin ordered the Germans to leave Western France with the exception of strong defenses at Toulon, Marseilles, and several important ports on the Atlantic.[95] Fully aware of the withdrawal order, General Truscott implemented the Task Force Butler plan on August 17th. The disparate units assembled on August 17th and were ordered to move west and then north along on August 18th toward Grenoble in an effort to cut off the retreat of the German *Nineteenth Army*.[96] Task Force Butler reached Gap by August 20th. General Truscott changed the objective on August 20th ordering it to turn west and move 25 miles to the Montelimar area near the Rhone River by the next day.[97]

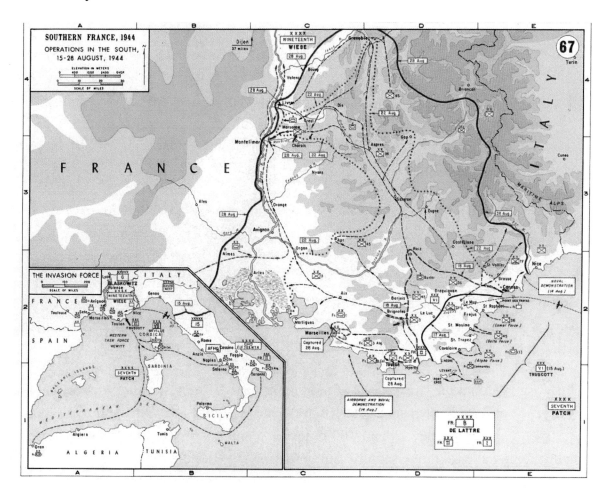

Figure 2.16 DRAGOON Invasion Force Progress After D-Day South,
Source: Map of Southern France During Operation DRAGOON !5-28 Aug 1944 *Pinterest*, retrieved from ww2db.com

The rapid advance ended in the Montelimar square on August 21st. This 250 square-mile area was bounded by the towns of Montelimar and Crest and the Rhone and Drome rivers. Task Force Butler arrived in the area ahead of the retreating Germans. Butler ordered 753d's commander, Lieutenant Colonel Felber, to lead an advance party into Marsanne, a town in the center of the square. Marsanne was a chokepoint that the Germans would have to move through. Felber positioned his force on the key terrain to stop the German move. Felber's force made initial contact with the Germans in the afternoon of August 21st. Truscott moved the 36th Infantry Division with an infantry regiment from the 45th Infantry Division into the area. The battle for the Montelimar Square lasted eight days.[98] It was neither a decisive victory for US VI Corps nor an entirely successful German withdrawal. Some units retreated in good order and others were badly mauled by US forces. The 753d Tank Battalion moved 235 miles with Task Force Butler in 10 days, inflicted heavy German casualties, and destroyed supplies.[99]

September 11, 1944, found the *OVERLORD* force that had landed at Normandy linking up at Saulieu, France with the *DRAGOON* force that had moved north from the French Riviera. Now there was a common front from the English Channel to the Mediterranean Sea.[100] The new allied line resulted in changes of command structures and boundaries. US VI Corps faced fierce fighting during the fall and winter in the Vosges Mountains. It is part of the same geological mass that forms the Black Forest in Germany. This brought back memories of winter fighting in Italy. [101]

US VI Corps began approaching the Vosges from the west on September 20. 1944 when it crossed the Moselle River.[102] The 100th and 103d Infantry Divisions joined US VI Corps and were to enter combat for the first time in this region adding full strength and newly arrived divisions to reinforce the 36th and 3rd Infantry Divisions that had been in combat since Sicily.[103] Company A of the 753d along with an attached platoon from D Company were detached to support the 100th Division and the battalion minus continued supporting the 36th Infantry Division.[104]

The Vosges Mountains are a series of mountains (low Vosges, middle Vosges, and the high Vosges) between the Moselle and Rhine Rivers southwest of Strasbourg in France and Stuttgart, Germany. They extend 100 miles long and about 40 miles wide in Eastern France located parallel to the Alsatian Plain bordering the Rhine.

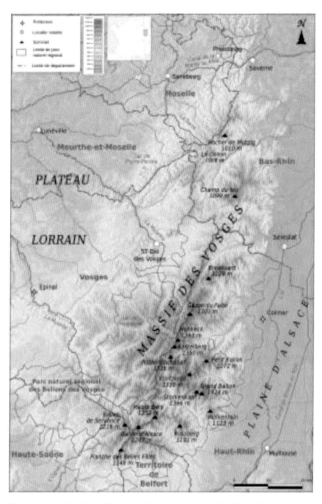

Figure 2.17 The Vosges Mountains: St Die des Vosges and Belfort Gap,
Source: WineGeo: Grès des Vosges, April 7,2017 from <u>WineGeo: Grès des Vosges | The Bubbly Professor</u> June 6, 2023

Wissembourg is the northern tip of the Vosges and Belfort in the high Vosges, is the southernmost point. In addition to Belfort, other key towns in the Alsatian Plain that were designated objectives by the allied command included Saverne, Strasbourg, and Colmar.[105]

St Die des Vosges (Figure 2.17 center) along the Meurthe River was an important objective about midway across the Vosges. Operation *DOGFACE* was the US VI Corps plan to seize St Die beginning on 15 October 1944 to be followed subsequently by a November attack by the US Sixth Army Group east over the Vosges and onto the Alsatian Plain through the Belfort Gap (Figure 2.17 bottom center).[106] The 36th Infantry Division added the 442d Infantry Regimental Combat Team (RCT) – the Japanese-American Nisei regiment to its order of battle for *DOGFACE*. This unit was supported by Company B of the 753d Tank Battalion. The 442d and 143d Infantry Regiments were to lead the main attack of the 36th Division into the Vosges. The remainder of the division occupied defensive positions.[107] One significant action during this period was the 753d's October 24-30 participation in the battle to rescue the 36th Division's 1st Battalion 141st Infantry Regiment (1-141) – "The Lost Battalion."[108]

The 36th Division commander ordered the 1-141 Infantry into an attack. The Germans encircled the battalion. During the next 48 hours, the 2-141 and 3-141 attempted to break through the German lines failed to reach the 1-141. There were 275 soldiers trapped by the Germans. They were resupplied by an Army Air Corps fighter squadron. Although the 442d had been moved to the rear from vigorous fighting earlier, the 36th division commander ordered it back for a final attempt to reach the 1-141. The 442d rescued 211 of the battalion's soldiers at the cost of more than 800 killed, wounded, and 44 taken prisoner by the Germans.[109]

Following the US VI Corps plan, Operation *DOGFACE*, the 36th Infantry Division fought through heavy rains, snow, low temperatures, and a determined German defense in October 1944 Operation in the mountains toward Bruyeres and Brouvelieures, France. The units fought over mountainous terrain and narrow rain-soaked roads hampering tracked and wheeled maneuver to secure Bruyeres on October 18th. The 36th Infantry Division continued fighting through the Vosges until November 10th and never captured St. Die although other US VI Corps units did reach the banks of the Meurthe River near the objective.[110]. In addition to combat casualties during *DOGFACE*, non-combat casualties included pneumonia and cold weather injuries. The 36th Infantry Division had advanced 20 miles since the September 20th Moselle crossing. [111]The 36th Infantry Division, still in the Vosges, was within seven miles of the Alsatian Plain near Selestat (Figure 2.17 upper right side) by November 26th.[112]

The US VI Corps movement to seize Selestat began on November 30th. German resistance in the town ended on December 4th. Although units of the 36th were among the first to reach the Alsatian Plain and participate in Selestat's capture, over half of the division was still making its way through the Vosges. For this reason, the Corps commander assigned the 36th Infantry Division to reinforce the French 2d Armored Division move south to Colmar while the rest of the Corps moved north.[113] The US Sixth Army Group Commander General Jacob Devers, reassigned the 36th Infantry Division and 3d Armored Division from 7th US Army to the First French Army on December 5th to end the fighting against the German *19th Army* in the southern Alsace.[114] Strong German opposition in the Colmar Pocket, bad weather, and trafficability caused this operation to be exceedingly slow. Additionally, the 36th Infantry Division Commander asked that his unit be removed from combat for rest and refitting as it had been in the line constantly since the October move through the Vosges. The 3rd Infantry Division which had been in the rear recovering from combat action replaced the 36th on December 15th.[115]

Into Germany and on to Austria

The German Ardennes offensive that began on December 16th against the allied 12th Army Group caught all allied forces by surprise and resulted in major mission changes across the front in response to the German attack. The US Sixth Army Group's offensive operations toward the Rhine River stopped and unit responsibilities changed to stabilize the front. Once the German attack was defeated there, another plan to stop the advance into Germany from the west by attacking into the Group's area south of the Ardennes became an option. Operation *NORTHWIND (NORDWIND)*went into high command planning on December 21st.[116] The objective was to attack south from Saarbrucken, Germany to drive a wedge in the US Seventh Army and clear the Alsace. The attack would be two pronged. The first would penetrate US defenses along the Sarre River and the second would attack through the Vosges. Their reserves would be in the Saarbrucken area. [117]

General Eisenhower had new intelligence about the German preparations in the south. He ordered his commanders to pull back to the eastern slopes of Vosges with the French insisting that holding major population centers in the Alsace including Strasbourg be in the defensive plans.[118]

To strengthen the defense in this area of concern, the Sixth Army Group Commander ordered the French 2d Armored Division to return to US Seventh Army control and that three new infantry divisions newly arrived in the theater at the beginning of December 1944 be sent forward to join in the defense although they had not seen any combat yet. They were the 63d, 42d, and 70th. The divisions arrived in the Strasbourg area with only their infantry units. Lieutenant General Patch, the Seventh Army commander, organized each of the units into a task force commanded by the respective assistant division commanders. Additionally, he strengthened his force by converting support soldiers into infantrymen to mitigate personnel shortages that were caused by the demands of responding to the German attacks in the Ardennes. [119]

The 753d's tank companies were divided to support Task Force Harris, (63rd Infantry Division), Task Force Linden (42d Infantry Division), and the advanced elements of the 70th Infantry Division units under the command of the assistant division commander,

Thomas Herren that took his name as Task Force Herren upon their arrival.[120] The green troops prepared for battle and fought enthusiastically learning from the experienced veterans. Operation *NORTHWIND* began on New Year's Eve 1944 and continued until January 5, 1945. This was the first of five major attacks that lasted until January 25th.[121]

Examples of Company A's experiences during early January that tested the veterans and their equipment are a single brief case study in the 753rd's World War II combat experiences from Sicily to the Rhine. First, the company had to consolidate into two platoons because of battle damage and mechanical breakdowns before year's end. Second, Company A was attached to Task Force Harris on New Year's Day. This changed on January 2d when it was ordered to join Task Force Herren. The company commander learned that his tanks would join the 3-274 Infantry Regiment. Then on January 3rd, the company was attached to the 2-274 Infantry. Company A was relieved of the previous day's assignment on the 4th and ordered to join the 399th Infantry Regiment of the 100th Infantry Division on January 5th for an upcoming attack[122].

The company's tanks underwent continued maintenance and were whitewashed for camouflage on January 6th. Reconnaissance was the mission for the company's leaders on the 7th. The company moved from its assembly area at 5am on January 8th. One platoon supported two companies of the 399th on the right and the second platoon supported the one company on the left. Both the Germans and the US troops were dressed in white camouflage. The attack on the left bogged down after moving about 400 yards due to heavy enemy direct fire from an 88mm gun. The route of march was across an uncovered or concealed ridgeline in direct view of the Germans. the Germans had strong defensive positions and heavy fire could not dislodge them. The lead tank threw a track on the narrow and slippery trail and the tank platoon leader ordered his tanks and infantry to rear at their LD to reorganize and resume the attack. Both platoons supporting their assigned infantry companies repulsed German counterattacks.

The 399th's commander ordered one tank without infantry to move across the reverse slope of the ridgeline. The Germans opened fire destroying the tank and three crewmembers were believed to have been captured. The Commanding General of US XV Corps relieved A Company of its assignment to the 399th RCT on January 10th and the tankers returned to their original company area to the control of the 753rd Tank Battalion.[123]

Company A returned to the 141st RCT 36th Infantry Division on January 18th after performing maintenance and training as well as returning its 3rd tank platoon to the unit structure. During this period, the tankers showed the differences between their newly acquired M4A3E8 tanks and the M4A1s that the infantry had been used to on January 24th.[124]

The 753d continued fighting along the Rhine through February and broke through the Siegfried Line in March with the 36th Infantry Division. VI US Corps fought near the northern tip of the French Vosges at Wissembourg which was the center of a 3.5-mile-wide gap that historically provided an invasion route into Germany on the Western bank of the Rhine River plain.[125] Key German cities in this region included from north to south: Worms, Mannheim, and Karlsruhe. The battalion crossed the Rhine on March 31st at Mannheim and was placed under US VI Corps.[126] Figure 2.18 displays the advance of the US VI Corps units.

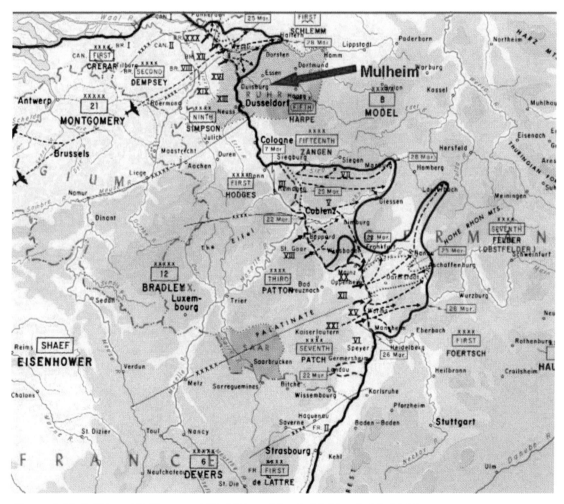

Figure 2.18 St Die to Heilbronn, Allied Lines March 22-March 28, 1945
Source: image 2 of 3Tony's Mission Log: March 2015 (juansrandommusings.blogspot.com),

The 753d continued fighting along the Rhine through February and broke through the Siegfried Line in March with the 36th Infantry Division. VI US Corps fought near the northern tip of the French Vosges at Wissembourg which was the center of a 3.5-mile-wide gap that historically provided an invasion route into Germany on the Western bank of the Rhine River plain.[127] Key German cities in this region included from north to south: Worms, Mannheim, and Karlsruhe. The battalion crossed the Rhine on March 31st at Mannheim and was placed under US VI Corps (Figure 2.18).[128]

The battalion then joined the 63rd Infantry Division in pursuit of the collapsing German defense on a route that took them first to Heilbronn where Company C fought the *17th SS Panzer Division*.[129] The battalion then proceeded along an axis from Augsburg and Bad Tolz into Austria reaching the Kufstein area by V-E Day, May 7th. This was the first occasion when the entire unit was reunited after landing in France. Daskevitch states that the battalion had been in combat for more than 260 days with at least one of its companies in contact.[130]

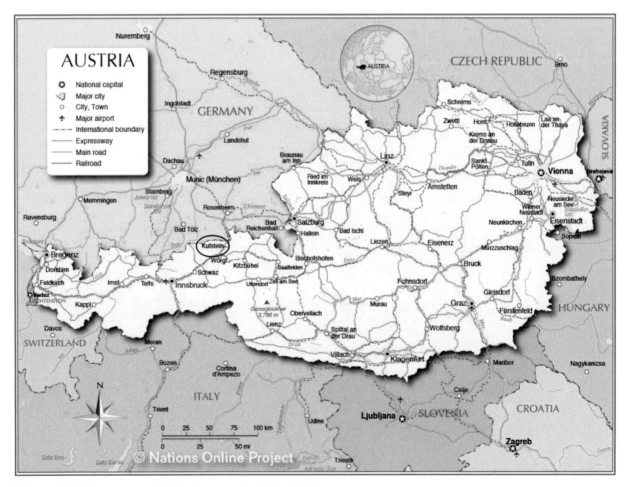

Figure 2.19 Germany to Kufstein, Austria, May 1945
Source: Download Map of Southern Germany and Austria Major Tourist Inside X, retrieved from
Pinterest https://pinterest.com/pin/3721180356703279400/

Table 2.5 summarizes the 753d's combat in France from the beginning of Operation DRAGOON in August 1944 until the German surrender on May 7, 1945.

753d Unit	Supported Unit	Dates	Location	Comment
753d Tank Bn	36th Infantry Division, VI (US) Corps, 7th US Army	August 15-17, 1944	French Riviera Green instead of Red Beach vicinity Ste Raphael	
	Task Force Butler Brig Gen Fred Butler Dep VI Corps commander	August 17	Montelimar (26 Aug), Gap, and Loriel	Opposed German 19th Army retreating. Advanced 235 mi in 10 days
		15 Sep		
B Co	442 RCT	15 Oct	Bruyeres	Operation DOGFACE
A Co w/D co plt	100th ID	~mid Nov 1955		
Cos of 753d	TF Harris (63rd ID); TF Linden (42d ID); (TF Herren) 70th ID	Late Dec 44	Vic Strasbourg	25-mile front; stopped Operation Nordwind German Attack into Alsace
			Along Rhine plain	
		Mar 31, 1945	Mannheim	Crossed Rhine into Germany
	Detached 36th ID and attached to 63d ID VI Corps	-		Moved 200 miles + across south Germany during April 1945
C Co	253d Inf Rgt, 63d ID		Vic Heilbronn	17th SS Panzer Div
753d	Attached to 36 ID	April 28		Augsburg, Bad Tolz
		May 7	Crossed Alps into Kufstein, Austria	VE Day
753d		May 10	Kufstein, Austria	Bn reunited ;260 days in combat since landing in France

Table 2.5 753rd Tank Battalion in France, Germany, and Austria,
Source: adapted from Colonel Anthony F. Daskevich II, Strategy Research Report: Insights into Modularity 753rd Tank Battalion in World War II, Carlisle, PA, US Army War College March 15, 2008, pp 27-31.

Table 2.6 displays the 753d's varied missions from January 1945 after it crossed the Vosges mountains from the vicinity of St Die des Vosges, France through the Belfort Gap into the flat plain of the Alsace Lorraine leading to crossing the Rhine River into Germany in late March 1945 and then across southern German to Kufstein,

January 1945	Location: Strasbourg	Unit				
753 Tank Bn C) 42d Inf Div 1-4 January Task Force Linden	Strasbourg			1 company NFI Task Force Harris 70th ID	1 Co NFI TF Herren, 63rd ID	
753d Tank Bn CP,36th Inf Div January 4- 31	Strasbourg to Mackwiller	A/753	B/753 Control	C/753 Bn Control	D/753	X Btry (Tanks used in indirect fire role reinforcing direct support artillery bn usually 133 FA Bn)
February 1945 Bn CP Weitbruch	Weitbruch	Spt 141st RCT, then to 142 RCT then to Bischweller	Spt 142 142 RCT	Spt 143 RCT In reserve at Bischweller	Bn Control with 1 plt to 141 RCT	
March 1945 March 1-14 Schwindraztsheim 14 March Adv CP Ringeldorf	Schwindraztsheim 1-14 March; 14 March Adv CP Ringeldorf Mission: attack across Siegried Line cross Rhine into Germany	In reserve trng & maint with RCT. 14 March move into attack with RCT	In reserve trng & maint with RCT. 14 March move into attack with RCT	In reserve trng & maint with RCT 14 March move into attack with RCT	In reserve trng & maint with 753d 14 March move into attack under 753 control	In reserve trng & maint with 753d 14 March move into attack under 753d control
April 1945 April 1; April 2 63rd Inf Div; Rapid move from Rhine to Danube	April 1 Implingen; April 2 Heidelberg via Stuttgart south to Zimmern	254 RCT, 63d Inf Div	255 RCT, 63rd Inf Div	253 RCT	255 RCT	
Bn CP May 7, 1945, VE Day Kufsten, Austria	Kufstein, Austria	Kufstein, Austria	Kufstein, Austria	Kufstein, Austria	Kufstein, Austria	Kufstein, Austria

Table 2.6 753rd Tank Battalion Diary January – May 1945,
Source: adapted from 753rd Tank Battalion (8753 TB10/c) January-May 1945, Ike Skelton Combined Arms Research Library, Digital Library retrieved from 753rd Tank Battalion. - World War II Operational Documents - Ike Skelton Combined Arms Research Library (CARL) Digital Library (oclc.org)

World War II was over for the 753rd Tank Battalion. The commander of the 36th Infantry Division, Major General John Dahlquist, wrote the following letter to the battalion at the end of their long relationship:

The mutual respect, the comradeship, and the esprit de corps which together we have developed as a result of our victorious campaigns on the many fields of battle and in the face of continued hardships will be long valued and forever cherished. Yours is an enviable record and I am proud to have had the 753rd Tank Battalion as a part of my command...you wear the "T" Patch with as much pride and proprietorship as any other unit in the Division.[131]

Chapter 3: The Cold War

Introduction

The Cold War between the United States with its Western allies and the Soviet Union and its allies began shortly after the glow following the defeat of Nazi Germany and imperial Japan faded in 1945. It became clear that the nations of eastern Europe were being brought under Soviet control by internal communist cadres and in several cases, this was aided by the presence of the Red Army. Winston Churchill, on March 6, 1946, at Westminster College speech in Fulton, Missouri, delivered his speech about an Iron Curtain descending on Europe from Eastern Germany across Poland, Czechoslovakia, Hungary, Romania, Albania, Yugoslavia, and Bulgaria. Figure 3.1 shows the division of Germany by the Allied victors.

Figure 3.1 Post-WWII Occupation Zones of Germany 1945
Source: Germany: Map of the Occupation Areas retrieved from https://cdn.mapmania.org/original/ zones of occupation 1945/ 1945_zones_of_occupation_for_germany_map_105985.jpg (2947×2414) (mapmania.org) June 13,2023.

Setting the Stage

George F. Kennan who was serving as the deputy head of the US mission in Moscow sent a telegram to Secretary of State James Byrnes on February 1946 reporting that Soviet refusals to enter into postwar international agreements were traceable to Stalin's personal objections but grounded in Russia's historic fear of being surrounded by enemies. This telegram became the Mr. X article when it appeared as "The Sources of Soviet Conduct" in the July 1947 edition of *Foreign Affairs*.[132] Kennan argued that communism would always be an enemy of capitalism and that social democracies and progressive organizations were enemies also. The solution he proposed was containment of the Soviet Union.

The U.S. Army in Europe following the German surrender and the redeployment of the troops back home included only the 1st Infantry Division and the U.S. Constabulary. The 1st Division was the one combat unit remaining in Germany and it was deployed throughout the American occupation zone. Thirty-two thousand soldiers were assigned to the Constabulary and were organized into 27 squadrons consisting of five company-sized troops. Three of the troops had M-5 or M-8 armored cars and two troops had jeeps. The squadrons were subordinate to three regiments. In addition to the three troops, each squadron had a light tank company equipped with M-24 Chaffee tanks, nine fixed-wing liaison aircraft, a motorcycle platoon that patrolled the roads, and a 30-man horse platoon that did the same over difficult terrain. Vaihingen, Germany near Stuttgart was the Constabulary's headquarters. The three regiments eventually became the 2nd, 6th, and 14th Armored Cavalry Regiments.[133]

The allies' expectations in the East were founded on observing Soviet unkept promises. One promise had been to dissolve the provisional governments that were installed as the Red Army moved west to be replaced by governments that were to be elected democratically. Another unfulfilled promise was the continued existence of coalition governments that would include communists in liberated nations already having communist parties with close ties to the Soviet Union. Generally. these nations bordered the Soviet Union.

The pace of the post-WW II transition in Europe devolving from an alliance fighting one revolutionary power to a single nation standing steadfastly militarily with its atomic arsenal was swift. The Economic Recovery Act of 1948, better known as the Marshall Plan provided assistance to rebuild western Europe against a new revolutionary threat not only expanding westward, but also to the east, and South.

To the east, the Chinese communists began their revolution in 1928 against the nationalists. The two formed a unified front against the Japanese from 1937 until 1945.

The civil war resumed after WW II and ended on October 1, 1949, when Mao Zedong declared the People's Republic of China to be established on the mainland.

Further northeast in Asia, Kim Il-sung who had joined the Chinese Communist Party began fighting the Japanese in Manchuria and Korea in the 1930s. He returned to Korea in 1945 with the Soviet army that was sent to accept the Japanese surrender and repatriate the Japanese home to Japan. The United States occupied South Korea for the same purpose. The Soviet and American armies withdrew in 1948 with the Republic of Korea (ROK) being created on August 15, 1948, and Kim announced the establishment of the Democratic People's Republic of Korea (DPRK) on September 9, 1948.

In southeast Asia, Ho Chi Minh, a committed Marxist-Leninist in Moscow since the 1920s, focused on expelling the French from their colony in Vietnam. He sought assistance from the Soviet Union and Stalin provided some, but he was concentrating on consolidating his hold in Eastern Europe. Ho and his military organization, the Viet-Minh, fought the Japanese in Vietnam while they occupied Indochina. Promoting himself as a nationalist and hiding his connection to the Soviets, Ho turned his attention to opposing the return of the French. His army defeated them militarily at Dien Ben Phu on May 7, 1954, and again between An Khe and Pleiku on June 24th and 25th. A final French defeat occurred at a mountain pass midway between Buon Me Thuot and Pleiku three days before the July 20th ceasefire was signed. The French departed Hanoi on October 9th.[134]

Ho visited Mao Zedong and Zhou en Lai during the late 1940s seeking assistance fighting the French. Mao wanted to use his Peoples War model as an exemplar for other Asian states. Qiang Zhai, author of *China and the Vietnam Wars, 1950-1975* stated in a 2001 interview at the Wilson Center that his book was the first publication in English of Chinese documents that had been released by the government. His observations included that the Chinese provided political, agricultural, and organization of the Vietnamese financial and national defense systems after France's 1954 departure but wanted the region to cool down because the Korean War affected China's capability to pursue its own goals. The Soviet Union advised the same to Ho.[135]

Numerous other sources argue the same position for the United States. President Eisenhower did not want to fill the vacuum created when France left Indochina abruptly so close to the 1953 Armistice between the Koreas, but he did send several hundred advisors as part of support pledge to noncommunist South Vietnam to assist President Ngo Dinh Diem. Former French President Charles de Gaulle visited President John Kennedy in May 1961 and during their meeting, he urged Kennedy avoid involving the US in Vietnam.[136]

Kennedy did not follow De Gaulle's advice and ordered more advisors and Army Special Forces troops to Vietnam that same month.

President Johnson who succeeded President Kennedy in 1963 did not want another Korean War in Vietnam. Johnson had domestic policy objectives he wanted to achieve including civil rights and the Great Society. Secretary of State Dean Rusk supported expanding the US presence in South Vietnam to prevent more dominoes from falling to communists. Rusk who along with Andrew Goodpaster in August 1945 were the two individuals who proposed the 38th Parallel to divide the Koreas into the zone where the Soviets would accept the Japanese surrender and the zone in which the United States would do the same.

Western Europe

Meanwhile in Europe, the western allies merged their occupation zones into a single entity in April 1949 and formed the North Atlantic Treaty Organization (NATO) that same month. This allowed their portion of Germany to establish the Federal Republic of Germany (FRG) on May 23, 1949 and the October 6, 1949 signing of the Mutual Defense Assistance Act of 1949 was the first US step to provide assistance for the NATO members' collective security.[137] West Germany was established on May 23, 1949 as the Federal Republic of Germany (FRG). The German Democratic Republic (GDR), East Germany, was created on October 7, 1949.

In the western allied occupation zones of Germany, the allied military presence was an empty threat to the Soviets. Initially, the United States possessed the atomic bomb that had proven itself to be a deterrent after its two uses against Japan in August 1945. Massive retaliation became the American leverage against further Soviet expansion in Europe.

The incredibility that nuclear weapons would be used against the Soviets as they consolidated their new position in Europe was a different strategic problem. Expelling the western allies from their sectors in Berlin became one of Stalin's goals. The Soviets stopped all road, rail, and canal traffic into Berlin in June 1948; however, they did not include closing the air corridors. The result was the 14-month Berlin Airlift beginning on June 24th that sent 2,343,301 tons of food, coal, and other essential commodities into the city by late September 1949.[138]

Senator Joseph McCarthy rose to prominence during this portion of postwar American domestic politics when he charged that the State Department was full of spies and this included the Secretary of State George C. Marshall whom Churchill declared was World War II's "...true organizer of victory...."[139] McCarthy emphasized the five years after the War's end which included the accused Soviet spy. General Marshall was President Truman's special envoy to China and arrived in the country in December 1945. His efforts to settle the civil war failed in early January 1947. Later that same month, he was confirmed as the Secretary of State and served until January 1949. The Soviets exploded their first atomic bomb on August 29, 1949 and China became Communist on October 1st. McCarthy ignored Marshall's role in rebuilding western Europe through the Marshall Plan.

The 1945-1955 decade was evidence to western leaders that Soviet communism was monolithic worldwide. In Europe, the Berlin Airlift kept the city under joint allied control. The Soviets started along another path in 1957 when they attempted to bring the entire city of Berlin under GDR control. At first, East German authorities began interfering with Berliners who had been permitted to travel freely between the eastern and western sectors. The second step was the threat to prevent entry into Berlin from the west.[140]

Nikita Khrushchev replaced Stalin after the latter's death in 1953 following a short period of political intrigues and consolidated his hold on power in 1954. In November 1958, he issued an ultimatum to the western allies that the Soviets would withdraw from Berlin within six months and allow it to be absorbed into the GDR. and presenting the appearance of no direct Soviet control His tactic was to propose that the United States, United Kingdom, and France could stay in Berlin if they wished but they would have to negotiate new treaties with the East German government. After posturing, threats and international conferences in Geneva, the Soviet ultimatum faded away. It resurfaced in 1961 shortly after the inauguration of President John Kennedy.[141] During the three-year interim over control of East Berlin, the city became the avenue of escape for East Germans fleeing to the West.

President Kennedy and Premier Khrushchev met twice on June 4, 1961. The Soviet leader said it was time to recognize the two Germanies with a peace treaty. The second meeting was a private one between the two. Kennedy stated that the United States was committed to the Berliners and to keeping its access to the city open. Khrushchev replied that if the US stayed in Berlin after the peace treaty he was determined to sign six months later in December, then the USSR would have no choice other than to aid the GDR militarily. President Kennedy addressed the people of the United States from the Oval Office on July 25th stating that the US would not be driven out of Berlin.[142]

President Kennedy announced the following: the strengths of US Army, Navy, and Air Force would be increased with the Army reaching 1,000,000; the tours of duty of those nearing the end of their service obligations would be extended; increased draft calls would be implemented; and he ordered the activation of some reserve component units and the deployment of three Army divisions from the U.S. to West Germany. In East Germany, four Soviet divisions deployed from their garrisons and encircled Berlin.[143]

There were 120 crossing points between East and West Berlin. The flow of Germans moving through the city to the west increased significantly. To stem the tsunami of escapees, the East German government announced that all but 13 points would be closed on August 12th. The next morning, armored vehicles including tanks closed the east-west border between the Soviet and allied sectors and construction equipment and materials were delivered signaling the beginning of the Berlin Wall.[144]

President Kennedy ordered a show of force to demonstrate the resolve of the allies not to be forced out of the city and to retain access to Berlin from West Germany. On August 18th, the US Army Europe Commander ordered the 1st Battle Group, 18th Infantry, 8th US Infantry Division to move from its garrison at Mannheim to Helmstedt, the last West German city on the autobahn before crossing into the GDR and then to continue on to Berlin.

The infantry battle group with an engineer company, artillery battery, and a military police platoon departed Mannheim on August 19th. The move to Berlin started on August 20th at 6:30 am after enduring routine Soviet military bureaucratic challenges. The column reached Berlin that afternoon where the soldiers passed by Vice President Johnson and retired General Lucius D. Clay, President Kennedy's special representative in Berlin. Clay had led the Office of Military Government, United States and was respected by the Germans for many of his decisions during his tenure that began in 1947 including his role during the Berlin airlift.[145]

There were three final pieces to fill out the beginning the US-Soviet Cold War in Germany and worldwide. First was the sequence of events beginning on August 22d when the Soviets announced that allied military traffic could only enter East Berlin at the Friederichstrasse crossing point named Checkpoint Charlie. Checkpoint Alpha was the crossing point at Helmstedt. Checkpoint Bravo was the entry point into Berlin.[146] Confrontations and challenges to western allied access into East Berlin continued into October 1961.

Second was the increase in bases and troop strength of the US Army in West Germany. This began in 1951 when much of the Army was in Korea. The Army acquired four major training areas. Grafenwoehr, encompassing 17,700 acres and the 40,738-acre Hohenfels area both northwest of Regensburg were the largest. Wildflecken, much smaller than the first two training areas covering 17,760 acres was about 20 miles southeast of Fulda. U.S access to Baumholder originally in the in French zone in 1951 began as a shared training area. Vilseck, near Hohenfels, was a military training school[147]

US V Corps was designated as the counterattack force and had its subordinate commands' headquarters at Mainz, Bad Kreuznach, and Baumholder. These units would strike a Soviet advance through the Fulda Gap. The Corps was headquartered in Frankfurt. The 4th Infantry Division and 2nd Armored Division joined the 1st Infantry Division beginning in 1951.[148]

The US VII Corps protected the East German-Czechoslovak border. Its units were the 28th and 43rd Army National Guard Divisions. The 14th Armored Cavalry Regiment screened from Hersfeld in Hesse to Bamberg in Bavaria. The 2nd Armored Cavalry's sector was in Bavaria. It began at Bamberg and extended to Regensburg. The 6th Armored Cavalry patrolled from Regensburg to Landshut which is in Bavaria also.[149]

Third was the shift in U.S. civil-military relations. Until the US (and NATO) – USSR (and Warsaw Pact) period until the dissolution of the East European bloc including the USSR by 1991, The US historically kept a small standing regular army with the states' militias (Army National Guard) and US Army Reserve units. These reserve components were comprised of civilians training for possible activation to perform state and federal missions in the case of the militias and federal missions when the Army Reserve was mobilized.

Cold War US Army Force Structure Evolution

The Cold War demanded the retention of a much larger active-duty force supported by the draft until 1973 when the volunteer Regular Army returned. The role of the reserve components began to change. Worldwide alliances to contain communism had changed the historic American civil-military paradigm.[150] Although the end of conscription resulted in a smaller standing Regular Army. There was no reduction in the Army's missions.

Table 3.1 displays changes in the Army's manpower over time. The Cold War's origins provide the backdrop for Steel Tigers' evolution from the end of World War II to the 1990s.

Army Active Duty Manpower 1920 - 1997

				World War II	Cold War Begins	Korean War Begins		Korean War Armistice				
Year	1920	1939	1941	1945	1948	1950	1951	1953	1954	1955	1956	1957
Manpower	204,282	180,839	1,462,315	8,266,373	554,030	593,167	1,531,774	1,533,815	1,404,598	1,109,926	1,025,778	997,994

			753rd Tank Battalion	Berlin Crisis; Ft Carson, CO, 5th ID with 1-77th Armor actvtd		US Army Troops to RVN; 5th ID has 1-& 3-77 Armor		1-77 Deploys	1-77 Deactivated		US Army leaves RVN and Draft Ends	
Year	1959	1960	1961	1962	1963	1965	1966	1968	1971	1972	1973	1974
Manpower	861,964	873,078	858,622	1,086,404	975,916	969,066	1,199,784	1,570,343	1,123,810	810,960	800,973	785,330

	Saigon Falls			Berlin Wall Falls	USSR dissolves, Warsaw Pact terminated, & Kuwait restored							
Year	1975	1980	1985	1989	1991	1992	1993	1994	1995	1996	1997	
Manpower	784,333	777,036	780,787	769,741	710,821	610,450	572,423	541,343	508,559	491,103	491,707	

Table 3.1 U.S. Army Active Duty Manpower Strengths 1920-1997
Source: adapted from Source Table 2-11, Department of Defense, Active Duty Military Personnel: 1789-Through Present, Department of Defense, Selected Manpower Statistics, Fiscal Year 1997, DIOR/M01-97 (Washington, DC: Directorate for Information Operations and Reports) November 1997, pp. 46-53, and John B Wilson, Maneuver and Firepower: the Evolution of Divisions and Separate Brigades, CMH Publication 60-14-1, Washington, D.C. Center of Military History, pp 305-6 and The Army Lineage Series, 1997.

Army force structure planners had to design a force that would defend US interests across the globe within manpower, equipment, and armament limits. All of the nation's military missions had to be without the blank check of World War II, responding to the surprise war in Korea, and keeping the Soviets at bay in Europe. The Defense Department approached the challenges by developing and acquiring weapons and equipment with enhanced capabilities that allowed reducing manpower levels to stay within a budget dictated by the threat and the how the services would operate in a nuclear war environment.

The Steel Tigers fought World War II and the Korean War using the 18,804-man 1948 infantry division organization that included three 3,774-man infantry regiments with one

148-man tank company in each regiment and one 667-man tank battalion. There were 68 Army divisions by 1957. Fifty-six were combat divisions of which 18 were Regular Army, 27 Army National Guard, and 11 Army Reserve. Twelve were training divisions, During the Korean War, there were eight divisions in the Far East, five in Germany, and seven in the United States as part of the General Reserve.[151]

The United States began the Cold War with a monopoly on atomic and followed by hydrogen bombs. The post-Korean War national defense strategy was initially one of massive retaliation. Nuclear weapons carried by the newly established US Air Force were to be the first line of deterrence against all enemies.

The Army had to compete with the other services for its share for the defense budget. There were several infantry, armored, and airborne divisions designed during the post-Korean War years. The 77th Armor Regiment was part of infantry divisions beginning in World War II and continuing through to the end of the Cold War after which one of its battalions joined the 1st Armored Division.

Two of three infantry division organizations among several that Army planners designed entered testing during the second half of the 1950s. The first was the 1954 Atomic Field Army Infantry Division that the planners wanted to assess by 1956. It was authorized 13,542 officers and men. It was divided into three combat commands. There were seven 1,019-man infantry battalions and one 611-man tank battalion with its tanks mounting 90-mm main guns. A second test of this division raised the number of tank battalions to two[152]

The second organization was the Pentomic Infantry Division. The Table of Organization and Equipment for this entity was published in February 1960. The design authorized the division 13,748 officers and men. Its combat units were five 1,356-man battle groups (battalions) each with five rifle companies, and one 760-man tank battalion.[153]

The ROAD Division and Separate Brigade

The third infantry division design was the Reorganization of Objective Army Division (ROAD) 1961-1965. It was designed in response to the reconceptualized national strategy of Flexible Response introduced by President John F. Kennedy and his national security team. Massive retaliation to any international conflict no longer presented a credible deterrent to potential adversaries because an eruption involving the United States could occur anywhere with any kind of armed force, symmetrical or asymmetrical, opposing the existing US force structure.[154] Additionally, the Army fielded tactical nuclear weapons beginning in the 1950s with the Honest John unguided missile, a truck-transported erector, and launcher with nuclear and nonnuclear capability and the Davy Crockett recoilless rocket system that could be fired from a tripod or a wheeled and tracked vehicle. Both weapons systems were planned to enhance firepower capabilities on the European battlefield.

The capability to perform missions that implemented the Flexible Response national strategy began emerging not only with the 1961 Berlin Crisis in Europe, but also with a response to the Cuban Missile Crisis in October 1962 that would have included deploying elements of the 1st Armored Division from Fort Hood, Texas into Cuba.[155]

In addition to responding to the continuing need to defend Western Europe and South Korea in 1965, came new missions: Vietnam, Central America, and maintaining the strategic reserve in the US. While preparing units for deployment to South Vietnam that began in May, a brushfire crisis erupted on April 28th in the Dominican Republic causing dispatch of the 82d Airborne Division.

The 173rd Airborne Brigade located in Okinawa was the first Army unit to arrive in Vietnam on May 7th followed in July by the 1st Infantry Division's and 101st Airborne Division's 2nd Brigade and 1st Brigade, respectively. Additional units followed. Force structure planners had to find a solution to keep the strategic reserve capable of responding to future missions as the Army's troop commitment to Vietnam increased.

The ROAD Division was the solution from which future variations evolved. It was established with a common infantry, mechanized infantry and armored divisional base. There was a division headquarters group with one division commander and two assistant division commanders one for maneuver and the other for support, three brigades, one military police company, an aviation, signal, and engineer battalion, a reconnaissance squadron, the division artillery, and a support command with the division headquarters company, administrative company, band, medical, supply and transport, and ordnance battalions. The building blocks were battalions of 842-man, 868-man, and 574-man infantry, mechanized infantry, and tank battalions, respectively. These modules gave the ROAD design its flexibility for the modifications required to conduct operations in any area worldwide.

The division's armor, infantry, and mechanized infantry combat battalions could be tailored depending on the projected mission, enemy capabilities and terrain. One division might have all infantry battalions, and another a mix. Each of these battalions had a headquarters and headquarters company, a combat support company, and three tank, infantry, or mechanized infantry companies. For example, the 9th Infantry Division placed a brigade of three infantry battalions aboard naval patrol boats in the Vietnam's Mekong Delta to conduct operations in conjunction with four other divisional infantry battalions and two mechanized infantry battalions divided into two brigades operating on the land.[156]

Organizing the Army into the ROAD framework was delayed because of the Berlin Crisis described earlier. It was not until January 1962 that the Secretary of Defense authorized the implementation of the ROAD structure. The first unit that reorganized was the 1st Armored Division at Fort Hood Texas on February 3, 1962. The second ROAD division formed was the 5th Infantry Division (Red Devils) at Fort Carson, Colorado. The first and third brigades were to be activated at Fort Carson. The new organization necessitated the Third Brigade headquarters to become the division's headquarters. Only one of the tank battalions and six infantry battalions were filled with men and equipment initially. Another tank battalion was stationed at Fort Irwin, California where it supported test and evaluation activities as part of the Combat Developments Command. The division's second brigade with three infantry battalions was stationed at Fort Devens, Massachusetts. By summer 1962, the Army established the building blocks of the three division types. The mechanized infantry division was to have three tank battalions originally and seven mechanized infantry battalions. The 5th Infantry Division's armor battalions activated on February 19, 1962 were the Steel Tigers of the 77th Armor Regiment's 1st, 2nd, and 3rd battalions; however, the 2-77 Armor was deactivated on October 1, 1963.[157] It took about three years for the ROAD Division structure to evolve and to implement not only throughout the regular force, but also in the Army Reserve's combat divisions. The ROAD framework also called for special purpose combat brigades that could be assigned missions inappropriate for divisions.

The 5th Infantry Division's pre-Vietnam organization completed its ROAD development on July 1, 1965. Initially, it was set at 10 battalions: eight infantry and the 1st and 3rd Battalions of the 77th Armor. No mechanized infantry battalions were authorized.

There was no standard structure established for the special purpose brigades. Instead. They would be organized to perform the missions they were assigned. There were 17 maneuver brigades activated with six in the Regular Army, seven in the Army National Guard and four in the Army Reserve.

Table 3.2 displays the Army's ROAD Division structure at the beginning of Fiscal Year 1966 (July 1, 1965) and before US divisions were deployed to South Vietnam. Table 3.3 presents the ROAD structure for the special purpose separate brigades at the beginning of Fiscal Year 1966.

The ROAD Division July 1, 1965

Regular Army

Location	Armored Divisions	Tank Bns	Inf Bns	Mech Inf Bns	Airmobile Bns
US	1st Armored	0	5	4	
US	1st Cavalry (Reorg to airmobile div June 30)	2	5	2	8
US	2nd Armored	5	4	0	0
FRG	3rd Armored	6	0	5	0
FRG	4th Armored	6	0	5	0

Army National Guard

Location	Armored Division	Tank Bns	Inf Bns	Mech Inf Bns
US	27th Armored	5	0	4
US	40th Armored	6	0	4
US	48th Armored	5	0	4
US	49th Armored	5	0	4
US	50th Armored	5	0	4

Army Reserve

Location	Armored Division	Tank Bns	Inf Bns	Mech Inf Bns
US	0	0	0	0

Regular Army

Location	Infantry Divisions	Tank Bns	Inf Bns	Mech Inf Bns
US	1st Infantry	2	5	2
US	2d Infantry	2	5	2
FRG	3rd Infantry	3	0	7
US	4th Infantry	2	5	2
US	5TH INFANTRY	2	8	0
ROK	7th Infantry	2	5	2
FRG	8th Infantry	3	4	3 Abne
FRG	24th Infantry	3	0	7
US	25th Infantry	1	6	1

Army National Guard

Location	Infantry Divisions	Tank Bns	Inf Bns	Mech Inf Bns
US	17	2	6	0

Army Reserve

Location	Infantry Divisions	Tank Bns	Inf Bns	Mech Inf Bns	Airborne
US	6	2	6	0	0

Airborne

Location	Divisions	Tank Bns	Inf Bns	Mech Inf Bns
US	82nd	1	9 Abne	0
US	101st	1	9 Abne	0

Table 3.2 ROAD Division Structure, July 1, 1965
Source: NOTE: 5th Infantry Division in the large font included the 1-77 Armor and 3-77 Armor. Adapted from John B Wilson, Maneuver and Firepower: the Evolution of Divisions and Separate Brigades, Table 24. Maneuver Division Mix of Divisions ROAD Reorganization June 30, 1965, p. 308, CMH Publication 60-14-1, Washington, D.C. Center of Military History, pp 310-11 and The Army Lineage Series, 1997, and Timothy S. Aumiller, United States Army: Infantry, Armor/Cavalry, Artillery Battalions, 1957-2011, (Takoma Park, MD: Tiger Lily Publications) March 19, 2008, pp 131-132.

The Army Separate Brigade ROAD July 1, 1965

Regular Army Brigades Location	Armored Brigade	Tank Bns	Inf Bns	Mech Inf Bns
US	194th Armored	1	0	0

Army National Guard Combat Brigades Location	Armor	Tank Bns	Inf Bns	Mech Inf Bns
US	53rd Armored	3	0	2
US	86th Armored	2	2 Abn	0

Army Reserve Combat Brigades Location	Armored Brigade	Tank Bns	Inf Bns	Mech Inf Bns
US	0	NA	NA	NA

Regular Army Brigades Location	Infantry Brigade	Tank Bns	Inf Bns	Mech Inf Bns	Airborne
US-AK	171 Infantry	1 co	1	1	0
US-AK	172 Infantry	1 co	1	1	0
Okinawa	173rd Infantry (Abn)	1co	0	0	2
Canal Zone	193 Infantry	0	1	1	1
US	197 Infantry	1	2	1	0

Army National Guard Combat Brigades Location	Infantry	Tank Bns	Inf Bns	Mech Inf Bns	Airborne
US	6 Brigades	1 or 2 bns	1-4 bns	1 or 2 bns	

Army Reserve Combat Brigades Location	Infantry Brigade	Tank Bns	Inf Bns	Mech Inf Bns	Airborne
US	**157TH INFANTRY**	2	1	1	0
US	187th Infantry	1	3	0	0
US	191st Infantry	2	1	1	0
US	205th Infantry	1	3	3	0

Table 3.3 Separate Maneuver Brigades ROAD Reorganization July 1, 1965
Source: NOTE: 157th Infantry Brigade in bold font included the 4-77 Armor. Adapted from John B Wilson, Maneuver and Firepower: the Evolution of Divisions and Separate Brigades, Table 24. Maneuver Division Mix of Divisions ROAD Reorganization June 30, 1965, p. 308, CMH Publication 60-14-1, Washington, D.C. Center of Military History, pp 313 and The Army Lineage Series, 1997, and Timothy S. Aumiller, United States Army: Infantry, Armor/Cavalry, Artillery Battalions, 1957-2011, (Takoma Park, MD: Tiger Lily Publications) March 19, 2008, pp 131-132.

Impact of Vietnam on Force Structure

Late spring and summer 1965 began the major commitment of US Army troops to South Vietnam and the first worldwide test of the ROAD organizational structure. The United States was the backbone of the NATO defense against the Warsaw Pact in Germany, the defense of Japan and South Korea from the Soviets, Chinese, and North Koreans in northeast Asia, and now a rapidly expanding conflict in southeast Asia. The first Regular Army unit ordered to South Vietnam was the 173rd Airborne Brigade. It arrived in May 1965. The 2nd Brigade, 1st Infantry Division, and the 1st Brigade, 101st Airborne Division followed the 173rd in July.

The 2nd Infantry and 1st Cavalry Divisions exchanged regimental colors in South Korea and at Fort Benning but without reassigning their soldiers and equipment. The 1st Cavalry Division was redesignated the 1st Cavalry Division (Airmobile) and deployed from Fort

Benning to Vietnam reaching there in September 1965. The remainder of the 1st Infantry Division arrived in October.[158]

South Vietnam became the priority theater for the Army. Although, no units were reassigned from NATO and South Korea. Planners had to meet the challenge of the keeping the units in conflict at full strengths. The solution was to use the commands in the US-based Strategic Reserve as well as NATO and South Korea as sources of officers, senior non-commissioned officers, and enlisted soldiers with special skills for the combat theater. The commands giving up these individuals had to replace them with officers and men junior in rank and less experience. For example, more than 1800 officers and men were leaving US units in West Germany monthly for units in South Vietnam. Staffing in Regular Army units used junior officers and non-commissioned officers awaiting or returning from their 12-month tours of duty in Vietnam or serving the remainder of their service obligations before release from active duty. Captains filled majors' positions and lieutenants filled positions authorized for captains. Lower ranking enlisted soldiers fresh from basic training were assigned to units in the US before going to Vietnam, and the combat veterans went to US units their before release from active duty Additionally, the Army identified three Army National Guard infantry divisions and six separate infantry brigades for increased readiness. These units were named the Selected Reserve Force. Their manpower and training were to be increased so that they could move to mobilization stations following a one-week activation order. [159]

Taking the general description of the Strategic Reserve above and summarizing it specifically in one of the two Steel Tigers battalions at Fort Carson, the following personnel and training programs occurred in 1967. Lieutenant Colonel John. M. Pickarts had been the 1-77 Armor's battalion commander for the entire year. His first executive officer was selected to attend the Army's Command and General Staff College to begin during the summer, and his second executive officer arrived as the replacement remained until the Steel Tigers were alerted for deployment in 1968. A captain performed the duties of the battalion personnel officer and logistics officer simultaneously from January until Second Lieutenant Carl Fellhauer arrived in May to become battalion personnel officer which was a captain's position. There was no intelligence officer until September when another second lieutenant was appointed to the position. There were four operations officers that year. In sequence, there was one major, a first lieutenant, a captain, and the same first lieutenant a second time between January and December. Two captains each commanded Companies A and B in 1967, and one captain followed by a second lieutenant commanded Company C. Three captains commanded the Headquarters and Headquarters Company (HHC). Two hundred recruits arrived in the battalion directly from basic and advanced individual training. This proved a challenge because some were assigned to the HHC which required specialized skills. On-the-job training directly supervised by non-commissioned officers fulfilled this requirement.[160]

Training during 1967 included tank gunnery which ended in April. Thirty-one crews qualified, which was higher than the number of crews in the 3d Battalion 77th Armor that year. Gunnery was followed by the 5th Infantry Division Command Maintenance Management Inspection (CMMI) in May. Platoon training followed by tests was the next phase of the training year. The US Fifth Army CMMI, the annual company unit training tests, the Battalion Army Training Test and a 1st Brigade field training exercise followed by a command-post exercise completed the training year for this Strategic Reserve battalion. The battalion successfully passed all segments of its internally and externally administered training. [161]

Force Structure and Domestic Missions

The Strategic Reserve in the United States was not a manpower and equipment pool to reinforce overseas commitments only. It had a specific domestic mission: preserving the domestic tranquility. The US Army had been used repeatedly through its history to restore order from political violence within the nation's borders.

During World War II, the emphasis was on preventing labor strife to disrupt the war effort. Immediately following the war came President Truman's authorization for the Army to operate the US railroads to prevent a threatened railroad workers' strike in 1946 and then the implementation his order in 1950. The formation of the Department of Defense in the National Security Act of 1947 the Army Organization Act of 1950, and subsequent Army regulations replaced the executive orders and gave the Army the mission of restoring order in the country.[162]

The 1950s also ended school segregation in the country. When the Army National Guard could not restore order, regular units were deployed. Paul Scheips in his *The Role of Federal Military Forces in Domestic Disorder* states that the Guard was employed over 30 times in response to civil strife from 1945 through 1957 when 1,000 federal troops were sent to Little Rock Arkansas to enforce school integration.[163] Further racial violence erupted in the south in the 1950s and then in the 1960s in Los Angeles, California, Newark, New Jersey, Detroit Michigan, and Washington, D.C.

The Army gained experience restoring civil order during the increased number of domestic deployments. One of the considerations among all policymakers with roles in preserving domestic security was the threat of extremists from seizing the initiative from unorganized and spontaneously appearing mobs without leaders and moderates attempting to regain control of their locale. One of its corrective actions was to reduce the response time between an outbreak of violence and the arrival of regular troops to restore order. The operations during the civil rights years during the early-to-mid-1960s were plans with the code name *STEEP HILL*. The name was changed to Operation *GARDEN PLOT* in 1967 when opposition to the war in Vietnam was inserted into the civil rights demonstrations and violence.[164]

The solution was to earmark regular Army units within the United States to be trained in riot control and be ready depart their home bases. Initially, each continental army region was to designate seven brigades (21,000 soldiers) with a manpower deployment ceiling set at 15,000 in 1963 for a single disturbance within its region.[165] By the time of the April 1968 riots following the Rev. Dr. Martin Luther King's assassination on April 4th, an eighth brigade from each army region had been added. The plan estimated that 4,000 to 25,000 troops could be available for a single eruption of violence. Controlling these units were six task forces: US XVIII Airborne Corps that was responsible for the First and Third Army areas and Washington, DC; US III Corps that was earmarked for cities in the Fourth, Fifth, and Sixth Army regions; and the 5th Infantry Division at Fort Carson, 82nd Airborne Division at Fort Bragg, and the 2nd Armored Division at Fort Hood.

The size of each force began with a reinforced 100-200-man company that could depart its home station within six hours, to be followed in 12 hours by a battalion with 600-800 soldiers, and by an 1,800-2,400-man brigade 24 hours later. Fifteen major U.S. cities were designated priority one. More than 105 smaller population centers were placed into priorities two-to-four.[166] Deployment packets were prepared for each of the population centers. These contained maps and other necessary information for commanders to know when their units were alerted. The brigades were responsible for updating the city packets for their army areas' missions and the packets were distributed to the battalion intelligence officers within each brigade.[167]

1968 was a singularly demanding year for the US armed forces. The North Vietnamese attack on Marines stationed at the Khe Sanh Combat Base (KSCB) in northwest Quang Tri Province began in earnest on January 21st following nearly a year of skirmishing. Also, on the 21st, North Korea attempted to assassinate the President of South Korea, and seized the US Navy's intelligence gathering ship, the *USS Pueblo* on January 23rd. The Tet Offensive began throughout South Vietnam on January 30th. In the United States, Martin Luther King was assassinated in the early evening of April 4th, and rioting broke out in nearly 130 population centers almost simultaneously across the country. All of the brigades in the Strategic Reserve including the 1st Brigade, 5th Infantry Division (Mechanized) that was training for deployment to South Vietnam were alerted by April 5th.[168]

The 5th Infantry Division's 2nd Brigade flew from Peterson Field which has since been renamed Peterson Space Force Base to Bolling Air Force Base outside of Washington, D.C. on April 8th. The 3rd Brigade, originally alerted to go to Cleveland on April 6th and then diverted to Chicago on the 7th left Peterson for a naval base near Chicago on April 7th.[169] Vietnam deployment training for the 1st Brigade stopped abruptly when it was ordered back to garrison for two purposes: to send troops to the other two brigades bringing their battalions to full strength and to undergo riot control training while awaiting the order to move to Peterson Field and board C-141 Starlifters for the mission to reinforce the National Guard and police in another city suddenly torn by civil strife. The 3rd and 2d Brigades began returning to Ft. Carson on April 13th and 16th respectively where the soldiers returned to their 1st Brigade units.[170]

Additional domestic violence erupted at Chicago's Democratic National Convention in August and The Warsaw Pact invaded Czechoslovakia later in the year beginning on August 20th.

Force Structure in the Post-Cold War and Voluntary Service Era

The Warsaw Pact dissolved on July 1, 1991 and the Soviet Union was renamed six months later. These two events brought the Cold War with its military threat of a massive war in Western Europe to an end. Before this, however, the US Army faced five challenges to its worldwide capabilities as the United States withdrew from Vietnam beginning in 1969, and national conscription ending in 1973. These events marked the end of the need for continuing the quarter-century-old paradigm of maintaining large active-duty armed forces.

The end of the draft caused four categories of challenges for the Army. First, planners had to determine how to deter the Warsaw Pact without relying on tactical and strategic nuclear weapons at the outset of conflict in Europe. Second was how to sustain the Army's worldwide missions during annual manpower reductions and lower budget appropriations following 1973. Third was the occurrence of smaller scope actions requiring ground force interventions that demanded swift reaction but not by units with the same structure as those earmarked for the European battlefield.

Fourth, the Army had to renew itself. Planners across the Army had to design a new strategy with new unit organizations and tactics to take maximum advantage of the new technologies being introduced into combat, combat support, and combat service support organizations so that smaller forces could defeat larger Warsaw Pact ground forces in Europe. The choice to merely add new equipment with new technologies to an existing force structure employed piecemeal and responding reactively to unanticipated events on the periphery of the Soviet Union would repeat errors of the past.

Finally, the reexamination included command and control. Rapid deployments necessitated correcting problems from the policymaking to the individual unit levels that had been observed over the years.

Five international events reinforced the necessity of the new approach: first, the 1973 Yom Kippur War. John B. Wilson states that the Egyptians and Syrians lost more tanks in the 18-day war with Israel than the US had on the ground in Europe.[171]

The second and third events occurred in 1979. Fifty two American diplomats at the US Embassy in Tehran were taken hostage on November 4th, and the Soviet Union invaded Afghanistan on Christmas Eve.

The fourth event was the 1982 conflict between the United Kingdom and Argentina over ownership of the Falkland Islands (Malvinas). Argentina's military government that took power in the 1976 coup in their country seized the Malvinas Islands in the southwest Atlantic on April 2, 1982 in a move to offset increasing civilian opposition against the military's rule. Having been British since 1833 but always contested and 8,000 miles from England, Argentina's leadership did not believe England would respond. Unexpectedly, Prime Minister Thatcher ordered the armed forces to reestablish British sovereignty. With its small armed forces dedicated to NATO, the British cobbled together a ground force of two light infantry brigades, 127 naval and civilian vessels, and air support. Argentina's defenders surrendered on June 14th. The British humbling of the Argentine armed forces led the country's military government to cede political power back to civilian control the next year.[172]

Fifth, the United States invasion of Grenada in October 1983 was ordered by President Reagan and occurred almost overnight. The US deployment to Grenada began on October

25th, two days after a truck bomb killed more than 200 Marines in Beirut. Conventional wisdom had it that this terrorist attack was the cause for the 82nd Airborne Division being alerted for movement to Lebanon. This was the assumption within the 82nd also. Instead, the 82nd's and the 8th USMC Regiment's three missions were to follow two Army Ranger battalions into Grenada, to rescue U.S. students attending medical school there, return the Cuban-supported revolutionary civilian government to a democratically elected government, and expel Cuban military and civilian workers from the island.[173]

The reexamination of the Army's organization, equipment, personnel, strategies, and tactics began in 1969 when Secretary of Defense Melvin Laird stated that the United States would continue its capability execute its assigned missions through modernizing its equipment, increasing readiness, and integrating the reserve and state militias into military missions so more could be done with less. Named the Division Restructuring Study (DRS), the initial force would be a combination of heavy divisions with armored and mechanized infantry battalion building blocks built on the ROAD division concept of a standard division base. A force of 13 Regular Army and eight Army National Guard divisions augmented by 13 Army National Guard and eight Army Reserve combat brigades would be in place to defend Western Europe by 1973 employing tactics named the Active Defense. There were three additional Regular Army brigades that had special missions assigned: one in Alaska and the Canal Zone which were infantry and the 194th Armored Brigade at Fort Knox, Kentucky, The 194th s combat battalions were assigned to support the Armor School.[174]

The Department of the Army had to reduce the manpower assigned to a division to under 17,000.[175] Air defense units replaced their existing systems with the Chaparral anti-air missile and Vulcan anti-air gun systems. Computers enabled automated data processing for logistical, maintenance, and personnel support. The Army's use of aircraft in Vietnam led to the addition of aviation companies to armored and mechanized infantry divisions. The anti-tank capability of infantry units that had depended on the French-developed wire-guided antitank missile with a range of 400 to 2 kilometers and the 106mm recoilless rifle (1,500-6,900 meters range) with the Tube-Launched Optically tracked, Wire-Guided (TOW) missile system that could deliver a missile capable of penetrating 30 inches of armor more than 3 kilometers. Battlefield intelligence was enhanced by merging the Army Security Agency's signals intelligence capability with the historic divisional tactical military intelligence company into the Combat Electronic Warfare Intelligence (CEWI) organization which could look far ahead of the forward edge of the battle area to give commanders advanced information and employ electronic warfare tactics to disrupt an enemy's capabilities. When combined with a target acquisition battery at the division artillery level, the look forward reached 31 miles.[176] The problem with the 21 Division - 21 Brigade structure (Tables 3.4 and 3.5) was that the Army met the goal by 1974 at the same time the Army's manpower level reached 785,330 from 1971's 1,123,810 strength and the Army Chief of Staff, General Creighton Abrams, a combat-experienced tank battalion commander during World War II in Europe and more recently the former commander of US forces in South Vietnam wanted to increase the total to 24 divisions.[177]

Structure of the 21 Division Army 1971-1974

Regular Army Divisions

Location	Armored Divisions	Tank Bns	Inf Bns	Mech Inf Bns
FRG	1st Armored	6	0	5
US	1st Cavalry	4	0	2
US	2nd Armored	4	0	4
FRG	3rd Armored	6	0	5

Location	Infantry Divisions	Tank Bns	Inf Bns	Mech Inf Bns
US	1st Infantry	5		5
ROK	2d Infantry	2	4	2
FRG	3rd Infantry	5	0	6
US	4TH INFANTRY	4	0	6
FRG	8th Infantry	5	0	6
US	9th Infantry	1	7	1
US (Hawaii)	25th Infantry	0	6	0

Location	Airborne Divisions	Tank Bns	Inf Bns
US	82nd	1	9 Abne

Location	Air Assault Divisions	Tank Bns	Inf Bns
US	101st	0	9 Air Aslt

Army National Guard Divisions

Location	Armored Divisions	Tank Bns	Inf Bns	Mech Inf Bns
US	49th Armored	6	0	5
US	50th Armored	5	0	4

Army National Guard

Location	Infantry Divisions	Tank Bns	Inf Bns	Mech Inf Bns
US	6	1	8	1
US	1	4	0	6

Army Reserve Divisions

Location	Armor	Infantry	Airborne
US	0	0	0

Table 3.4 The 21 Army Division Structure: 1971-1974
Source: NOTE: 4th Infantry Division in bold included 1-77 Armor, Adapted from John B Wilson, Maneuver and Firepower: the Evolution of Divisions and Separate Brigades, Table 32. The 21-Division Force, June 1978, CMH Publication 60-14-1, Washington, D.C. Center of Military History, pp 362 and The Army Lineage Series, 1997, and Timothy S. Aumiller, United States Army: Infantry, Armor/Cavalry, Artillery Battalions, 1957-2011, (Takoma Park, MD: Tiger Lily Publications) March 19, 2008, pp 131-132.

Structure of the 21 Army Separate Brigade 1971-1974

Regular Army Brigades

Location	Armored Brigade	Tank Bns	Inf Bns	Mech Inf Bns
US	194th Armored (School Support)	0	0	0

Regular Army Brigades

Location	Infantry Brigade	Tank Bns	Inf Bns	Mech Inf Bns	Airborne
US (AK)	172 Infantry	0	3 Lt Inf	0	0
US (Canal Zone)	193rd Infantry	1	0	2	0
US	197th Infantry	1	1	1	0

Army National Guard Combat Brigades

Location	Armor	Tank Bns	Inf Bns	Mech Inf Bns
US	30th Armor	2	0	1
US	31st Armor	1	0	2
UA	155th Armor	1	0	2

Army National Guard Combat Brigades

Location	Infantry	Tank Bns	Inf Bns	Mech Inf Bns
US	1 Infantry Brigade			2
US	8 Infantry Bdes		3	
US	6 Mech Infantry Bdes	1		2

Army Reserve Combat Brigades

Location	Armor	Location
US	0	

Army Reserve Combat Brigades

Location	Infantry	Tank Bns	Inf Bns	Mech Inf Bns
US	157th Infantry (Mech)	1	0	2
US	187th Infantry	0	3	0
US	205th Infantry	0	3	0

Table 3.5 The 21 Army Separate Brigade Structure: 1971-1974
Source: adapted from John B Wilson, Maneuver and Firepower: the Evolution of Divisions and Separate Brigades, Table 33. The 21 -Brigade Force, June 1972, CMH Publication 60-14-1, Washington, D.C. Center of Military History, pp 363 and The Army Lineage Series, 1997, and Timothy S. Aumiller, United States Army: Infantry, Armor/Cavalry, Artillery Battalions, 1957-2011, (Takoma Park, MD: Tiger Lily Publications) March 19, 2008, pp 131-132.

Structure of the 24 Division Army, 1978

Regular Army Divisions

Location	Armored Divisions	Tank Bns	Inf Bns	Mech Inf Bns
FRG	1st Armored	6	0	5
US	1st Cavalry	5	0	4
US	2nd Armored	6	0	5
FRG	3rd Armored	6	0	5

Location	Infantry Divisions	Tank Bns	Inf Bns	Mech Inf Bns
US	1st Infantry	5	0	4
ROK	2d Infantry	2	4	2
FRG	3rd Infantry	5	0	6
US	4TH INFANTRY	5	0	7
US	5TH INFANTRY	3		3
US	7th Infantry	0	6	0
FRG	8th Infantry	5	0	6
US	9TH INFANTRY	1	1 Abne	7
US	24th Infantry	2	0	4
US	25th Infantry	0	6	0

Location	Airborne Divisions	Tank Bns	Inf Bns
US	82nd	1	9 Abne

Location	Air Assault Divisions	Tank Bns	Inf Bns
US	101st	0	9 Air Aslt

Army National Guard

Location	Armored Divisions	Tank Bns	Inf Bns	Mech Inf Bns
US	49th Armored	6	0	5
US	50th Armored	6	0	5

Army National Guard

Location	Infantry Divisions	Tank Bns	Inf Bns	Mech Inf Bns
US	5 divisions	1	8	1
US	1 division	5	0	6

Army Reserve Divisions

Location	Armor	Infantry	Airborne
US	0	0	0

Table 3.6 The 24 Army Division Structure: 1978
Source: NOTE: 4th Infantry Division included 1-77 Armor; 5th Infantry Division included 3-77 Armor, 9th Infantry Division included 2-77 Armor., Adapted from John B Wilson, Maneuver and Firepower: The Evolution of Divisions and Separate Brigades, Table 35. *The 24-Division Force, 1978*, CMH Publication 60-14-1, Washington, D.C. Center of Military History, p. 368, and The Army Lineage Series, 1997, and Timothy S. Aumiller, United States Army: Infantry, Armor/Cavalry, Artillery Battalions, 1957-2011, (Takoma Park, MD: Tiger Lily Publications) March 19, 2008, pp 131-132.

Structure of the Army 24 Separate Brigade 1978

Regular Army Brigades

Location	Armored Brigade	Tank Bns	Inf Bns	Mech Inf Bns
US	194th Armored	2	0	1

Army National Guard Combat Brigades

Location	Armor	Tank Bns	Inf Bns	Mech Inf Bns
US	30th Armor	2	0	1
US	31st Armor	1	0	2
US	149th Armor	0	0	0
US	155th Armor	0	1	2

Army Reserve Combat Brigades

Location	Armor
US	0

Regular Army Brigades

Location	Infantry Brigade	Tank Bns	Inf Bns	Mech Inf Bns	Airborne
US (AK)	172 Infantry	1	1	1	0
Canal Zone	193rd Infantry	1	0	2	0
US	197th Infantry	1	0	2	0

Army National Guard Combat Brigades

Location	Infantry	Tank Bns	Inf Bns	Mech Inf Bns	Arbn Bns
US	8 Infantry (3 Rnd Out)	0	3	0	0
US	3 Infantry	1	0	2	0
US	5 Mech Infantry (1 Rnd Out)	1	0	2	0
US	1 Airborne	0	0	0	0

Army Reserve Combat Brigades

Location	Infantry	Tank Bns	Inf Bns	Mech Inf Bns
US	157th Infantry	0	2	1
US	187th Infantry	0	3	0
US	205th Infantry	0	3 Lt Inf	0

Table 3.7 The 24 Army Separate Brigade Structure: 1978,
Source: Adapted from John B Wilson, Maneuver and Firepower: the Evolution of Divisions and Separate Brigades, Table 36. *The 24- Brigade Force ,1978*, CMH Publication 60-14-1, Washington, D.C. Center of Military History, p. 369 and The Army Lineage Series, 1997, and Timothy S. Aumiller, United States Army: Infantry, Armor/Cavalry, Artillery Battalions, 1957-2011, (Takoma Park, MD: Tiger Lily Publications) March 19, 2008, pp 131-132

General Donn Starry another armor commander who had commanded V US Corps in West Germany prior to assuming command of the US Amy Training and Doctrine Command (TRADOC) in 1977 presented the Division 86 (Div 86) Army's projected force structure plan. Its original organization of the European battlefield designed heavy armored and mechanized infantry division presented five alternatives that would have a manpower level between 19,000-20,500 officers and enlisted soldiers. The problem that presented itself, to all was a total Army personnel strength of 836,000 would be needed to support the force.[178] Table 3.1 above displays that the Army's personnel ceiling went from 800,973 in 1973 after Vietnam to 710,821 in 1991 at the dissolution of the Warsaw Pact.

Army planners were forced to reduce the ratio of support troops to combat troops to reduce the manpower levels and to integrate more new and more lethal equipment to replace older systems. For example. Armored units received the M-1 Abrams tanks along with the Bradley fighting vehicle family of systems. Until the new equipment was available for more and more units, the M-113 family of vehicles remained in units possessing the M-60 series of tanks.[179]

Another step taken was to stress teamwork and unit cohesion within units whether training or performing a garrison housekeeping task was instituting a new regimental affiliation system in 1981. The overall goal was to increase unit readiness rather than assigning soldiers as individual replacements. Initially, soldiers assigned to armor, air defense artillery cavalry, field artillery, and infantry regiments identified with the regiments and could expect to spend major portions of their Army service in that entity.[180]

Unlike the surprise attack in June 1950, the first battle of the next war could not repeat the Army's unready and piecemeal response to the North Korean surprise attack on June 20th. Starry's vision of the future battlefield was not one of fighting a defensive war that would be costly to the Soviets by trading space for the time to inflict maximum casualties and damage to attacking men and equipment before the threat of using tactical nuclear weapons arose. Field tests of the several configurations of the heavy division were conducted; however Starry assessed that the tests lacked thorough analysis for several reasons and that the force opposing the test division was not employing Soviet tactics.[181] Starry was correct.

William P. Baxter asserts in his *Soviet AirLand Battle Tactics* that opposing force combat tactics assumed by U.S. and its NATO armies would be very similar because the tactical tasks both sides face are the same, and this is a false assumption.[182] Baxter, a subject matter expert on the Soviet ground forces, went to Russian language publications to examine the Soviet Army's theoretical foundation. His research described the many differences between the Soviets and their probable Western opponents. The Soviets applied their concept of warfare which was conceived to be a social phenomenon definable by laws in the following categories: Marxism-Leninism which established the ideological base that capitalism is corrupt and must be destroyed; technology which provided the capabilities for conducting warfare and established that the Soviets must fight with the equipment what they designed, developed, and placed in their inventories following their own military doctrine; and history. It was the historical category that studied the relationships among each of the components in the first two categories. The laws were revised over time as assessed to be necessary. Input came from the Academy of Sciences, the Central Committee of the Communist Party (CPSU) and the Defense Council which was an advisory entity to the CPSU that was involved in implementing military policy.[183] Authority flowed from the top down. To emphasize this, Baxter cites the 1984 dismissal of Chief of the General Staff, Marshal of the Soviet Union Nikolai Orgarkov for disputing the decreed importance of using tactical nuclear weapons on the battlefield to defeat NATO forces.[184]

The Soviet armed forces had conscripted military service during the Cold War, and the draft was unpopular because it disrupted lives, and few remained on active duty following the ends of the obligations similar to their western counterparts. Serving was part of being a Soviet citizen. The Soviet education system was Marxist-Leninist and standardized across the country. Also, the USSR fought World War II on the Eastern Front without a coalition reinforcing it. Young Soviets arrived at the annual draft call believing that the west was corrupt and that the Soviet Army had to be victorious. Whether it was in Czarist Russia, the Soviet Union, or the present Russian Federation, one historic feature of the Russian socio-political culture as it addresses international politics has been that it the country is an island surrounded by enemies.

Starry believed that the first battle that occurred against the Soviets had to be decisive just as did the Soviets. A combination of the U.S. Army well-trained and well-supplied air and ground units using new technologies maneuvering over considerable distances from their home stations had to be massed at the location of the critical battle.[185]

The U.S. national political foundation for Secretary Laird's vision was not established until the mid-1980s with the introduction of the National Security Strategy of the United States of America (NSS) series published as required by each administration. The NSS was the Executive Branch's general guidance about its strategic priorities for the U.S. Congress and foreign governments. From it flowed the National Military Strategy (NMS) that guided the Department of Defense. The legal foundation of the NSS and NMS was the 1986 Goldwater-Nichols Act which streamlined the chains of commands in the services to eliminate interservice rivalries. [186] Its importance here is that the Act integrated improvements in command and control affecting all the armed forces as an additional dimension into the Army's reexamination that solidified the *Active Defense* doctrine (also known as *The Air Land Battle) in 1982[187]*.

The Army Division 1989 Structure

Regular Army Divisions

Location	Armored Divisions	Tank Bns	Inf Bns	Mech Inf Bns
FRG	1st Armored	6	0	4
US	!st Cavalry	3	0	2
US	2nd Armored	5	0	4
FRG	3rd Armored	6	0	4

Location	Infantry Divisions	Tank Bns	Inf Bns	Mech Inf Bns
US	1st Infantry	6		4
ROK	2d Infantry	2	0	2
FRG	3rd Infantry	5	0	5
Ft Carson	4TH INFANTRY	5	0	4
US	5th Infantry	3	0	3
US	6th Infantry	0	3	0
US	7th Infantry	0	0	9 (Lt Inf)
FRG	8TH INFANTRY	5	0	5
US	9th Infantry	1	2 Lt Inf	0
US	10th Mountain	0	6(Lt Inf)	0
US	24th Infantry	3	0	3
US	25th Infantry	0	9 Air Aslt	0

Location	Airborne Divisions	Tank Bns	Inf Bns
US	82nd	1	9 Abne

Location	Air Assault Divisions	Tank Bns	Inf Bns
US	101st	0	9 Air Aslt

Army National Guard

Location	Infantry Divisions	Tank Bns	Inf Bns	Mech Inf Bns
US	3 divisions	1	8	1
US	2 divs	5	0	5
US	1 div	2	8	0
US	1 div	0	9 Lt Inf	0
US	1 div	3	6	1

Table 3.8 The Army Division 1989 Structure,
Source: NOTE: 4th Infantry Division included 1-77 Armor in 1989 only; 8th Infantry Division included 3-77 Armor and 5-77 Armor. Adapted from John B Wilson, Maneuver and Firepower: the Evolution of Divisions and Separate Brigades, Table 37. *Divisions 1989* CMH Publication 60-14-1, Washington, D.C. Center of Military History, p. 404-5, and The Army Lineage Series, 1997, and Timothy S. Aumiller, United States Army: Infantry, Armor/Cavalry, Artillery Battalions, 1957-2011, (Takoma Park, MD: Tiger Lily Publications) March 19, 2008, pp 131-132.

Structure of the Army Separate Brigade 1989

Regular Army Brigades

Location	Armored Brigade	Tank Bns	Inf Bns	Mech Inf Bns
US	194th Armored (School Support)	0	0	0

Regular Army Brigades

Location	Infantry Brigade	Tank Bns	Inf Bns	Mech Inf Bns	Airborne
US (AK)	172 Infantry	0	3 Lt Inf	0	0
US (Canal Zone)	193rd Infantry	1	0	2	0
US	197th Infantry	1	1	1	0

Army National Guard Combat Brigades

Location	Armor	Tank Bns	Inf Bns	Mech Inf Bns
US	30th Armor	2	0	1
US	31st Armor	1	0	2
UA	155th Armor	1	0	2

Army National Guard Combat Brigades

Location	Infantry	Tank Bns	Inf Bns	Mech Inf Bns
US	1 Infantry Brigade			2
US	8 Infantry Bdes		3	
US	6 Mech Infantry Bdes	1		2

Army Reserve Combat Brigades

Location	Armor	Location
US	0	

Army Reserve Combat Brigades

Location	Infantry	Tank Bns	Inf Bns	Mech Inf Bns
US	157th Infantry (Mech)	1	0	2
US	187th Infantry	0	3	0
US	205th Infantry	0	3	0

Table 3.9 The Army Separate Brigade Structure 1989
Source: adapted from John B Wilson, Maneuver and Firepower: the Evolution of Divisions and Separate Brigades, Table 38. *Brigades 1989* CMH Publication 60-14-1, Washington, D.C. Center of Military History, p. 406, and The Army Lineage Series, 1997, and Timothy S. Aumiller, United States Army: Infantry, Armor/Cavalry, Artillery Battalions, 1957-2011, (Takoma Park, MD: Tiger Lily Publications) March 19, 2008, pp 131-132.

Five tank battalions wore the crest of the 77th Armor Regiment during the Cold War. The 1st, 2d, and 3rd Battalions were activated at Fort Carson beginning on February 19th, 1962. The 2d Battalion activated in 1962 but deactivated 20 months later returned to the active roles of the Army on August 21, 1977 at Fort Lewis, Washington as part of the 9th Infantry Division. The 4th Battalion was activated on January 17, 1963 and assigned to the Army Reserve's 157th Infantry Brigade in Upper Darby, Pennsylvania. The 5th Battalion was activated in Bad Kreuznach, West Germany and was part of the 8th Infantry Division beginning on April 4, 1984.[188]

The 5th Battalion 77th Armor moved 52 miles southeast to Mannheim. It remained active until 1995 when it was deactivated. Its commanders included Lieutenant Colonel Daniel R. Zanini (1983-1985); Lieutenant Colonel Joseph B Morgan (1985-1987); Lieutenant Colonel Thomas A Morton (1987-1989); Lieutenant Colonel Phillip A Allum (1989-1991); Lieutenant Colonel Hank Sharpensburg (1991-1993); and Lieutenant Colonel Patrick J. Flynn (1993-1995).[189]

The Steel Tigers' 1st Battalion was deactivated in Vietnam in August 1971 during the reduction of the US presence there. The 5th Infantry Division (Mechanized) (Red Devils) was renamed the 4th Infantry Division (Ivy) in 1970 and cased its colors.[190] Then, the 5th Infantry Division consisting of two infantry battalions returned to the active unit list at Ft Polk, Louisiana in 1974.[191] It was stationed there until November 1992 when it became the 2d Armored Division.[192] The division moved from Louisiana to Ft Hood, Texas in 1993. While at Fort Polk, the 5th Infantry Division was part of the Operation *JUST CAUSE* force that invaded Panama in December 1989 to restore the internationally recognized Panamanian government that was overthrown by General Manuel Noriega who was commander of the country's armed forces. He was arrested for criminal activity including drugs and money laundering. The Red Devil division was stationed there until November 1992 when it was renamed the 2d Armored Division and deactivated again. The division moved from Louisiana to Ft Hood, Texas in 1993.[193]

The 1st Battalion 77th Armor was reactivated at Fort Carson in March 1973 where it began in 1962 when it replaced an infantry battalion to make the 4th Infantry Division a more formidable force if deployed to Europe. It was joined by the 2nd Battalion in June 1986.[194]

While part of the 9th Infantry Division Guard at Fort Lewis, the Steel Tigers 2nd Battalion performed the Army's standard peacetime training year consisting of tactical, maintenance, and administrative elements and supporting Army National Guard tank units undergo annual tank gunnery training at the Yakima, Washington Firing Center. The battalion also deployed to West Germany in the 1978 Return of Forces to Germany (REFORGER) exercise demonstrating of the Army's capability to react to a Warsaw Pact invasion.[195] The two battalions remained with the 4th Infantry until January 16, 1996 when the 2d Battalion left the Army's active roll. The 1st Battalion remained subordinate to the 4th Division until December 15, 1989 when it was deactivated only to be reactivated again and subordinated to the 1st Infantry Division Forward in West Germany.[196] The 4th Division moved to Ft. Hood Texas in 1995 to replace the now inactive 2d Armored Division. The 4th Division returned to Fort Carson in 2009.[197]

The Soviet Union and the Warsaw Pact dissolved in 1991. The Cold War ended with 18 Regular Army Divisions (including the 82d and 101st Airborne Divisions) and 20 Army National Guard, 4 Regular Army, and three Army Reserve brigades on the U.S, Army's active role in 1989.[198]

Table 3-1 above showed that the US Army's 1989 manpower ceiling was 769,741. The peace dividend reaped from the end of the Cold War resulted in Congress setting a reduced manpower level for the Army to reach at 495,000 by 1996.[199] The Army had 491,103 soldiers on active duty by that deadline. How the Army reached this goal was systematic but also dramatic as the force planners had to deal not only with manpower reductions, but also new combat actions.

The major intervention was in response to the Iraqi invasion of Kuwait in August 1990. The 1st Armored (minus its 1st Brigade) and 3rd Armored Divisions, along with the 3rd Brigades from the 2d Armored and 3rd Infantry Divisions were moved to Southwest Asia from Germany. The 1st Cavalry Division, 1st Infantry Division (minus the 1st Infantry Division Forward), 24th Infantry Division, 82nd Airborne, and 101st Airborne Divisions, and 197th Infantry Brigade were deployed from their U. S. garrisons to prepare for Operation *DESERT SHIELD* followed by Operation *DESERT STORM* in January-February 1991.[200]

Later in August 1991, the 1st Infantry Division Forward in Germany was deactivated.[201] The 8th Infantry Division was deactivated and renamed the 1st Armored Division on January 17, 1992 in a ceremony at Baumholder Germany. The Division included the 3rd Brigade's 5th Battalion, 77th Armor that was activated on April 1, 1982 and garrisoned in Mannheim at Sullivan Barracks, and the 3rd Battalion 77th Armor that was activated on June 16th, 1986.[202] The battalions were organized under the Division 86 structure of a battalion headquarters and four tank companies with three platoons of four M-60A3 tanks each and two tanks in the company headquarters. There were also two tanks in each battalion's headquarters. Both battalions were assigned to the 1st Armored Division when the 8th Infantry Division was deactivated following the dissolution of the Warsaw Pact. The two battalions were later removed from the active unit roll on April 16, 1995 after the end of the Cold War.[203]

After Operation *DESERT STORM*, the 3rd Armored Division, 3rd Brigade, 2 Armored Division, and US VII Corps were deactivated in the winter of 1992-1993 and the 2nd Armored Cavalry Regiment returned to the United States. The US Army's presence in NATO was reduced to US V US Corps, two brigades each of the 1st Armored and 3rd Infantry divisions, and the 11th Armored Cavalry Regiment[204]

The 4th Battalion, 77th Armor activated on January 17, 1963 at Horsham, Pennsylvania and then moved to Reading was assigned to the 157th Infantry Brigade, US Army Reserve. In addition to the Steel Tigers' 4th Battalion, the 157th Brigade included the following combat units: the 6th Battalion 68th Armor located at Bethlehem and Indiantown Gap Military Reservation (IGMR); the 1st Battalion 313th Infantry headquartered at IGMR, Annville, and Lock Haven; the 1st Battalion 314th Infantry (Mechanized) at Bristol and Warrington; and the 1st Battalion 315th Infantry in the Philadelphia. The Department of Defense sought to remove all combat units from the Reserve to keep them in the National Guard. One of tools used was to send the 4-77's tanks and the 3-414's mechanized infantry and their support vehicles to Israel following the June 1967 Six-Day War. Political pressure in Congress caused withdrawing three infantry brigades from the drawdown including the 157th. Nonetheless, the 157th converted its mechanized infantry and tank battalions to infantry one of which was the 4th Battalion 77th Armor. The personnel were merged into the 6-68th Armor. The Steel Tigers were deactivated on January 31, 1968.[205]

Chapter 4: The Korean War

Introduction

The 753d Tank Battalion went home after VE Day and was deactivated along with much of the rest of the US Army. The discharged veterans pursued their post-war goals while others remained on active duty. World War II was fought as a crusade with the federal bureaucracy, industry, and the people united behind the armed forces. While the lessons learned from combined tank and infantry operations were studied by the Army's leadership, the soldiers' experience evaporated and the nation demobilized. In addition to the loss of experience, the American industrial base shifted to peacetime products.

The 1946 Stilwell Board examined the use of tanks and concluded that the best antitank weapon was another tank.[206]. The board added one tank company to every infantry regiment and one tank battalion to every infantry division. The 1950 Army Field Manual FM 7-20 included this change.[207] The lesson of World War II that tanks and infantry worked well together became set in Army theory; but the problem of the drastic reductions in the Army's budget did not allow for the tanks and necessary support organizations to be trained and manned, and new equipment to be designed, tested, produced and maintained. No new tanks were coming off the assembly line in the United States. The Army had 28,000 tanks in 1945. By 1950, there were 3,400 M-24 Chaffee light tanks and 3,200 M4A3E8 Sherman Tanks that were veterans of World War II. Most of the M-24s and about half of the Shermans were inoperable.[208] In addition, the authorization for armored organizations to be placed into infantry regiments and divisions could not implemented. The 1949 and 1950 budgets forced the elimination of the infantry regimental tank company, the reduction of the infantry division's tank battalion to one tank company for the entire division, and the loss of one infantry battalion in every infantry regiment[209]

Prelude to War

The mission of the Army following World War II was occupation duty in Germany, Austria, Japan, and South Korea. The 753rd Tank Battalion reemerged as the 77th Medium Tank Battalion. It was assigned to the 7th Infantry (Bayonet) Division after the division moved from Korea to Japan in 1948. This division began World War II protecting the US west coast in the San Jose, California area. Its entry into World War II in earnest was against the Japanese-held Aleutian Islands of Attu in May 1943 and then Kiska in August.

The 7th proceeded south to the next battle in the Marshall Islands at Kwajalein in January 1944 followed by Eniwetok in February, and on to Leyte in the Philippines in October. Its final battle began on April 1, 1945, against the Japanese on Okinawa. It ended on June 21st. The 7th Division was ordered to South Korea from Okinawa to accept the Japanese surrender following the August 14th announcement of Japan's unconditional surrender.

Japan's rule of Korea began in 1907 after defeating the Chinese in the 1894-1895 Sino-Japanese War and the Russians in the 1904-1905 Russo-Japanese War. Following the conclusion of the latter conflict, the Japanese stayed in Korea. The Japanese demobilized the Korean military and assumed control of the country's administrative and political institutions. By 1907, they controlled the country and dealt swiftly and violently to suppress resistance and uprisings.

Korea's future was discussed by the allies at the Potsdam Conference, July 17-August 2, 1945, but no decisions were made. The United States dropped the first atomic bomb on Hiroshima on August 6th. The Soviet Union declared war on Japan on August 8th. Once the US used the second atomic bomb against the Japanese at Nagasaki on August 9th, the Soviet Far East Command attacked the Japanese with 1.6 million men and more than 5500 tanks. Japan's complete collapse was nearly immediate.

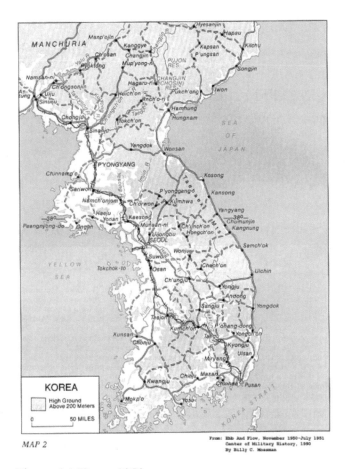

Figure 4.1 Korea 1950
Source: Korean War Project Army Maps, Map 2 Korea 1950 NOTE: from Ebb And Flow, November 1950 - July 1951 - The United States Army in the Korean War, Center of Military History, United States Army, Washington, D.C., 1990, retrieved from Korean War AMS Topo - Map 2 - Korea

In addition to Manchuria, the Soviets considered Korea to be their strategic area of interest. The *25th Army* seized its first objectives in northern Korea on August 11th and then moved south to its new headquarters in Pyongyang where it began occupation missions. The Soviets also moved into the South Sakhalin and Kuril Islands. They placed communist governments in all conquered areas.

Restoring Korea's social, economic, and political systems were not major U.S. national policy concerns at the July 17-August 2, 1945 Potsdam Conference with President Harry Truman, British Prime Minister Clement Attlee, and the Soviet Union's General Secretary of the Communist Party and Chairman of the Council of Ministers, Joseph Stalin. The mission of the US forces in Korea was to accept the Japanese surrender and nothing extending beyond that. The US did not want to occupy a large portion of the country because General Douglas MacArthur the Supreme Commander for the Allied Powers (SCAP) was emphasizing the occupation of Japan and concentrating US forces there.[210]

Stalin's sudden and swift expansion into the Far East promoted the importance of the Korean peninsula to the top of the list of post-war defense priorities facing United States policymakers. How to counter Moscow's unanticipated penetration of northeast Asia and where to stop the Soviets became two challenges for the US foreign policy community. Dividing Korea at the 38th Parallel was the product of two Army staff officers assigned to the War Department: the future Secretary of State Colonel Dean Rusk, and future Eighth Army Commander Colonel Charles H. Bonesteel III. This line would divide Korea nearly in half. They were allowed about 30 minutes during the night of August 10th, 1945 to deliver a recommendation to War Department planners. Neither was a Far East expert. They agreed that Korea's capital, Seoul, should be in the US-controlled area. Their only aid was a *National Geographic* map and they saw no natural barrier in the region that could serve as a physical dividing line between the US and Soviet forces. They recommended using the 38th Parallel. Once approved at the War Department, the Bonesteel-Rusk choice had to be staffed through the rest of the U.S. national security establishment before being submitted to President Truman. While the Soviet Army began entering Korea on August 11th, the closest U.S. forces other than those on occupation duty in Japan were in Okinawa.

President Truman approved using the 38th Parallel division of the country on August 15th. North Korea's area (46.540 square miles) was nearly the same as Mississippi's (48,434 square miles), and South Korea's area (38,691 square miles) is nearly the same as Indiana's (36,418 square miles). It was transmitted to Moscow and accepted by Stalin on August 16th and the Soviets did not go further south than the 38th Parallel.[211] In the United States, the 38th Parallel runs from the Pacific coast through Stockton, California between Utah and Arizona, Colorado and New Mexico, through the southern thirds of Kansas and Missouri, and the southern tip of Illinois, West Point, Kentucky near Fort Knox, West Virginia, Maryland, and Milford, Virginia which is between Richmond and Fredericksburg and then across into the Chesapeake Bay and Atlantic Ocean.

The allies agreed that the Soviets would receive the Japanese surrender in the north and the US in the south of the dividing line. General MacArthur received instructions to include Korea in his occupation responsibilities with Japan.[212] He had to organize a military force and then place it on the ground to demonstrate US resolve in Korea. He looked at the nearest US forces not presently engaged in occupation duties in Japan: the 7th Infantry Division in Okinawa.

MacArthur ordered Lieutenant General John R. Hodge, the commander of the US XXIV Corps to be in charge of the occupation as the Commander of United States Army Forces in Korea. The Corps arrived between September 4-8, 1945 from Okinawa.[213] Hodge appointed Major General Archibald V. Arnold to be the Military Governor of South Korea on September 12, 1945.[214] Hodge also commanded the 7th US Infantry Division.

US forces entering Japan and Korea for occupation had four missions including 1) reducing Japanese opposition; 2) gaining control of political communications centers and sea lines of communication; 3) controlling food supplies and the land and coastal lines of communication, and 4) recovering and repatriating allied prisoners of war. To accomplish these missions, the occupation forces would have to gain control of the Japanese armed forces by disarming and demobilizing them and destroying hostile elements; gain tactical unit control of internal routes of communications; and to prepare for the transfer of responsibilities from military occupation forces to post-war government agencies.[215].

Major General Paul Mueller wrote in his *2007 Occupation of Japan-A Progress Report* that the occupation of Japan began by entering a country where industry had been destroyed, food shortages caused by reduced rice and fishing harvests, and the lack of timber impacted the capability to rebuild. In accordance with the Cairo and Potsdam conferences, Japan retained control of the following large islands: Hokkaido and Honshu in the north and Shikoku and Kyushu in the southwest.[216]

The occupation progressed more smoothly in Japan than in South Korea. The Japanese civilian population expected the United States to exact vengeance on them for the war. There were 1.7 million former members of the armed forces and another 3.2 million civilian defense volunteers with weapons when the nation surrendered.[217] The overarching cause for the smoother occupation was General MacArthur's recognition that to maintain order and prevent resistance movements from erupting, it would be necessary to integrate the Japanese into rebuilding their country at all levels from technocratic management to those doing the work at docks, railyards, and elsewhere.

In his role as the SCAP, MacArthur accomplished the successful transition from a historically autocratic nation to a democracy. He agreed with the Japanese to allow Emperor Hirohito to remain as the head of state and not be held accountable for war crimes. A second key cause was the conduct of US occupation troops. MacArthur stressed to all that they were on the world stage. The examples that they set by their behavior on- and off-duty would determine the success or failure of their goal: a peaceful occupation. When violent opposition to the allies did not occur, the abolishment of all vestiges of Japanese militarism and the disarming of the military and paramilitary forces proceeded peacefully. MacArthur changed the Japanese constitution to introduce representative government and other democratic instruments into the Japanese political, economic, and social systems.

Japan's first free elections in its history occurred on April 10, 1946 as testimony to the success of MacArthur's approach.[218]

The occupation was much rougher in Korea. On the US side, no one spoke the language and the units were combat troops. No one was trained in military government and civil affairs. The Japanese had not included Koreans in the administration of the country, and this resulted in no technically trained Koreans available to manage transportation and communications when the Americans arrived. Korean civil outrage and demonstrations occurred when the US commander approved allowing Japanese technocrats to fill the necessary positions. When the Koreans replaced the Japanese, inefficiencies and incompetence were the result.

North and South Korea established their respective governments in 1948 and the last Soviet troops departed back to the Soviet Union at the end of the year. They left behind large stockpiles of armaments and military equipment including T-34 tanks (Figure 4-2).

Figure 4.2 North Korean T34 Medium Tank,
Source: retrieved from https://www.gettyimages.com/photos/north-korean-t-34-tank, May 18, 2023

The 7th Infantry Division remained in Korea until the beginning of 1948 when it deployed to Japan. The 17th and 32nd Infantry Regiments and elements of the 1st Battalion, 31st Infantry Regiment were assigned to Honshu Island. Other 31st Infantry Regiment's units, including the 77th Tank Battalion, occupied Camp Chitose near Sapporo on Japan's northernmost island, Hokkaido. Figure 4.3 displays A Company's 3rd Platoon during the late winter-spring 1950 period at Camp Chitose. The firing ranges and airbase were located about 25 miles away.[219]

Figure 4.3 3rd Platoon, Company A, 77th Heavy Tank Battalion, Camp Chitose, Japan,
Source: retrieved from 77th Armor Association Archives May 22, 2023

Divisional units conducted cold weather training and other military skills training during the winter of 1949. After receiving 800 replacement enlisted soldiers (300 from basic training in the US and 500 first-term enlistees from the First Cavalry Division) training began again in April 1949. In addition to tactical training, remedial education courses were also ordered for those soldiers who scored low on the written portions of their proficiency tests as the average education level for enlisted soldiers was eighth grade. The Division also initiated unit leader training because of a shortage of noncommissioned officers. Training including range firing continued through the summer of 1950.[220] In spite of the training and freedom from occupation missions, unit readiness was degraded as officers and enlisted were reassigned to the US, and military budget reductions impacted all aspects of readiness including the replacement of fuel and lubricants, ammunition, parts to service vehicles, and other items.

The 77th Armor was organized in accordance with *Part 4, Tank Battalion, Infantry and Airborne Divisions, Field Manual 17-33*, September 1949.[221] Its organic units on paper were a battalion headquarters and a headquarters and service company, three medium tank companies with four platoons of five tanks each, and a medical detachment In addition, each tank company had two command tanks. The headquarters and service company contained the personnel, vehicles, and equipment for the administrative, supply, and maintenance of the battalion.[222] The battalion was authorized 39 officers and 597 enlisted.[223] Each tank company was authorized twenty 30.3 ton M4A3E8 Sherman Medium Tanks with 76 millimeter (mm) main guns (Figure 4.4) and two M4A3 Sherman tanks with 105 mm howitzer main guns (Figure 4.5). The battalion headquarters was authorized two M4A3E8 Shermans.[224] In reality, the battalion had 20.2 ton World War II M-24 Chaffee Light Tanks because the heavier tanks could not travel on Japanese roads and bridges without damaging them.[225]

Figure 4.4 M4A3E8 Sherman Medium Tank 76mm
Source: retrieved from File:M4A3E8.JPG - Wikimedia Commons

Figure 4.5 M4A3 Sherman Medium Tank 105mm Howitzer,
Source: M4 Sherman tank - Flickr - Joost J. Bakker IJmuiden.jpg Retrieved from
https://commons.wikimedia.org/wiki/File:M4_Sherman_tankM4 Sherman - Wikipedia

June 1950 Surprise Invasion

US Army to Korea

No one anticipated another conflict a short five years after the end of World War II, and none recognized the Korean conflict for the first limited war contest of the Cold War. The North Koreans attacked South Korea during the night of June 25, 1950. The North Korean attack caught everyone by surprise. There were four infantry divisions with occupation missions in Japan that were available to respond at the outbreak of the Korean War were understrength. There was a great gap between the image of the divisions' combat potential manifested by their physical proximity and their real combat capability. The divisions were the 24th Infantry Division, 25th Infantry Division, 1st Cavalry Division and the 7th Infantry Division. These units were about 7,000 men below their authorization of 18,900 soldiers. Two of the most important problems were personnel and equipment.

The personnel shortage problem caused by annual budgets, missions, and priority when balanced against Army requirements in Europe was that division shortages were exacerbated when they were ordered to fill units to deploying to Korea.[226]   The 24th Infantry Division was the first to be assigned to South Korea in response to the North's attack. Despite its reduced manpower levels, the other three divisions were levied for troops to bring the 24th up to its authorized strength. This requirement reduced unit proficiency and cohesiveness as well as already reduced unit strengths in the other divisions.[227]   The 7th Division's manpower strength reached a low of 7,900 men in August 1950.[228]

Another example of the personnel problem also highlights the equipment problem the Army faced in the chaotic weeks after the North Korean invasion: assigning a tank unit to the 24th Infantry Division from the 7th Division.

Lieutenant Samuel R. Fowler, a platoon leader, and 14 members of his unit in Company A, 77th Medium Tank Battalion, 7th Division were reassigned to the deploying division as the 8064th Provisional Heavy Tank Platoon. The platoon had been training on the M-24 Chaffee Light Tank (Figure 2.3) that was armed with a 75-millimeter main gun in the 77th. The 8064th's mission was to go into combat with three 46-ton M-26 Heavy Tanks armed with 90-millimeter main guns that had been discovered on June 29, 1950 in a Tokyo army depot (Figure 4.5).[229]

Figure 4.6 M26 Pershing Heavy Tank, 90 mm
Source: Josh Hallett - Flickr: Tanks at the USS Alabama - Mobile, AL, CC BY-SA 2.0,
https://commons.wikimedia.org/w/index.php?curid=18150779 retrieved from
https://en.wikipedia.org/wiki/M26_Pershing#/media/File:Tanks_at_the_USS_Alabama_

Fowler and his tankers first had to make the M-26s operational. The tanks had been sent to Japan after being used in an exercise in Latin America. Extensive repairs were needed before they could move. One example of the state of deterioration was that the fan belts had rotted and replacement belts had to be fabricated. The cobbled-together-unit left for Korea before the new belts arrived from the United States. The platoon fired the tanks' main guns for the first time once they arrived in the theater. They were the only U.S. tank unit in Korea. The fan belts failed and three tanks were lost on July 31, 1950 in a combat action during which Lieutenant Fowler was killed. Alvin Clouse, a member of Lt Fowler's platoon recalled that he was a tank crewman whom Lt Fowler replaced with a mechanic named Anderson for the deployment. Clouse later found four members of his platoon who told him that five other members of his Steel Tiger platoon had been killed in action that day along with Lt Fowler [230]

The 24th Infantry Division's 1st Battalion, 21st Infantry deployed to Pusan (Busan) on June 30-July 1st by air. This unit is more commonly remembered as Task Force Smith. It had two infantry companies, a battery of 105mm howitzers, and 75 mm rifles and bazooka rocket launchers that provided the antitank capability. It took up defensive positions between Suwon and Osan and came under attack on July 5th.

The next unit also came from the 24th Division. It consisted of two understrength battalions of the 34th Infantry Regiment that were alerted on July 1st and moved immediately to port. This unit arrived in Pusan, South Korea on July 2d, checked its equipment, and began moving into positions south of Osan to stop the invading force on July 4th This unit was attacked on July 6th. [231]

The 25th Infantry Division arrived in Korea on July 13th. It brought the 89th Tank Battalion ashore which was the first full strength armored unit to enter the war. The First Cavalry Division landed on July 18th. Next, three independent tank battalions debarked on August 7th. The 6th, 70th, and 73rd Tank Battalions. The 6th Tank Battalion with four companies of 48.5-ton M-46 Patton tanks mounting 90 mm main guns had been part of the 2d Armored Division at Ft Hood (Figure 4.7).

Figure 4.7 M-46 Patton Medium Tank, 90mmSource: retrieved from
en.wikipedia.org/wiki/M46_Patton#/media/File:M47_Patton-Army.mil-2007-04-20-164919.jpg

The 1st Cavalry Division received the US Army Armor School's 70th Tank Battalion (two companies of M4A3E8s and one company of M-26s that arrived from Fort Knox. The third was the 73rd Tank Battalion that had been a unit of the 3rd Infantry Division at Ft Benning, Georgia and it operated as an independent tank battalion initially in South Korea. It had three companies of M-26 Pershing tanks. It joined the 7th Infantry Division at Inchon in September. The 2nd Infantry Division reached Korea with its 72nd Tank Battalion. This battalion was equipped with a combination of M4A3E8s and M-26s on August 16th.[232] Subsequently, the 3rd Infantry Division was alerted to deploy to Korea and replaced the 73rd Tank Battalion with the 64th Tank Battalion that had been reassigned from the 2d Armored Division.

An immediate remedy to overcoming the US Army's manpower shortage was the creation of the Korean Augmentation to the United States Army (KATUSA project) shortly after the war began. This stopgap project became a program that still exists. Its authorization was a verbal agreement between the South Korean President Syngman Rhee and General MacArthur. The KATUSAs belonged to their South Korean army but were integrated into American units in various occupational specialties and served alongside their US Army counterparts. In addition to increasing the strengths of the US units, they also could assist in identifying North Koreans and contribute their knowledge of the terrain.[233]

The first 1,857 KATUSAs were sent from South Korea to Japan to join the 7th Infantry Division in August 1950 about two weeks before the division deployed to Korea. They had no prior military training. Receiving and integrating the South Koreans posed a major problem for the division. There were no South Korean interpreters, and no US personnel could speak Korean. Additionally, the soldiers brought with them unfamiliar diseases and different sanitation standards. The 31st Infantry Regiment reported that all of its KATUSAs were fully integrated by September 9th.[234]

George Goebel and Michael Borske were assigned to Company A, 77th Medium Tank Battalion at Camp Chitose on Hokkaido. Goebel wrote that the battalion existed as a unit until the beginning of the Korean War, but the unit was broken up on June 25th. The battalion remained active on paper with a warrant officer as its commander, but the three tank companies were assigned to the 7th Division's three regiments. A Company retained is unit designation and was assigned to the 31st Infantry Regiment. The other two companies became part of the 32nd Infantry Regiment, and the 17th Infantry Regiment were named Tank Company, 32 Infantry Regiment and Tank Company, 17th Infantry Regiment in the official documents at the National Archives and Records Administration (NARA) in College Park, Maryland. Borske added that the A company commander was Captain Robert E. Drake, and the First Sergeant was Clifford G. Keck. The warrant officer battalion commander joined the rest of A Company when it departed for Korea in September 1950.[235]

Captain Drake was originally from Pasadena, California and graduated from the United States Military Academy on June 6, 1944. His initial assignment was as a platoon leader in Company B, of the 9th Tank Battalion, 20th Armored Division fighting in the European theater. He became the commander of Company A, 77th Medium Tank Battalion (A-77 Armor) when the 7th Infantry Division moved to Japan. The company was assigned to the 31st Infantry Regiment on June 25, 1950. Drake stayed with his unit throughout 1950. Subsequently, he returned to the U.S. to attend the Armor School at Fort Knox, Kentucky. He remained at Fort Knox serving on the Army Field Forces Board #2 after graduation and then left to continue his career.[236]

Deployment from Japan

The 31st Infantry Regiment's alert that it would depart for Korea came on September 6, 1950. The soldiers traveled by rail to Gotemba station and the vehicles road marched directly to Camp Fuji on Honshu Island in Shizuokua Prefecture near the base of Mount Fuji. From there, they went to the Port of Yokohama on September 7th. Goebel wrote that

Company A's tankers would receive M-4A3E8s Sherman Medium Tanks to replace their M-24 light tanks when they joined the rest of the division at the port of Yokohama.[237]

The 31st Infantry Regiment including A-77th Armor boarded the assault transport, *USS General H.W. Butner* (AP-113) on September 8th and sailed away from the docks. The *Butner* went into anchorage in the Yokohama port where the regiment initiated administrative guard duties and a 10-day, eight hours per day training program to begin once the ships were underway to Inchon (Incheon).[238] The convoy reached Inchon at about 11:30 am on September 16, 1950, and anchored 10 miles outside of the port (Figure 4.8).[239]

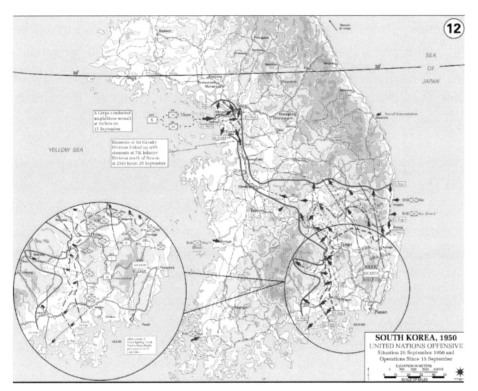

Figure 4.8 Inchon Landing and Pusan Breakout September 1950
Source: Kennedy Hickman, Korean War: Inchon Landings, ThoughtCo, Apr. 5, 2023, retrieved from Inchon Invasion in the Korean War (Operation Chromite) (thoughtco.com) June 21, 2023.
The Inchon landings took place September 15 through 19, 1950.

The invasion force consisted of 70,000 troops and 230 naval vessels.[240] Codenamed Operation *CHROMITE,* this amphibious assault was planned by General MacArthur to land forces behind the North Korean invasion force in a surprise move to achieve a strategic turnaround for the UN forces who by September had been pushed back to a small perimeter around Pusan in southeastern South Korea. MacArthur's plan was to attack the North Koreans to the north and south of Inchon destroying fighting units and severing supply lines between them. The major US command taking part in the landings was US X Corps

(Xth Corps) commanded by Major General Edward M Almond who was also MacArthur's Chief of Staff. The Xth Corps included the 1st Marine Division led by Major General Oliver Smith and 7th Infantry Division commanded by Major General David Barr. The Corps was supported by non-divisional artillery and engineer units.[241]

Before the US forces began attacking south from Inchon and Seoul into the North Koreans' rear, the US Eighth Army broke out of the Pusan Perimeter when it crossed the Naktong River in the Waegwan vicinity and began attacking north on September 16th (Figure 4.8). The main attack used a central to western axis from Waegwan, through Kimch'on, and Taejon (Daejeon). The objective was Suwon where the leading force would meet the US X Corps advancing from the north. Suwon is 19 miles south of Seoul and is now a major commercial center and it is the capital the country's most populous province. Before the North Korean invasion, the Suwon area included what had been a US Air Force base that had to be abandoned on June 30th as the North Koreans advanced. Regaining control of the airfield was the 7th Infantry Division's objective.[242]

The 1st Marine Division landed initially on September 16th and began liberating Seoul from the North Koreans. The 7th Infantry Division, less its 17th Infantry Regiment which was diverted to Pusan to go into Eighth Army reserve, began landing on September 17th with the Division Headquarters, Company B of the 73rd Medium Tank Battalion followed on the 18th by the 7th Division's 32nd Infantry Regiment, 7th Reconnaissance Company, and Companies A and C of the 73rd. This tank battalion went initially into an assembly area and formed Task Force Hannum named after the 73rd Armor's commander, Lieutenant Colonel Calvin S. Hannum. The Task Force included Company B-73 Armor, a rifle company from the 31st Infantry Regiment and a light artillery battery. *The* 73rd Tank Battalion was placed under the control of the 7th Infantry Division on September 2, 1950.[243]

The journey of the 73rd Armor to the 7th Infantry Division where it joined the 77th Armor's tank company is only one example of the US rapid response to the surprise North Korean invasion on June 25th. The 73rd Armor fought in World War II through southern France as the 756th Tank Battalion alongside with the 753d, and was deactivated. It was reactivated on August 1, 1946 and then reorganized and redesignated the 756th Heavy Tank Battalion on January 15, 1948.

The 756th was renamed again becoming the 73rd Heavy Tank Battalion on January 10, 1949, and assigned back to the Third Infantry Division at Fort Benning, Georgia. The unit's name was changed again to the 73rd Tank Battalion on July 14, 1950, and ordered to Korea as an independent unit. It left Fort Benning on July 15th. The battalion arrived in Korea in August. It was committed immediately to the defense of the Pusan Perimeter.[244]

The 73rd's Company C joined the 27th Infantry Regiment which itself had been a subordinate unit of the 25th Infantry Division, but which Lieutenant General Walton Walker, the Eighth Army commander, detached and used as well as other units as an independent quick reaction reserve to plug gaps in the line wherever they occurred. One of these missions provided support for the 24th Infantry Division in the Punchbowl battles between August 15-21st 1950.[245] Company A of the 73d guarded the Main Supply Route (MSR) near Ulsan, Korea, and Company B moved first to Kyongju (Gyeongju-si) to support one task force and then to Kigye to assist another regiment.[246] The 73d Armor was assigned to the Eighth Army reserve on September 2, 1950 and began a road march to Pusan where with the 1st Provisional USMC Marine Brigade it began preparing for the Inchon invasion and loaded onto tank landing ships (LSTs).[247]

The 31st Infantry Regiment entered Inchon harbor on September 17th. Units of the 31st Infantry Regiment began departing their ship on September 19th beginning about 8:45 pm. Once on the Inchon landing beach, they moved into an assembly area for the night. The Regimental Command Post became operational at 12:45 pm on September 20th.[248] The 31st was designated the 31st Regimental Combat Team (RCT) on September 7, 1950.[249] The attached units included the Regiment's three battalions, the 57th Field Artillery Battalion, and Company C, 13th Engineers (Combat).[250].

The lead elements of the 31st RCT began moving southeast toward Suwon on September 22d with the 32nd Infantry Regiment to retake control of the former US air base from the North Koreans.[251]

The 73rd Tank Battalion's first mission as part of the 31st RCT was to move toward Suwon on the 22nd. Elements of the regiment entered the heavily defended town on September 23d. The 7th Infantry Division controlled Suwon by September 25th. Once this occurred, its area of operations expanded to include Osan which is about 8.5 miles south.[252] All of the 31st's battalions were deployed to prevent North Korean forces with armored and other mechanized vehicles retreating north in the face of the Eighth Army's advance from breaking through. The Division ordered units to conduct reconnaissance, establish roadblocks, and occupy the high ground around the town and airfield. Company A-77th Armor did not complete unloading its equipment at Inchon until September 24th and the first platoon began moving to Suwon. It arrived by noon that afternoon and the remainder of the company was expected by noon on September 25th.[253]

US Army liaison aircraft and patrols reported sightings of North Korean troops beginning at 9:15 am on September 26th. Contact between the North Koreans and 7th Infantry Division occurred at 11:52 am and intensified at 12:50 pm. The 31st RCT experienced heavy enemy action throughout September 26th and 27th. Company A-77th Armor (A-77 Armor) attached its 2nd and 3rd Platoons to the 2nd Battalion, 31st Infantry during this battle. Company A 73d Armor had three of its platoons attached to the 2d Battalion also, and one platoon attached to the 3rd Battalion, 31st Infantry. Reports from Xth Corps that the Eighth Army's 1st US Cavalry Division was nearing the 7th Infantry Division in the 31st RCT's sector from the south and orders were issued not to fire into this friendly unit. The 31st Infantry and the 7th Cavalry Regiment of the 1st Cavalry Division US units established contact at 11:40 pm on September 26th on the Osan-Suwon road that linked X Corps and Eighth Army.[254] The final attack on the North Korean units occurred with a combination of ground and air attacks on September 28th. [255]

The 31st RCT declared in its Unit Report dated 291800I Sep50 that organized resistance to US Army operations had ended. Although only the 2nd Battalion captured prisoners of war (POWs) above a railroad tunnel near Suwon, reconnaissance missions by the 1st and 3rd Infantry Battalions reported no enemy contacts.[256]. There was no further contact with the North Korean Army into early October. The 31st RCT stopped preparing defensive positions and began sending out patrols to locate the enemy. The Xth Corps commander began applying lessons learned since landing at Inchon in live-fire training exercises. The purpose of the training was to improve combat skills. Also, Xth Corps sent an alert to its subordinate commands on October 2nd to be ready to move into an assembly area upon receipt of an order to prepare for a new assignment. This included the 31st RCT and its reunited A-77 Armor. Until receipt of the order, units would remain in a defensive posture by sending out patrols and screening.[257]

Into North Korea

Suwon to Pusan to Iwon (Riwon)

On October 3rd, A verbal warning order from 7th Division headquarters was issued to all its units to be prepared to relocate to the assembly area and begin preparations to roadmarch 500 miles south to Pusan. Two regiments of the 1st Cavalry Division would replace them in the Suwon-Osan area. [258] The 7th Division completed entry into the assembly area by 8 pm that night. The division would leave its Suwon assembly areas for Pusan on order. The 31st RCT's Operations Order 13 that was issued on October 4th specified that the 31st RCT's tank company, A-77, and the 73rd Tank Battalion would move together. The units began leaving their assembly area at 4 am on October 5th.[259]

The 31st RCT reached Pusan on October 7th. Regimental Commander Colonel R.P. Ovenshine, who brought the 31st from peacetime occupation duty in Japan to wartime Korea turned over his command temporarily to the executive officer Lieutenant Colonel Richard F. Reidy.[260] Colonel Allan D. MacLean assumed command on October 10th.[261] The Regiment began an extensive training program that included platoon and battalion-scale attacks, night attacks, mountain warfare, communications, and control, blocking amphibious landings, and coordinating and controlling artillery, mortar, and individual weapons fire. The Regiment also performed maintenance and an inventory of all equipment and clothing.[262]

The 31st RCT issued Operations Order Number 16 on October 17th.[263] This document outlined the next campaign for US forces in Korea. US Eighth Army would attack north and northeast toward Pyongyang from Korea's western coast. The Xth Corps would conduct an amphibious operation from the east coast near Wonson with the 1st Marine Division landing first on the south side of the town and port of Wonson to seize its objectives. The 7th Infantry Division would follow the 1st Marines, and advance to the west, seize its initial objectives, and then protect the Corps' right flank as it moved to linkup with the Eighth Army moving toward Pyongyang. The first unit of the 7th Infantry Division scheduled to land was to be Task Force Whirlaway which included the 17th Infantry RCT, the 73rd Tank Battalion, and the 7th Reconnaissance Company. Figure 4.9 displays a political map of North Korea identifying population centers that were objectives of US Eighth US Army and Xth Corps.

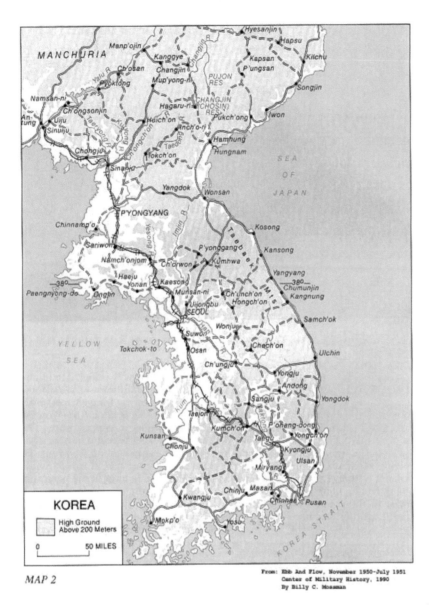

MAP 2

Figure 4.9 UN Offensive into North Korea October 1950
Source: Korean War Project Army Maps, Map 2 Korea 1950   NOTE: from Ebb And Flow, November 1950 - July 1951 - The United States Army in the Korean War, Center of Military History, United States Army, Washington, D.C., 1990, retrieved from <u>Korean War AMS Topo - Map 2 - Korea</u>

Simultaneous with US Xth Corps' preparations for its missions into North Korea, General MacArthur's vision of this phase of the war changed during the last half of October. MacArthur's goal became unifying Korea by destroying all remaining North Korean forces by the end of 1950. He alerted General Almond that should Eighth Army move faster than anticipated and seize Pyongyang before his force established physical contact, then Xth Corps units would change direction and attack north to the Yalu River. MacArthur sent his mission change on October 17th. The Eighth Army was in Pyongyang by October 20th and this was almost a week before X Corps sailed from Pusan. The 31st

RCT's Operations Order 17 published at Pusan on October 22nd reflected the change of plan.[264]

The 17th RCT's axis of advance changed from Wonson east of Pyongyang to the new objective, Hyesanjin, located at the Yalu River nearly 100 air miles northeast of the Chosin Reservoir. Once the rest of the 7th Infantry Division disembarked, it would follow the 17th Infantry north. The only exception was the 31st RCT's tank company, A-77 Armor. Order #17 contains no reference to it.[265]

The landings were to begin in mid-October but were delayed because the North Koreans had mined Wonson's harbor and a mine-clearing operation had to be initiated. This delayed the landings by about two weeks. While the 1st Marine Division disembarked at Wonson on October 27th which had been secured by the First Republic of Korea (ROK) Corps on October 17th.The 7th Infantry Division moved its landing beaches to Iwon approximately 100 air miles to the north at the end of October[266] Getting the division ashore minus its tanks began on October 29th and was completed by November 9th.[267]

The 31st Tank Company began appearing again in the 31st RCT's subsequent orders and reports again on November 16th. The 31st RCT's War Diary for November 16th states that the Steel Tigers landed at Iwon and moved into positions near the village of Shunghang-ni on the 18th.[268] The movement delay occurred because the Steel Tigers and the 73rd Tank Battalion had been ordered by the 7th Division Commander to remain in Pusan and continue training and maintenance. One of the reasons that may have contributed to this was because a new track was not available in the Pusan supply depot at the time for all models of tracked vehicles. The armored units needed to replace the existing track on their vehicles which was worn too severely for further operations.[269] The supplies of track had to be replenished and then installed.

The 17th RCT minus the 73rd Tank Battalion began moving north toward its objective Hyesanjin which is about 60 air miles from Iwon on the Korean bank of the Yalu River that separates North Korea and China.[270] The 32nd RCT, the final unit to leave the ships began reaching the shore on November 4th. After delays serving as the force protecting the Iwon beachhead and serving as the division's reserve, the 2nd and 3rd battalions began moving north toward Singjalpin on the Yalu but along a different route.[271] The 32d's first battalion was located near the town of Kujong-ni, several miles west of Pukchong. It did not move with its parent unit because it had to wait for truck transportation.

The 17th RCT's axis to the Yalu River was Iwon-Pukchong-Pungsang-Hyesanjin The 32d RCT's route was Iwon-Hamhung-Pukchong and turning to the northeast of the Chosin and Fusen Reservoirs toward Kapsan and then on to Singjalpin which would place it west of the 17th RCT along the Yalu. The First Marine Division's Fifth Marine Regiment was positioned along the eastern shore of the Chosin Reservoir. The 7th Marine Regiment was located on the western shore in the vicinity of the village of Yudam-ni. By November 18th, the 17th RCT reached Hyesanjin on the Yalu River in the east and the 32d RCT was near Kapsan which was 30 miles south of its objective.

Examining the geography of North Korea, today's town map names in English do not correspond to the towns and villages used on the 1916 Japanese- made maps of the area used by US forces in 1950. For example, "Chosin" is the Japanese pronunciation of the reservoir where the Chinese stopped the US advance to the Yalu River. Changjin" is the Korean pronunciation. Also, existing satellite imagery does not capture the dramatic differences in weather, elevation and trafficability between the coastal region, the inland roads and towns, and the steep ascent into the central Korean highlands.

Iwon to Hungnam to Chosin

Figure 4.10 displays the 60-mile route to the Chosin Reservoir from the Hamhung-Hungnam 500-foot coastal lowlands through the narrow Funchilin Pass rising to 4,000 feet on the Koto-Ri Plateau at the 4,500-foot level.

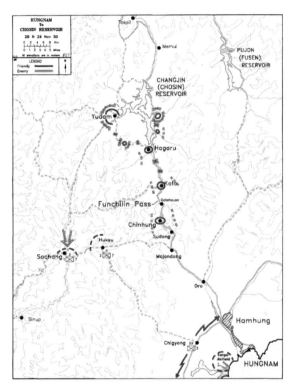

Figure 4.10 Hungnam to Chosin Reservoir
Source: Libertas, The Marines of Autumn: Review, July 13, 2017 retrieved from <u>The Marines of Autumn: Review | (masculineepic.com)</u>, June 21, 2023.

The 7th Infantry Division's operating zone encompassed three regions containing 11 towns or villages in the story of the Chosin Reservoir: seacoast. piedmont, and the mountainous region of the Koto-ri Plateau where the Taebaek mountains are located. The mountain range extends from South to North Korea. These mountains form the Korean Highlands with peaks rising to more than 8,000 feet above sea level between the east and west coasts of North Korea. The Taebaeks prevented physical contact between the Eighth Army and Xth Corps.

Principal towns along the seacoast are Wonson, Hungnam, Iwon, and Songjin (Kimchaek). Elevations in the seacoast region ranged from sea level to 500 feet. An example of daily November average high and extremely daily low temperatures at Songjin were 48 degrees Fahrenheit (F) and two degrees (F) respectively in 1950. The December high and extremely low temperatures were 35 degrees F and minus seven degrees F. The coastal roads permitted two-way military traffic.[272]

The piedmont region had two axes. The 17th RCT and 32d RCT followed the Iwon-Puckchong-Pungsan-Kapsan-Hyesanjin and Singjalpin routes. Pungsan's elevation is 3,900 feet above sea level. The average daily high temperature in November 1950 was 35 degrees F. In December, it was 20 degrees F. The extreme daily minimums for the same months were minus 17 and minus 26 degrees F. Although Hyesanjin's altitude was 2,300 feet above sea level, its daily average high temperatures in November were 35 degrees F and 16 degrees F in December. November's extreme minimum low was minus 25 degrees. The extreme minimum low in December was minus 40 degrees F.[273] There was no mountainous area weather data available from the divisional data used; however, the weather appendix was especially careful to state that its data was taken from observation points that were in sheltered areas along main roads and in larger towns.[274]

The population centers marking the second axis of advance were through the piedmont from the Iwon beachhead through the towns of Pukchong and Hamhung into the mountainous third region on the Koto-ri Plateau. Once on the plateau, Hagaru-ri, a 4,000-foot above-sea-level mountain village was about 1.5 miles south the Chosin Reservoir. The 1st Marine Division's area of responsibility placed the 5th Marine Regiment from Hagaru-ri to the sawmill town of Sasu-ri along the east bank, and the 7th Marine Regiment from Hagaru-ri to Yudam-ni on the west bank. The 1st Marine Regiment secured the road from the beginning of the Koto-ri plateau to Hagaru-ri. In 1950, the road distance from Hamhung to Hagaru-ri was 60 miles and it was two-way until it reached the beginning of the Funchilin Pass that ran up to the Koto-ri Plateau and on to Hagaru-ri.

This final segment of the Pass was a one-way trail rising about 2,800 feet over eight miles. Once the road reached the plateau that was about 4,500 feet above sea level, it became a one-way and very narrow dirt and gravel trail that engineers widened somewhat. It had many curves and traversed wetlands, streams and rivers requiring bridges. There was a narrow-gauge railroad running from Hagaru-ri on the plateau that went nearly to the Fusen Reservoir east of the Chosin Reservoir. The temperature at Hagaru-ri on November 14. 1950 was minus eight degrees F with winds up to 35 miles per hour. This combination resulted in a wind chill of almost minus 60 degrees F.[275]

The Xth Corps' landings began on October 26, 1950 at Wonson with the Corps units and headquarters along with the 1st Marine Division.[276]

On November 1st, the 31st RCT minus its tanks left Pusan and sailed the 830 miles north. The ships arrived the next day at about 8:00 am and the team began going ashore on November 3rd at Iwon.It completed disembarking on the 5th.[277] The 1st Battalion occupied blocking positions. The 2nd Battalion established squad and platoon-sized strong points with wire communications between them, and the 3rd Battalion was attacked by North Korean Army units on its way to its objective[278]

The 3rd Infantry Division to which the 73rd Armor had been assigned in the United States was alerted to deploy to Korea in August 1950. The division headquarters and its 15th Infantry Regiment were at Fort Benning, Georgia. The 7th Infantry Regiment was stationed at Fort Devens, Massachusetts. The division had only 7,494 soldiers. It began sailing from San Francisco to Japan on August 30th. The last troop ship arrived on September 16th. The 65th Infantry Regiment of the Puerto Rican National Guard was called to federal service and rounded out the division to its authorized three infantry regiments. The 65th Infantry sailed on August 25th through the Panama Canal directly to Pusan. It arrived on September 22nd. The 64th Tank Battalion was sent from the 2nd Armored Division to Fort Benning to replace the 73rd Tank Battalion.[279]

The 3rd Division landed at Wonson on November 5th and became the Eighth Army's reserve. The 65th Regiment was the first unit to join the Xth Corps. Its mission was to keep the roads open between the two ports of Wonson and Hamhung[280].

The intelligence was present that a PLA force was in North Korea. Following the landing at Iwon, the 31st RCT continued moving toward its assigned objectives near Pungsan. The 1st and 2nd Battalions reached them and sent out patrols without incident. The 3rd Battalion reported engaging a PLA infantry unit on November 8th. It was armed with 45- and 80-millimeter mortars and heavy machineguns. The contact began at 4:30 pm and continued through the night until about 5:30 pm on November 9th. The regimental commander directed that all units send out day and night patrols and keep one-third of every unit awake at all times. The unit reported three US soldiers and 50-75 Chinese killed.
[281]

The 3rd Battalion captured two Chinese prisoners. Each stated that he had moved to the Manchurian border by train about 30 days prior and then marched into North Korea arriving in the area where the contact was made with the 31st Infantry about 10 days prior.[282]

The 31st RCT's intelligence and reconnaissance platoon linked up with the right flank of the 1st Marine Division's 5th Marine Regiment at about 1:45 pm on November 7th and they had not made enemy contact. However, the 7th Marine Regiment reported that it engaged the *370th, 271st,and 372nd* PLA regiments The report added that these regiments were part of the *124th* Division.[283].

The 31st RCT and the 7th Marine Regiment reported their engagements with the PLA up the chain of command to Far East Command in Tokyo. The problem was that no one at these higher echelons anticipated the Chinese would move into Korea. Those in Tokyo were victims of groupthink, faulty reasoning, and successes following the Pusan breakout coupled with the Inchon end run.

Before the 31st RCT's encounter on November 8th, the PLA had stopped two Eighth US Army ROK divisions and the First Cavalry Division's Eighth Cavalry Regiment that were leading the Eighth Army north toward the Yalu after seizing Pyongyang. This battle began on November 1st, and it continued through November 6th at which time the regiment's 3rd Battalion was decisively defeated and was no longer an organized unit. This PLA attack stopped the Eighth Army advance near Unsan and forced it to withdraw about 70 miles. Unsan is about 50 miles west of Hagaru-ri and Hungnam in the Xth Corps zone that is separated by the Taebaek mountains. The 8th Cavalry was attacked by the *116th* and *115th* PLA divisions that were a part of a force of 30 divisions (300,000 soldiers) that had crossed into Korea undetected in October.[284] The Chinese units disappeared into the mountains after this action.

First contact with the PLA that moved into the to the Xth Corps zone was established by the 3rd ROK Division's 26th Infantry Regiment on October 25 and it captured one prisoner of war. Another contact between the PLA and the 26th occurred three days later.[285] General MacArthur's headquarters in Tokyo did not believe any of the reports that the Chinese had entered Korea in force. The captured Chinese were assessed to be volunteers. The stage was set for the US-PLA confrontation at the Chosin Reservoir.

The Far East Command sent a revised plan to Xth Corps on November 16th, about a month after General Mac Arthur notified General Almond that Xth Corps would attack north instead of west of Wonson. The main attack would be led by the 1st Marine Division from the west side of the Chosin Reservoir north to the town of Changjin about 35 miles away where it would turn west and interdict the road leading from the Yalu River into the Eighth Army's axis of advance.[286] No units of the 31st RCT reported contact with the North Koreans on 16-17 November.[287]

Planning and coordination by Far East Command and Xth Corps was completed on November 24th. General Almond issued the order to Xth Corps on November 25th to move into position by noon the next day to begin the attack on the 27th. This two-day period gave the 5th Marine Regiment located on the east side of the Reservoir the time to rejoin the rest of the division on the west bank near Yudam-ni. The challenge was moving the 7th Infantry Division units. The 17th and 32nd RCTs except for the 1st Battalion 32d Infantry were nearly 100 miles away.[288]

Almond also wanted an infantry regiment from the 7th Infantry Division to replace the Marines on the east bank. General Barr had to choose his troops from those closest to the route to the Chosin Reservoir to form this regimental combat team. The 31st RCT was securing the division's rear and MSR. It was available to perform this mission, and Barr gave it to Colonel MacLean. MacLean had only his 31st RCT's 2nd and 3rd Infantry Battalions immediately available. Ordering the A-77 Armor to rejoin its parent unit was part of the rapid assembling of the force to perform the mission.[289]

Because the 1st Battalion of the 32d Infantry commanded by Lieutenant Colonel Don C. Faith was positioned near Pukchong at the town of Kujang-ni having not yet not been transported to join the rest of the 32d RCT, Barr added it to the 31st RCT's order of battle on November 26th which brought his force up on paper to its authorized strength of three infantry battalions.[290] In addition to the infantry and the Steel Tigers, the 57th Artillery Battalion and D Battery of the 15th Anti-Aircraft Artillery Automatic Weapons Self-Propelled (AAA AW SP), two units which had been subordinate to the 31st RCT since its arrival in Korea, remained available to Colonel MacLean to reestablish his command in the confusion of readjusting unit positions over great distances, traffic jams on narrow roads, and a finite number of trucks in the various transportation units that were available to move the infantry if all was to be ready to initiate the Xth Corps attack by MacArthur's designated jumping off time - the 27th.[291]

The 7th Infantry Division's 17th and 32nd RCTs were ordered to remain at their locations well over 100 miles away and be prepared to continue to attack to the west initially. The 7th Division's had the 17th Infantry RCT continuing to Hyesanjin and the 32d moving to the west of the 17th to seize another town along the Yalu - Singalpaljin[292]

Almost simultaneous with Far East Command's November 16th plan to Xth Corps, the Navy began planning an evacuation of the Corps from Hungnam port. Rear Admiral James Doyle, Commander of Combined Task Force 90 received the order from Vice Admiral Turner Joy, Commander of Naval Forces, Far East on November 13th.

Doyle was given control of the amphibious ships, protection of other naval, shipping, naval gunfire, Marine ground- and Naval carrier-based air support. Initially, Admiral Doyle had two amphibious groups under his command. One was designated for Hungnam and Xth Corps in the east. The other would evacuate US Eighth Army in the west from the Pyongyang area. A third amphibious group was ordered to operate at Inchon. Amphibious Group One went to Korea shortly after the war began to train Eighth Army units in amphibious operations thereby establishing a working relationship with Army units that had little amphibious logistical and operational skills. Doyle's units supported the Inchon and Iwon landings.[293]

There are several excellent books about this historic battle. Two were used in the research for this study. First is Martin Russ' *Breakout: The Chosin Reservoir Campaign, Korea 1950*.[294] This book concentrates on the Marine Corps' effort on the west side of the Reservoir in the vicinity of Yudam-ni with references to the 7th Infantry Division's effort on the Reservoir's east bank. The second book, Roy Appleman's *East of Chosin: Entrapment and Breakout in Korea, 1950,* recounts the Army's role in the battle with references to the 1st Marine Division.[295] Both books combine to tell a heroic tale in great detail that is out of the scope of this effort. This narrative concentrates on the role of the 31st RCT's tank company, A-77 Armor, before and during the battle, and how it reinforced the Army and the Marines in the combined withdrawal to the port of Hungnam for transport to Pusan. This author used both books for reference but relied on original 7th Infantry Division unit records that were digitized from microfilm at the National Archives and Records Administration (NARA)'s Korean War Project.[296]

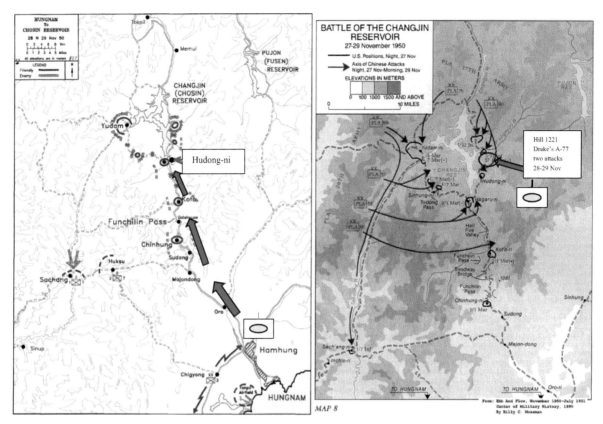

Figure.4.11 UN Offensive and Chinese Counteroffensive, November 1950
Source: Adapted from Hungnam to Chosin Reservoir from The Marines of Autumn: A Review, July 13, 2017, retrieved from The Marines of Autumn: Review | (masculineepic.com), and adapted from Battle of the Changjin Reservoir, US Army Map, retrieved from Battle of Chosin Reservoir in the Korean War (thoughtco.com) June 24, 2023

Captain Drake received orders for his tank company to join its regimental combat team at the Chosin Reservoir on Thanksgiving Day, November 24th. Company A-77 Armor along with the rest of the RCT began moving toward the reservoir on the 25th with the exception of the 2nd Battalion 31st Infantry which did not receive its orders until November 27th. Captain Drake, First Sergeant Keck, and the men of A-77 travelled 70 miles by rail to Hamhung and then roadmarched 60 miles to the Koto-ri Plateau. The Steel Tigers arrived at the RCT's rear command post at Hudong-ni on November 27th. Colonel MacLean selected this location. It was formerly a village and in November 1950 consisted of only ruins and an abandoned school. Hudong-ni was located about a half mile north from Sasu-ri across the Paegamni River and about four miles northeast from Hagaru-ri. The single modern bridge along the trail from Hagaru-ri along the east bank of the reservoir was across the river separating Hudong-ni and Sasu-ri and it had been destroyed in the US air strikes. The river was fordable nearby.[297]

The 31st RCT's second battalion never arrived at the reservoir. It began moving along the same route as the A-77 Armor to Hamhung by rail but was redirected to other locations because no trucks were available to move the unit to join the other two infantry battalions. The lack of trucks continued until November 30th when vehicles finally moved the battalion to the road leading up to Koto-ri. The column was attacked by the PLA early in the movement on this road. The infantrymen counterattacked and pushed the Chinese back. Following a night attack, the second battalion reached the plateau and was placed under the control of the 1st Marine Regiment that was defending Koto-ri. It launched a night attack against which the Chinese responded.[298] .

By the 27th, the 31st RCT's other units were moving also onto the plateau with the exception of the 2nd Battalion. Movement was delayed as it had to wait for the 5th Marine Regiment to clear the access route to the Chosin. The Steel Tigers halted at Hudong-ni and Captain Drake began traveling to forward locations in search of Colonel MacLean for further orders. Drake met with Lieutenant Colonel Faith during the search. Faith recommended that he not move the tanks at night along the narrow road, but that he should depart Hudong-ni on the morning of the 28th which would be coincident with the beginning of the 7th Division's attack north. Drake and MacLean never met.[299]

The 31st RCT's units were distributed between the northern-most unit, 1st Battalion 32d Infantry, and Hagaru-ri – the southern base of the Chosin Reservoir about 14 miles apart. The location of the RCT's rear command post and the A-77 Armor at Hudong-ni were about four miles north of Hagaru-ri on the reservoir's east bank. South of Faith's battalion were the regimental forward command post and heavy mortar company. The next major units, the 3rd Battalion, 31st Infantry, D Battery of the 15th AAA AW SP and two batteries of the 57th Field Artillery were about halfway between Hudong-ni and the 1st Battalion 32d Infantry on the high ground above the inlet where the Pungnyuri River fed into the reservoir. The 57th Artillery's service battery arrived late on the 27th and established its position with the rear command post (CP) at Hudong-ni. The senior officer present on November 27th was Brigadier General Henry I. Hodes, Assistant 7th Division Commander. The division's commander, General Barr, sent him to the reservoir to oversee the 31st RCT's operation and to speak on-site for him.[300]

The 31st RCT's Medical Company reached Hudong-ni after A-77 Armor closed into the rear CP and Captain Drake's return after failing to find Colonel MacLean. The medical company's commander wanted to move forward and Drake urged him to wait until morning. He told Drake that he would press on to be at the 3rd Battalion 31st Infantry's location where it could support both this unit and Lt Col Faith's 1st Battalion 32nd Infantry to the north that was scheduled to lead the attack in the morning. The company was ambushed by the PLA at a sharp bend in the road about a mile beyond Hudong-ni. Three medics, including the company's first sergeant, returned on foot to the rear CP, but damaged vehicles blocked the road.[301]

The PLA initiated its counteroffensive against the 1st Marine Division and the 31st RCT during the night of November 27th and throughout the next day. The Chinese attack began against Company A, 1st Battalion 32nd Infantry and then spread to the rest of the battalion's positions. The PLA began attacking the 3rd Battalion, 31st Infantry and the 57th Artillery units in their positions after midnight on the 27th.[302]

The fighting continued throughout the daylight hours of the 28th, but airstrikes helped the forward battalions to restore their perimeters. Meanwhile, The Steel Tigers were ordered by the 31st RCT's operations officer to move from Hudong-ni to reopen the road to the 3rd and 1st infantry battalions. Captain Drake formed a combined arms team of three tank platoons and a composite unit of soldiers from the rear command post to fight as infantry. He left his 4th tank platoon to defend the rear CP and one of his two M4A3(105) command tanks which were M4 Sherman tanks that were armed with 105mm howitzers. Importantly, the radio configuration in these tanks enabled the tank commander to communicate with headquarters beyond the company instead of only with the other 20 M4A3E8s and their 76-millimeter main guns. Accompanying Captain Drake were General Hodes and the first sergeant of the 31st Medical Company.[303]

The Steel Tigers advanced about a mile over the narrow road that was initially level and then followed the terrain and crossed a river. They located the site where the PLA attacked the medical company and turned it into a roadblock. Drake estimated the Chinese force at one entrenched infantry battalion. Two platoons were sent cross-country to the dominant terrain feature. One moved through soft low ground before reaching the slope and was attacked by PLA infantrymen who climbed on to the tanks. Other tanks viewing this development fired their machineguns at the Chinese soldiers on the tank decks. This platoon was able to withdraw undamaged. The second platoon moving off the road was able to avoid the soft low ground and started up the hill's slope. One of these tanks slid downward and fell over a bank. A second tank threw a track. The platoon could not move uphill on the ice and snow. When the third platoon following the road reached the site of the destroyed medical company's vehicles, it began receiving fire. The two leading tanks were struck by antitank rockets. One blocked the road and the second slipped over a bank. Supporting tanks placed machine gun fire into the enemy and crew members were able to escape. The battle continued until the afternoon when Drake began withdrawing toward the regimental rear command post. The battle losses were 2 officers and 10 enlisted men wounded with four tanks lost.[304]

Because FM radio communications were poor-to-nonexistent, General Hodes returned to Hudong-ni before the tank company's attack ended to find a location where he could request additional assistance both air and ground. For safety reasons considering the advancing Chinese and the radio configuration in command tanks, he took A-77 Armor's second command tank. Both tanks permitted talking with the next higher command echelon. Hodes departed Hudong-ni for Hagaru-ri to find support for the 31st RCT. He conferred with Major General Oliver Smith, commander of the 1st Marine Division.[305]

Appleman states that Drake could see Chinese on horseback moving south along the higher ridgelines about 2 miles away, but Drake had no contact with the forward battalions. The two infantry battalions had no radio contact with the tank company and only sporadic and garbled communications with Hudong-ni. Appleman's interviews revealed no one heard the battles being fought by the infantry in defense or tank battle to rescue them. One of the reasons for this, according to Appleman, were the mountains blocking the transmissions. Another reason is that radios in use at the time had different frequency bands for infantry, armored, and artillery units.[306]

Colonel MacLean and Lieutenant Colonel Faith agreed that the 31st RCT would move south to consolidate at the location of the 3rd Battalion about four miles south. Faith ordered all vehicles to prepare to carry the wounded, move in blackout drive, and begin at 4:30 am on the 29th.[307]

Approaching the low ground at the inlet of a tributary flowing into the reservoir almost immediately below the positions of the 3rd Battalion, the Regimental Commander was lost when he attempted to stop troops who were moving and shooting toward the battalion's positions. MacLean thought they were friendly. Instead, they were PLA. Appleman states that several witnesses from different locations recounted the same events. MacLean fell several times and then could not be found. Released US prisoners of war remembered that they aided him as they were marched northward toward a prison camp and that he died of his wounds after four days. Lieutenant Colonel Faith assumed command of the 31st forward units which became known as Task Force Faith. This entity did not include the Steel Tigers and the others at the rear command post.[308]

Another event occurred on November 28th that no one in the reservoir area knew about. General MacArthur convened a meeting of principals at his Tokyo headquarters to assess the situation with Eighth Army in the west and Xth Corps in the east. The commanders of these two entities were present as were the commanders of Naval Forces Far East and the Far East Air Force. Other attendees were MacArthur's chief of staff and his intelligence and operations chiefs. The PLA had been attacking the Eighth Army since November 25th. MacArthur issued no orders at the meeting, but on November 29th, he told the Eighth Army's commander, Walton Walker, to hold Pyongyang if he could. He gave Walker the discretion to act as required to prevent the PLA from enveloping him. MacArthur instructed Almond to withdraw Xth Corps to the Hamhung-Hungnam area. Upon Almond's return to his headquarters, he ordered that command of all troops on the Koto-ri plateau would pass to General Smith, the 1st Marine Division commander, at 8:00 am on the next morning.[309]

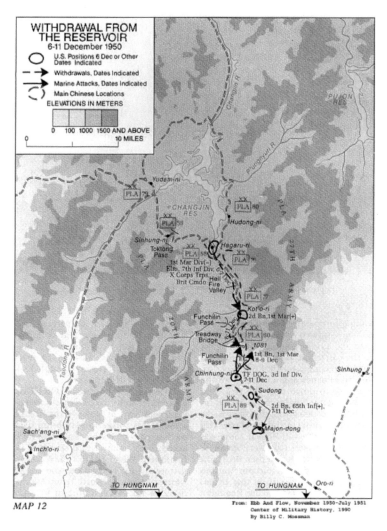

Figure 4.12 The UN Allies Withdraw from the Reservoir

Source: US Army Center of Military History retrieved from http://www.history.army.mil/brochures/kw-chinter/chinter.htm. June15, 2023

Almond met with his 1st Marine and 7th Infantry division commanders and General Hodes in the morning of November 30th. He ordered them to abandon the reservoir and withdraw. General Barr flew to meet with Colonel Faith to tell him he would have to fight his way out with only air support to reinforce him to get him to Hagaru-ri. The Hudong-ni regimental rear CP would not be there.[310]

The Steel Tigers repeated their attack of the 28th at about 8 am on the 29th with the 2nd, 3rd and 4th tank platoons, an engineer platoon, an antitank platoon, and another composite group of soldiers from the rear CP serving as infantry. Two platoons reached their initial objectives and then began unsuccessfully to move up the icy slope of the same hill as the day before but received heavy fire from an estimated two PLA battalions. The infantrymen suffered the most casualties. The third platoon searched for an overland route behind the enemy positions. The platoon leader and two tankers were killed in this mission and the company lost two more tanks. Captain Drake stopped the attack and ordered the team to return to the rear CP.[311]

Other action on the 29th included the 7th Infantry Division units except for those at the Chosin Reservoir to assemble at Hamhung by truck and rail transport. All the units began moving including the 17th and 32nd RCT's that were at or near the Yalu River. Advanced 7th Division units began reaching Hamhung late in the afternoon of December 3rd. This included the 73rd Tank Battalion.[312]

Lieutenant Colonel Berry K Anderson, 31st RCT's operations officer assumed command of the units at Hudong-ni on November 30th and he was now under the command of the 1st Marine Division. The Steel Tigers were ordered to withdraw to Hagaru-ri at 4:30 pm that day. The unit began towing two of its disabled tanks but had to abandon them because it slowed the column. Upon reaching Hagaru-ri at about 5:30 pm after encountering heavy enemy fire while serving as the point and rear guard for the 31st RCT's rear CP unit. The company was attached to the 1st Marine Division's 1st Tank Battalion at Hagaru-ri and placed on the perimeter of that battalion's defensive position. A PLA battalion attacked the perimeter at the tank company's sector and was repulsed leaving an estimated 100 Chinese killed while suffering one tanker wounded.[313]

The PLA began its nightly assault on Task Force Faith at 8:00 pm on the 30th. The Chinese withdrew after daylight in previous attacks but not on December 1st. They continued firing into the position throughout the day. Appleman states that Faith ordered that the units begin moving once airstrikes had been completed and that meanwhile the wounded need to be prepared for movement as well as continuing defense of the perimeter[314].

When the units began moving at about 1 pm, one supporting aircraft released its napalm bomb early falling on friendly troops. As the day progressed, other aircraft supported Task Force Faith in relays of four to six aircraft. Faith's forward air controller was directing the planes to attack at danger-close ranges using napalm as well as other ordnance as close as 50 feet at times because of the intensity of the fighting.[315]

Task Force Faith continued moving toward Hudong-ni and on to Hagaru-ri. Gradually, command and control broke down as the intensity of the fighting increased. With officers and NCOs being killed and wounded, the troops began attacking the Chinese in groups as they confronted them instead of organizing to use the small unit tactics that they learned in training. Lieutenant Colonel Faith personally did his best to rally and direct his men and the column advanced almost to the abandoned Hudong-ni rear CP. Meanwhile, his soldiers were enduring withering enemy fire and this continued destroying unit integrity. Ammunition was low generally and some had none. Faith was wounded about 2 am by a hand grenade. He was placed in a truck cab and died later about two miles north of Hagaru-ri. The 31st RCT was combat ineffective. Soldiers, individually and in small groups, found their own withdrawal routes to friendly lines and most lost some or all of their equipment along the way.[316]

Figure 4.13 is a diagram of the plan used by X US Corps to withdraw from North Korea

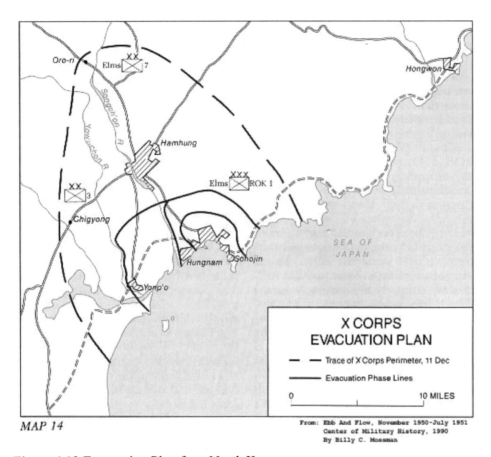

MAP 14

From: Ebb And Flow, November 1950-July 1951
Center of Military History, 1990
By Billy C. Mossman

Figure 4.13 Evacuation Plan from North Korea,
Source: US Army Center of Military
History - https://history.army.mil/books/korea/maps/map14_full.jpg,
Hungnam evacuation map December 1950, 2 January 1990, retrieved from File:Hungnam evacuation map.jpg - Wikimedia Commons, June 15, 2023

When the order was given to initiate the withdrawal to the Hamhung-Hungnam area from MacArthur's headquarters to Xth Corps, Admiral Doyle ordered the ships in his command to be on a two-hour sailing alert. They left Japan on November 30th and December 1st. Doyle's plan was to evacuate support troops and unnecessary supplies first while keeping combat units in sectors defending the port's perimeter. As combat soldiers began leaving, the perimeter was tightened systematically. Hungnam as well as Wonson were being defended by air support, minesweepers, and naval gunfire to keep the PLA and North Koreans at bay. Hungnam port closed on December 24th. When all that was being removed was on the ships, all remaining buildings and other facilities were destroyed by explosives. The results of this effort saved 105,000 soldiers, 91,000 civilians, 17,500 vehicles, and 350,000 tons of supplies. The ground, air, and naval gunfire from the offshore ships including the USS Missouri prevented the PLA from making a determined attack against the port during this operation. [317]

Headquarters and Service Company of the 73rd Tank Battalion arrived in Hungnam on November 30th. Units of the battalion conducted road reconnaissance missions between Hungnam and Hamhung beginning on December 2nd and the battalion expanded its missions to include reconnoitering the suitability of the terrain for tank deployments north and northwest of Hamhung On the 4th, the 73rd began selecting firing positions to initiate counterattacks against Hamhung if required.[318]

Meanwhile on the 2nd, A-77 Armor was sent from Hagaru-ri on a reconnaissance to find members of the 31st RCT's forward units. The company rescued about 20 wounded soldiers while under heavy antitank and small arms fire.[319]

The Steel Tigers were attached to the 5th Marine Regiment on December 3rd. Together with a British Royal Marine detachment, they went to the western bank of the Chosin Reservoir toward Yudam-ni where they were to support the withdrawal of the 5th and 7th Marine Regiments to Hagaru-ri. The units were ordered to return before they completed their mission.[320]

Other units of the 7th Infantry Division were traveling toward Hamhung from November 29th. The 17th RCT retraced its route to the Yalu by leaving Kapsan for Pukchong on December 2d . The 32nd RCT began moving from Pukchong to Hamhung on the 3rd and by late that afternoon on December 3rd, 7th Infantry divisional advanced units entered Hamhung. The 73rd Tank Battalion was designated to be the division's reserve in the Hamhung vicinity and ordered to initiate a counterattack on order.[321]

The 7th Infantry Division made preparations to receive the soldiers of the 31st RCT arriving at Hamhung from the Chosin Reservoir. The men were to be fed hot meals, provided medical attention, and warm tents to sleep in. Once in the assembly area, replacements would begin joining the 31st and new clothing and equipment would be issued. Veterans of the units at the Chosin Reservoir whose wounds and injuries were not as severe as others would be assigned to the units suffering greater numbers of casualties [322]

The 31st RCT used the time to reorganize after it descended from the plateau and began moving to Hamhung. The RCT began reaching the port by 11:00 pm on December 5th less the Steel Tigers who were still attached to the 1st Marines. It took 3 more days for the 31st's second and third battalions to arrive because of the lack of transportation and not enemy action. All of the 31st was at Hungnam by December 12th. Once the troops had been cared for, the members of the 31st joined in the defense of Hamhung.[323] Colonel John A. Gavin assumed command of the 31st RCT on December 5th.[324]

The 7th Division Operations Order 31 issued on December 6th, assigned the 31st RCT to participate in the defense of Hamhung The 31st RCT, 73rd Tank Battalion, and the 7th Reconnaissance Company were placed in Division Reserve while the soldiers of the 32d and 17th RCTs, Division Artillery, 13th Engineer Battalion and a provisional battalion of military police, quartermaster, ordnance, and signal units were in sectors of the defensive perimeter.[325]

Chosin to Pusan

The 31st RCT's tank company was assigned to serve as the 5th Marine Regiment's advance and rear guard when the 1st Marine division withdrew from Hagaru-ri. The company engaged the PLA along the route to Koto-ri and went into the perimeter defense there until December 10th when the column began moving down the pass enroute toward Hamhung which it reached the next night at about 11:00 pm without any serious incidents. The Steel Tigers moved on December 11th from Hamhung to Hungnam, entered their assembly area and began to rest, reorganize and prepare for embarkation. The withdrawal from the Chosin Reservoir was completed.[326]

Embarkation Order 3-50 stated that the division would begin leaving Hungnam at 8 am on December 10th and complete its departure by midnight on December 18th. The 31st Infantry Regiment was in the 1st group to embark.[327] The main body of 31st Infantry Regimental Combat Team soldiers loaded onto the *USNS General Freeman* in Hungnam harbor on December 14th. Vehicles and equipment were loaded onto cargo ships. The Steel Tigers left North Korea for Pusan.[328]

The 31st RCT reached Pusan and debarked on 17-18 December. The soldiers were transported by rail and the vehicles roadmarched toward their new assembly areas. The 31st RCT tank company remained in Pusan where the tankers offloaded their tanks and other vehicles between the 18th and 20th. Ordnance units inspected and began rehabilitating the vehicles. Also, the tankers prepared to test fire their tank weapons in association with the 30th Ordnance Company. Although the morale of the 31st RCT was reportedly excellent, its combat efficiency was assessed to be at 35 percent. Its losses at Chosin rendered the 31st combat ineffective. [329]

December 23rd was a significant milestone for the regiment. Except for the Steel Tigers who remained in Pusan undergoing vehicle maintenance, certifications of combat readiness, and training, the 23rd was the first day since November 27th that the 31st's infantry battalions were in the same place.

All of the RCT, including the Steel Tigers, trained in accordance with Training Memorandum Number 29. The soldiers underwent all sorts of activities during a six-day workweek from general soldier skills including physical training and road marches, to care of clothing and equipment, cold weather training and personal care, military courtesy, crew-served weapons and individual weapons range firing, individual weapons, and specialist training for cooks, mechanics, medics, and communications personnel. Also, ordnance personnel inspected individual weapons and repaired those that they could and replaced unserviceable weapons with new ones. Gradually, the addition of patrolling to the training schedule indicated that the division was preparing to return to combat.[330]

Veterans were cross levelled among the infantry units and replacements were assigned. The first six-months of the Korean War ended with a command inspection of all 7th Division units except the Steel Tigers by the Xth Corps and 7th Infantry Division commanders. The combat efficiency of the division was assessed to be 57 percent on New Year's Eve.[331]

Year's end also saw Lieutenant General Matthew B. Ridgway assume command of Eighth Army on December 26th following General Walker's December 23rd (December 22nd US time) death in an automotive accident. Ridgway was the Army's Deputy Chief for Operations and Administration at the Department of the Army in Washington. MacArthur had asked the Army Chief of Staff for him to succeed Walker in routine contingency succession planning earlier. Ridgway left Washington the next night and arrived late in the evening on Christmas where he met with MacArthur on the 26th. During their meeting, MacArthur removed himself and his staff from its previous operational decision-making role of the Eighth Army.[332]

Walker had established a defensive line generally along the Imjin River in the west to the 38th Parallel across much of the rest of the way to Korea's coast following the withdrawals of Eighth Army and X Corps. This line was named Line Bravo. Intelligence estimates indicated that the Chinese would attack Line Bravo on Christmas Day. The attack did not occur that day. New Year's Eve was assessed as the next likely date and that assessment proved correct. The 174,000 soldiers of the PLA's *XIIIth Army Group* with its 6 field armies and three corps of 65,800 North Koreans launched the main attack against the UN forces in the west on an axis from Uijongbu to Seoul. Another axis of attack was also in the west from Kaesong to Munsan-ni to Seoul. The entire front extended for 45 miles from west to east where supporting attacks attempted to envelop the defenders.

Ridgway ordered a withdrawal from the Seoul area on January 3rd to Delay Line Cthat ran generally along the Han River south of Seoul and Inchon and then northeast to the coastal city of Wonpo-ri. He ordered the move to Delay Line Don January 4th. This line extended in the west from P'yongt'aek which was below Osan and then ran northeast through Ansong, Changhowon-ni, and then to Wonju and Wonpo-ri.[333] Two more defensive lines were planned on January 8th. Delay Line E would run 25 miles south of Line D and Line F would be 65 miles south of Line D.[334]

UN Command

Twenty-nine members of the United Nations contributed combat, medical, and other support to the war in Korea. Of these, one nation's contribution is noteworthy not only for the 1,017 troops it sent to Korea in November 1950 and remaining there through the July 1953 armistice, but also in its next deployment to Indochina from South Korea in October 1953.

This foreign battalion was a volunteer infantry force that was assigned to the 23rd Infantry Regiment of the US 2nd Infantry Division that was part of Xth US Corps fighting in the center portion of Eighth Army after January 1st, 1951, against the Chinese and North Korean offensive. The unit was the French Korea 1 Battalion (*Bataillon de Coree*) ..It fought with distinction in the same Corps zone as the Steel Tigers and the 31st RCT that were part of the 7th Infantry Division in the battles of Wonju, Twin Tunnels, Chipyong-ni, and Heartbreak Ridge, among others. The unit was awarded two Korean Presidential Citations, three US Distinguished Unit Citations, and one Distinguished Service Cross awarded to Sergeant Louis Misseri, a squad leader in the battalion at Heartbreak Ridge. Colonel Paul L. Freeman who was the 23rd Infantry's commander at the time and later the Commander, United States Army Europe, stated, "When you order them in defence, you're sure they'll hold the position. When you show them a hill to be seized, you're sure they will manage to get atop. You may leave for two days, storms of shells and waves of enemies may swarm over them, the French are still there."[335]

Ridgway had three challenges facing him: operational and reestablishing the Eighth Army's self-confidence and instilling resolve to defeat the North Koreans and Chinese. Operationally, the Korean War went through two phases from December 31, 1950 to

November 11, 1951: first, a United Nations' controlled withdrawal trading space for time moving south from Line Bravo until Ridgeway could initiate an offensive action against the PLA. Phase II would follow the offensive and result in securing a northern boundary for South Korea while not seeking to reunite the entire peninsula. The purpose of the war would change from defeating the North Koreans and driving the Chinese back across the Yalu into a war of limited objectives.

Ridgway's second challenge meant that he had to change mindsets and raise the low morale among the officers and men of the UN Command including the Eighth US Army and Xth Corps following the battles of November and December. These units also needed the time to refit and receive and train replacements. Once he achieved this goal, his plan was to initiate an offensive against the Chinese and North Koreans and drive them out of South Korea. If he was unable to accomplish this task, then a decision would have to be made in Washington whether to stay in Korea or depart.[336]

The third challenge was a combination of strategies: national security including those of US allies, national defense, and national military, This challenge was determined first. The decision meeting occurred on January 15th in Tokyo. Generals J. Lawton Collins, and Hoyt S. Vandenburg the chiefs of staffs of the Army and Air Force, respectively met with MacArthur. They related a meeting with President Truman to delay withdrawing from Korea as long as possible without endangering Eighth Army or Japan and to give UN forces the chance to punish the Chinese. Following the meeting in Tokyo, Collins, Vandenburg, and Ridgway had follow-up meeting in the latter's Taegu headquarters where the failure of the Chinese and North Koreans to cross the Han River indicated that the PLA's counterattack had run out of steam. Collins announced that UN forces would not evacuate South Korea.[337]

Among the preparations to defend against the Chinese attack was Ridgway's orders to Xth Corps to accelerate its preparations to return to action. The Corps' order of battle would again be the 1st Marine Division, and the 7th Infantry and 3rd Infantry Divisions. The latter Army unit commanded by Major General Robert Soule had not yet completed its withdrawal from Hungnam.[338] The order of battle later varied according missions assigned by Ridgway.

Walker had established a defensive line generally along the Imjin River in the west to the 38th Parallel across much of the way East following the withdrawals of Eighth Army and X Corps. This line was named Line Bravo. Intelligence estimates indicated that the Chinese would attack Line Bravo on Christmas Day. The attack did not occur. New Year's

Eve was assessed as the next likely date and that assessment proved correct. The 174,000 soldiers of the PLA's *XIIIth Army Group* with its six field armies and three corps of 65,800 North Koreans launched the main attack against the UN forces in the west on an axis from Uijongbu (Uijongbu), location of the 1970s movie and subsequent television series *M*A*S*H,* to Seoul. Another axis of attack was further to the west from Kaesong to Munsan-ni to Seoul. The entire front extended for 45 miles from west to east where supporting attacks attempted to envelop the defenders.

The tactic employed by the Chinese and North Koreans since the beginning of the war was to fix the defenders in position while enveloping them on both flanks and maneuvering behind and beyond the units being engaged to advance as deep into the rear areas as possible. The battles at the Chosin Reservoir indicated that the Chinese could not exploit their initiatives because their supply lines were extended too far. The momentum of their offensive actions had to be slowed after every 10-14 days. Analyzing Chinese tactics, Ridgway noted that the Chinese forces' real strength was its numbers. The PLA did not employ artillery, tanks, and air power against the UN Command's ground forces in any appreciable numbers. The North Korean ground forces continued using their Russian T-34 tanks.

Ridgway ordered a command-wide withdrawal without breaking contact with the enemy from the Seoul area on January 3rd to Delay Line C that ran generally along major roads and terrain features from the Han River south of Seoul and Inchon and then northeast to the coastal city of Wonpo-ri. Next, he ordered withdrawing south again to positions along Delay Line D. Ridgway's orders to his subordinate commanders were to not allow gaps to occur between allied units on the ground from coast to coast that would permit further PLA and North Korean advances along unit boundaries or turn flanks. The UN Command's goal during the first half of January was to stabilize its lines.[339]

In the east, the Xth Corps' and 7th Infantry Division's missions were to stop the North Koreans' effort coming from the north and northeast. The threat to the UN forces in this area was the loss Wonju from the 2nd Infantry Division and then moving further south along the Corps' MSR seizing Tanyang, Andong, and Taegu (Daegu). The last was the location of the Ridgway's command post. The advance of the North Koreans and Chinese in this sector was so serious that Ridgway moved the eastern end of Line D into a straight line 40 miles to the south from Wanpo-ri to Samchok on the coast.[340]

Among other units, the 7th Infantry Division's 32nd and 31st RCTs and the Steel Tigers were ordered to move to the narrow Tanyang Pass to reduce the enemy roadblocks at the

Pass, to prevent larger North Korean forces attacking from breaking through, and to keep the MSR open for UN commands. The 31st RCT was south of the Pass at Andong and the 32nd RCT was located in defensive positions along the Pass. The most intense period of the combat began on January 8th and lasted to the 15th. Throughout this period, units of the 31st RCT reinforced as well as relieved 32nd RCT units. Elements of the North Korean *2nd and 10th divisions* remained opposite the 7th Division but did not attack on the January 16th. The 7th Infantry Division ordered the 32nd RCT to attack north and northeast the next day to clear out the enemy and reduced the size of the force defending the Tanyang Pass to the 2nd Infantry Battalion of the 31st RCT.[341]

Figure 4.14 displays the thrusts by the North Koreans during the New Year Offensive and the locations of the 7th Infantry Division's 31st RCT with A-77th Armor, its tank company, 32 Infantry RCT, and 17 Infantry RCT on January 7th and 8th.

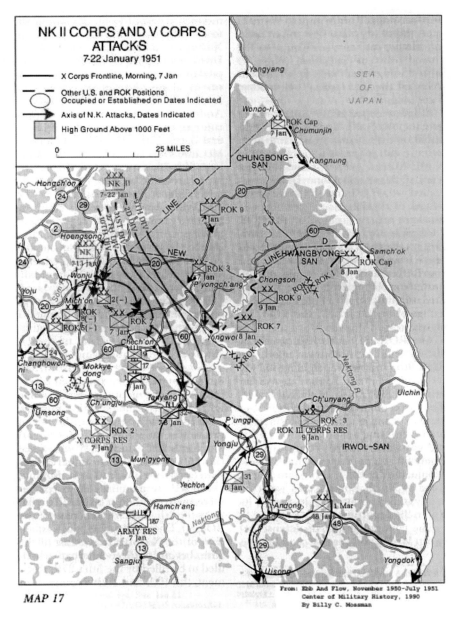

Figure 4.14 7th Infantry Division January 7-8, 1951 locations,
Source: adapted from map17_full.jpg (563×745) (army.mil), June 16, 2023

Simultaneous with trading space for time, Ridgway wanted to determine the enemy situation facing him. The second week of January 1951 began the series of UN operations initially conceived to be reconnaissance in force. Operation WOLFHOUND (January 15 – January 20) was to be initiated by I Corps in the east primarily by the 25th Infantry Division toward Osan and Suwon. Task Force Johnson (January 22) was comprised of a task force of infantry, armor, and engineers led by the IX Corps' 70th Tank Battalion of the 1st Cavalry Division's, 8th Cavalry Regiment. The task force's 24-hour mission was to determine enemy locations. Operation *THUNDERBOLT* (25 January-February 11) which began as a reconnaissance in force but turned into an attack north toward the Han River to thwart the movement of two Chinese divisions from *the XIIIth Army Group's 38th Army* that intelligence indicated had suddenly move from an assembly area where it had been reequipping and absorbing replacements in a likely move to stop the UN advance.

Operation *ROUNDUP* (February 5-18) initially ordered I and IX Corps to approach the Han River by February 8th to hold the positions they seized. Xth Corps received and responded to the expected Chinese and North Korean offensive to that captured of Hoengsong (Hoengseong) east of Seoul and north of the major road junction city of Wonju (Weonju). There were three battles for this strategic city beginning on January 7th. The first occurred when the New Year's Eve Chinese counteroffensive began that drove the UN Command's forces 60 miles south of Seoul. Wonju was a critical point to defend because it was the junction of east-west roads connecting Seoul to Kangnung on the east coast, and northern cities of Chunchon, Kumwha, Hoengsong, the strategic Hwachon (Hwacheon) Resevoir, and Taegu to Pusan in the south. This north-south route became the Xth Corps MSR in its zone.

The second battle began on January 8th. The 2d Infantry Division accomplished the X Corps order to retake Wonju on January 20th. The third battle for Wonju was February 13th through the 18th and it included the 2nd Infantry Division's 14th-16th defense of Chipyong-ni by its 23rd RCT reinforced by the 1st Battalion 5th Cavalry Regiment. [342] This operation was designed to stabilize the Xth Corps' zone. The 7th Infantry Division's three regiments were part of the effort in the Wonju area. Following the battle, the 7th Division was in the vicinity of Pyongchang (Pyeongchang-gun) northeast of Wonju and about 95 miles east of Seoul and was ordered to move to Chechon below Wonju to protect the Corps' MSR to the south [343]. The enemy's defeat Chipyong-ni was the deepest penetration that was made into South Korea for the rest of the war. This victory and that at Wonju was the turnaround for the Eighth Army that Ridgway had hoped for after its expulsion from North Korea in December and withdrawal below Seoul when the Chinese and North Koreans launched their counteroffensive. US units were capable of defeating much larger enemy forces.[344]

Ridgway's vision since assuming command was that the primary objective of the war was to destroy enemy formations wherever they were discovered, not to give them the time to reorganize and refit, and not to emphasize that the UN mission was gaining territory only. He sought MacArthur's concurrence more than once on the last item. In keeping with Ridgway's guidance, IX Corps continued toward the Han meeting little opposition through February 18th. Ridgway put his staff to work on another operation to be launched this time from the Chipyong-ni (Jipyeong-ri) vicinity before that battle had concluded. Its purpose was to block Chinese and North Korean withdrawal routes preventing them from breaking contact without giving them respite from their most recent combat actions. Operation *KILLER* began on February 21st and continued through March 7th.[345]

The attack included IX and X Corps advancing along two major highways east of the Han River. I Corps and the 24th Infantry Division protected the west flank and the ROK III Corps with its 7th Infantry Division moving in its zone along the X Corps route and its other two divisions blocking lateral routes into the X Corps main axis from enemy attacks. The 7th US Infantry Division, on the right (east) portion of the Corps' zone, was to attack north, seize a road junction linking the IX Corps route, and seal the enemy's escape route north to a line designated Arizona a short distance north of Hoengsong.[346]

Operation *KILLER* achieved mixed results. First, the commander of IX Corps died of a heart attack soon after his helicopter crashed and had to be replaced. Second, the area experienced an abnormal rise in average temperatures from below freezing to above with rain during the day. This combination turned the routes of advance to mud during the days and they froze at night.[347] The attack ended by March 7th with the UN forces reaching their assigned objectives while inflicting substantial casualties on the enemy. However, the Chinese and North Koreans were not defeated decisively.[348] Operation *RIPPER* followed immediately on *KILLER's* heels.

Operation *RIPPER* intended to destroy the Chinese and North Korean forces around Seoul and the towns to the east and west without seizing Seoul directly.[349] Instead, the UN flanking attacks were to force the enemy to withdraw north of the 38th Parallel. Ridgway's planned objective was first to seize the banks of the Han River eight miles east of Seoul with I Corps, and then shift northeast near the 38th Parallel in the IX Corps zone with the Xth Corps zone beginning at the northern most point and the extending southeast to the coast. The estimate of the enemy forces between Seoul in the west and the Taebaek Mountains in the east were six Chinese field armies and four North Korean Corps.[350] The plan included a deception portion that would suggest that the UN Command would include another Inchon-like flanking amphibious operation behind the defending forces to the enemy. US Navy ships employed naval gunfire, sent in minesweepers along the coast, and deployed cargo and troop ships sailing from Inchon.[351] The UN Command began its attack on March 7th and it continued through the 31st.

March 15th marked a major change. All was going smoothly in the UN forces' zones as the commands moved forward, however, intelligence had identified seven new Chinese armies and four North Korean corps with 14 divisions entering Korea from Manchuria beginning in January. Added to the enemy already in North Korea and delaying rearward, the evidence that a counterattack was in the planning stages. General Ridgway ordered phase II of *RIPPER* on March 13th [352] Aerial reconnaissance (March 12) and ground unit patrols entering Seoul indicated that North Korean troops had all but withdrawn from the South Korean capital. Ridgway ordered his forces to take control of dominating terrain to the north and west of the city but not to continue the attack on March 15th.[353]

The North Koreans and Chinese withdrew successfully during the last half of March avoiding destruction. All of the UN units reached their assigned objectives between March 15th and occupied major towns and other areas where resistance had been expected to be strong but did not materialize. Long-range ground and aerial reconnaissance continued to discover indicators of an enemy counteroffensive forming.

Operation *COURAGEOUS* was planned to attack the Chinese *26th Army* and North Korean *I Corps* in the western part of South Korea along a line generally from Uijongbu, and the western-most part of the Imjin River where it meets the Han. The goal was to prevent these units from escaping over the Imjin River. An attack by I Corps and an airborne assault by the US 187th Airborne Regimental Combat Team near the village of Munsan-ni located at an Imjin crossing point were included in the plan. I Corps moved in front of the 187th's drop zones on March 22d.[354] Enemy resistance was light, the ground advance was hindered by minefields, and the airborne force experienced an aircraft failure disrupting command and control were among the problems. All of the indicators suggested that the North Koreans in the Munsan-ni area either had withdrawn or had not been there recently.

The situation near Uijongbu was different. The US 3rd and 25th Infantry Divisions encountered strong resistance on March 23rd and 24th compounded by minefields, poor roads, and heavy rain. Ridgway changed unit areas of operations to add more Eighth US Army divisions to the advance including the 1st Cavalry and 1st Marine Divisions. By March 28th, Operation *COURAGEOUS* advanced to or near to the 38th Parallel without engaging and destroying Chinese and North Korean ground forces and equipment in detail. These units were available for future action. This line was designated Line IDAHO. It ran from above Seoul to the northeast and below Uijongbu to the northwest northeast to Chunchon and then sloping southeast toward the coast[355]

Two additional operations were planned to begin in April once X Corps and ROK III Corps had reached their objectives where I and IX Corps had been since late March. Operations *RUGGED and DAUNTLESS* were to begin in April even though continuing reconnaissance reports convinced General Ridgway's intelligence staff that the beginning of the expected enemy counteroffensive was near. Two of the indicators were the identification of new Chinese units and that no new delaying positions were being built. Despite this, Ridgway wanted to keep the pressure on the enemy by destroying their capability to continue the war   The UN Command would move about 10 to 20 miles across the 38th Parallel.[356]

Simultaneous with the planning in Korea, the Parallel took on a new political importance. The question arose in Washington and UN whether China and North Korea might agree to end the war where it began as it was apparent that they could not win a military victory. President Truman scheduled an announcement and the Joint Chiefs of Staff notified General MacArthur on March 20th. He told General Ridgway on March 22d. MacArthur ordered Ridgway not to cross the Parallel. He could move the Eighth Army north only with MacArthur's permission. MacArthur blindsided President Truman on March 24th when he announced that he would be amenable to negotiating with his military equivalent.[357]

Ridgway revised his plan for a strong attack across the Parallel. Operation *DAUNTLESS* would threaten but not seizing three cities: Pyongyang, Chorwon (Cheorwon), and Kumwha (Gimhwa-eup). Nicknamed the Iron Triangle, they contained a complex of road and rail networks extending as far east as the Wonson port and southwest to Seoul among other places. Operation *RUGGED* was to regain contact with the enemy. Mac Arthur approved the plan.[358]

Operation *RUGGED* began on April 1st and Xth Corps of which the 7th Infantry Division and the Steel Tigers remained in the order of battle were not involved. The objective was to move to LINE KANSAS generally along the 38th Parallel from the confluence of the Imjin and Han Rivers in the west about 115 miles across the country east to the seacoast city of Toepo-ri through the Taebaek Mountain north of the Hwachon Reservoir in the center which was Seoul's source for electricity and water.[359] Operation *DAUNTLESS* began on April 11th with I and IX Corps. This occurred on the same day that President Truman relieved General MacArthur replacing him with General Ridgway who was replaced by Lieutenant General James Van Fleet.[360]   The UN Command's advance, including that of the US X including the 7th Infantry Division, and ROK III Corps reached Line KANSAS near Hwachon and the Hwachon reservoir by April 9th.[361]

Van Fleet's plan was to continue inflicting as much damage on the Chinese and North Koreans even if they launched the counterattack that the UN Command expected. He was prepared to order a coordinated rearward delay as far south as necessary until the offensive played itself out and the UN Command could move north again.[362] There were no surprises in the enemy's tactics when it came on April 22d. Their main strength was their manpower. UN intelligence estimated about 700,000 troops were in North Korea and that about 350,000 were in the attacking formations. The Chinese and North Korean infantry attacked in waves and were supported by a limited number of artillery and the North Koreans also used tanks. They struck during the night to avoid UN air attacks.[363]

The communists' main effort was directed in the west to cut Seoul off from UN control with a secondary attack in the center in the Yonchon-Hwachon area. The enemy's goal was the same as UN Command's after General Ridgway took command: to destroy UN forces and equipment. Initially, the attack forced the UN forces to give up their recent gains and fall back to Line KANSAS. The withdrawal was coordinated and when a gap occurred, troops were immediately available to fill them. UN forces held the enemy advance at a new line that was designated NO-NAME-LINE a few miles north of Seoul.[364]

The Chinese and North Koreans did not cross the Han or reach Seoul where they stopped although there was intelligence that they would mount a new attack. Van Fleet ordered his command to begin patrolling and then attacking north to keep the pressure on the enemy. They seized Uijongbu on May 6th[365] UN forces used the time to strengthen their lines while Fifth Air Force and 1st Marine Air Wing attacked The Chinese and North Koreans further north. The UN kept the pressure on until the enemy continued the offensive during the night of May 15-16.[366]

The Chinese attacked the central sector of the UN Line against the Xth Corps. North Korean divisions attacked the western and eastern flanks of the UN forces. The Chinese threw 23 manpower-heavy divisions against the center against UN ground forces who were reinforced by air and heavy volumes of artillery fire. All units on both sides fought tenaciously. The forward movement of the Chinese and North Koreans slowed by May 20th. To relieve the pressure in the center against US IX and Xth Corps, General Van Fleet initiated planning for his counterattack to strike the enemy's flanks on May 18th.[367] Nevertheless, the communist forces continued to move units toward ROK units and Van Fleet had to stabilize the UN Command's line. The attack plan was broadened to emphasize not only destroying enemy forces and supplies wherever found, but also to seize main road junctions and hubs. With IXth US Corps on the left of Xth US Corps, the 7th Division's mission was to attack in the Xth US Corps zone and then relieve the 1st Marine Division in the US IX Corps Zone along Route 29 and to continue the attack along Route 29 from Chunchon back to Hwachon where it had reached before the April counterattack.[368]

Planning for Operation *PILEDRIVER* which was a IX and I Corps offensive forward to destroy North Korean and Chinese forces, entered the planning stage in late May 1951. A three-division I Corps attack began on June 3rd. The I Corps' mission was to secure the Iron Triangle's two base towns of Kumwha in the east and Chorwon and continue west to the Imjin. This attack began on June 3rd.[369]

The three-division IX Corps mission was to extend the UN lines back to Line WYOMING by securing the roads from Highways 29 and 17 in the west from Kumwha to the west side of the Hwachon reservoir east between Highway 17 and the Pukhan River. The IX Corps attack launched on June 5th. The 7th Infantry Division moved north on June 7th. The division's mission was to seize the road leading into the Iron Triangle from the town of Hwachon. The UN Command controlled the terrain Lines KANSAS in the west to the juncture of KANSAS and WYOMING in the east slightly above the roads meeting in the Inje-Yanggu area and then moving east along a redrawn LINE KANSAS to the coastal city of Kansong at the end of June. This line passed the future battle sites of Pork Chop Hill And the Iron Triangle in the west and Heartbreak Ridge and the Punchbowl in the East[370] The further north that Van Fleet's forces moved, the stronger the defenses became. There was no renewed Chinese and North Korean attacks south except for continuing to infiltrate soldiers whose mission was to guerrillas disrupting rear areas as they had been doing since the war began. Instead, air and ground reconnaissance reported that the defenses north of the UN's positions were growing stronger.[371]

The UN Command's Operation *PILEDRIVER*'s reached all of its LINE KANSAS-WYOMING objectives by June 10th [372] There were forays north of KANSAS. I US Corps sent two armor and infantry task forces to the outskirts of the Iron Triangle, Pyongyang, on June 13th. The city was empty of defenders but the enemy held the key terrain to the north so the units returned to the UN line.[373]

May 1951 was another turning point in the Korean War for the Steel Tigers as well as the rest of the forces in the UN Command when US and United Nations policymaking came into conflict with the military's mission. General Ridgway wanted to continue to destroy all communist forces he came into contact with to protect the achievements of the UN alliance in Korea while redeploying units to defend Japan against a Soviet attack should one occur. There was no indication that an attack was imminent. Instead, he was contingency planning for such an event[374] Throughout May, diplomatic activity occurred in numerous locations including the New York, Washington, Ottawa, Moscow, and Paris.[375]

Simultaneous with the diplomatic effort, Generals Ridgway and Van Fleet were exploring options to continue attacking north beyond the KANSAS-WYOMING Line to continue keeping the Chinese and North Koreans off-balance and destroying their capability make war. Moving north to establish a line from Pyongyang to Wonsan was one option. They also assessed optimal lines to strengthen to defend South Korea if a ceasefire occurred and agreed that the Line KANSAS-WYOMING was the best choice because of the terrain. Ridgway ordered that two more lines be established and strengthened. The first 10 miles beyond KANSAS would be an outpost line, the ceasefire line separating the two Koreas would be 10 miles in front of the first line.[376]

One of the reasons leading to President Truman's April 11th relief of General MacArthur was his scuttling of Truman's March offer to the Chinese and North Koreans that it was time to enter into negotiations to end the fighting because the communists would never defeat the UN's effort. Mac Arthur returned to the United States where he addressed a joint session of Congress on May 3d where he identified steps to be taken to end the war. The United Nations' Security Council, the US National Security Council, and the US Joint Chiefs of Staff examined the UN Command's mission in Korea.[377]

General Ridgway received a new mission from Joint Chiefs on June 1st that included four parts. First, end the war with an armistice agreement acceptable to all combatants. Second, establish South Korean authority over all of the country along an agreed line that was no farther south than the 38th Parallel. Third, prepare plans for a phased withdrawal of all non-Korean UN troops. Last, rebuild the South Korean military force structure to stop a new North Korean attack on the country.[378] The Soviet Ambassador to the UN stated on June 23rd in a brief statement that the USSR agreed that a settlement was possible. The Chinese stated its support on the 25th. North Korean Premier Kim il Sung agreed to the talks on July 1st. The first meeting of the armistice negotiating group met in Kaesong, Korea on July 10, 1951.[379] There was no ceasefire agreed to and the war continued until 10:00 pm on July 27, 1953 when the ceasefire became effective after being signed 12 hours earlier.[380]

The Defense Department gave Ridgway the authority to continue the attack northward using the Pyongyang-Wonsan plan should the initial negotiations fail; however, he opted to keep US casualties as low as possible especially if the UN Command fought for terrain that an eventual ceasefire would force them to withdraw from and give to the North Koreans.[381]

When the negotiations opened at Kaesong, the balance of forces was more than 550,000 in the UN Command and 459,000 Chinese and North Koreans. The UN manpower advantage was illusory because there were no reserves immediately available. The 459,000 Chinese and North Koreans distributed among 13 Chinese armies and seven North Korean corps could rely on an additional 749,000 Chinese across the border in Manchuria.[382]

Tank Company, 31st Infantry Regiment (RCT)

The Steel Tigers remained integral to the 31st RCT's missions during the first nine months of 1951. They kept the MSRs open during the advances and counterattacks when enemy units penetrated the 7th Division's sectors seeking to move behind the regiment through gaps in the line. They trained replacements and received training themselves in tanker specialties including the indirect firing of their tanks' main guns by artillerymen. Soldiers enjoyed rest and recuperation periods in Japan and at secure locations in South Korea. They had vehicle maintenance and weapons care between missions. When the 7th Division advanced as part of Ridgway's strategy to destroy the North Koreans formations and equipment wherever found, the men of the 31st Infantry's tank company worked together with the regiment's infantrymen to perform reconnaissance, establish, organize, and strengthen blocking positions to defend against possible counterattacks, and to conduct reconnaissance-in-force patrols task organized into teams forward of the regiment's temporary lines to stay in contact with the enemy.

The 7th Infantry Division's 32nd RCT defended the Tanyang Pass south of Wonju in early January as the North Koreans and Chinese attacked south during the first battle for that strategically critical road hub in the Xth Corps zone. The 31st Infantry was ordered to secure the Corps MSR, Route 29, at Andong by January 8th. This road intersected with Highway 48 that ran east to the coast. The 31st's mission was to prevent enemy forces moving from Wonju around the Tanyang Pass any further south than Andong by strong patrols.[383] The 1st Battalion of the 31st RCT moved forward to relieve the 32d RCT on January 11th and returned to the 31st RCT's control two days later.[384]

The 31st Infantry spent the first week of Operation *KILLER* in March 1951 by serving in the Xth Corps reserve The Steel Tigers patrolled in the Corps' zone including along the MSR, it established a replacement training center and it improved its blocking positions. Often a tank platoon was attached to one or more of the 31st' infantry battalions to give added firepower to the patrols venturing beyond the forward divisional line at the time to keep in contact with the enemy. At other times, the 31st tank company had the reconnaissance platoon of the 73rd Armor attached for MSR patrols. The regiment's units conducted on-the-job training, and care and cleaning of their equipment when not otherwise patrolling or training the new members of the unit. The regiment was also responsible for maintaining daily contact with the 7th ROK Infantry Division.[385]

During Operation *RIPPER* that followed immediately on the heels of Operation *KILLER*, the Steel Tigers experienced the heavy rains that slowed the advance of the rest of the 7th Division in its zone across the Han River and to the north. The mountainous terrain compounded by bad weather that turned the already deteriorated roads into mud also allowed the enemy to withdraw northward with their equipment. The Steel Tigers had to be reassigned to serve as the regimental reserve on one occasion when only two tank platoons could inch their way along the dirt roads for several days. which had already been cratered by mines and no enemy contact had been made. Patrolling was left to the infantry during this period. About 4,000 men were working on road repair on March 28th. Overall, the road conditions affected everything. Snail-paced forward combat unit movement and the delays in resupply of food, fuel, and water did not allow the entire Xth Corps to reach its objectives until early April.[386]

The Steel Tigers were part of the offensives that pushed north during April during Operation *RUGGED* in April and then during the defensive missions that responded to the North Korean and Chinese counteroffensive beginning April 22nd. The Tank Company, 31st Infantry attacked north again on June 5th as part of Operation *PILEDRIVER* with one tank platoon attached to each of the regiment's battalions. Units attached to the 31st RCT were the 57th Field Artillery Battalion, C Battery 15th AAA AW SP Battalion, and a prisoner of war interrogation team. The RCT reached its objectives in the vicinity of Line KANSAS by June 23rd.[387]

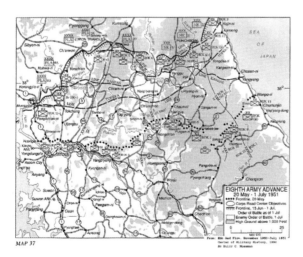

Figure 4.15 Eighth Army Northward Movement Stops
Source: Eighth Army Advance, 20 May- 1 July 1951 | A Military Photos & Video Website (militaryimages.net) June 16, 2023

The 31st Infantry became the 7th Division's reserve during July. The regiment cleared its zone of civilians and harvested the barley crop in the area. It was also responsible for preparing its area for a United Services Organization show by the movie, radio, and later television star Jack Benny and his troupe on July 8th. During this period, 16 officers and 336 enlisted men earned enough points to rotate out of the regiment. All units participated in strengthening their Line KANSAS defensive positions and the field fortifications. Each battalion spent the first half of the month planning, rehearsing and conducting an intensive demonstration of an infantry battalion defending its positions for units of the division. The exercise was named Operation *BUNKER HILL*. The Steel Tigers and the regimental heavy mortar company supported the iterations of the demonstration. Positions along Line KANSAS were the setting for the exercise. There was an enemy attack countered by long-range, final protective, and in-position indirect fire and a friendly infantry counterattack. Specialist training for cooks, mechanics, signal and other specialists took place as did command inspections by the regimental commander of the soldiers and their equipment. No enemy contact occurred during July except that the engineers destroyed several anti-personnel mines that were found. The month closed with a regimental command post exercise during July 27-29. [388]

August began with the 31st ordered to relieve units of the 2nd Infantry Division on August 8th. Until then, there had been no enemy contact. Meanwhile, the units continued improving their defensive positions and said goodbye to eight officers and 93 enlisted men who rotated out of the regiment. The Steel Tigers led the 31st's move on August 7th relieving the 5th Regimental Combat Team on Line WYOMING. The rest of the regiment followed on the 8th and went into a static defense until August 30th when it was ordered forward. The mission was a limited objective night attack to a ridgeline overlooking the Hudong-ni valley and searchlights were used to guide the units. No enemy contact occurred and the attack was successful.[389]

September found the 31st Regiment occupying the same ridgeline that now was extended to overlook the Pangdangdong-ni Valley too. The terrain was rugged . The *238th Infantry Regiment of 80th Division* that was subordinate to the *IXth Army Group's 27th Army* drove the 31st's 1st Battalion from its position on September 1st. The battalion regained its position the next day reinforced by the 2nd Battalion. The Chinese did not initiate any further attacks from September 4-30, but the *27th Army* was replaced by the *598th Regiment of the 67th Army's 200th Infantry Division* on September 12th. The *67th Army* entered the war after the Chinese November 27th counterattacks against Eighth US Army and Xth Corps.[390]

The Steel Tigers launched a strong tank patrol on September 9th that penetrated 12 kilometers into the Chinese lines. The operation caught the Chinese by surprise and resulted in the destruction of bunkers and supplies. It also resulted in mine damage to two tanks and one tank retriever. The vehicles were recovered the next day but also resulted in the loss of a second retriever when it drove into a mud pit and broke a track. Despite receiving small arms fire from the Chinese, there were no US casualties. Missions from September 11th through the 30th were daily combat patrols.[391]

The Steel Tigers Deactivated

October and November 1951 were eventful for the Steel Tigers. The 31st RCT fought the *596th* and *598th* regiments of the *67th Army's 199th infantry Division* from October 1-7. On the 8th, the regiment moved into reserve and remained there until October 12th when it was ordered to fill a gap in the 6th ROK Infantry Division's front for a short period. Next the regiment relieved the 2nd Infantry Division's 9th Infantry Regiment. Generally, the Chinese did not mount a determined defense against these patrols and now was facing another new PLA army: the *610th Infantry Regiment* of the *204th Infantry Division* that was part of the *68th Army*.[392] Although the war continued, the Steel Tigers were relieved from their assignment to the 31st Infantry Regiment, 7th Infantry Division on October 10, 1951 and deactivated on November 10, 1951 in South Korea.[393] The 73rd Tank Battalion was assigned to the 7th Infantry Division that same day.[394]

Figure 4.16 displays the lines between North and South Korea on the date the armistice was signed.

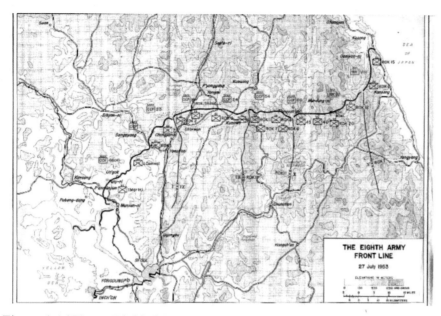

Figure 4-16 Korea Divided June 27, 1953
Source: from joon Chang, retrieved from <u>Blogger: User Profile: Joon Chang</u> July 18, 2023

Army tours of duty for soldiers drafted during the Korean War averaged nine to 12 months. Conscripts served their two-year obligations which included training. The 7th Infantry Division landed at Inchon in mid-September 1950. It was time for the original Steel Tigers to rotate back to the United States. There was no mention of the change of unit designations in any of the regimental command reports for October through December 1951 that this research could identify. It is very likely that the veterans who deployed from Japan 13 months prior went home and those who had not reached their end-of-tour eligibility were reassigned to tank companies in the 73rd Armor. The reports of the 31st Infantry Regiment continue to refer to *tank company* and *Tnk Co 31st Inf* in the November and December 1951 reports. Historically, the bond that was formed between the 77th Armor and the 73rd Armor when the two units met after the Inchon landings remains as both units remain active in 2022 as the 1st Battalion 77th Armor and the 5th Squadron 73rd Cavalry.

There were four individuals whose careers in the first six months of the Korean War intersected again when the 77th Armor arrived in South Vietnam: Second Lieutenant John Max Pickarts, Second Lieutenant Carmelo P. Milia, Lieutenant Colonel Raymond Davis USMC, and Sergeant Joe D Offutt.

Lieutenant Pickarts enlisted in the Marine Corps in World War II and fought in the Pacific. He attended the University of California, Santa Barbara beginning in 1946 and was commissioned in the US Army at graduation. His first assignment was to the reconnaissance battalion of the 2nd Infantry Division. He reported to Fort Lewis, Washington after graduation in June and was told he was on alert and could not leave the post even to tell his wife. The division arrived in Pusan and went into combat. He suffered a war-ending wound in the side and lost a finger within the first few weeks of his arrival. He was evacuated for treatment. Lieutenant Colonel Pickarts was the 1-77 Armor Battalion Commander when it was alerted for deployment to South Vietnam. He trained the Steel Tigers at Fort Carson, Colorado, and took it into combat.[395]

Second Lieutenant Carmelo P. Milia graduated from the United States Military Academy in June 1950 He joined the 3rd Infantry Division's 64th Armor as a tank platoon leader. His unit's mission was to keep the roads open for Xth Corps units moving south from the Chosin Reservoir to the redeployment port at Hungnam. Lieutenant Colonel Milia was originally the deputy commander and operations officer of the 1st Brigade 5th Infantry Division (Mechanized). He assumed command of the 1-77 Armor from Lieutenant Colonel Pickarts. He applied his experience traversing the rugged terrain of Korea's Taebaek Mountains in March 1969 when he led a tank-heavy task force with artillery, combat engineers, and others in a reconnaissance-in-force mission to the Laotian border past the Khe Sanh Combat Base that had been besieged during the North Vietnamese 1968 Tet Offensive.[396]

Lieutenant Colonel Raymond Davis commanded the 1st Battalion, 7th Marine Regiment, 1st Marine Division at the Battle of the Chosin Reservoir for which he received the Medal of Honor. He fought in the Pacific Theater during World War II at Guadalcanal, New Guinea, and Peleliu. Major General Davis commanded the 3rd Marine Division that operationally controlled the 1st Brigade, 5th Infantry Division (Mechanized) in Quang Tri Province, Republic of Vietnam.[397]

Sergeant Joe D. Offut was a tank commander with 4th Platoon, A Company, 73rd Tank Battalion. Initially a tank driver when his battalion reached Korea, he earned command of his own tank. He was captured by the Chinese and escaped. The 73rd was part of the Eighth Army drive from Pusan that linked with Xth Corps near Suwon after it landed at Inchon. During the drive north to the Yalu, his unit arrived from Pusan shortly before Thanksgiving Day on November 25th and became the 7th Division's reserve located at Hamhung port at the beginning of the Chinese counterattack on November 27th. First Sergeant Offutt was the first sergeant of Company A, 1ˢᵗ Battalion 77ᵗʰ Armor at Fort Carson, Colorado and in Vietnam.[398]

These four professionals prepared and led the next generation of Steel Tigers in Vietnam.

The Enemy

The Korean War was a symmetrical war between the combatants. The North Korean People's Army (NKPA) began the war with five army corps of 20 infantry divisions with 11,000 men assigned in each and one 6,000-man tank brigade of 150 T-34 medium tanks mounting the 85-millimeter main gun. There were three more corps of nine infantry divisions in Manchuria. Appleman estimates that the 135,000 North Koreans invaded the south on June 25th.[399]

Mossberg states that the UN Command in Tokyo estimated in October that there were about 12 Chinese divisions with 70,000 PLA troops in North Korea. The estimate did not change. In reality, the Chinese had more than 300,000 troops positioned to stop MacArthur from reaching the Yalu River in November 1950. The Chinese moved at night remaining hidden during the day, and air reconnaissance never detected them at the Yalu River crossing points.[400]

The Chinese People's Liberation Army committed the 120,000-man *IX Army Group* with its four armies of 20,000-30,000 men each having four infantry divisions against Xth US Corps in the east at the Chosin Reservoir on November 27th. Elements of the *XIII Army Group* that had six armies of three divisions each had already stopped the US Eighth Army's advance along the western approach to the Yalu in the November 1-6 battle at Unsan and then disappeared back into the mountains.[401]

The Chinese *XIII Army Group's 42ⁿᵈ Army* with its *124ᵗʰ, 125ᵗʰ, and 126ᵗʰ divisions* had crossed the Yalu in October into the western area of the Chosin Reservoir mountains to protect the flank of the rest of the Army Group when it attacked the Eighth Army along Korea's west coast. The Marines identified the *IX Army Group's 79ᵗʰ, 80ᵗʰ, 81ˢᵗ, and 90ᵗʰ* divisions of *27th Army*, and the *20ᵗʰ Army's 58ᵗʰ, 59ᵗʰ, 60ᵗʰ* and *89ᵗʰ* divisions in the Yudam-ni sector of the west bank of the Reservoir prior to the attack.[402]

Mossberg states that a 1950 Chinese division had 8,000-10,000 men each, and a regiment had 3,000. A Chinese division had one 122-mm artillery battalion with 12 howitzers, twenty-four 76-mm guns, one battalion of 12 Su-76 self-propelled 76-mm guns, twelve 45-mm antitank guns, and thirty-six 14.5-mm antitank rifles. Regiments had six 120-mmm mortars four 76-mm gun, and six 45-mm antitank guns. In Infantry battalions had nine 82-mm mortars and two 45-mm antitank guns. Infantry companies had 60-mm mortars for immediate indirect fire support. In addition, individual units brought various US weapons to Korea because they had been captured from the Chinese Nationalists during the civil war that ended in 1949.[403]

Summary

The 1949 edition of Field Manual 17-33, Tank Battalion addressed the roles of armored units. One of the lessons learned from World War II was that tank units could support infantry units in attacks, counterattacks, exploiting successes and increasing the depth of an infantry unit's antitank capabilities in offensive and defensive operations. Force structure planners attached a tank battalion to each infantry regiment that would provide the regimental commander maximum flexibility for organizing the regiment to accomplish the assigned missions in accordance with the enemy situation on the ground, the terrain, and the commander's plan. The tank battalion might have infantry attached or, the tank battalion could be divided into companies being attached the infantry battalions.

A tank company instead of a battalion attached to an infantry regiment could still add its shock effect of vehicles and firepower, increase the infantry's antitank capability and generally support the infantry's mission.[404]

The 77th Tank Battalion existed on paper when it joined 31st Infantry Regiment in March 1949, but it went to war with only its Company A. The Steel Tigers were known officially as Tank Co (or Tnk Co), 31st Inf. One of the advantages that the services had in June 1950 was the large number of World War II veterans. Not only were there regulars who remained in the military following V-J Day, but also reservists were recalled to active duty. Both were able develop the draftees. The percentage of the experienced Army soldiers in Korea by December 1950 was 82 percent.[405]

Korea was a come-as-you-are war. It was not even dignified as a war at the time. The president called it a police action. Public support was high when the North Koreans attacked but unlike World War II interest diminished as the war continued especially once the peace talks began in July 1951.

Moreover, the difficult terrain caused many leaders to assess Korea as unsuitable for tanks. Captain Robert McCaleb's January 1951 "Facts, Not Prejudice" letter to the editor of *Armor* called Korea "a battle of the road nets." Unlike World War II where armored units took full advantage of good roads and favorable terrain wherever possible, the road networks in Korea were not developed. Tanks and other vehicles could move from one location to another and then go off into a position. Cross-country movement was impossible especially when the temperatures were above freezing. McCaleb argued that the Chinese and North Koreans were able to withdraw successfully in the face of the UN Command's advances because they were lightly armed and did not have to endure bumper-to-bumper traffic.[406]

Others argued that the M4A3E8 Sherman tank with its 76mm main gun was ineffective against the T-34's 85mm used by the North Koreans. Colonel William Withers a staff officer in the Eighth Army's Armor Section argued the opposite in "Report from Korea". He presented data from tank engagements during September and October 1951 as the Eighth Army began moving north from Pusan before the amphibious landings at Inchon by the Xth Corps and 1st Marine Division. He stated that that the M4A3 and M4A3E8 tanks proved superior to the Russian tank in all tank vs. tank engagements. Tank crew casualties were few in these tank-on-tank fights and some of the damaged Shermans were repairable. He noted that the North Koreans learned not to expose their tanks to the US tank units and surrendered to US armor units when they ran out of fuel and parts. He assessed that the Sherman M4s were fine tanks when they were properly maintained, inspected before departing on missions, and employed wisely.[407]

Captain Drake, the Steel Tigers' first commander in Korea was assigned to the Army Field Forces Board Number 2 at Fort Knox after returning from Korea. He wrote about tanks that were part of infantry units in "The Infantry Regiment's Tank Company." From his position at Fort Knox, he was responding to a debate within the Army over whether to keep the tank company in the infantry regiment's organization or to the addition of a second tank battalion.[408]

Drake stated that keeping the tank company in the regiment had many advantages primarily because many infantry commanders were unfamiliar with tanks and their capabilities. For this reason, the company commander was the regimental commander's armor advisor. His continued presence and dedicated support educated the regimental commander and built trust and confidence between them. He made the following additional points. First, the issue of communications between the infantry battalion, regiment, and division arose at the Chosin Reservoir. Only the tank company's command tanks could link with the 7th Infantry Division, tactical air support, and artillery forward observers. It was stated that the division's assistant commander commandeered one of Drake's two command tanks to call for reinforcements for Task Force Faith.

Second, it took 18 hours for the 5th Marine Regiment to roadmarch the six miles from the command post at Hagaru-ri to Koto-ri in order to move down through the pass to reach Hamhung. The Chinese had the high ground on both sides of the narrow road. The Steel Tigers were the front and rear guard and Drake stated that tank fire up and into Chinese contributed greatly to preventing them from closing the road.

Third, the tank company worked with the regiment. It did not have to be detached from current operations and moved distances before it could arrive to provide support to another divisional entity. When issues arose, primarily maintenance, the problem was at the division level because the ordnance company's lack of tools, parts and the mechanics' training to support an armored unit regardless whether it was a second tank battalion or the regiment's tank company.

Fourth, the tank company was part of the regiment. The unit's pay, administration, awards, casualty, promotions, and replacements were processed by the regiment. The infantrymen and tankers knew each other. Additionally, the presence of tanks providing antitank fire instead of an infantryman exposing himself to fire his antitank weapon was a confidence builder and it reinforced the bond among them.[409]

In the end, it was the tankers themselves who achieved success. First Lieutenant Robert L Brown wrote that tank crews always face problems caused by weather and terrain. It was the intelligence and creativity of those who took their tanks into battle that made the difference. Tank units could perform reconnaissance to find routes around filled rice paddies. The problem in the winter with Korea's snow and ice was remedied by the crews carrying straw mats on their tanks to gain traction when required. Brown believed that the tanks could do anything "…except float and fly."[410]

Chapter 5: Vietnam - 1968

Introduction

The first decade of the Cold War (1945-1955) established in the framework of national security policy and defense and military strategies that Soviet communism was monolithic and threatened the western democracies. There was ample evidence of this in Europe following World War II. The communist movements in Asia and Africa were caught up also in post-WW II decolonization. Movements existed throughout East Asia including Indochina, Malaysia and Indonesia. Histories written in the subsequent second and third decades began appearing that included the two currents rather than the one. They agreed that while Ho Chi Minh was a devout communist, he was a product of Vietnam's evolution toward a national identity that began in 208 BC when the Viets who had moved into the northern region of Vietnam from Mongolia opposed China's occupation of the entire area. The Chinese and Vietnamese did not integrate over the subsequent centuries and the latter rebelled periodically against Chinese domination. The Vietnamese clung to their own identity.

Indochina included Cambodia, Laos, and Vietnam. Ho Chi Minh's interests focused only on Vietnam. The 1945-1955 decade is named the First Indochina War against the French. The 1954 Geneva Accords signed in July 1954 established Laos, and Cambodia as separate countries and partitioned Vietnam temporarily into two countries until elections could be held in 1956. The Second Indochina War against the US and its allies began in 1955 and lasted until 1975. While the wars against the French and the US might not have been directed from Moscow or Beijing, Ho Chi Minh's ruling leadership was a revolutionary body that neither tolerated dissent from the varied socio-political groups comprising the population in the north nor did his southern governing entity the Central Committee of the People's Revolutionary Party. This organization was better known as the Central Office for South Vietnam (COSVN) by the Americans and its allies. The military arm of COSVN was the People's Liberation Armed Forces of South Vietnam (PLAF), better known the Viet Cong (VC) enforced compliance among South Vietnamese civilians as well as fought the Army of the Republic of Vietnam (ARVN) and other Government of Vietnam (GVN) military entities: the US, Australia, South Korea the Philippines, Thailand, Cambodia (later the Khmer Republic), and Laos. The People's Army of Vietnam (PAVN) was the military arm of the North Vietnamese army during the war. Its name was shortened to the North Vietnamese Army (NVA).

French interests in Vietnam began in earnest in the mid-1800s during the reign of Napoleon III as other European nations were colonizing portions of East Asia. Ho Chi Minh was educated in Vietnam and France and was firm in his opposition to his homeland being a French colony. The French perceived that their indigenous opposition were simply bandits.[411] Ho traveled between the Soviet Union and China during the 1930s and then returned home in 1941 to fight the Japanese.

Before the 1941 Japanese attack on Pearl Harbor and France's surrender to Germany on June 22, 1940, The Japanese requested that the French government allow its forces to attack China through its Indochina colony and stop the pass-through of US supplies to Chiang Kai-Shek entering at Haiphong harbor.[412] Approval from Paris did not occur and the Japanese invaded Indochina by land and sea September 22-24, 1940. Vichy France under Marshal Petain consented to allow the Japanese presence to remain.[413]

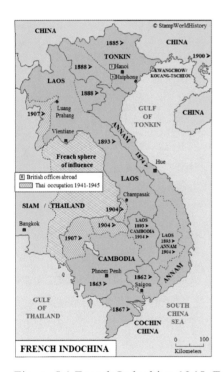

Figure 5.1 French Indochina 1945, Enemy in the Mirror, Source: Our Enemies ~ Ourselves, Vietnam After World War II, November 9, 2017, Ho Chi Minh and the rise of Vietnam-World War II- One Minute History, You Tube retrieved from Vietnam 1945 (enemyinmirror.com), July 20, 2023

Ho Chi Minh and Vo Nguyen Giap, also a communist, created the Viet-Minh as a nationalist movement and began operating in remote northern areas of Vietnam in 1944.[414] Ho hid his communist ideology so his efforts would attract all Vietnamese patriots.[415] His goal was that his opposition to the Japanese would be the gift of independence for Vietnam from the allied powers at the end of the war in the Pacific.

Stanley Karnow recounts in his 1991 *Vietnam: A History* that Vietnam, Laos, and Cambodia were ancillary to the Allied effort in World War II. President Roosevelt and Prime Minister Churchill declared in the 1941 Atlantic Charter that states whose sovereignty had been taken from them would see them re-established. Roosevelt promised the Free French in 1942 that their overseas colonies would be returned in an effort to urge General De Gaulle to increase his effort against Germany. This was revised in 1943 to propose that the French reoccupation would carry with it the guarantee of future independence. Before his death in 1945, Roosevelt next promised to return the three nations of Indochina to the Chinese. President Truman following a debate within the State Department between its European and Asian branches over the future of Southeast Asia finalized the decision in favor of France in May 1945.[416]

In summary, there was no post-war vision for Vietnam or the rest of Indochina in the western capitals. Regardless of the allies' foreign ministries and heads of state, the pre-war colonial empires ended with VE and V-J Days in 1945. At the time of the Japanese surrender, there was no French presence in the colony and Ho Chi Minh and his Viet Minh organization filled the power vacuum. The Indochinese Communist Party (ICP) met on August 13, 1945, and agreed to do the following:

- Disarm the Japanese before the French and any external states entered the country.
- Grant permission as Indochina's governing authority to foreign forces entering Indochina for the purpose of disarming the Japanese.

The ICP proclaimed Indochina to be a republic in September 1945 and the French negotiated with its leadership to reenter Indochina in February 1946. During this window of opportunity, the Viet-Minh consolidated its control of the country by subjugating and eliminating Vietnamese who did not want the communists or the French.[417]

The Indochinese wars against the French and Americans with their allies were not simply about the restoration of western colonialism following World War II in the case of the French and replacing them with a new set of colonial nations after 1954. Opposition to Ho's communist ideology was widespread especially in the north among Roman Catholic and Buddhist Vietnamese who were opposed to the atheistic communists not only because of religion, but also the socio-cultural customs of the country where the family was the focal point of social interaction. Younger members were expected to internalize that the obligations they owed their parents were enormous and never ending. Buddhist opposition extended to some of the Vietnamese leaders in the south as well.[418]

The best example of the enmity between the communists and those opposing not only them, but also all foreign occupiers of their country is the post-1968 Tet Offensive discoveries in Hue following the VC and NVA invaders' retreat. The North Vietnamese's leadership had expected the southern civilian population to rise up and join them when they entered the former imperial capital city. There was no massive civilian uprising and Vietnamese and US troops found mass graves where the communist invaders murdered about 3,000 men, women, and children and many were buried alive.[419]

The Cold War and Korean War chapters presented general facts about the creation of Vietnam out of Indochina. One French unit that fought in the Korean War and against the Vietnamese communists after France reestablished its pre-WW II colony is an exemplar of the differences between fighting a symmetrical war where the two opponents employ similar types of armaments and tactics in a linear war. Analyses of the US involvement there focused historically on the French defeat at Dien Bien Phu on May 7, 1954. The better example of symmetrical versus asymmetrical warfare in Vietnam was mainly in the Central Highlands during 1954 (Figure 5.2).

Figure 5.2 Central Highlands, South Vietnam, Not-to-scale sketch by author

This story of the Steel Tigers from the Regiment's 1940 activation to the end of the Cold War in 1992 examines what one foreign combat-experienced and distinguished infantry battalion encountered when it left what was then a conventional linear battlefield and reached Vietnam where the combat environment was unconventional, and the alignment of opposing forces was asymmetrical. The French ground forces already in Vietnam had various models of wheeled and tracked military vehicles supported by air power. Ho's troops led by Giap destroyed 398 of the vehicles between 1952 and 1954, and they employed various types of mines and booby traps against 84 percent of those.[420] The Red Devil Brigade entered this form of conflict where there were no front lines and where objectives were seized but then abandoned in the summer 1968.

The Korea 1 battalion presented earlier as part of the 2nd US Infantry Division's 23rd Infantry Regiment reached Saigon on November 1, 1953. It expanded into a second battalion (Korea 2) from its own resources and was named the *Le Regiment de Coree* (Korea Regiment). It joined other units that were veterans of Indochina combat including an artillery regiment, the 43rd Colonial Infantry, and the 3d Squadron, 5th Armored Cavalry. The entire unit went on the French Army's active role as *Groupement Mobile* (Mobile Group) Number 100 (G.M.100) on November 15, 1953, near Saigon where it began to train. The Group numbered 3,498 officers and men. It entered action on December 4, 1953, searching the creeks and ditches of the Saigon River delta for Viet Minh supplies and weapons caches and discovered quickly that warfare in this theater was different from Korea. The French had tanks, armored cars, artillery, and air support. The Viet Minh had the element of surprise and broke contact when G.M. 100 could use its firepower and other assets effectively. The first casualty occurred on December 4th when a soldier stepped on a mine almost as soon as the operation began. From that day on, G.M.100 was vulnerable to ambushes, boobytraps, and night attacks throughout its area of operations (AO) in the central highlands bounded by Buon Me Thuot in the south and Pleiku in the north. Even when the French expected a Viet Minh attack at a certain location and prepared for it, the surprise was in the timing of the attack.

G.M. 100 was rendered combat ineffective as a unit on June 24-25, 1954. Mobile Group 42 (G.M.42) several kilometers closer to Pleiku received G.M.100 survivors and continued the retreat toward Pleiku which they reached on June 29th. G.M. 42 added remnants of the Korea 1 and 2 battalions and other G.M.100 survivors to its own order of battle. It began a new operation on July 14th and was defeated on July 17, 1954, at a mountain pass midway between Buon Me Thuot and Pleiku. Korea 1 was the rear guard of the column and was the only unit in the column that was ambushed in the pass. It had been in continuous combat in the performance of various missions within its AO for seven months. The battalion had 107 members remaining of which 57 were in a military hospital.[421] A reconstituted Korea battalion was renamed and sent from Vietnam to Algeria in the summer of 1955.

Ho Chi Minh was the head of state in North Vietnam and Ngo Dinh Diem was the President of South Vietnam. The Demiltarized Zone (DMZ) separating the two entities was located near the 17th Parallel along Quang Binh Province's southern border, and Quang Tri Province's northern border. The Ben Hai River bisected the DMZ in the east. Gio Linh was the last military base before reaching the DMZ, and Dong Ha had the largest population nearest the DMZ in the south. The Cua Viet River emptying at Cua Viet Port east of Dong Ha formed the south's first natural barrier. The border extended west past Khe Sanh to the Xe-pon River crossing into Laos that was the border of the two countries at the time (Figure 5.3).

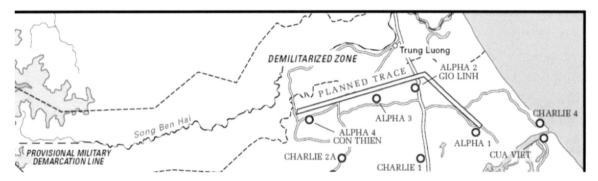

Figure 5.3 Separation of North and South Vietnam,
Source: Adapted from Supporting the Marines, January -June1967 Retrieved from Supporting the Marines, January-June 1967 :: EC-47 (ec47.com) August 4, 2023

True to the communist practice and that of other totalitarians, Ho began consolidating his control over the north. Refugees flowed south once they witnessed the draconian measures he implemented to control the population including this author's Virginia neighbors. This Roman Catholic family lived in Hanoi until 1954 and then near Saigon when they lost everything a second time in 1975.

Pre-Deployment

The Cold War chapter stated that US troops in the United States formed the strategic reserve in the US and the mission of those in the FRG was to defend western Europe along with NATO's European members from a Warsaw Pact attack westward that would be spearheaded by the Soviet Group of Forces Germany and the Central Group of Forces in Czechoslovakia.

Army officers and enlisted men in Europe and the US fell into one of three groups: serving until ordered to Vietnam as individual replacements; serving following the 12-

month tour in Vietnam until their obligated military service ended and they returned to civilian life; and those career soldiers who were serving the mandatory year between Vietnam assignments.

March 1968 was especially significant for U.S. policy and strategy in Vietnam. Following the allies' military victory over the North Vietnamese during the Tet Offensive that began at the end of January in which as many as 40,000 communist troops were killed, General Westmoreland, COMUSMACV requested in February that 206,000 more troops be sent to South Vietnam by July. Despite the South's victory, General Westmoreland's request for more troops added to the growing domestic US discontent over the war's increasing cost in US lives took its toll on the Johnson administration. The Department of Defense, at the order of President Johnson and his advisors, denied the troop increase in those numbers which would have increased the US troop presence to 700,000 but approved sending 15,500 that included the 3rd Brigade, 82nd Airborne Division from Fort Bragg, NC, and a brigade of the 5th Infantry Division Mechanized (M) from Ft Carson. President Johnson announced the increase on March 31, 1968.[422] Also, in the fallout from the Tet Offensive, Secretary of Defense Robert McNamara resigned. He had been in office since President Kennedy appointed him in January 1961. McNamara lost confidence that the US could defeat the North Vietnamese. Johnson appointed Cyrus Vance, Sr. to replace him. Vance who supported the war initially, counselled the President that it was time to seek a negotiated settlement and withdraw from Vietnam. General Westmoreland's reassignment to Washington to become Army Chief of Staff was announced on March 22d with the subsequent appointment of his deputy General Abrams announced on April 11th. Abrams became COMUSMACV on June 10th.[423]

Johnson announced the following in a speech to the nation on March 31st: deployment of the two brigades, the end of bombing North Vietnam north of the 20th parallel (running south of Hanoi and across the top of Hainan Island), an offer to begin negotiations with the North Vietnamese with Averell Harriman leading the US diplomatic effort in Paris, and that he would not run for reelection.

The President added to his March 31st statement he made about no longer bombing North Vietnam on October 31,1968. He stated that effective the next day, all air, naval, and artillery bombardment of North Vietnam above the DMZ would end. [424] These developments signaled that the US was turning the war over to the Vietnamese and beginning its disengagement. The policy became known as *Vietnamization* after President Nixon succeeded Johnson on January 20, 1969. The first Paris meeting to negotiate an end to the war occurred on May 10, 1968, and the negotiations continued for four years.

This author was stationed at Fort Leonard Wood, Missouri in 1968. He received a phone call from the armor assignment officer at the Army's personnel center in early-to-mid-March notifying him to report to Fort Carson, Colorado on March 28th to join a unit preparing to deploy to a classified location.

Captain Neil T. Howell, who had served in the Army for nine years, left to go to college, and returned to active duty as a finance officer in the Air Force. He spent four years in that role before transferring back into the Army as an armor officer. He was a new tank company commander sent to Fort Knox, Kentucky in November 1967 to gain experience as a tanker. He was told that he could expect to serve there for about a year. The armor assignments officer called him again at 2 am on a Tuesday in early March 1968 ordering him to report to Fort Carson on the following Monday. Major Donald Pihl and First Lieutenant Laurie Ledoux, also at Fort Knox, received their calls at about the same time. This scene was replayed for officers stationed elsewhere to bring the Steel Tigers as well as the other brigade units to their authorized strengths in the proper ranks.[425]

The Steel Tiger battalion commander received word that it was on alert to move from Fort Carson to Vietnam at a regularly scheduled commanders' meeting in the office of the 5th Infantry Division 's 1st Brigade commander on March 25th. He informed his battalion commanders of the order. The 1st Brigade would cease being a major subordinate command of the 5th Infantry Division (M) (Red Devils)) where the brigade was a headquarters that controlled only three maneuver battalions: the 1st Battalion 77th Armor (1-77 Armor) (Steel Tigers), the 1st Battalion 61st Infantry (Mechanized) (1-61 Inf (M), and the 1st Battalion, 11th Infantry (1-11 Inf). It would transform into a separate brigade organized using the ROAD concept of constituent elements meeting a specific theater's needs discussed earlier. The Red Devil Brigade's new structure would include a base consisting of the headquarters with the commander, deputy commander for intelligence and operations, executive officer, and a headquarters and headquarters company; A Troop, 4th Squadron, 12th Cavalry (A/4-12 Cav); 5th Battalion 4th Artillery (155mm) (SP) (5/4 SP Arty); 75th Support Battalion (75th Spt); Company A, 7th Engineer Battalion (A/7 Eng); 532nd Signal Platoon (Forward Area) (532 Sig Plt); 1st Detachment, 5th Military Intelligence Detachment, (1/5 MID); 86th Chemical Detachment (86th Chem Det); 48th Public Information Detachment (48th PI Det); and the 407th Radio Research Detachment (407th RR Det). The Brigade's total strength was 4,790.[426] Once in Vietnam, the structure would be modified as the military situation evolved. The brigade commander also informed his battalion commanders that Colonel Richard J Glikes would arrive from Fort Hood, Texas to assume command of the 1st Brigade.

Three of the four individuals who learned warfare during the first year of the Korean War interacting with Company A, 77th Armor came together during this last week of March 1968 to become key leaders of the Red Devils. Lieutenant Carmelo P. Milia, who in the Korean War was one of the tank platoon leaders in the 3rd Infantry Division's 64th Armor whose mission was to keep the roads open for US Army and Marine units moving to the evacuation port of Hungnam. He became the Brigade's Deputy Commander for Operations (S3) and Intelligence (S2) and later the second commander of the Steel Tigers in Vietnam.[427]

The 1-77 Armor Commander, Lieutenant Colonel John M. (Max) Pickarts, was the second of the four veterans who interacted in 1968. He was a World War II Marine Corps Raider combat veteran who joined Army's 2d Infantry Division at Fort Lewis, Washington in June 1950. He was a reconnaissance platoon leader and was seriously wounded and evacuated from the theater before the Eighth Army linked up with US Xth Corps following the Inchon Landing.

The third veteran of the Korean War who would help prepare the new generation of Steel Tigers to go to war was Joe D. Offutt. He was A Company's First Sergeant, who had been a tank crewman and tank commander in the 73rd Armor when it joined the 7th Infantry Division in 1950 for the push from Inchon to the Yalu River. He had been captured and then escaped from the communist forces.

The fourth Korean War veteran in the group was in South Vietnam already. He was Marine Major General Raymond Davis who was the Deputy Commander of the Phu Bai-based Provisional Corps Vietnam (PCV) in I Corps that included Thua Thien and Quang Tri Provinces.[428] Davis had commanded the 1st Battalion, 7th Marines at the Chosin Reservoir where he earned the Medal of Honor. He also fought at Guadalcanal and Peleliu among other World War II battles. As stated in the Korean War chapter, the Steel Tigers supported the 5th and 7th Marine Regiments during their move off of the Koto-Ri plateau.

Colonel Pickarts returned to his headquarters following the one at the First Brigade's headquarters and met first with the battalion's Sergeant Major George Showell. Next, he told the executive officer, Major Joyce Downing, and the adjutant, 2nd Lieutenant Robert Forman about the brigade commander's meeting. The battalion's other officers were notified at a 1 pm meeting that same day. One of the first tasks that had to be completed was reassigning about one-third of the battalion to other units because they were ineligible to go to Vietnam for the reasons stated earlier. The new contingent of officers and men began arriving by the end of the week and the transfer of responsibilities began.[429] The battalion's authorized strength was 614: 37 Officers, 3 Warrant Officers, and 574 Enlisted.[430]

Major Donald Pihl became the new Executive Officer and Major Jerry Thomas was the new Operations (S-3) Officer. Captain James Herrington, Captain Arthur McGowan, and Captain Darrell Blalock assumed command of A, B, and C Companies, respectively. Colonel Pickarts appointed Captain Karl Schwarz to be the new Headquarters and Headquarters Company Commander and Captain Neil Howell to command the Service Company, also known as D Company. Lieutenant Forman moved from the adjutant's job to become the 4.2-inch mortar platoon leader.[431]

The battalion staff included the Executive Officer, Personnel Officer (S-1), Intelligence and Security (S-2), Operations (S-3), and Logistics, (S-4). A new brigade and battalion staff position was authorized for the Red Devils: Civil Affairs (S-5). The portfolio for this section included the impact of civilians and military interacting within the battalion, and brigade operational areas. Captain Warren Elahee was the first Steel Tiger to hold this office. More about him below, but at the time he was assigned to the S-3 staff section as an assistant operations officer primarily because no one had had experience with the functions of a civil affairs section in previous assignments, and the operations section was a busy place. Captain Elahee and his driver with the authorized M-151 utility one-quarter ton light truck (jeep) were welcome additions.[432]

The Steel Tigers began their 13-week training program on March 30th. Tank gunnery was the first milestone to complete. It began in garrison and moved to the gunnery ranges. The battalion had 54 M-60 Main Battle Tanks. Each of the three tank companies had three platoons of five tanks each with two tanks in the company headquarters section for the company commander and the artillery forward observer. The battalion headquarters tank section had an additional three tanks. The battalion also had one platoon equipped with four M-106 mortar carriers each carrying one 4.2-inch mortar, a fire direction center contained inside one M-577A1 Command Post Vehicle, and three forward observers each of whom rode in a jeep. The entire 1st Brigade was at the top of the list of priority units in the United States. Presumably, it was untouchable for other missions. The other two Red Devil brigades and the division's headquarters remained in the strategic reserve to be ready for a crisis in Europe or elsewhere.

Gunnery was initially planned to take the month of April.[433] The battalion and its tank companies' first training increment was to progress through the non-firing and firing exercises of tank gunnery that began by boresighting and zeroing the M-60 tank's turret mounted and tank commander's machineguns and the 105-mm main gun. The final exercise was the Tank Crew Qualification Course (TCQC). This exercise had day and night phases. Individual tanks followed a designated course where they engaged diverse stationary and moving targets with either the main gun or one or both of the machine guns. A grader rode in each tank recording accuracy and the time required to engage each target. The ranges used were in the Fort Carson training area that began at Colorado Springs and extended south almost to Pueblo. Ranchers grazed their cattle in the training area, so the first requirement was to alert the owners to clear the area within the right and left limits of the firing ranges.

A new imperative superseded the entire 5th Division (M)'s activities that changed the Steel Tigers' focus completely. Martin Luther King was assassinated in the early evening of April 4th. Units from the Division's 2nd and 3rd brigades were sent to the cities where rioting broke out as discussed in the previous chapter. The Red Devil Brigade was ordered to return to the cantonment area immediately, send soldiers to fill other battalions that were deploying, and begin unit riot control training with the soldiers who remained in preparation for future on-order deployments. Air Force transports were on the ground at Peterson field ready to receive the troops.

The order to move to the airfield was never issued to the 1st Brigade. The civil disorder and urban violence began subsiding enough within several days that Regular Army units were released to their home stations. The 1st Brigade resumed pre-deployment training when its soldiers returned to their parent units at Fort Carson. The tank companies went back to tank gunnery training again where they left off as soon as the ranchers herded their cattle back to the safe areas.

Following tank gunnery, unit tactical training began in May for the battalion including the tactical and support units. One difference introduced was the attachment of one mechanized infantry company from the 1-61 Inf (M) to the Steel Tigers and the reciprocal attachment of a tank company from the Steel Tigers to the infantry. Unlike World War II and the Korean War where armored and infantry units trained independently and were later cross attached in the combat theater according to mission requirements, the Red Devil Brigade integrated its armor and infantry units before deployment to allow the officer and non-commissioned officer leadership and the soldiers to interact. All learned each other's capabilities and limitations and gained mutual trust before leaving Fort Carson. The B companies of the two battalions were identified to come under the operational control (OPCON) of the 1-77 Armor and 1-61 Inf (M).

Occurring also in May was the dispatch of an advanced party under the leadership of the brigade's executive officer, Lieutenant Colonel John D Smythe, to South Vietnam to discover where the brigade would be located initially and identify additional equipment and other items to bring. A group of about 15 officers and senior non-commissioned officers travelled in temporary duty status for about a three-week period aboard civilian airliners that were booked by the Fort Carson travel office. The team left the civilian airport in Colorado Springs with weapons in the duffle bags for Denver, and then to San Francisco where there was a four-hour layover before boarding the Pan American Airways flight to the civilian airports in Hawaii, Guam, and finally to Ton San Nhut International Airport near Saigon. Passengers packed the plane from San Francisco to Hawaii. Fewer flew to Guam. Only the Red Devils went on to South Vietnam. The flight attendants moved the group to First Class, served First Class only meals and beverages, and played movies during the final hours of the trip. When the airliner's doors opened and the pressurized air was replaced by Saigon's humidity, the first view of Vietnam for those wearing eyeglasses was moisture-covered lenses. This civilian flight became a military charter for the return trip filled with armed forces members whose tours had ended.

The group had to fly aboard military aircraft from Bien Hoa airbase to the PCV headquarters at Phu Bai, 57 miles north of Da Nang and 7 miles from Hue, the old capital city. The VC celebrated Ho Chi Minh's May 19th birthday by attacking major American bases across the country including PCV and the headquarters of the units that the Red Devil team visited. It was not on the scale of the Tet 1968 attacks that began on January 30th. Nonetheless, the group began visiting and receiving briefings at the headquarters of 1st Air Cavalry Division, 101st Airborne Division, 3rd Brigade, 82d Airborne Division, 3rd Marine Division (3MARDIV}, and one of its regimental headquarters at Camp Carroll beginning on May 20th. The 1st Air Cavalry Division Personnel Officer (G-1) at Camp Evans, who was bandaged from wounds received during the rocket attack on Camp Evans told the group that the division commander's barber had been the one who identified the division headquarters' targets for the enemy. Following these briefings, the information-gathering team travelled individually to talk specifics with units in Quang Tri Province.

The Steel Tigers' representative spent two days with the 9th Infantry Division's 3rd Squadron, 5th Cavalry (3-5 Cav) headquartered at Wunder Beach which was about 10 miles southeast of Quang Tri City (Figure 5.4).

Figure 5.4 Wunder Beach , May 1968
Source: By NARA photo 111-CCV-2-CC8205-https://wwwfold3.com/image/245159135, Public Domain, https:/commons.wikimedia.org/w/index.php?curid-90274906

Wunder Beach became an alternate logistics depot on the shore of the South China Sea that was established at the beginning of March 1968 following the Tet Offensive that began on January 31st. It was located at the end of the road leading east from Hai Lang, the district capital, which sits astride Highway QL-1. This highway begins in Saigon and extends north through Quang Tri Province to Hanoi. Wunder Beach was selected for the depot because it could be more easily defended than the port at the Dong Ha's Cua Viet Naval Support Facility should post-Tet attacks occur.

Some of the specifics discussed with the commander, Lieutenant Colonel Hugh Bartley and executive officer, Major Michael Mahler, and members of the squadron's staff included the response times for the logistics chain to send repair parts for tanks, the M-113 armored personnel carrier family of vehicles, and all wheeled vehicles to tactical units. Another was what parts from major end items to those that were consumable in any theater such as various vehicle filters wore out especially fast in Vietnam because of the country's terrain and weather.

Figure 5.5 shows Quang Tri Province's three geographic regions in the post-Tet1968 period while the 1st Air Cavalry Division was in the province: flat lands with sand and dirt from the South China Sea past the QL-1 the main north-south highway, followed by piedmont with vegetation, and then a mountainous region also with dense vegetation. It was important especially that the advanced party member focusing on armored vehicles learn as much as possible about the effects of sand and dust on the engines and drive trains of tracked and wheeled vehicles. Another danger especially to vehicles operating off the roads and trails in the piedmont and mountainous areas were the craters from earlier B-52 bombing raids that were covered by tall elephant grass that had grown around and inside the holes where strikes were not recent. The final area discussed with the 3-5 Cav leaders and staff were their thoughts and suggestions about extras that the Red Devil Brigade should bring from Ft. Carson based on their combat experiences with battle damage in Vietnam compared with other assignments elsewhere during their careers.[434]

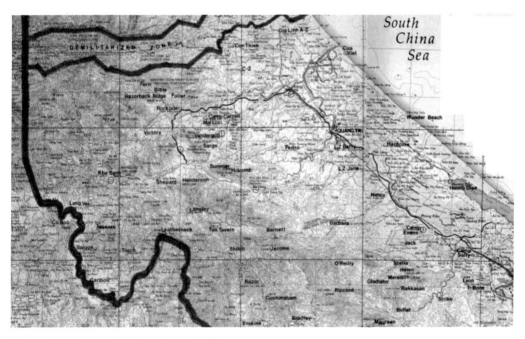

Figure 5.5 Quang Tri Province, 1968
Source: Quang Tri Province, Map (506infantry.org)

Highway QL-1 in addition to being the main north-south highway through the province was known also as *La Rue Sans Joie* (The Street Without Joy) from Hue in Thua Thien Province to the Demilitarized Zone beyond Dong Ha. It received its name by French soldiers from the many ambushes of French convoys along the road during Ho Chi Minh's campaign against them. It became the title of and a chapter in Bernard Fall's 1961 book, *The Street Without Joy: The French Debacle in Indochina*.[435].

The French fought a major battle there in 1953 integrating land, sea, and air forces. The terrain from the South China Sea beach region began as hard flat sand in the beach area. Sand dunes followed ranging in various heights, ditches, fishing villages in a two-kilometer-wide portion, and at the time a series of cemeteries, small villages, that were short distances apart around which there were vegetation, fences, swamps, and rice paddies filling the area to the district headquarters in Hai Lang.[436] Parallel to Highway 1, there was another very narrow road between Hai Lang and the sea with the route number 555 in 1968 and now named QL-49. It ran from Hue to Quang Tri City in Trieu Phong District.

The 3-5 Cav fought a new battle on the Street on June 27-28, 1968, which was about a month following the departure of the Red Devil fact finding visit and one week before the Red Devil Brigade's' July 3rd advanced party arrival at Quang Tri. The contact began along the seacoast about between Dong Ha and Quang Tri City outside the village of Binh An.

The squadron's mission was to provide security for this area of the South Vietnamese coast from the Wunder Beach area to the Navy and Marine logistical base where the Cua Viet River meets the South China Sea at Dong Ha that was about 12 miles north.[437] Contact was made by one of the squadron's troops moving south from Dong Ha toward Wunder Beach. What began as small arms fire from positions outside of the village revealed a well dug-in NVA battalion of 300 soldiers. Soon reinforced by two infantry companies from the nearby 1st Air Cavalry Division, the Army troops encircled the village on the land. The sea was the only exit, and naval combat ships off the coast closed that route. Army artillery and naval gunfire was fired into the village interspersed with cavalry-infantry sweeps through the village. NVA attempts to escape during the night failed. About two-thirds were killed and the remainder became prisoners of war.[438] The 3-5 Cavalry moved on to new missions in the province.

In addition to the briefings and individual information-gathering tasks, the group was flown over the portion of western Quang Tri Province where the Khe Sanh battle was fought. Some of the team stayed at Phu Bai to begin coordinating the preparations for receiving the brigade, and others had one more destination.[439]

The last stop on the group's itinerary before returning to Fort Carson was a visit to the Army's Military Assistance Command, Vietnam (MACV) headquarters in Saigon where they were told that the Red Devils would be deployed in a portion of Quang Tri Province and be operationally controlled by the 3MARDIV. The division's new commander was Major General Raymond Davis who had moved from PCV that was renamed the U.S. Army's 24th Corps (US XXIV Corps) at Phu Bai to Quang Tri Combat Base (QTCB). An aside comment during a USMC briefing within two or three days following the Ho Chi Minh birthday attack that destroyed several buildings at the regimental Camp Carroll base demonstrated the new approach that General Davis brought to the division. He was briefed that rockets had been seen being fired into the base causing casualties and damage to buildings and other structures. He asked the regimental commander what he did about it, and the answer was he had requested artillery and airstrikes. General Davis told the commander words to the effect of don't sit inside the wire; send out infantry to find and destroy the rockets![440]

One piece of information that the advanced group learned during the trip was the about color of the unit patches. While appearing to be incidental, it was important to the Red Devil Brigade. Army units wore subdued patches on their combat uniforms except for the 101st Airborne (Airmobile) Division and the 82nd Airborne Division's 3rd Brigade. These units wore full color patches because their commanders wanted the enemy to know exactly who they were fighting. The team recommended to Colonel Glikes that the Red Devil Brigade wear the red 5th Infantry diamond shoulder patch instead of the subdued black diamond. He approved the recommendation. It was not until brigade members left Vietnam for other assignments that they began wearing the subdued black diamond on their fatigues in compliance with the Army's uniform policy at the time. [441]

The returning team members boarded another civilian airliner that arrived from the US and stayed on the ground only long enough to debark its passengers and load another group of end-of-tour veterans returning home as a military charter. The aircraft took off from the Ton San Nhut terminal with an Air Force fighter escort and flew directly to Clark Air Force Base in the Philippines to be serviced and refueled. The team returned to Colorado Springs late at night and went directly to the Fort Carson training area for the final field training exercises the next morning.

The team briefed the brigade's officers and senior noncommissioned officers about their trip and the information they gained after the training exercises ended. That was followed by railoading vehicles and other equipment stored in shipping containers formally named continental express shipping containers but better known as CONEX containers for transport by train to a west coast port for the sea voyage to Vietnam. The Colorado Springs evening television news showed film of the departing trains for several days. Their destination was unknown according to the reporters.

The 1-77 Armor was told early that it would turn its M-60 tanks in at Fort Carson and draw M48A2C tanks once in Vietnam. The M-60 carried 385 gallons of diesel fuel and had an operating range of 288 miles.[442] The M48A2C used gasoline. It had a 335-gallon fuel tank and an operating range of about 160 miles. It weighed 52 tons combat loaded.[443] The M-60s were turned over to the 3rd Battalion 77th Armor.[444]

The brigade's advanced party including the battalion commanders departed Fort Carson at the end of June and arrived in Vietnam on July 3rd to begin their year-long tour. The role of this contingent was to prepare the area for receipt of the brigade later in the month. The 4-12 Cav provided security for the advanced party. The main body of the brigade at Fort Carson was divided into two groups and permitted to take a staggered two-week leave. Once the leaves ended, all were confined to Fort Carson until their unit departure dates. All were in Vietnam on July 31st.[445]

Deployment

The Steel Tigers flew on Lockheed C-141 Starlifters from Colorado. Some were configured with palettes on which reclinable airline seats were fixed in rows. Others had red webbing that ran the length of the fuselage. The route was Colorado Springs to Alaska for refueling only and next to Yokota Air Force Base near Tokyo where everyone could walk to a cafeteria, eat something hot instead of the box lunches provided on the aircraft, and use a real restroom. Military chartered civilian planes were on the ground at Yokota also with service personnel in the cafeteria either going to Vietnam and Korea as individual replacements or returning at the end of their tours.

One of the C-141s deviated from the route. This Starlifter with passenger seats had to land at McChord Air Force Base next to Ft Lewis Washington for repairs and then refueling. It bypassed the stop in Alaska. The final leg of the trip was to Da Nang which was receiving indirect fire from Vietnamese rockets when the plane landed. The pilot ordered everyone to run off the loading ramp at the rear to nearby C-130 turboprop transports warming their engines for the flight to QTCB's airfield. Once each C-130 landed, the passengers entered a building and processed into Vietnam with one of the steps being exchanging US currency for military script that substituted for greenbacks outside of the US. From that building, the group loaded onto trucks for Camp Red Devil where a rest area had been established with cots and tents to sleep until dawn. The group ate a hot breakfast and loaded onto trucks once the daily minesweeping of the roads was finished to go to the end of the trip from Colorado where Colonel Pickarts and the other members of the Steel Tigers' advanced party met everyone at Wunder Beach.[446]

The maximum Army commitment to South Vietnam totaled seven divisions and four separate brigades by July 1968. The Red Devil Brigade was the last major unit sent to Vietnam.[447]

Wunder Beach was where the 1-77 Armor received its M-48A2C tanks, M-113 family of armored vehicles including the armored personnel carrier, M-106 4.2-inch mortar carriers, M-577 command, and other vehicles, and CONEX containers full of equipment via Naval transports beginning in August. The tanks arrived on August 2nd.[448] The Steel Tigers began preparing to enter the Vietnam War. The tank companies boresighted, prepared, and tested their tanks for combat. Each tank commander's weapon, the M2 Caliber .50 M2 Heavy Barrel machine gun, was mounted on a pintel on top of the cupola instead of inside the cupola mounted on its side. This was to improve the tank commander's field of vision and reduce jamming and the time required to clear a jammed weapon. The M-73 7.62mm turret machine gun was mounted coaxially to the main gun.[449]

The mortar and reconnaissance platoons prepared their weapons and vehicles for action also. Other activities included unloading the CONEX containers and organizing the items inside them to become functional in the proper battalion units and acclimatizing to the drastically changed temperatures from Colorado. General Creighton Abrams who replaced General Westmoreland as the COMUSMACV during June welcomed the Red Devil Brigade to Vietnam at QTCB.

Colonel Pickarts ordered a combat vehicle identification scheme using geometric figures along with the vehicle's standard Army unit naming convention on the front and rear of each. Headquarters and Headquarters Company had a triangle stenciled on the vehicles' sides. The figure was placed on the sides of the tank turrets. Company A displayed a diamond; B Company used the circle, and C Company applied the square. Each vehicle's number was inside the geometric figure .Various other figures and words were painted on the tanks' main gun tubes except in Company B. Captain McGowan ordered each gun tube to have the same title on the left and right sides - *Steel Tigers*. He continued the Ft. Carson practice of placing a yellow circle painted at the M60's main gun's muzzle with a second on the company commander's so everyone would know where the commander was located. On the M48A2C tanks, the circles were around the bore evacuators at the front of the main gun tubes behind the flash suppressors. Additional circles were added to each main gun when the entire company completed a major combat operation. [450]

Figure 5.6 Steel Tiger Vehicle Markings
Source: Company A commander's tank, courtesy William Rosevear and Company B commander's tank, courtesy Joseph Davis

Wunder Beach to Leatherneck Square

The combat battalions went into positions along the Demilitarized Zone where General Westmoreland had planned to position a brigade in 1967.[451] The 1st Brigade 5th Infantry Division (M) headquarters, combat support, and combat service support units were located at Camp Red Devil that was part of QTCB and midway between the cities of Dong Ha and Quang Tri. Not only was QTCB the headquarters for the Brigade and the Third Marine Division (3MARDIV). It was also the headquarters for the Second Regiment, 1st Infantry Division, Army of Viet Nam (ARVN). Following the Tet 1968, Major General Ngo Quang Troung became the division's commander. Troung was a combat rather than a politically oriented commander who focused on defeating the enemy. His headquarters was in Hue. Andrew Wiest states in his 2008 *Vietnam's Forgotten Army* stated that US General Norman Schwarzkopf called Troung a most brilliant commander.[452] Under Troung, the 1st ARVN Division had the reputation at the time of being the best in the South Vietnamese Army. The Division's Second Regiment's area of responsibility began on the 1st Brigade 5th Infantry Division (M) eastern border a short distance west from QL-1.[453]

Leatherneck Square August to October 1968

The combat elements of the Brigade were ordered to relieve the 3MARDIV units occupying the 54-square mile Leatherneck Square that was formed by the following population centers and military bases: Cam Lo Resettlement Village along the east-west QL-9 six miles west of from Dong Ha to the north-south Highway 561 crossing the French-built C-3 Bridge across the Cam Lo River, past the firebases at C-3, C-2, C-2 Bridge and the water point, and then branching off along Highway 606 to A-4 at Con Thien that was

9 miles north of Cam Lo and 1.9 miles south from the beginning of South Vietnam's portion of the Demilitarized Zone (DMZ). This route was the MSR from Camp Red Devil to A-4.

A-4 was the western most point of the McNamara Line that extended northeast past firebase A-3 to firebase A-2 at Gio Linh which was the northernmost military position in South Vietnam. Gio Linh was located on the QL-1 Highway. The square turned south and closed at Dong Ha that was about 10.5 miles south of Gio Linh. The C-1 firebase along QL-1 was south of Gio Linh and about 7 miles north of Dong Ha. Figure 5.7 displays much of the Marines' Tactical Area of Operations (TAOR) in which the Steel Tigers began sharing responsibility.[454]

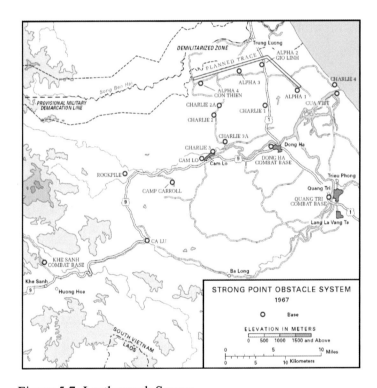

Figure 5.7 Leatherneck Square
Source: Supporting the Marines, January -June1967 Retrieved from Supporting the Marines, January-June 1967 :: EC-47 (ec47.com) August 4, 2023

Leatherneck Square was a nickname. Originally the 3MARDIV's sector ran from Gio Linh to the south bank of the Ben Hai River which was in South Vietnam's portion of the DMZ across the country to the Laotian border and then south across QL-9.

The 3MARDIV assigned its regiments to perform missions in TAORs that were given names. Leatherneck Square was known as TAOR KENTUCKY when the Red Devils arrived at Wunder Beach. Prior to July 1968, the larger TAOR KINGFISHER had been divided into KENTUCKY and LANCASTER that encompassed the western DMZ, south across QL-9 along which Camp Carroll, the Rockpile, and Ca Lu were centrally located in the western portion. Further west was the Khe Sanh Plateau leading west to Laos.[455]

Leatherneck Square's significance was that it was also the Eastern portion of a barrier to stop the cross-DMZ movement of NVA forces that was named the McNamara Line. This defensive concept originated in response to the failure of US airpower's bombing campaign in North Vietnam to stop the infiltration of Ho's forces into the south. Secretary of Defense McNamara convened a committee during late 1965 and early 1966 to construct a 47-mile wall from the South China Sea to the Laotian border in two parts . The first shown in Figure 5.7 above would be a series of military strong points beginning at the South China Sea that extended inland to A-4 past the firebases mentioned earlier through a 200-to-600-meter-wide zone cleared of vegetation, structures, and people less than a mile below the DMZ. It was named The Trace. Outside of Leatherneck Square there were two more strong points. A-1 was east of Highway 1 and midway to the coast. The second was C-4 that was on the north bank of the Cua Viet River at its junction with the South China Sea. Ground troops were to live in fortified bunkers and patrol in their first portion sectors to stop the NVA.

The second portion of the line would continue west beyond A-4 to the Laotian border employing electronic motion, heat sensing, acoustic detectors, gravel antipersonnel and other various minefields, and defensive razor-sharp concertina wire to detect vehicle and troop movements. The base at Khe Sanh and the Lang Vei Special Forces camp along QL-9 were included in the plan, but the Tet 1968 offensive throughout South Vietnam ended work in this portion of the barrier. The entire project ended in October 1968 when General Abrams, ended the program along with the dismantling the remainder of Khe Sanh combat base and destroying the bridges and fording points leading from the piedmont region to the mountains on the Khe Sanh plateau.[456]

The Red Diamond Brigade was ordered to relieve USMC 3MARDIV units in Leatherneck Square in mid-August. Figure 5.8 below is a combination of two map sheets showing the same areas at two different degrees of resolution to display where operations in Leatherneck Square occurred during the fall of 1968 and subsequently.

153

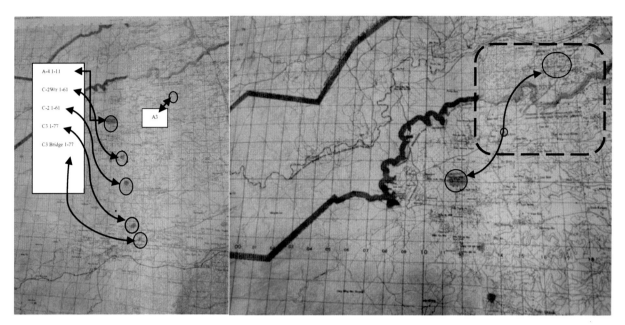

Figure 5.8 Operations SULLIVAN, RICH and Others, Fall 1968
Source: Map, Courtesy of Lawrence Wills; graphics by author

The 1-11 Inf with two platoons of A/1-77 Armor attached, was to move first to C-3 and then to A-4 at Con Thien and send a company to secure the Brigade's headquarters at Camp Red Devil. The third platoon of A/1-77 was attached to Task Force 1-61(M) whose mission was to occupy C-2 and secure C-2 Bridge and the water point.[457]

The first 1-77 unit to enter combat was A Company's 3rd Platoon during Operation KENTUCKY. Before the Red Devils relieved the USMC units, a Marine reconnaissance team made contact with the NVA unit that surrounded the team on August 14th. A reaction force to rescue the team was organized by the 1st Battalion, 1st Marine Regiment, (1-1 USMC). For this operation, the 3rd platoon was attached to the 1- 1. Second Lieutenant Everett Nagel's tank, A-36, was in maintenance and not available. [458]

The reaction force departed A-4 on the 15th. The 1-1 USMC infantry team made contact with the NVA who directed their small arms and mortar fire at the tanks. Nagel rode on the back deck of tank A-35 from which he could direct the fire of the platoon into the NVA positions. The reinforcements enabled the reconnaissance team to reach the tanks. During the fighting, Platoon Sergeant Merton Teixeira ordered his tank A-34 driver, Kevin Dunne, to go to A-35 because there were wounded. There were four friendly casualties: two members of the reconnaissance team and two third platoon soldiers including Lieutenant Nagel whom Dunne assisted until the medical evacuation helicopter arrived. Teixeira assumed command of the platoon. [459]

The remaining Steel Tigers elements received the order to relieve the Leatherneck Square Marines on August 19, 1968. Operations Order 2-68 gave the 1-77 Armor the mission to occupy and secure the Cam Lo district headquarters, the C-3 Bridge, and C-3. B/1-61 (M) was to be the first Steel Tiger unit to occupy C-3. A/1-77 Armor would move to C-3 on order and C/1-77 Armor was to secure the C-3 Bridge. The Cam Lo River ran north northeast (NNE) to south southwest (SSW) through this area. Company C established its main position at C-3 Bridge on the south side of the western approach to the bridge with the third platoon on the northern approach. Troop A/4-12 Cav (A/4-12 Cav) was ordered to move to the C-3 area when it received the order.[460]

Two daily mine sweeps beginning at C-3 were ordered. The first was to clear Highway 561 south to Cam Lo and then along QL-9 east to Dong Ha and turning north to A-3 on QL-1. The Duster section's mission was to support this requirement. The second mine sweep began at C-3 and went north on Highway 561. Tm B provided tactical support for the engineer squad of the requirement and Team C provided the minesweeping team.

The battalion's organization is listed below:

- Team A: A/1-77 Armor
- Team B: B/1-61 Inf(M) (-)
    o   1/C/1-77 Armor
    o   2/C/1-77 Armor
    o   Reconnaissance (Scout) Platoon

- Team C: C/1-77 Armor (-)
- 2/B/1-61 Inf (M)
- Team D: A/4-12 Cav
- Battalion (Task Force) Control
    o   3/A-7 Engr
    o   Duster Section (two M-42 40 mm Self-Propelled Anti-Aircraft Guns)
    o   1 Light Observation Helicopter (LOH)

- Mortar Platoon: General Support[461]

The 1-77 Armor was renamed Task Force 1-77 Armor (TF 1-77 Armor) because it was no longer a tank-pure battalion. Fragmentary Order (Frag Order) 5 to Operations Order 2-

68 dated 311700 Aug 68 directed the Task Force be in position to begin the mission between 6:00 and 7:00 am on September 2, 1968.[462]

The units moved from Wunder Beach on September 1st as soon as the QL-1 and the other roads had been swept for mines. This meant that all the equipment from tents to typewriters were packed and loaded on vehicles during the night of 31 August-1 September. Some equipment had to be left at Wunder Beach for subsequent moves to the area of operations. The task force headquarters moved into its temporary position at the Cam Lo District headquarters in the late afternoon of September 1 and on to C-3 the next morning where the engineers bulldozed protected positions for the M-577A1 command tracks that TF 1-77 Armor would occupy during the base's transition from Marine to Army control.

The USMC handover of C-3 to TF 1-77 Armor required several days to complete. Meanwhile, the S-3 and S-2 sections initiated 24-hour operations in two 12-hour shifts on September 2nd. The two M-577s were positioned as designed for deployment in the field with empty five-gallon fuel cans placed so that the vehicles' rear cargo ramps rested levelly on them instead of being lowered angularly onto the ground. This enabled each staff section to increase its work area. The cargo ramp was raised and lowered by a steel cable activated by a small motor and latch at the rear of the driver's position. Normally, it required two-to-four individuals to move the gate manually. The cargo ramp had a door for an individual to enter or leave the vehicle with the ramp raised. The night shift in both staff sections had little reporting to record after midnight except for periodic communications checks with the maneuver companies and the brigade headquarters. Once each shift's activity became routine, the night hours became tedious except for one early morning when the new arrivals in Vietnam learned the difference in sound between incoming indirect fire explosions and outgoing fire from artillery.[463]

Present at C-3 was a Marine battery of six M-114A1 155mm towed howitzers.[464] The range of this weapon was 9.1 miles and was within the distance to the southern half of the DMZ. Harassment and Interdiction (H&I) unobserved artillery fire had been employed since World War I. This artillery tactic was firing a predesignated number of rounds during the day and night at preestablished times. The targets were randomly chosen. There were few rounds fired at any one time. The purpose of this tactic was to hinder enemy vehicles and troop movements.

One early morning somewhere between 2-4 am, the C-3 battery began to fire. All in the command center immediately alerted from their drowsiness and Master Sergeant

Robert Geer, the S-3 Operations Non-Commissioned Officer-in-Charge jumped up from his chair and raised the S-3 M577's cargo ramp single-handedly before the driver could turn around in his seat to raise the ramp mechanically.

Operation *SULLIVAN*, September 11

Although Operation *SULLIVAN* was the not the first Steel Tiger action in Vietnam, it was the first one ordered by the Red Devil Brigade, and it was also the first to use a code name. The 1-77's first mission occurred on September 11th. The 1-11 Infantry relieved the Marines of their responsibility for the defense and operations at Con Thien on September 1st as did the other Red Devil battalions at their respective firebases. Company A/1-77 was attached to 1-11 Infantry. Lieutenant Colonel Little ordered D/1-11 to respond to an NVA unit 2.5 miles north of Con Thien at the Marketplace on September 11th. One of A-/1-77's platoons supported the infantry.[465] Another of the earlier missions included Team B/1-61(M) and Team C/1-77 Armor conducting a search and destroy mission with the task force's command group in the area west of C-3. One of the more memorable events of that operation was that the command group was on the 4.2-inch mortar gun-target line and one round exploded to the rear of Colonel Pickarts' tank. He gave the order to cease fire.[466]

Operation *SULLIVAN*'s mission was to sweep through a suspected NVA position that was north of Con Thien about 1.25 miles into the DMZ and about 1.1 miles south of the Ben Hai River. The intelligence indicated the *138th Independent Regiment* was in the area. A B-52 bomb strike (ARC Light) was ordered before the operation began, and Task Force Steel Tigers was to search and destroy any enemy remaining in the area several hours afterward and perform a bomb damage assessment (BDA).

Operation *SULLIVAN* had one command headquarters. Colonel Pickarts led not only Task Force 1-77 Armor but also Task Force 1-11 Infantry commanded by Lieutenant Colonel Selby F. Little, Jr. Operation *SULLIVAN*'s organization is below:

1. TF 1-77 Armor

     1-77 Armor minus Company B and 1st Platoon/A Company
   a. B/1-61 Inf (M)
   b. D/1-11 Inf
2. TF 1-11 Inf
   a. A/1-11inf
   b. A/4-12 Cav

    c. 2/A/1-77 Armor

    d. Plt, A/7 Engr[467]

Planning included an aerial reconnaissance by Pickarts. Initially, he requested a helicopter but was given a Forward Air Controller's (FAC) aircraft piloted by the 1-61 (M) air controller whose radio callsign was *Barky 2*. An initial map reconnaissance of the area indicated that following one route into the objective and a second route from it was desirable to achieve total coverage of the target. The aerial reconnaissance revealed bomb and artillery craters, many filled with water, throughout the Con Thien region since the rainy season had begun. Compounding these obstacles were natural bogs near what would become intermediate objectives.[468]

During the reconnaissance, the pilot told his passenger that a flight of F-4 Phantom fighter bombers was returning from a raid in North Vietnam loaded with ordnance the F4s could not release. The squadron commander asked permission to deliver a strike in the general area where Operation *SULLIVAN* would occur. *Barky 2* agreed and marked targets with his rockets. After the F-4s departed, Colonel Pickarts told the pilot that he did not see indications of NVA activity. *Barky* told Pickarts to keep his eyes open, and the pilot cut his engines went into a dive, glided over the area, and began receiving ground fire. The two counted several bullet holes in the fuselage when they landed at the airfield.[469]

The reconnaissance shaped the plan into its final form. The vulnerability of the tanks to the weather and the trafficability of the terrain given the physical obstacles reduced the desired two-route option to one route. Pickarts also wanted to focus directly on the maneuver force. He delegated the combat service support function including ammunition and fuel resupply to Major Pihl, the XO.[470]

Pihl moved the battalion support group that included the medical aid station, recovery section, M-548 cargo carriers with gasoline and diesel fuel, and the 4.2-inch mortar platoon from C-3 to A-4 at dawn before the tactical units left C-3. A fueling point was established at A-4 that refueled the task force in 42 minutes and extended the operational time of TF 1-77 by an hour.[471] The mortar platoon was guided to a position on the west side of Con Thien where it positioned itself for action. Each M-106 mortar carrier contained a basic load of 88 4.2-inch rounds most of which were high explosive along with some white phosphorous and illumination rounds.[472]

Under radio silence, TF 1-77 departed C-3 led by Team A/1-77 and followed by the Command Group comprised of the TF commander's and Sergeant Major's M48A2C tanks, and the Jump Command Post which was the S3 Air's M-113. Next, was Team B/1-61, then Company D/1-11, riding on the Scout Platoon's Armored Cavalry Assault Vehicles (ACAV) which were modified M-113s) and three M-113 Armored Personnel Carriers (APC) borrowed from Task Force 1-61 Inf (M). and finally, Team C/1-77. The Jump-CP carried the S-3Air and the Artillery Liaison Officer. The S-3, Major Thomas, oversaw *SULLIVAN* from a helicopter and updated Colonel Pickarts, who commanded it from his tank. Once the plan became active, the unexpected began to occur. First, the heavy rains made the Cam Lo River at C-3 Bridge unfordable. The high water was washing over the bridge. Captain Blalock informed Pickarts on secure radio of the situation and suggested his company use the bridge. It was built by the French and cornerstone dated it 1894. It was wide enough for a tank to cross, but it had a nine-ton weight classification. Pickarts knew that it would hold a 30-ton vehicle, but a 52-ton combat loaded tank was a gamble. He told Blalock to place one tank on the bridge at a time to make a danger-close crossing moving slowly straight across without steering. The bridge held and Team C was on its way.[473]

Task Force 1-77 Armor and Task Force 1-11 Infantry arrived at the points where they would cross their lines of departure (LD). The battleship *USS New Jersey (BB-62}* that was on station off of the coast fired its 16-inch guns on the objective area in preparation for the ground units' movement forward. The task forces departed at 7:00 am which was the set time in the operations order. Both moved in columns for speed and surprise more so than dictated by the terrain. TF 1-77 Armor travelled immediately east of A-4 and proceeded northeast. There were two intermediate objectives, ALPHA, and TANGO. Task Force 1-11 Inf departed A3 for Objective ROMEO and was prepared to move to Objective SIERRA (Kinh Mon - a destroyed village) on Order.[474]

Team A encountered three incidents. The first was some small arms fire before reaching ALPHA. The second was the shock wave from the *New Jersey's* preparatory fire. Dan Decker the loader on 1st platoon leader Jim Davis's tank, A-16, did not have the open loader's hatch locked to the turret's top and the naval gunfire caused the hatch to swing shut severing his fingers. A medical evacuation helicopter (medevac) was required. Third was the discovery that A-16's main gun did not work. Team A continued moving forward with Davis's tank carrying a three- instead of four-man crew and no main gun.[475] Team A encountered no resistance at ALPHA and continued toward TANGO which it reached at 8:00 am. The scale and suddenness of TF 1-77's arrival at TANGO surprised the NVA at the objective. An estimated NVA platoon opened fire and others went into bunkers. Company A's M-88 Medium Tank Recovery Vehicle (M-88 VTR) threw a track. The Scout Platoon carrying D/1-11 was behind Team A and was unable to move forward. Then at 8:15 am, Tm C and the TF 1-77 command group arrived at TANGO. Team A found another route beyond TANGO and proceeded toward SIERRA. Team B/1-61(M) held Objective ALPHA behind the TF 1-77 column until the units ahead began moving again. While at ALPHA, One of Tm B's M-113s hit a mine wounding three soldiers who had to be transported to the rear by a medevac flight. Objective TANGO was not secured during *SULLIVAN*. Pickarts parked the force on top of the NVA to keep as many as possible from mounting an organized counterattack that would threaten the mission. [476]

Team A maintained a column formation as it approached Objective SIERRA. Enroute, it encountered two bogs. Five of Team A's 11 tanks were able to move past the second bog. Captain Herrington halted his team's forward movement and called for preplanned artillery fire while he waited for the infantry to catch up. Team B moved from ALPHA to the SIERRA area followed by D/1-11 and the Scout Platoon. They reached the objective at 12:30 pm, left their vehicles, and began their sweep. During this same period, the NVA fired small arms and indirect fire from the northwest at Tm C and the command group at TANGO. The battalion's mortar platoon and the 5/4 Artillery returned fire and the FAC called for a close air support mission that dropped napalm.[477]

Teams A and B and D/1-11 found equipment items but nothing indicating recent use; however, NVA artillery began falling on to Sierra and three rounds landed between Captain Herrington's and First Sergeant Offutt's tanks. Herrington ordered his vehicles to pull back about 220 yards and the infantry remounted their APCs. The artillery fire lessened, and Pickarts told Herrington not to search further because it was time for TF 1-77 to begin its withdrawal. Company A departed Sierra at 1:50 pm. It passed through Tm at TANGO enroute to the Marketplace at 3:40pm where it went into position to cover the withdrawal of Tm C.[478] Tm B and D/1-11 withdrew directly from SIERRA to A-4.[479]

The TF 1-77 XO had moved from Con Thien already to retrieve the disabled tanks. Captain Blalock ordered Tm C to withdraw from TANGO at 4:11pm and one of his M-113s threw a track. The leader of the rear-guard platoon was retrieving that vehicle while the Tm B XO moved through TANGO at the same time. Meanwhile, NVA activity had responded to *SULLIVAN* at TANGO and began moving south to close the withdrawal route of these TF 1-77 units. The FAC directed an air strike that dropped ten 500-pound bombs in the TANGO area destroying ten bunkers and an inflicting an unspecified number of casualties. The last elements of the task force moved through Tm A at the Marketplace at 5:30 pm. One of Captain Herrington's tanks then hit a mine resulting in another delay that was covered by another air strike of eight 500-pound bombs. The FAC estimated destroying seven bunkers and an automatic weapons position and causing a large secondary explosion. Team A left the Marketplace after 6:00 pm and closed at C-3 by 7:40pm.[480]

Task Force 1-11 crossed its LD from A-3 through the McNamara Line TRACE north northeast toward Objective ROMEO. Enroute, an A Troop 4-12 Cav M-113 ran over a mine blowing off three road wheels and wounding three soldiers who required a medevac. The NVA present at ROMEO skirmished with TF 1-11. Maneuvering from a herringbone to a line formation, 2/A/1-77 placed tank A-25 on the far left, A-24 on the right, and one of the A/4-12's tanks in the middle. There was a berm the abandoned rail line that ran west of QL-1 to the right with a culvert in the middle. The tank commanders saw NVA running into the culvert and their platoon leader, Lieutenant Warren (Hap) Trainor, gave his gunner, Sergeant Larry Darnell, a main gun fire command and he sent high explosive rounds into and at the top of the culvert.[481]

Four US soldiers were wounded and eight NVA were killed. Three 82mm mortars with 168 rounds of ammunition were found along with 300 more rounds of 82-mm and 60-mm mortar ammunition elsewhere on the objective. One rocket-propelled grenade launcher (RPG) and two antitank rockets were added to the captured equipment. All was destroyed. Objective ROMEO was secured at 9:30 am.[482]

There were four US airstrikes against the NVA on September 13. One dropped napalm and the others were 500- and 750-pound bombs. Four medevac missions were required. Lieutenant Forman recalls firing his 4.2mm mortars all day, mostly responding to requests from Tm B/1-61(M). He had to be resupplied with ammunition twice and that proceeded smoothly because of the pre-operation planning. The second resupply borrowed 4.2-inch ammunition from the mortar platoons at A-4 and C-2. Forman estimated firing nearly 500 rounds. The after-action report states 405 rounds. The lesson learned was that all in the platoon performed excellently and adapted their procedures to the volume and intensity of fire requests without errors. No TF 1-77 soldiers were killed-hostile-action (KHA) and 25 were wounded-hostile-action (WHA). Task Force 1/11 suffered three US KHA and at least three WHA.[483]

Pickarts assessed Operation *SULLIVAN* as a typical penetration operation with the exception that the same route had to be used to enter and leave the objective area. The task forces executed it without deviation. He recommended for future similar missions that a second dismounted infantry company be assigned to complement the sweep force.[484]

Two Leatherneck Square Vignettes

Shortly after *SULLIVAN*, a typhoon stormed through the region. Part of the damage it caused was washing away the C-3 Bridge and raising the water level of the Cam Lo River above fording depth. This was the moment for Captain Warren Elahee, the 1-77 S-5 (Civil Affairs) to emerge from the S-3 section with a solution in mind to the dilemma by the location of the Brigade's combat service support being located at Camp Red Devil south of QL-9 and the maneuver battalions across the river north of the highway. Ammunition, fuel, water, and food were at a premium until the river subsided. Elahee negotiated with a local fishing village moored in the Cam Lo River to ferry soldiers and supplies across the river. The engineers built a temporary military bridge when the weather cleared to enable resupply convoys to move north of the river.

Figure 5.9 Resupplying Red Devil units in Leatherneck Square, Fall 1968.
Source: Photo courtesy of William Rosevear

Eventually, wheeled and tracked vehicles could ford the receding river. Then, a second typhoon struck the engineer's bridge and destroyed it., Captain Elahee negotiated a second contract with the fishing village and that remained in force until the engineers constructed a more permanent bridge.

During the typhoon period, a 1-61 mechanized infantry company was returning from a mission to its base at C-2. An enemy unit ambushed the column that was moving along a ridgeline. The first M-113 APC that was attacked was the company commander's. Its twin antennas were the physical giveaway about who was riding in it. The NVA destroyed that vehicle seriously wounding the company commander. This threw the unit's command and control into chaos. Reinforcing the column from C-2 by Task Force 1-61 that included

B/1-77 was impossible because of the torrential rain and mud. The weather was severe enough that close air support could not respond. Task Force 1-77 was unable to do anything to rescue the unit for the same reasons. All anyone could do in the 1-77 operations center was keep the command radio nets open and simply listen to the 1-61 Infantry battalion commander talk with the company's lieutenants amidst the ferocity of the NVA attack. Eventually, one of the lieutenants emerged as the leader and organized the unit into a defense. The brigade operations center was listening to the action as well. Finally, the brigade's aviation officer unable to simply listen went on his own initiative to a brigade helicopter, flew to the fight, and began evacuating wounded. He flew several sorties.

Operation *RICH*, October 23-27

Operation *RICH* was the second major mission in which the Steel Tigers played a role. *RICH* was a reconnaissance-in-force in the DMZ south of the Ben Hai River and expanded the area covered beyond the objectives of *SULLIVAN* on September 13th. Task Force 1-61(Mechanized) was the controlling headquarters and Lieutenant Colonel Bernard D. Wheeler was the commander. The organization is below:

Task Force 1-61 Inf (M)

- 1 – 61 Infantry (M)
- B/1-77 Armor
- D/1-11 Inf
- B/5-4 Arty (155 SP) (Direct Support)
- A/1-40 Arty (105SP) (General Support)
- 2/A/7 Engineers
- 1 Light Observation Helicopter (LOH)
- 2 Scout Dogs[485]

The most current intelligence identified the *138th Independent* (also known as the *132nd Independent*) and the *27th Regiments* to be operating in the area. Only the *138th* was reported for the TF 1-77 Armor's September 13th mission.

Colonel Wheeler's plan contained three phases. The first began on October 23rd at 3:00 am with three infantry companies and the scout platoon all departing dismounted from A-4 and A-3 and generally moving on-line. The LD for Company B/1-61, commanded by Captain Jack Langston, the scout platoon, and the engineer platoon was at A-3. Companies A/1-61 and C/1-61 commanded by Captains Walter Haddingan and Glenn Mutter, respectively crossed their LD at Con Thien (A-4). The Steel Tigers' Bravo Company, commanded by Captain Arthur McGowan and D/1-11 commanded by Captain Donald Smallwood remained at Con Thien providing security.

Company B, 1-61 Inf made the initial contact with the NVA at 7:38 am on October 23rd when it began receiving mortar fire. Small arms fire described as short but intense was directed at the unit as it attacked toward the mortars' location. After destroying the location of the mortars. The company seized its first objective at 8:04 am. Company C/1-61 Inf secured its first objective at 8:24 am and A/1-61 Inf did the same at 8:30 am. A and C companies did not encounter any NVA; but B and C companies discovered NVA bunker complexes various types and calibers of weapons and ammunition including mortars, RPGs, rice, miscellaneous personal equipment, mines, and documents. There was no indication of recent enemy activity at Company A's objective.[486]

The dense underbrush slowed the forward progress of the three companies as they moved toward the DMZ. Two of the three companies (B and C) secured their second set of objectives at 3:00 pm. Company A reached its second objective by 3:45pm having been slowed by the terrain and vegetation. Further movement north was halted when the TF 1-61 FAC's aircraft crashed killing the pilot near C Company's location. The pilot's remains and three soldiers with heat injuries were evacuated. After this event, the units began moving to their night defensive positions (NDP).[487]

Task Force 1-61 resumed its sweep toward the Ben Hai River in the companies' individual zones on October 24th. C/1-61 made the day's first enemy contact at 6:55 am. A/1-61 began receiving fire at 8:09 am. B/1-61 received the most intense fire starting at 10:00 am. Some came from NVA in the area followed by mortar and automatic weapons fire from two NVA platoons in the Ben Hai River area. A/1-61 discovered an NVA battalion headquarters at 11:25 am. A Company found a platoon sized camp with ammunition, rice and live animals including chickens and pigs. B/1-61 discovered a North Vietnamese field hospital in its zone along the Ben Hai's south bank at 12:55pm and then began receiving heavy fire from the Ben Hai's north bank. Air strikes and the USS New Jersey responded to this development. Meanwhile, the B-1/61 search of the river's south bank uncovered NVA fortifications and supplies.[488]

The NVA's resistance to TF 1-61's movement north toward the Ben Hai River increased throughout the day. Individuals firing their small arms and automatic weapons along with a mortar or two mortar firing gradually grew into NVA squad and platoon-sized engagements by 10:00 am. The companies engaged occasional snipers in spider holes, reacted, and destroyed ammunition, weapons, and supplies as they swept northward. Calls for artillery and air strikes were made as the intensity of the engagements grew in numbers. The task force withdrew from the river's south bank in preparation for establishing their NDPs for the night. Colonel Wheeler directed a false message to be sent over an insecure radio net ordering the companies to move south to A-4.[489]

During the early morning of October 25th, TF 1-61 received a report that the NVA were moving south toward Troung Luong on the south bank of the Ben Hai. Operation *RICH*'s second phase began at 7:00 am when the task force was ordered to move to Kinh Mon which was a new Objective 9 directed by Colonel Glikes, and about the same area as Objective SIERRA in TF 1-77's September 13th Operation *SULLIVAN* a month earlier. Company A/1-61 moved north along the river toward the boundary between the 1st Brigade 5th Infantry Division (M) and the 2nd Regiment, 1st ARVN Division (2-1 ARVN) just east of the abandoned railroad tracks that ran at parallel to QL-1 as far as Gio Linh and then turned northwest toward the Ben Hai. A/1-61 turned south along the tracks to secure the east portion of the objective. Company B/1-61's route was south and then turning north parallel to the abandoned railroad to seize the western half of the objective.[490]

A/1-61's advance was slowed when it received a heavy volume of mortar and automatic weapons fire at about 8:39 am as it was forced to cross a wide stream using immediately available equipment. The intensity of the NVA attack forced A Company to establish a defensive position. Artillery and air strikes were called on enemy positions as within 16 yards of A Company's positions. The NVA continued pouring heavy automatic weapons and mortar fire on the company especially at the stream crossing. This resulted in the platoons separating. Captain Haddigan first ordered his company to escape the incoming mortar fire's impact area by attacking southeast. That did not work so he ordered the company to move in a different direction to take the high ground and establish a defensive perimeter so it could reorganize.[491]

Wheeler ordered Langston to move B Company that was crossing the same stream as A Company had to the north to relieve the pressure on A Company by enveloping the enemy force attacking Haddigan's men. B Company's aggressive attack was so rapid that it took the unit into an NVA company-sized bunker complex where the enemy fired into B Company from all directions and the opposing troops were in close combat with each other. This bunker complex was between the two companies which prevented Langston and Haddigan from linking their troops together. The NVA attacked A/1-61 when about half of the unit had reached the high ground and the other half was still on the move. The NVA launched an attack at 10:19 am against the remaining units of the company still on the low ground. Mortar fire wounded Captain Haddigan at 10:45 am.[492]

Lieutenant Colonel Wheeler committed the Steel Tigers supported by a rifle platoon from D-1/11 to move from A-4 at 11:45 am on Road 561 to Kinh Mon. Captain McGowan had 10 tanks available. Two tanks were lost to anti-tank mines between 12:25pm and 12:27 pm and a third tank was lost later also to an anti-tank mine. The first tank to run over a mine caught fire because the explosion ignited the gasoline fuel. Enroute B/1-77 encountered an NVA platoon attempting to move around the TF 1-61. McGowan engaged the platoon. The Steel Tigers destroyed two squads and dispersed the remainder. The company continued its attack and entered the TF 1-61's perimeter on the eastern flank. They forced pockets of NVA to flee from their positions and into the open under the guns of Companies B and C. The tankers continued attacking north and northwest and secured Wheeler's east flank by establishing contact with C/1-61 and together destroying two NVA platoons. The NVA withdrew by 6:30 pm and TF 1-61 established its NDPs.[493] McGowan related later that B Company's tankers buttoned up and sprayed each other's back decks with coaxial machinegun fire on several occasions to clear them of NVA soldiers who had climbed aboard to destroy the tanks.[494]

The morning following the second Kinh Mon battle, TF 1-61 was resupplied at 6:30 am for the first time since Operation *RICH* began. Lightly wounded casualties and a POW who had tried to escape from a spider hole within the task force's perimeter were sent back to QTCB on the resupply helicopters. Meanwhile, the task force began a sweep of the Kinh Mon battlefield searching for more bunkers, equipment, and NVA. One of the bunker complexes found was battalion-sized with sleeping areas and fighting positions linked by a trench line and well camouflaged. This site and the others located were facing south in anticipation of an attack from that direction. Ammunition, personal items, food, and weapons were found during this sweep and destroyed.[495]

A report of the POW's debriefing was sent to Wheeler stating that the soldier had been seeking medical aid when he left his hiding place. He stated that he was a member of the *132nd Independent Regiment* and that one of the companies in his battalion was located in nearby Tan Bich about 2 miles southeast of Kinh Mon and Tan Lich that was 0.5 miles beyond the first location. [496] Companies B and C moved with Company A in reserve attacked at 11:00 am toward Tan Bich with B/1-77 protecting the right flank of TF 1-61. The Steel Tigers were fired on by about a squad of NVA at 1:30 pm. The tankers killed three NVA and captured their weapons. B/1-61 uncovered a supply point with pigs, chickens, cooking pots, pans, etc., and small shovels that soldiers use. There was no further enemy contact on the October 26th and TF 1-61 went to A-3 and established the NDPs. The Steel Tigers returned to A-4.[497]

The final phase of Operation RICH started at 9 am the next morning when the three infantry companies conducted a final sweep of Leatherneck square which ended at Con Thien at 3:00 pm.[498]

One of the lessons learned from the operation was that the NVA lacked flexibility in reacting to the unexpected. Wheeler noted that previous operations into the DMZ area were conducted in daylight. *RICH* began at 3:00 am and TF 1-61 did not occupy their NDPs until after dark. Also, the NVA defenses anticipated attacks from the south. The TF attacked Kinh Mon from the West.

Captain McGowan added another ring around the company's main gun barrels signifying a major combat action. Further rings were added after similar operations. As stated earlier, the company commander's tank always had an extra ring.[499]

October 25: The Next Mission and the Unanticipated

At about the same time as the Battle of Kinh Mon began the morning of October 25th, the Steel Tigers encountered the finely-honed skills of Ho Chi Minh's sappers (combat engineers). Highway 561 was a well-travelled improved dirt road that was two-lanes wide. As stated above, it was the MSR from QTCB to Con Thien. The daily mine sweep of the road from C-3 north to C-2 Water Point and Bridge had been without incident since arriving in Leatherneck Square. The sweep team with their mine detectors and the security force began their daily assignment on October 25th as they had since September 2nd when the mission was passed from the Marines to the Red Devils. The roadway was clear on both sides with no vegetation providing concealment for an enemy ambush. The sweep team passed C-3 and once out of site of the C-3 observation tower, a member of the team stepped on an antitank mine that was buried in the road with no evidence that the ground had been disturbed.

Colonel Pickarts was giving the Task Force 1-77 Armor leadership a warning order about the next operation when he received word of the explosion, He sent Major Pihl to direct assistance. Lieutenant Forman's driver was returning from the headquarters company bunker in his jeep. Major Pihl stopped the driver and directed him to drive to the site of the explosion. The XO sent Forman's jeep back and directed the driver to send his jeep and the battalion surgeon to the location of the explosion. Bob Forman went to the scene with one of his mortar carriers to assist.[500] Next, Dennis Tripp, the XO's driver, drove his jeep over another antitank mine buried in the road that exploded near where the first mine detonated. Again, there was no evidence that the ground had been disturbed. Dennis was killed and the XO was wounded as was the battalion surgeon.

There were three tasks that had to be accomplished immediately: reporting the second mine explosion and the casualties, requesting evacuation of the wounded by helicopter (medevac), and identifying a helicopter landing site away from the minefield. The site selected was off to the right (east) side of the road and was cleared of further mines by one person looking meticulously and expeditiously for disturbances in the road's surface. The rescue action proceeded without further incident. The medevac flew the wounded to the naval hospital ship stationed offshore for immediate medical care and the damaged equipment was removed, and the remains of the victims were recovered and sent to QTCB.[501] Major Pihl recovered from his wounds (burst eardrums) and the surgeon suffered eye injuries. Pihl was reassigned to the Brigade headquarters as the S-1 and the physician did not return to the 1-77 Armor. Major Richard Benson, the Brigade's Inspector General, became the new Executive Officer.[502]

The mission that Pickarts was presenting at the time of the explosion was to have occurred north of the Cua Viet River to the Ben Hai River along the South China Sea's beach-. The 3/5 Cav was being ordered to return to its parent 9th Infantry Division in the south of the country in the post-Tet tactical environment and giving up its mission of securing the Street without Joy. The squadron would board ships at the Cua Viet naval base. The Steel Tigers with the same models of vehicles and thus presenting the same vehicle signatures would roadmarch to the same port and appear to blend in with those of the 3/5 Cav. and then initiate their surprise attack northward into the east region of QL-1 through Firebases A-1, C-1, and east of Gio Linh to the Ben Hai. The S-3 and S-2 made a helicopter reconnaissance of the routes and area of operation following the commander's warning order.[503]

The plan was stopped suddenly when President Johnson ordered an end to be bombing all of North Vietnam beginning November 1st in his October 3rd address to the nation. Additionally, ground operations were to be severely restricted. General Abrams implemented the President's decision by halting missions into the DMZ to interdict NVA movement to the south. Abrams added his touch to the directive by stating that the armed forces would maintain active surveillance and respond to NVA units moving south of the DMZ and into the South Vietnam from their safe havens in Laos and Cambodia. In addition to the President Johnson's order, Abrams changed the emphasis from Westmoreland's strategy of inflicting unacceptable casualties using major US units on Ho Chi Minh's and General Giap's forces because thisapproach had been unsuccessful.

Instead, Abrams initiated a new military strategy – pacification of populated areas and attacking North Vietnamese formations in coordinated single-force efforts. Abrams believed that U.S units could be used more effectively by assisting the South Vietnamese military and paramilitary to gain the confidence of local populations by demonstrating Saigon's commitment to them that the Saigon government was capable defeating the north.[504]

In I Corps (Quang Tri and Thua Thien Provinces), the single force would combine Army, Marine, and Vietnamese regulars and militias in single-purpose joint operations instead of ordering missions in separately designated areas of operations. This step signaled the US' operational implementation of Vietnamization. Primarily, its goal was to inspire local civilian loyalty to the South Vietnamese central government by removing the north's influence and demonstrating that the South could keep the population safe. One of the first steps in the coordinated single force concept was to keep tactically important firebases manned and closing unnecessary installations. Two of these to be abandoned included C-3 and A-3.[505]

Leatherneck Square to LZ Nancy

The tactical situation in I Corps by mid-1968 made a repeat of the Tet Offensive unlikely. This allowed General Abrams to move the 1st Cavalry Division to another part of the South Vietnam. Leaving the defense of Quang Tri and Thua Thien Provinces to the 3rd Marine, 101st Airborne, 1st ARVN Divisions, and the 1/5 Inf Bde (M), The Red Devil Brigade's areas of responsibility expanded in Quang Tri as did those of the 101st Airborne Division with the attached 3rd Brigade, 82nd Airborne Division in Thua Thien.

The Brigade moved its tactical battalions south from Leatherneck Square while retaining the region in its AO, with TF 1-11 and TF 1-61 (M) settling into Landing Zone (LZ) Sharon, and TF 1-77 occupying LZ Nancy to the south of Sharon and Quang Tri City. Figure 5.10 presents the new areas of responsibilities for the Red Devils.

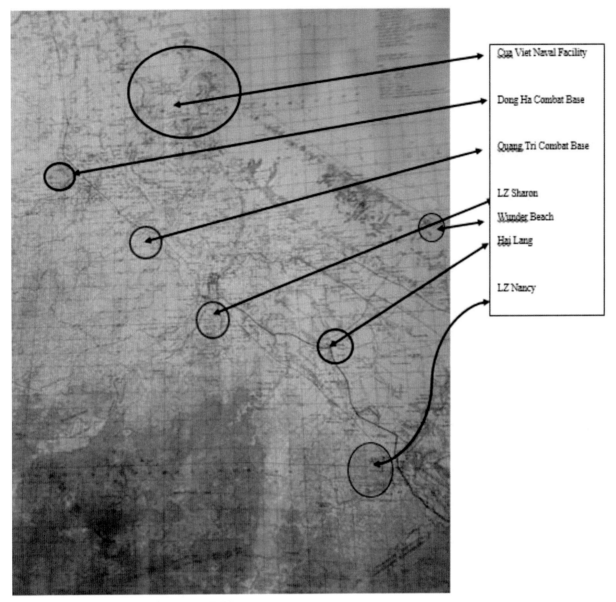

Figure 5.10 Steel Tigers move to LZ Nancy
Map courtesy of Lawrence Wills; graphics by author

LZ Sharon was the closest Red Devil base to QTCB. Nearby was the town of La Vang which was the location of the Basilica of Our Lady of La Vang. This Roman Catholic landmark is the site of the appearance of the Virgin Mary and the Christ Child to the community of Vietnamese Catholics who had assembled there for safety from one of the anti-Catholic persecutions in 1798. Clothed in a Vietnamese traditional *ao dai* (a woman's dress with panels in the front and back and worn over slacks). The vision was seen several times comforting those present. Pope John XXIII assigned it the honorific of minor basilica in August 1961 because of the visions seen there 163 years before.[506] The ARVN and US as well as the NVA, and VC respected the site by avoiding any conflicts on its grounds.

Colonel Pickarts moved two of the three Steel Tiger tank companies and the scout and mortar platoons to LZ Nancy. He told Major Benson to move the battalion trains comprising the unit's combat service support elements as soon as the equipment could be organized, packed, and loaded onto the 40 wheeled and tracked vehicles in this battalion entity. Pickarts also told Benson that a 3MARDIV unit would occupy C-3. As soon as the USMC unit arrived, Benson was to send the third tank company to LZ Nancy and to use the Marines for security. The Executive Officer reported that the replacement unit had not arrived yet so he could not release the tank company and that the 77th trains were still assembling. Pickarts changed his order to move the 77th Armor units immediately and leave C-3 unoccupied.[507]

Benson ordered the trains and the front and rear guards to move from C-3 in the late afternoon and took the route through QTCB instead of east on QL-9 to Dong Ha and turning south on QL-1 through the city of Quang Tri. He halted the roadmarch on the base to give the soldiers time for a hot supper meal in any mess hall that would feed them. The move continued at dark after the short break. When the column reached the exit of QTCB, the USMC gate guard refused to open the gate because 3MARDIV policy was that no US troops left the base after sundown. Benson ordered the guard to open the gate and the guard refused without the permission of a superior. The column remained stopped as the Steel Tiger XO's order went up the gate guard's chain of command to the QTCB duty officer. This individual approved opening the gate and the 1-77 trains proceeded along QL-1.[508]

The column's next unanticipated stop occurred at bridge over a river emptying into the South China Sea about midway between QTCB and LZ Nancy on the Street Without Joy. The bridge had barbed wire on steel frames closing both ends of the bridge and spotlights on either end used for searching the river near the bridge and the QL-1. The bridge's guards were either members of the local part-time Vietnamese Popular Force (PF) responsible for securing local villages or the full-time Regional Force (RF) that was a militia available for missions throughout a province. These guards, nicknamed Ruff-Puffs (RF/PF) refused to open the barriers. Major Benson who had been an advisor to ARVN during his first combat tour, ordered the soldiers to open the barriers in Vietnamese which they did. The column closed at LZ Nancy at about 11 pm that night.[509] For the first time since arriving in Vietnam, the entire battalion was reunited.

The unit south of the Steel Tigers was the 101st Airborne at Camp Evans who took the base over from 1st Air Cavalry Division. Each firebase bordered QL-1, The areas of interest of each battalion extended east to the coast and west into the more mountainous regions where it met the units of the 3MARDIV at Camp Carroll and Vandegrift Combat Base

(VC. Steel Tiger units rotated securing the abandoned Wunder Beach location in case it was needed again. TF 1-61 units replaced the 3/5 Cav's mission protecting the naval port at Cua Viet.

The forms of TF 1-77's operational missions changed when it reached Nancy. Instead of search and destroy sweeps through the area close to and inside the DMZ, before President Johnson's restrictions, the first single force operation was a cordon and search. It used South Vietnamese intelligence resources and a 1st ARVN Division battalion searching the area while US troops established a perimeter around the targeted population sites to prevent VC or NVA elements from escaping. To the west, TF 1-77 and the other brigade task forces initially performed various missions within their established boundaries designed to block the enemy from reentering populated areas or transporting food, medical supplies, and ammunition to VC and NVA units west from the QL-1 villages.

The first cordon and search operation ordered by the 3MARDIV took place in the Street Without Joy area. It was part of the single war strategy and began on November 1st. Its name was *Operation Napoleon Saline II & Marshall Mountain AO*. This operation will be addressed in more detail in Chapter 6; however, the Steel Tigers' role was contained in Operations Order 11-68 dated November 29th. It stated that there would be three phases and that the TF main Command Post would be 5.5 Kilometers southeast of Quang Tri City. Highway QL 1 ran through the AO. The length was about 8 kilometers, and it was about 5 kilometers wide. Phase I would be a seven-day cordon (December 1-7) in one area. Phase II would last five days (December 7-11) in the second area, and Phase III would cover December 11-14 in the final sector. The order of the cordons would be the same in each of the three areas with B/1-61(M) in the 11-to-3 o'clock position C/1-77 in the 3-to-8 o'clock position, and B/1-77 in the 8-to-11 o'clock position. The 3rd Battalion 1st Regiment of the 1st ARVN Division(1-1 ARVN) would be the search, destroy, and sweep force. The operation start time was set at 4:30 AM and the start point was the LZ Nancy gate. There were two routes. C/1-77 was to use route 1 east of QL 1 through the center of the zone from LZ Sharon. B/1-77 and B/1-61(M) with the mortar platoon were assigned route 2 along the west side of QL 1 from LZ Nancy. The 3d Platoon of Company A, 7th Engineers was in General Support. Perimeter security for LZ Nancy was provided by A/1-77 and A/4-12 Cav.[510]

Following this cordon and search mission, the Steel Tigers returned to LZ Nancy and the Brigade underwent changes of command. Colonel Glikes turned over the Brigade to Colonel James Gibson. Glikes went to 24th US Corps at Phu Bai. Lieutenant Colonel Carmelo Milia, the former Deputy Brigade Commander for Operations and Intelligence, assumed command of the Steel Tigers from Colonel Pickarts who moved to Camp Red Devil as the Brigade Executive Officer.

The Enemy

Lessons Learned

The Steel Tigers learned how to prevail in an asymmetrical warfare environment during the first six months of 1968 as did the North Vietnamese and Viet Cong The latter were used to infantry sweeps conducted by infantry (USMC) who had been delivered to landing zones by helicopters. Fighting from prepared defensive position with their backs to the Ben Hai River, regular North Vietnamese units were surprised by the Red Devil mobile formations comprised of tanks and armored personnel carriers moving into their areas swiftly under the cover of USAF and Naval air and artillery support. US support was comparatively far superior to that available to the French ground forces in the previous two decades.

The Steel Tigers learned that the enemy observed routes being taken to an objective and then moved to the flanks of the route to avoid contact and then planted mines in back of the column or other combat formations. It was probable that a vehicle would detonate a mine sometime in the future when the route was used again.

A second lesson learned by Red Devil mechanized formations was to always sweep the area around a night defensive position to assure that an enemy infantry-sapper attack on the position would be unlikely during the night. One technique employed was to move into a site, go through the establishment of a defensive position including the sweep, and then move to another site after dark where the unit would remain until morning.

The Steel Tigers learned quickly never to take any situation for granted, even when in a base camp. The North Vietnamese and Viet Cong always were searching for a place and opportunity to seize the initiative.

Land navigation was a lesson to be learned not only in Vietnam, but also earlier by previous Steel Tigers in the earlier wars. Tracked vehicles especially could not be bound by roads. Weather, the enemy, river crossing points whether fords or bridges, other choke points, time available, and the assigned missions dictated routes to an objective. Terrain capable of bearing tracked and wheeled vehicles were subject to mines, booby traps, and command detonated explosive devices that could be emplaced by small teams who went undetected.

The second half of the battalion's first year in Vietnam was spent partially operating in populated areas along Highways QL-1 and QL-9 supporting the forces of South Vietnam demonstrate that the central government could protect civilians and keeping the NVA and VC off balance in remote sections of Quang Tri Province. This included reducing the numbers of enemy ambushes of civilian automobiles, trucks, and busses filled with noncombatants traveling along main thoroughfares and depriving the enemy of covered and concealed routes from base areas in the western mountainous regions to the eastern cities of Dong Ha and Quang Tri and the villages close to them.

Infusion

Not long after the Steel Tigers arrived in Vietnam, the term *infusion* became a daily reality. The Red Devil Brigade had trained together, deployed together, and fought initially together; however, personnel policy was that the standard armed forces combat tour was to be 12 months long with a year-long break between them. Keeping the original Red Devils together would have meant that the Army would have to redeploy the brigade to the US in the June-July 1969 period, and a replacement unit from Europe or the US would needed to be identified, trained, and deployed to assume the brigade's missions. This was impossible given the Army's responsibilities at the time and that neither the Army Reserve had been placed on active duty nor had the Army National Guard been brought into federal service from the states and placed on active duty. Infusion began as a program in the theater before the Red Devils arrived.[511]

The solution was to reassign members of the brigade to other units in South Vietnam and receive replacements from other entities resulting in staggered rotation dates. The program began in the 77th Armor in late October. Infusion concerned the battalion's leadership because the commander had no input as to the individuals selected. Those reassigned were officers and enlisted of various ranks and categories of military occupational specialties.[512] The Red Devils' cohesion forged at Fort Carson was impaired most at the company, platoon, and squad levels where each soldier knew the others' strengths and weaknesses. The positive feature of infusion was that those more experienced in current service in the combat theater could disseminate their knowledge to the Red Devils who were still new to the theater.

Chapter 6: Vietnam - 1969

Introduction

January 1969 began a year of change in Vietnam for both the South Vietnamese and the US and its allies on the one side, and the North Vietnamese and South Vietnamese communists on the other. Politically, Richard Nixon was inaugurated on January 20th. During the Presidents Kennedy and Johnson administrations, US involvement grew from an advisory mission into a full commitment to defeat Hanoi's and COSVN's forces on the battlefield. After the rapid buildup of US forces to over 500,000 troops during the previous four years. The capability of the communists to launch the Tet 1968, albeit a military defeat for the communists, led to the national strategy level in Washington in the last year of the Johnson administration, recognizing that increased US domestic political opposition against the war demanded a reduction in US troop strength. A greater role for the South Vietnamese armed forces nation-building effort had to be undertaken that would draw the South Vietnamese population into a closer relationship with their government. This carried over into the presidency of Richard Nixon in January 1969. The revised strategy had to be implemented quickly. The goal was to demonstrate that the South Vietnamese could defeat the North's effort to win a victory. US military aid to the South would include equipment modernization, training, and armed air support.[513]

There was an additional US domestic political agenda occurring in the summer of 1968 before the presidential election between the US Congress and the Department of Defense that affected the Fiscal Year 1969 budget. Lewis Sorley, in his *Vietnam: A Better War* recounts a July 1968 meeting between General Ralph Haines who was en route from his position as Army Vice Chief of Staff to Commander, US Army Pacific, and General Abrams. Haines told Abrams about a demand from the Chairman of the House Ways and Means Committee and the Department of Defense to give up $3 billion in 1969 that would affect Vietnam indirectly through reductions in the training base, hospital support in Japan, and other areas. Abrams was concerned that the troops in Vietnam had to continue observing that they had the nation's support.[514]

The Communists believed that they had created a base of influence and conducted successful guerilla operations that extended their influence across the south by 1967. They were ready to launch a general offensive beginning with 1968's Lunar New Year that would cause the population to revolt against the Saigon government. Although the expected revolt did not occur when the southerners did not join them, and the major military defeats they suffered during Tet and again at Khe Sanh where the attempt failed to repeat their 1954 defeat of the French at Dien Bien Phu, Hanoi recognized the impact of their failures on the domestic morale within the United States. That the North could launch attacks on the scale that they did after continuous reports from Saigon and Washington that victory was near resulted in the nosedive of popular support for continuing the war and increased demonstrations of opposition.

During the last half of 1968 and first half of 1969, Hanoi replaced its units with soldiers and reequipped them. Some of this occurred in the safe areas north of the DMZ and other units were sent south along a 3,500-mile network of footpaths trails, and roads named the Ho Chi Minh Trail using safe areas inside a 30-mile-wide zone through Laos and Cambodia along their borders with South Vietnam . This route from North Vietnam into Cambodia was maintained and defended by NVA troop units stationed at way stations and each responsible for its sector and communications between them. William Nolan estimated that it took two months for one NVA increment to move from north to south. [515]

Military operations were limited to fighting the US and its allies as they did the French: picking their varied targets and employing proven tactics while avoiding confronting a better-equipped force on the battlefield. Although militarily weak during the first half of the year, the North Vietnamese could project the image of strength and manipulate public opinion in the South and among the US and its allies. The military-political goal was to inflict more allied casualties daily impacting troop morale and dragging out the Paris peace negotiations.[516]

The Red Devil Brigade's primary area of tactical operations in Quang Tri Province during 1968 had been in the Leatherneck Square beginning at the DMZ and then south to QL-9 and east to Dong Ha which intersected with QL-1.

Following the departure of the 1st Air Cavalry Division in the fall of 1968 from Quang Tri, allied forces stationed in the province by January 1969 had nearly the same area of responsibility with fewer troops. The 3MARDIV was headquartered at Quang Tri Combat Base (QTCB) with its three regiments: 3rd, 9th, and 4th. Major General Raymond Davis continued commanding the division until April 1969 when he turned the division over to Major General William Jones on the 14th.

The 1st Brigade, 5th Infantry Division (Mechanized) with two of its battalions at LZ Sharon and the Steel Tigers at LZ Nancy remained under 3MARDIV's OPCON received its new commander, Colonel James M. Gibson in December 1968 who turned the Brigade over to Colonel John Osteen on June 5, 1969. Osteen, in turn, gave up command on November 22, 1969, and was succeeded by Brigadier General William Burke.

The Brigade's order of battle changed somewhat during 1968 and into 1969 at the maneuver battalion level. The 1969 order of battle and the unit locations included the following: Task Force 1-11 Infantry had four of its own infantry companies and an attached tank company from the 1-77 Armor stationed at LZ Sharon. Task Force 1-61 Infantry (Mechanized) also at LZ Sharon operated as a mechanized infantry battalion with three mechanized infantry companies. While located at Sharon, the one 1-77 tank company supported both infantry battalions' missions. Away from Sharon, the task organization was governed by the mission of each battalion. A self-propelled 155mm howitzer artillery battery of the 5-4 Artillery (155mm SP) established Fire Support Base (FSB) Tombstone on the Sharon base.

Tank companies and the A/4-12 Cav were cross-attached for specific missions. The 1-77 Armor had two of its tank companies and either an infantry or a mechanized infantry company, again depending on the mission. The battalion also exercised OPCON of the Brigade's A/4-12 Cav troop. This occurred at LZ Nancy because Lieutenant Colonel Pickarts recognized that the tank battalion had the armored vehicle maintenance capability to better support the troop than did the 75th Support Battalion's maintenance company at Camp Red Devil. A second battery of self-propelled 155mm howitzers was at FSB Hardcore that was located within Nancy's perimeter.

The 5-4 Artillery (155mm SP) commander placed his third battery on FSB Hai Lang at the intersection of QL 1 and the road to Wunder Beach located near the Hai Lang District capital. The artillery battalion's headquarters, and support units were at Camp Red Devil that was part of QTCB. The battalion commander could displace his batteries to support various brigade missions throughout the Red Devil Brigade's Area of Operations (AO).

New units coming under the brigade's control during 1969 were the 3rd Squadron 5th Armored Cavalry (3-5 Cav); 79th Infantry Detachment (Long Range Patrol) renamed in February 1969 to P Company, 75th Infantry Regiment (Ranger); 298th Signal Company; 517th Military Intelligence Detachment; and the 77th Combat Trackers. The last unit contained five-man teams each with a Labrador retriever who operated in front of infantry patrols to reconnoiter for enemy, identify them, and call for infantry support to move forward to engage whoever they located. Scout dog units worked with infantry units and were present during the 1-61's Operation RICH in October 1968.

The following units remained unchanged from 1968: 75th Support Battalion; A/7th Engineer Bn (A/7 Engr); 86th Chemical Detachment; 407th Radio Research Detachment (RRD); 86th Chemical Company; and the 48th Public Information Detachment.

The 1st ARVN Division established a forward command post at Dong Ha. Assigned to the 1st ARVN Forward was the 2nd Regiment. It was stationed at Gio Linh (A-2) and its five battalions were located from A-2 across Leatherneck Square to Camp Carroll. Also, there was a Vietnamese Marine brigade.[517] It was the 3rd Battalion of the 1st ARVN's 1st Regiment that was the search and sweep force in the 1-77's December 1968 cordon and search operation.

Geographically, the Province included Khe Sanh; LZ Ca Lu-Vandegrift; Camp Carroll; Leatherneck Square; and Base Area 101 that extended through the Province's mountains to the Laotian border and included the Ba Long Valley. Quang Tri's most densely populated area was along the Street Without Joy where an estimated 180,000 lived.[518] QL-9 connected Dong Ha and the Laotian Border, and QL-1 connected the DMZ to Dong Ha and Quang Tri City and then through Thua Thien Province and across the Hai Van Pass to Danang in Quang Nam Province which was the headquarters of the III Marine Amphibious Force (MAF). This headquarters was responsible for all combat and pacification operations in I Corps which included Quang Nam, Quang Tin, and Quang Ngai provinces south of Thua Thien (Figure 6.1).

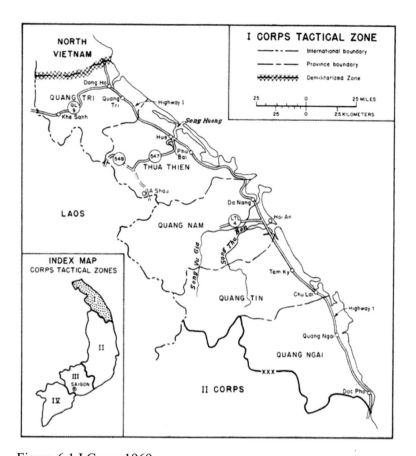

Figure 6.1 I Corps 1969
FileL File: I CTZ.gif, from Citizendium: The Citizens' Compendium_CTZ 1969.gif (600×639) August 10, 2023

The AOs in Quang Tri Province were divided as follows:

1) Red Devil Brigade: Coastal lowlands east of QL-1, and west of QL-1 into the piedmont region.

2) Third Marine Division: along the DMZ west to Quang Tri's border with Laos through Base Area 101 and then south into the mountainous and heavily vegetated areas generally beyond the border between Quang Tri and Thua Thien Provinces in Base Area 611.

3) Task Force Hotel (TF Hotel) which was name of the 3MARDIV (Forward) CP was located at LZ Vandegrift. It controlled operations to the Laotian border. The AOs extended above QL-9 north to the DMZ and south of QL-9 and into Quang Tri Province's Base Areas 101 (Route 926 Laos-616 South Vietnam) and Thua Thien Province's Base Area 611 that were entered from the Ho Chi Minh Trail along Route 922 in Laos that turned into Route 548 in Vietnam through the Da Krong Valley. The tactic employed was carving out fire support bases on the tops of dominant terrain where supporting

artillery was placed and infantry patrolled surrounding areas. Travel from Vandegrift-Ca Lu or from one base to another was by helicopter.

Thua Thien Province, immediately south of Quang Tri, was the location of the ancient capital city of Hue and the headquarters of Major General Ngo Quang Truong's 1st ARVN Division. Phu Bai that was the headquarters of US XXIV Corps. It was commanded by Army Lieutenant General Richard Stilwell to whom the III MAF Commander, a USMC lieutenant general, had delegated control of spoiling-attack combat, rice and other denial, and hearts and nation-building operations in Quang Tri and Thua Thien. Communist forces operated from the Ho Chi Min Trail into the mountains west of Hue in Base Area 114. The 101st Airmobile Division was located in the latter province at Camp Evans and Camp Eagle. The A Shau Valley and Dong Ap Bia (Hamburger Hill) were two geographic sites in Thua Thien that played major roles in 1969. Major General Melvin Zais was the division commander from July 1968 through May 1969 when he was promoted and became the new commander of XXIV Corps replacing Lieutenant General Stilwell.

Colonel Gibson began dividing the Red Devil Brigade to varied and simultaneous missions throughout Quang Tri Province ranging from supply and food denial operations near the populated areas to penetrating areas on the ground that had been accessible by US forces only by helicopter to destroy enemy combat units.

The era of the single-force strategy began for the Steel Tigers when the battalion arrived at LZ Nancy. It conducted a short-duration cordon and search mission across QL-1 from Nancy into the area around the village of My Chanh in November 1968. The 1-77 was the cordon element and local RF/PF troops were the search and sweep force. This first mission evolved into subsequent rice denial and demonstrations that the South Vietnamese could bring security and stabilization to populated areas. Lieutenant Colonel Pickarts, who trained the Steel Tigers at Fort Carson and took them into battle turned command of the 1-77 Armor over to Lieutenant Colonel Milia on December 6, 1968. He took the Streel Tigers to the Khe Sanh plain where many at higher echelons believed a combined arms armored ground force had no place. Lieutenant Colonel Lieutenant Colonel Thomas Miller assumed command of the Steel Tigers on June 23, 1969. Miller remained the battalion commander for nearly the remainder of 1969, when Lieutenant Colonel Niven Baird succeeded him.

Initially opposing the Red Devil Brigade across the Demilitarized Zone were the NVA *B-5 Front's 138th, 270th, 84th, 27th, 31st, infantry*, and the *126th Naval Sapper regiments*.[519]. Additional NVA units including the *304th NVA Division* began moving gradually from its Laotian safe areas back into Vietnam.

General Davis ordered the 3MARDIV to operate in the western regions of northern I Corps to prevent a repeat of Tet 1968 during 1969 New Year's celebration. By spring 1969, the Red Devil Brigade and regiments of the 1st ARVN Division joined the Marines for operations not only in Quang Tri but also in Thua Thien provinces with the 101st Airmobile Division.

LZ Nancy to Khe Sanh

Operation *NAPOLEON SALINE II* AND *MARSHALL MOUNTAIN*, November 1, 1968 - February 28, 1969

This was a food and equipment denial and nation-building operation in Hai Lang and Trieu Phong Districts: a hearts-and-minds demonstration that the central government in Saigon could protect and provide government services to its citizenry nationwide. It began following Tet 1968, Khe Sanh, and US forays into the DMZ operations of the North. The NVA left the *814th* and 808th main force and the *10th Sapper* battalions behind in Quang Tri to maintain contact with local *C-59th and H-99th Viet Cong* local force companies in the Trieu Phong and Hai Lang districts, along QL-1, respectively. These units supported the transport of rice to feed the main force NVA and VC main force combat units that were refitting with men and equipment in the remote areas of the province. Additionally, there were 234 small villages near the highway of which 74 were believed to be under communist control. Intelligence reported that there were an estimated 4,000 VC units of varying sizes distributed among them. Figure 6.2 shows the Trieu Phong and Hai Lang districts where the pacification efforts occurred.

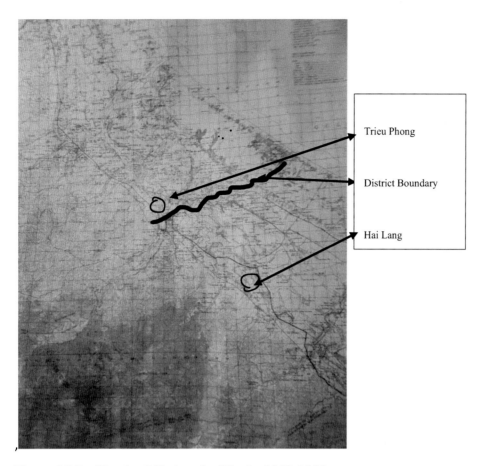

Trieu Phong

District Boundary

Hai Lang

Figure 6.2 Pacification Missions by District 1968-1969
Map Courtesy Lawrence Wills, Graphics by Author

The mission of allied forces was to interdict the supply routes to the enemy's combat units in the west that demonstrated Saigon's commitment to the pacification and security efforts to earn additional popular support for the government. North Vietnamese main force units were in Base Area 101 which was southwest of Quang Tri City in the mountainous and heavily forested Hai Lang National Forest Reserve. Units included the unlocated *7th Front* headquarters and the *812th regiment.*[520] *The 812th* and the NVA's *320th Division* suffered heavy losses of troops and supplies in the Tet 1968 and post-Tet combat actions during 1968. The US intelligence estimated North Vietnamese strength in the Base Area to be 36,800[521]

Instead of moving through populated areas from one to another in US-dominated battle formations, the tactics employed were small unit night ambushes, daytime patrolling, and focused searching, probing and using detection devices in cooperation with the 1st ARVN Regiment, RF/PF units, South Vietnam's national police, and a special force known as Provisional Reconnaissance Units (PRUs). Close coordination was essential so that the small units knew where other friendly forces were located, and no team began firing at another friendly entity. An example was the 1-61 Infantry (M). It averaged 30 ambush teams per night and the Vietnamese units averaged 60 nightly during this operation's period.[522] Even TF 1-77 Armor conducted night ambushes using not only the scout platoon as infantry, but also the tank companies positioning their platoons after dark and turning off the engines. If the movement were detected where civilians were not permitted to be after the nightly curfew, the engines and tank searchlights would be turned on and the ambush initiated. The nightly ambush plan was reported to the Brigade during daylight hours.

Intelligence analyses concluded that cordons and searches, widespread ambushes, and patrolling through the first quarter of 1969 had severely hindered NVA access to food and other supplies.

Some supply denial operations included the pacification initiative named Civil Action Projects (CAPs). These required close coordination with the local South Vietnamese leadership of the designated civilian villages and hamlets to deliver medical (MEDCAPS) and dental care (DENTCAPS) to villagers during cordons and searches as well as providing engineer assistance to local residents to accomplish a variety of construction and repair tasks.[523] The Operation *SALINE II & MARSHALL MOUNTAIN* after-action report lists 15,302 Vietnamese treated during MEDCAPS and 507 treated in DENTCAPS during the period. There were school and bridge construction projects, and distributions of food, clothing, soap, and school-kit projects that took place.[524]

The Operation *SALINE II & MARSHALL MOUNTAIN* period also found the Steel Tigers and A/4-12 Cav turning in their M48A2C gasoline-powered tanks and drawing M48A3 diesel engine tanks.[525] The new tanks had an improved operational range, fuel efficiency, increased horsepower (690hp vs 750hp), and the change from gasoline to diesel fuel reduced the likelihood of a fire. Although this was a positive development, there was also the negative effect of operating in the sandy terrain on tracked vehicle suspension systems with special mention of sprockets and track in the operation's after-action report. Sand being sucked into the engine and transmission assemblies during windy and dry weather resulting in an above number of failures of machined parts and clogged fuel pumps were also identified as problem areas.[526].

SALINE II AND MARSHALL MOUNTAIN found A/1-77 and C/1-77 performing missions denying the NVA access to the province's villages and towns. B/1-77 was securing Wunder Beach. In addition to tank platoon-sized patrols between the dunes and the seacoast. The latter unit conducted maintenance and supported the Hai Lang District military commander conduct a joint operation along route 555 during the three-day Tet 1969 holiday that began on February 23rd. B/1-77 was the security force while Hai Lang District RF/PFs searched for VC infiltrators. Although there were attacks near Saigon and Danang during this period, there were none in the Steel Tigers' AO.

Operation *MASSACHUSETTS BAY* April 23- June 15
Operation *ELLIS RAVINE* April 8 -15

March found Company B moving to LZ Sharon and attached to the 1-11 Infantry. The missions were a part of Operation *MASSACHUSETTS BAY* that continued the earlier pacification operations initiated in late 1968. The Steel Tigers denied NVA and VC access to populated areas and responded to infantry requests for armor support. The access denial mission began with tank platoons patrolling the area southwest of LZ Sharon on the south side of the Song Thach Han (Quang Tri) River within a zone established by the 1-11's commander, Lieutenant Colonel Thomas Britton. Subsequently, the mission expanded into a land-clearing operation using Rome Plows. Figure 6.3 is a photograph of this vehicle.

Figure 6.3 The Rome Plow
Source: 2d04419c54894d6097f1d7a5aeacbad3_medium.jpg (550×367) (pocketsights.com) August 8, 2023

These vehicles were Caterpillar D7E bulldozers modified with armor protection and each mounting a more than two-ton blade designed to cut trees and heavily vegetated terrain to six-inches above ground surface level to protect against erosion. The equipment was operated by the Army's 18th Engineer Brigade's 59th Land Clearing Company based at QTCB under the control of 3MARDIV.[527]

B Company rebuilt an abandoned French defensive position overlooking the river to secure the plows and their security. The site was named Landing Zone (LZ) Mohegan. Mohegan was an elementary school near Bridgeport, Connecticut whose students were corresponding with B/1-77 Armor.[528] This operation cleared a vast amount of acreage.

During this two-month operation, the platoons rotated with one in garrison performing maintenance while one platoon secured the engineers and a second swept the area being cleared each day. Gradually, concealed routes from the VC camps to the villages near LZ Sharon diminished and restricted the enemy's movements to draws and stream beds. Figure 6.4 displays the area where the Rome Plows operated.

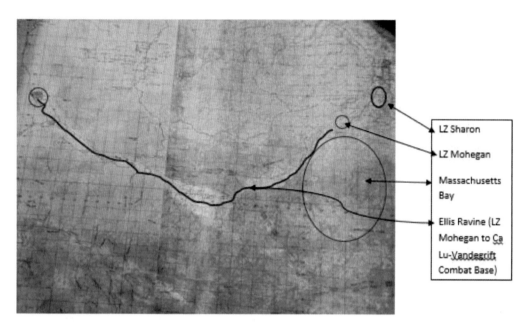

Figure 6.4 Operations Massachusetts Bay and Ellis Ravine
Map Courtesy Lawrence Wills, Graphics by Author

It was during this period that the five-day Operation *ELLIS RAVINE* was conducted. This mission was to rebuild and open Route 556 from B/1-77's LZ Mohegan west of LZ Sharon to the Ca Lu -Vandegrift Combat Base through the Ba Long Valley in Base Area 101. Figure 6.4 displays the route. The original road bordered the Song Thach Han (Quang Tri) River that flowed from Cua Viet past Dong Ha through Quang Tri and then southwest through the Ba Long Valley to the Ca Lu-Vandegrift complex next to QL-9. From there, the river went past the base of the Khe Sanh Plateau and turned south.[529]

There were two Red Diamond task forces in this mission. Task Force 1-11 Inf, comprising two 1-11 Infantry companies, A/4-12 Cav, and B/1-40 Arty (105mm SP) staged at LZ Mohegan and moved along the abandoned road to the southwest. Task Force 3/5 Cav included two cavalry troops, one 1-11 Infantry company, and a battery of 5-4 Arty (155mm SP). The two task forces met at the valley's west end and then proceeded to sweep the reopened Route 556 eastward.[530]

Task Force Remagen, March 16 – April 11

The Red Devil Brigade, 3MARDIV, and the 1ˢᵗ ARVN Division owned Quang Tri Province during the early weeks of 1969. The North Vietnamese had moved into Laos, Cambodia, and north of the DMZ to recover from their manpower and equipment losses in Tet 1968, the battle for Khe Sanh, and along the Street Without Joy. North Vietnamese units replaced their losses with fresh men and equipment.

Each major US and South Vietnamese command continued operating in their respective AOs. In keeping with General Abrams' one-war strategy of keeping the North Vietnamese off balance by taking the fighting to them, Major General Davis's tactic of getting his 3MARDIV units out of their firebases and deploying them to find and destroy enemy units were operations with general codenames that incorporated USMC, Army, and ARVN troops working together in assigned sectors.

Initially, the 3MARDIV assigned its 9ᵗʰ Marine Regiment to operate near and in Base Area 611 that was south of Quang Tri's Base Area 101 in January 1969. It led into southern Quang Tri and Thua Thien Provinces. The 9ᵗʰ Marines were ordered to cut Route 922 (Laos)-548 (Vietnam) west of the 101st Airmobile Division through the long and narrow Da Krong River Valley. The Da Krong is the principal route into the A Shau Valley. It is about 4.5 miles south of the Ba Long Valley. Other Marine regiments operated north of QL-9 toward the DMZ and to the south of QL-9 in Base Area 101. South of the highway the Marines reopened abandoned landing zones (LZ) left by the 1ˢᵗ Air Cavalry Division when it redeployed out of I Corps or established new positions on key terrain mountain tops and traveled to them using helicopters provided by III MAF assets at Danang. The LZs in Base Area 101 south of QL-9 at the Xe Pon River border crossing point were LZs Snapper, Whisman, Torch, Tenaru, Saigon, and Passport. Those LZs south in Base Area 611 included Henderson, Tun Tavern, Shiloh, Razor, Dallas, Cunningham, and Erskine.[531]

During this January operation. General Davis requested permission to pursue the North Vietnamese into Laos as an exception to the general national policy about not conducting search and destroy missions across the international border. US troops could maneuver into Laos only if engaged at the time to save the US force from an enemy counterattack out of the safe haven back into Vietnam and employ artillery and air strikes across the border against forces that posed a threat. The 9ᵗʰ Marines used these exceptions to justify initiating a raid.[532]

Not only were there intelligence indicators of increased NVA activity in Base Area 101 by March, but also three NVA regiments, the *27th*, *138th*, and the *246th* that had been in North Vietnam were stepping up searches for US and ARVN positions, employing ambushes, sapper attacks against small unit positions, and small unit reconnaissance patrolling south of the DMZ.[533] This activity dictated that the time was right to increase the effort to disrupt NVA initiatives as they moved south and west along the Ho Chi Minh trail in Laos back into South Vietnam. USMC Task Force Hotel at LZ Vandegrift ordered the 4th Marine Regiment to locate, attack, and push the *246th Regiment* that had moved beyond the DMZ into Quang Tri's northwestern portion beginning on March 1st in the area of the Rockpile (Elliott Combat Base).[534]

Meanwhile, Lieutenant General Stilwell, and Lieutenant Colonel Milia met at the Camp Red Devil Tactical Operations Center (TOC) on March 14th to discuss reopening the 16-mile segment of QL-9 from Ca Lu next to Vandegrift Combat Base to the Khe Sanh plain. Once there, the task force would move to the abandoned Khe Sanh Combat Base (KSCB) to begin a combined arms armored reconnaissance-in-force from there along QL-9 to the Laotian border and then conduct search and destroy operations.[535] Geographically, the area from Lang Vei to the international border and then south of QL-9 was known as the Vietnam Salient. It was the location where Vietnamese bulge extended into Laos.

General Abrams, as stated above, ordered the combat base to be abandoned and the QL-9 bridges to be destroyed about six months earlier. Weather caused erosion and landslides during the interim rendering the road to be even more impassable. For this reason, the mission had three phases: repair QL-9; perform reconnaissance in force missions along QL-9 from the north and northwest of the Khe Sanh airfield south to the border with Laos at the Xe Pon River crossing point with its Co Roc Mountains looking down on QL-9 from Laos into Vietnam near the abandoned prison and airfield complex of Lao Bao; and then turning south following the river to Route 926 (Laos) – Route 616 (Vietnam) located 8.1 miles south of the destroyed Lang Vei camp along QL-9 that was an entry route into Vietnam's Base Area 101 from the Laotian portion of the Ho Chi Minh Trail from Laos into Vietnam. Geographically, this area was known as the Vietnam Salient. It was the location where the Vietnamese bulge extended into Laos.[536]

The engineering task confronting TF Remagen was daunting. Initially, QL-9 was flat for 6.2 miles. It turned into a very narrow road with many tight turns for the subsequent 5 miles through a valley that was bordered on the south side by the Song Thach Han River and on the north side by mountains that ended at the edge of the road. The road was barely wide enough for a 12-foot-wide M48A3 tank to negotiate. The result was the tanks could neither rotate their turrets to the north nor elevate their main guns south toward the cliffs on the opposite bank of the river. Finally, the column had to climb a 45 percent grade to reach the plateau. It took three days for the task force to reform on the plain to begin the next portion of the mission.

Stilwell told Milia he could select the organization of his task force to perform the mission. Milia requested a mechanized infantry company, a reinforced company of armored engineers, and a section (two) of M42A1 twin 40-mm Self-Propelled Air Defense Artillery (ADA) Guns (Dusters). These were in addition to the 1-77 Armor's organic units.[537]

Instead of requesting an artillery battery from the Red Devil's organic 5th Battalion 4th Artillery which had 155mm SP howitzers, Milia asked that a battery of 105mm SP artillery be attached to the Task Force. His reason was that only this caliber of artillery ammunition had the *beehive* round in Vietnam. Beehive was the nickname of the M546 APERS-T 105mm anti-personnel round of ammunition containing 8,000 eight-grain steel flechettes (darts). Each had a tail for stability during flight. The artillery round had a fuse setting allowing the dispersal to occur as soon as the round passed the howitzer's muzzle and up to 100 seconds afterward. [538]

M48A3 tanks also had antipersonnel ammunition for their 90mm main guns. There were two types: first, the M336 90mm cannister antipersonnel tank cylindrical round covered by cardboard that contained 1,281 steel pellets which were spread out to 273 yards as soon as they left the muzzle. The second tank main gun antipersonnel round was the tank version of beehive. The M377 antipersonnel round held 5,600 flechettes controlled by a variable time fuse that could be adjusted to explode and disperse the tiny darts at the muzzle or out to 2.5 miles.[539] Both types of 90mm rounds were part of the basic load of the tank's main gun ammunition that also included high explosive (HE), high explosive antitank (HEAT), and white phosphorous (WP). The number of rounds of each ammunition type in a basic load was determined by the battalion commander who had to anticipate the organization and transport of the most likely enemy to be encountered: dismounted infantry, infantry in armored or other vehicles, tanks, and to mark targets or establish smoke screens.

The Task Force Remagen organization is below:

Team B:

B/1-61(-1plt) and 2/C/1-77, commanded by Captain David Porreca who replaced Captain Jack Langston.

Team C:

C/1-77(-1 plt) and 3/B/1-61(M), commanded by Captain Darrell Blalock followed by Captain Patrick Sullivan.

Task Force Control:

D/1-77 (-) commanded by Captain Emerson Addington

A/7 Engineers (-) led by First Lieutenant Lawrence Marlin.

Scout Platoon: led by First Lieutenant Bruce Goldsmith

Heavy Mortar (4.2inch) Platoon: led by First Lieutenant Rance Sopko who had been a tank platoon leader from Fort Carson to LZ Nancy

C/1-40 Arty (105-mm SP)

1-77 Armor Ground Surveillance Section (two AN/PPS-4 Ground Surveillance Radar sets each mounted in a M-113 APC).

Section /C/1-44 ADA (SP) [540]

The Task Force departed LZ Nancy at 8 AM on March 16th and moved to Fire Base Ca Lu at a bend in QL-9 that evening where its controlling headquarters became the 3MARDIV's Task Force Hotel. The first phase began the next morning with Goldsmith's five M-113 Armored Cavalry Assault Vehicle (ACAV) Scout platoon departing Ca Lu leading and securing the Lieutenant Marlin's equipment including two Armored Vehicle Launch Bridges (AVLB), minesweeping equipment, and bulldozers from the 11th Engineer Brigade.

The scouts swept the road for mines and fired into likely ambush sites. The engineers moved forward leapfrogging their two AVLBs each carrying a 62-foot (19 meters) scissors bridge mounted on a modified M60 tank. Engineer squads with their bulldozers followed working on every obstacle they encountered by building bypasses, emplacing culverts and removing weather- and manmade-caused blockages. When an AVLB was required before building the bypass, the scissors bridge was deployed on one side and then retrieved on the other side when the bypass was finished.

Eight checkpoints (A-H) were established for this phase. The goal was to reach Checkpoint G which was the only clearing along QL-9 wide enough for one vehicle to pass another and for the Heavy Mortar platoon and artillery battery to establish firing positions. It was also the last checkpoint on the valley floor. The scouts and engineers reached this position by the late afternoon of March 17th.[541] Checkpoint H was the location of a wide and unfordable river at the beginning of the climb to the plateau. Initially, a high-level truss bridge had been built and subsequently destroyed as were the abutments. A replacement pontoon bridge washed away where a bypass once existed. The width of the gap was unmeasurable using aerial reconnaissance because the bridge abutments no longer existed. Milia stated that when the AVLB placed its bridge, all present cheered because they had three feet to spare.[542]

The scout platoon and engineers reached the Khe Sanh plain by dark on the 18th. Below, the dismounted infantry of B/1-61 Inf (M) was securing the flanks of Checkpoint G, and C/1-40 105-mm SP was in its firing positions ready to provide fire support to the scout platoon and engineers 1250 feet above on the plateau.[543]

Captain Blalock began C/1-77 Armor's move with the TF's command group and combat trains following behind his company to the plain at 8:00am on the 19th. Goldsmith's scouts reached the destroyed Khe Sanh City (KSC) by 11 am where the TF Command Post would be located. The 86-tracked vehicle force with its tanks, APCs, M-88 VTRs, M-106 4.2-inch mortar carriers, M-577 Command Post Vehicles, and M-728 Combat Engineer Vehicle (CEV) reached KSC by 1 pm. When the AVLB at Checkpoint H at the base of the plateau was removed, TF Remagen could only be reached and resupplied by air.[544]

The Modified Table of Organization and Equipment (MTOE) under which the Steel Tigers were organized at Fort Carson provided for a support company (D/1-77). The value-added of this organization instead of combining the support functions into the control of a single headquarters and headquarters company (HHC) when the battalion went into combat on September 13, 1968, in Operation *SULLIVAN*. The S4 (logistics officer) was able to concentrate on his tasks of planning, procuring, and loading items for transport, and the D/1-77 Company commander could focus on his responsibilities to turn the plans into reality by distributing the supplies, parts, and exchanged equipment end items to where they were needed.

Figures 6.5 through 6.9 present the area of operations for Task Force Remagen and its follow-ons that occurred on the Khe Sanh plain during March 16 - July 1969.

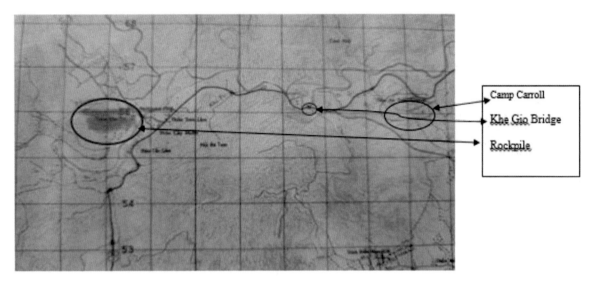

Figure 6.5 QL 9 to The Rockpile
Map Courtesy Lawrence Wills, Graphics by author

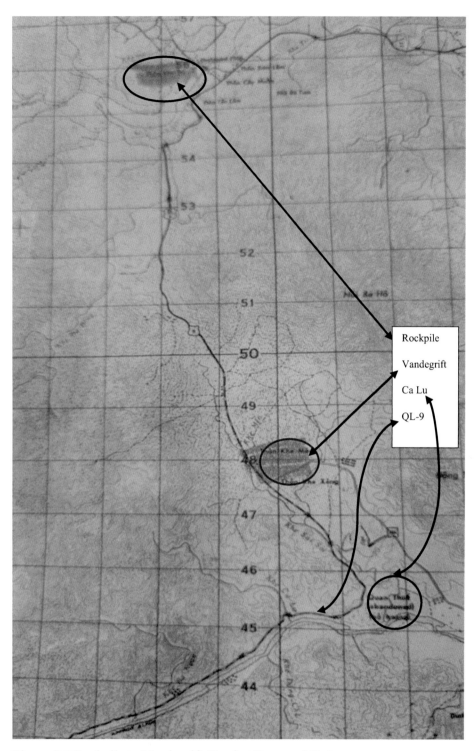

Figure 6.6 Rockpile to Vandegrift Combat Base and Ca Lu
Map Courtesy, Lawrence Wills, graphics by author

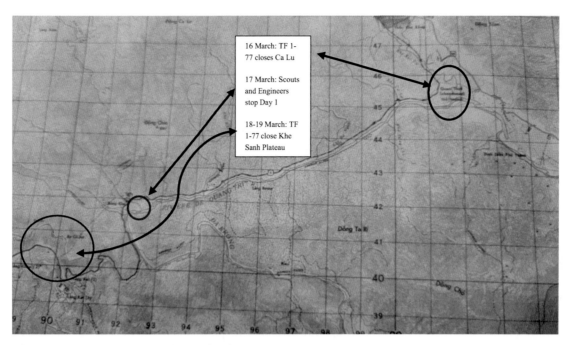

16 March: TF 1-77 closes Ca Lu

17 March: Scouts and Engineers stop Day 1

18-19 March: TF 1-77 close Khe Sanh Plateau

Figure 6.7 QL 9 Ca Lu to Khe Sanh Plateau 1969
Map Courtesy, Lawrence Wills, graphics by author

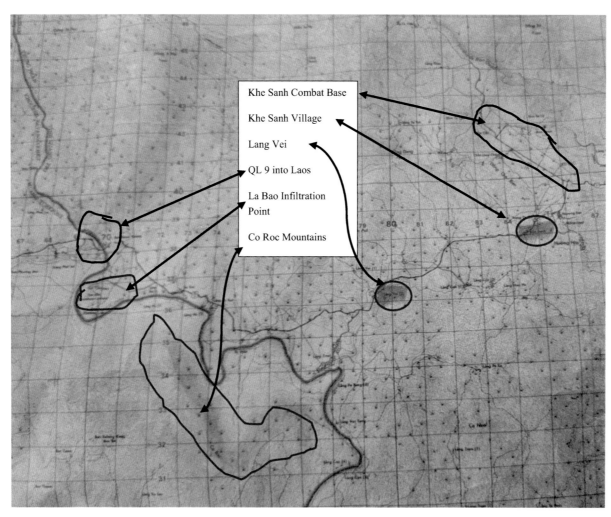

Khe Sanh Combat Base

Khe Sanh Village

Lang Vei

QL 9 into Laos

La Bao Infiltration
Point

Co Roc Mountains

Figure 6.8 Khe Sanh to Laos
Map Courtesy of Lawrence Wills, Graphics by Author

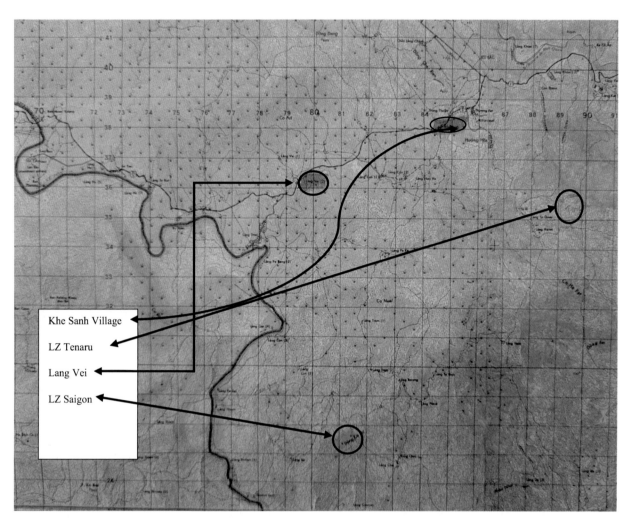

Figure 6.9 Lang Vei to 1969 Area of Operations
Map Courtesy of Lawrence Wills, Graphics by Author

Task Force Remagen proved the prescience of this force structure for the tank battalion of an independent brigade. The logistics required to support operations on the Khe Sanh plain was always present when it was needed. The Red Devil Brigade positioned a forward support element (FSE) at Ca Lu where the supplies of food, water, ammunition, fuel and repair parts required to support those on the plain could be positioned and prepared for helicopter transport. The task force's field trains were located there under the control of the 1-77's logistics officer. Captain Neil Howell. The combat trains on the plain which included medics in tracked medical vehicles, and mechanics and members of the support platoon in tracked support and recovery vehicles were under the command of Captain Emerson Addington, the commander of D Company.[545]

Table 6. 1 below summarizes the scale of resupplying TF Remagen.

Item	Quantity
Average CH-47 resupply loads	15
Rations	93 pallets
Fuel	76,000 gallons (gasoline and diesel)
Other petroleum, oil, and lubricants	2,000 gallons
Major caliber ammunition	18,000 rounds
Small arms ammunition	225,000
Major component repair parts	50 engines, transmissions, track, final drives, starters
Tracked vehicle engine repair	13; tank powerpacks transported by CH-47 to the FSE for direct exchange

Table 6.1 Logistics Requirement Summary: Task Force Remagen
Source: Adapted from Carmelo P Milia, "Task Force to Khe Sanh," Armor: The Magazine of Mobile Warfare Vol. 79, No 3 May-June 1970, p. 46.

Upon consolidating the task force at KSC, the reconnaissance-in-force began moving along QL-9. It stopped at the abandoned Lang Vei Special Forces and its four destroyed Soviet-made PT -76 Amphibious Tanks. Three NVA battalions with 12 PT-76 tanks overran a US Special Forces A-Team and its Vietnamese Civil Irregular Defense Group on beginning on the night of February 6-7, 1968.

Attacking the North Vietnamese in their safe areas across the borders of Laos and Cambodia was a desire of all US commanders in the histories of the Vietnam War. Exploiting success into a cross-border location where the enemy knew that they would safe was not a decision a commander on the scene was allowed to make. The rules of engagement stated earlier regarding the 9th Marines' cross-border raid in January permitted Lieutenant Colonel Milia to fire artillery from Vietnam into Laos. He requested approval to confirm that the rules were unchanged and received permission to proceed. He chose April 10th just before dark and moved his artillery battery secured by the scout platoon and the headquarters tank section from Khe Sanh into Lang Vei. He began an unobserved artillery raid into Laos at targets that had been identified by XXIV Corps artillery intelligence. He stated that the dark sky looked like a display of fireworks on July 4th when secondary explosions occurred. The artillery raid ended at about 11:30 pm and the column returned to its Khe Sanh night position.[546]

Milia added a footnote to this action. He had been an armor officer since June 1950. On the night of the artillery raid, he heard a sound from his tank for the first time. It was the noise a torsion bar in a roadwheel housing makes when it snaps. To move the tank at any speed would have resulted in a thrown track, so he ordered his crew to move it slowly back to the battalion's night position escorted by a scout section. He rode back to the battalion's location inside a scout platoon ACAV with the rest of column.[547]

Task Force Remagen reached Route 926-616 and conducted search and destroy missions from March 26th to March 30th.

Task Force Remagen April 11-April 29

Task Force 1-61 Infantry (M) commanded by Lieutenant Colonel David Hartigan relieved Lieutenant Colonel Milia and TF 1-77 Armor and became the control headquarters for TF Remagen on April 11th. Additionally, the 2nd troop of the ARVN 7th Cavalry Squadron (2/7 Cav ARVN) that was based at Camp Evans and reinforced by the 1st ARVN Regiment's reconnaissance company arrived on the Khe Sanh plain on April 20th and placed under the OPCON of Hartigan's command.[548]

During the March 16-April 11 phase when the Steel Tigers controlled Remagen, Milia estimated that the force operated within a 62 square mile area.[549] There was little North Vietnamese response during the period. A combined arms force of tanks, mechanized infantry, self-propelled artillery, armored engineers, and self-propelled ADA guns maneuvered where only dismounted infantry transported by helicopters had done so previously.

Losses during Phase 1 were minimal. There were 2 Killed in Action (KIA), 13 Wounded in Action (WIA), and one M48A3 tank, one M88 VTR, one M548 tracked cargo carrier, one M113 personnel carrier and one bulldozer were combat losses and buried at Khe Sanh.[550]

Lieutenant Colonel Milia reported that the daily resupply effort averaged 15 CH-47 Chinook helicopter missions This included the following: food, fuel (diesel and Mogas) and other various Petroleum, Oil, and Lubricants (POL), small arms and large caliber ammunition, and repair parts including major end items such as track, engines, transmissions, final drives for tanks and the M-113 family of tracked vehicles, and suspension system parts. He gave an example of three days in the lives of crews and mechanics maintaining their vehicles where they removed and directly exchanged 13 engines

The Steel Tigers' command group, mortar and scout platoons, and the Combat Service Company (D/1-77) departed the Khe Sanh plain at 1:45 pm for the 60.6 mile road march to LZ Nancy which they began reaching their base at 8:30 pm.[551]

Task Force Remagen's force structure remained the same for the second phase, but the order of battle changed. Blalock's C/1-77, now under the command of Captain Patrick Sullivan as of April 1st, remained on the plain and conducted search and clearing missions in the vicinity of Khe Sanh was replaced by A/1-77 commanded by Captain Jerry Brown, but remained on the plateau.. B Company of the 1-61 (M) replaced A/1-61(M). The latter remained on the plateau also with C/1-77 when both companies returned to LZ Nancy and LZ Sharon respectively on April 15th. Hartigan brought his battalion's scout and mortar platoons. The artillery support capability increased with the addition to C/1-40 Arty (105mm SP) of a 3-gun 5/4 Arty 155-mm SP Howitzer Battery and two USMC 8-inch howitzers which broke down before reaching Ca Lu. The Steel Tigers were the last serial in the order of march and towed the howitzers to the Khe Sanh plateau where they arrived that evening after End of Evening Nautical Twilight (EENT). Teams B/1-61, and C/1-77 that had remained at Khe Sanh after April 11th were under control of Lieutenant Colonel Hartigan. They departed the plain on April 15th for LZs Sharon and Nancy, respectively. They also took the 8-inch howitzers off the plain with them. The operable vehicles in the column moved along the recently reopened Route 556 through the Ba Long Valley. The inoperable vehicles were towed along QL-9 and then QL-1 to their home stations. [552]

On April 13th, A/1-77 moved from the Khe Sanh-Lang Vei area on QL-9 to find a road or trail south to move an armored column for the purpose of interdicting the Ho Chi Minh Trail entry crossing into South Vietnam along Route 926 from Laos (616 in RVN). This crossing point was about 2 miles south of LZ Saigon. The purpose of this new trail was to avoid moving along close to the Xe Pon River under the direct observation of the 304th NVA Division elements who were located in the Co Roc mountains and were watching everything. The original plan was to find a road south near Lang Vei which intersected with was eight miles north of Route 926-616.[553] There was none. Captain Brown had to build one without engineer support through the vegetation and mountainous terrain. The effort took several days to reach the Route 926-616 crossing point that was south of LZ Saigon on April 21st Brown established a night defensive position on the Ho Chi Minh Trail entry route and began his team's return to LZ Saigon on April 22nd as Team A/1-61 passed through Team A/1-77. The mechanized infantry spent the rest of that day searching and clearing east along Route 926-616 in the Vietnam Salient. Both companies began moving back slowly to KSC on April 23rd minesweeping the newly constructed road. They reached their destination on the 24th and began performing maintenance prior to the planned departure of TF Remagen from the plain on the 26th.[554]

A major enemy reaction to the second phase of TF Remagen did not begin until 3:30 am on April 25th when an estimated battalion attacked C/1-40 (105mm SP) and the 7th

ARVN located near the abandoned Khe Sanh Combat Base and KSC. The attack began with an hour-long mortar preparation and was followed by a ground attack using satchel charges, one flamethrower, rocket-propelled grenade (RPG) launchers, small arms, and Chinese hand grenades. The NVA broke contact at about 6:00 am. The retrograde operation from the plain was delayed until the 28th while US troops searched for the enemy. One A/1-77 tank was damaged and three ARVN personnel carriers were destroyed. US and ARVN losses included 2 US, 8 ARVN, and 1 Australian advisor Killed in Action; and 3 US, 40 ARVN, and 2 US advisors Wounded in Action[555].

A second attack began at 3:00 am on April 28th and this time it was directed against A/1-61 and A/1-77 with probing attacks against the Task Force command post area and the ARVN Cavalry Troop. The cavalry troop moved to the US units' position and began sweeping the area. The NVA broke contact at about 5:30 am leaving 34 Killed in Action behind and abandoning the same models of weapons employed on the first attack. US equipment losses included three damaged C/1-40 vehicles: two damaged 105mm SP howitzers and one M548 cargo carrier. One M48A3 tank , one M113A1 APC, one water trailer, and a second M548 loaded with 105mm artillery ammunition that had exploded were combat losses and destroyed.[556]

The second phase of Task Force Remagen began leaving the Khe Sanh plain at 7 am on April 29th. Anticipating that the NVA had mined QL-9 following the two previous attacks, the trip to Ca Lu was slow and very deliberate. The lead element reached Ca Lu at 12:46pm and began the 50-mile trip back to LZ Sharon. The last unit reached the home station at 9:50 pm.[557]

Operation *MASSACHUSETTS BAY*, April 23-June 15

Rice denial, interdicting NVA and VC troop movements, and pacification operations continued to be the missions of the Red Devil Brigade after Operation *NAPOLEON SALINE & MARSHALL MOUNTAIN* ended. the AO remained the same in eastern and southeastern Quang Tri Province. During this period, the brigade's task organization is listed below:

- TF 1-77 Armor (- Co B): A/1-77 Arm; C/1-77 A/4-12 Cav; and C/1-11 Inf;
- TF 1-11 Inf (- Co C) ((A/1-11, B/1-11, B/1-77 Arm))
- TF 1-61 Inf (Mech): 1-61 (Mech); C/1-40 Arty

• The Brigade's organic artillery battalion, 5-4 Arty (155mm SP), and the 2-94 Arty (8 inch, SP), and C/1-40 Arty (105mm SP) provided the artillery support for the operation.[558]

Task Force 1-77 Armor controlled the missions assigned to it for the operation. The composition of changed weekly during the operation beginning April 23rd and ending on June 14th. Initially, the only Steel Tiger unit in the task force on the first day of the operation, April 23rd was C/1-77 just recently returned from Task Force Remagen Phase 1 at Khe Sanh. A/1-77 joined C/1-77 on April 30th after the second phase of Khe Sanh concluded. These two Steel Tiger companies were core units of 1-77's missions. Other Red Diamond Brigade units joining the task force in one-week increments included the following: A/4-12 Cav; 1/A/4-12 Cav; 2/A/4-12 Cav A/1-11 Inf; C/1-11 Inf; A/1-61 Inf (M); B/1-61 Inf (M); C/1-61 Inf (M); and C/3-5 Cav.[559]

Supporting *MASSACHUSETTS BAY* were the Brigade Aviation Section's four UH-1H utility (Huey) helicopters used for reconnaissance, command and control, Ranger unit insertions and extractions, and backup Medevac missions. The four OH-6A Light Observation helicopters performed reconnaissance and command and control missions while 3MARDIV CH-47 and CH-53 helicopters were available for resupply where and when needed if overland resupply could not be employed or to augment it. Army, Navy, and Marine Air fixed wing and helicopter support were available on missions that were preplanned and immediate.

Artillery support was provided by two batteries from the 5-4 Arty (155mm SP), 2-94 Artillery (8-inch), and C Btry/1-40 Arty 105mm.[560]

There was little contact with the enemy beginning in 1969. By the time of *MASSACHUSETTS BAY*, POWs stated that units of the *7th NVA Front* were moving back into Base Area 101 at nearly full strength from Laos. One sapper(*K-10*), one infantry (*K-14*), and one artillery battalion (*K-34*) were identified, and it was likely that additional 7th Front units were in Base Area 101 also but had not been identified yet.[561] By January 1969, the *812th NVA Regiment* was present. This regiment was subordinate to the *324B NVA Division*.[562]

During the period following the March 17-April 29, the 3rd and 4th regiments of the 3MARDIV were operating between QL-9 and the DMZ in the north and Gio Linh (A2) in the east on QL 1 and the Laotian border in the west.[563]

Task Force 1-77 began *MASSACHUSETTS BAY* with an April 28 – May 3 cordon and search of the area along the Quang Tri-Thua Thien border by A/4-12 Cav and C/1-61 Inf (M). The other task force units, A/1-77, C/1-11, and C/3-5 Cav, performed search and destroy missions south and southwest of LZ Nancy. Contact with 15-20 NVA was made at 2:40 am on May 4th by C/3-5 with no results except blood trails. [564] One tank- and one infantry- heavy team initiated an attack to seize and search an area on May 8th. No enemy contact was made, but recently occupied bunkers and huts discovered indicated that an NVA unit had been there and moved on.[565]

Three 122mm rockets hit LZ Nancy from the south on May 17th. As LZ Nancy was the southernmost base in the 3MARDIV's area of responsibility, the indicator was that the NVA discovered the division's boundary with the 101st Airmobile Division and was using it as a route into populated areas.[566] Another rocket attack on LZ Nancy occurred on May 19th, but this time from the west. Task force units were sent to sweep both areas. In one, they found individual equipment including a pistol belt, canteen, and loose small arms ammunition. Several empty 122mm rocket containers. The sweep units captured three enemy soldiers. Four rockets were fired at LZ Nancy on May 25th, and the NVA launched a ground attack on the 5/4 Arty (155mm SP) battery stationed at the Hai Lang crossroad between QL 1 north to Quang Tri and the road east to Wunder Beach. This battery's position was secured by A/1-77Armor's second platoon. North Vietnamese combat engineers (sappers) attempted to penetrate the concertina wire surrounding the position but were unable to do so.[567]

The infantry companies that were part of TF 1-77 made contact with NVA small sized units and discovered NVA infiltration trails and bunker complexes during the Steel Tigers' portion of Massachusetts Bay between April 23d and June 9th. The NVA did not reveal themselves during the operation's remaining five days. Several captured NVA soldiers and documents identified the North Vietnamese units encountered all which were part of the 7th Front that retreated into Laos after Tet 1968 and were returning to Base Area 101 in Quang Tri Province.[568]

Operation *UTAH MESA*, Joint Task Force Guadalcanal, June 12-July 9

Intelligence collected during the late April-June 1969 period indicated that the *24th Regiment* of the NVA's *304th Division* with its three battalions had been moving into South Vietnam from Laos using Route 926, a short distance south of LZ Saigon and the Xe Pon River crossing point at Lao Bao on QL-9 where the enemy moved toward Lang Vei and east. A previously unknown independent Sapper company was also identified. The intelligence reports estimated that about 40 percent of the 2,430-man *24th Regiment* was not combat ready. Impacting readiness had been malaria, US and ARVN ground, air, and artillery strikes, lack of food, and inexperience because the troops completed basic training shortly before deploying south on the Ho Chi Minh Trail. Nonetheless, the *24th* and its support units was the second increment of the *304th Division's* to return to Vietnam.[569]

The Steel Tigers went to the Khe Sanh plain again beginning in June 1969. The name of the operation changed from Task Force Remagen to Operation *UTAH MESA*. This was much larger than the previous battalion-sized missions. *UTAH MESA* was a joint US and ARVN initiative controlled by Task Force Hotel also known as 3MARDIV Forward at Vandegrift. The Steel Tigers' Company B was attached to Lieutenant Colonel Hartigan's 1-61 Infantry (M). Task Force 1-61 was codenamed Task Force Mustang. The larger US part of *UTAH MESA* was named Joint Task Group Guadalcanal (JTTG) and included the 1st, 2d, and 3rd battalions of the 9th Marine Regiment.

1-61(M) (-1 Co)

Company B/1-61(M) commanded by Captain David Porecca

Company C/1-61(M) commanded by Captain William Starr

B/1-77 Armor commanded by Captain Donald Cummings

Section/1-44 Artillery (40mm SP)

Platoon/A/7th Engr

  2 Squads A/7 Engr

  2 AVLBs

  2 Bulldozers A/7 Engr

  1 Bulldozer 11th Engr

Additionally, there were five artillery batteries assigned to direct support. Four were 105mm and one was 155mm. Three batteries were from the 12th Marine Regiment. The USMC 105mm and the 155mm batteries were towed artillery. The fourth battery was the Army's B/1-40 Arty (105mm SP).[570]

The 3rd Battalion, 2nd ARVN Regiment arrived by helicopter at KSC bn June 12th and moved northeast of KSCB and QL-9 to begin search and destroy operations to the west.

The 2nd Battalion, 2nd ARVN Regiment landed on June 13th. The 1st Battalion 9th Marines (1-9 Marines) began its operations northeast of Khe Sanh on June 12th. This unit remained a component of *UTAH MESA* until June 23d. Initially, its mission was to secure the flanks of TF Mustang as it moved from Ca Lu up to the Khe Sanh plateau. From that day through the end of the 28-day operation, a unit or units in *UTAH MESA* engaged the enemy. The 1-9 Marines experienced its first encounter at about 10 pm on the 12th when a D/1-9 Marine detonated a booby trap hidden in a tree. [571]

June 15-16:

Task Force Mustang departed LZ Sharon, arrived at Ca Lu on June 15th, and began moving to the Khe Sanh plain the next morning beginning at 6 am. The Steel Tigers were the last serial in the march order. One of the maintenance tasks performed before beginning the movement was checking track tension. Despite the preparation, which included the column's moderate-to-slow speed and deliberate movement along the narrow portion of QL-9 even when tempered by foreknowledge of the road's narrowness and hairpin turns, the column came to a stop when one tank threw a track negotiating around a tree whose ground had been stirred loose by all of the previous tracked vehicles in the serials. There was no course of action except to repair it and that took what seemed to be days; nevertheless, B/1-77 closed into its night position on the plain at 7:45 pm on June 16th.[572]

The 2nd Battalion 9th Marines (2-9 Marines) and the 3rd Battalion 9th Marines (3-9 Marines) were controlled initially by Task Force Hotel from Vandegrift Combat Base. Control of 3-9 Marines by JTTG occurred when it relieved 1-9 Marines on June 23rd. This unit remained with *UTAH MESA* through July 7th. The 2-9 Marines joined the operation during the July 2-6 window.[573]

The command posts for Task Force Mustang and JTTG were collocated first at LZ Hawk. the abandoned KSCB, and later at LZ Tenaru south of Lang Vei. Lieutenant Colonel Hartigan kept one of his companies in reserve. Colonel Lewis R. Bauman, Deputy Commander of the 1-5 Inf Bde (M), commanded JTTG and kept the Red Devil Brigade's security platoon and the 407th Radio Research Detachment under his control at the command post located at KSCB.[574]

June 17: Team Armor secured the area around the destroyed KSC for the helicopter landing of the 1-9 Marines. It consisted of 3/B/1-77 and a mechanized infantry platoon each from Companies B and C, respectively. Team B with 1/B/1-77 Armor attached made contact with 4-5 NVA. The team employed its organic weapons and called for an artillery strike. A tank from 2/B/1-77 Armor that was attached to Team C detonated a mine but there were no casualties.

June 18: Team B was attacked by approximately 100 NVA beginning at 3:35 am. The NVA penetrated Tm B's perimeter. Fighting was at close quarters. Some climbed on the tanks to destroy them. Each tank defended itself and fired its machine guns at the neighboring tanks to clear the enemy from them. Platoon Sergeant Jesse Smith fired a High Explosive Anti-Tank (HEAT) round into an enemy soldier who was holding onto the flash suppressor of Tank 14's main gun as he attempted to climb over the front of the tank to attack one of the turret hatches with a satchel charge. He failed. The tank did receive an RPG round into the side of the turret. It blew Smith out of the tank commander's position onto the back deck. Although wounded and shaken, he returned to his position and continued fighting the tank. He insisted that he walk to the medevac helicopter later. The NVA withdrew at about 5:30 am.[575]

The North Vietnamese left 38 KIAs and took their WIAs with them. One POW was captured. Nine AK-47 assault rifles, 5, RPGs, 50 Chinese hand grenades, and 100 pounds of satchel charges were counted after the battle.[576]

There were 10 US soldiers killed in the battle including the Tank 15 commander, Sergeant Michael L. Hodge. Jim Wilsman, Hodge's gunner, took over and fought the NVA from the tank commander's position for the rest of the night. Sergeant Hodge and medic Specialist 4 James R. Dolvin were B Company's first fatalities since arriving in Vietnam in July 1968.[577]

Throughout the remainder of the 18th, Companies A and D/1-9 Marines received small arms fire beginning at 7:00am. Later, D/1-9 Marines was airlifted to Team B's location to reinforce it. Shortly after noon, a reconnaissance squad from C/1-9 Marines received fire from a 12.7mm (Soviet or Chinese) heavy machinegun. Although the squad destroyed the machinegun, reinforcements received fire all around their positions. This developed into a battle that lasted until 7:00 pm. [578]

June 19:

C/1-9 Marines found 60-70 bunkers and saw movement. Air and artillery strikes were requested. Team B made contact with an unknown size enemy force at 8:40 pm. A *Spooky* gunship (AC-47) was requested.[579] At 3:40 am next morning, the NVA initiated a second major attack Team B and D/1-9 that the NVA ended at about 5:40 am.

The Spooky gunship was a converted World War II Douglas cargo C-47 twin-engine fixed-wing aircraft that carried three left side-mounted Gatling guns capable of firing 2,000 7.62mm rounds per minute and 48 flares that illuminated the target area. Every fifth machinegun round was a tracer. These combined with the rate of fire made it look as though it was delivering red rain, hence the Air Force's nickname *Puff the Magic Dragon*. The NVA and VC called it the *Dragon Plane*. It could orbit at 3,000 feet with an air speed of 120 knots. Its range was 2,175 miles giving it a long loiter time.[580]

The Spooky aircraft was flown from the Air Force's the 14th Special Operations Wing located at Da Nang. It took immediate requests for air support time to arrive on station. The time lapse for Spooky to reach the Khe Sanh plain was about 30 minutes. The author visited the squadron enroute during his journey to Cam Ranh Bay to meet his flight back to the United States. After discussing the impact of the mission flown in support of Team Armor defending LZ Saigon later in Operation *UTAH MESA*, the pilots remarked that they appreciated the visit because they rarely received feedback about their missions.[581]

June 20: Team Armor was ordered to move from TF Mustang Reserve toward the road that A/1-77 Armor constructed to LZ Saigon during TF Remagen. The column stopped at Team B's location for a short time and then continued along QL-9 and went into a night defensive position at Lang Vei. The entry into the position was a narrow trail on a slight incline. It was searched and probed for mines. The NVA often buried mines deeper than mine detectors could register them. All of the APCs, the M88 ARV, and the first three tanks reached and deployed within the abandoned Special Forces camp. By this time, the tracks on the vehicles had churned enough of the dirt that the fourth tank detonated a mine. No crewmen inside the tank were wounded, but six soldiers nearby including three mechanics were. Medevacs were called and the tank had to be moved off the entry trail onto flat ground for repairs. Damage to the tank included three sets of two roadwheels each, three sets of support rollers, torsion bars, and track. All of the parts had to be flown from the Forward Support Element at LZ Vandegrift. The work began almost immediately by those at Lang Vei preparing the tank to be repaired[582]

Team Armor constructed its night defensive position and its forward observer prepared the artillery support fire plan. During the night, the infantry listening posts reported voices in the low ground concealed by foliage on the opposite side of QL-9. Artillery concentrations were requested and fired. On one occasion, the firing unit stopped its fire missions to recheck the firing plan data. Then, it fired two rounds from each howitzer to test the accuracy of these data. The rounds landed in the middle of the Lang Vei defensive perimeter. Fortunately, the forward observer knew there was an error when he was told the rounds had been fired and he began shouting cease fire into his microphone. The tank crews buttoned down inside their tanks and the infantry got into or crawled under their vehicles. The battery-two test mission of 12 rounds resulted in no injuries. Overall, the artillery fire stopped any probe or dedicated attack against the position.

June 22d:

Team Armor began repairs to the damaged tank as soon as the repair parts arrived. Later that day, D/1-9 Marines arrived to reinforce Team Armor. Team Armor received several visitors that day. Lieutenant Colonel Milia arrived to introduce his successor Lieutenant Colonel Miller who would formally take command on the 23rd . Lieutenant Colonel Pickarts visited to inspect the extent of the damage and progress on the repairs. Both Milia and Pickarts said farewell to B/1-77Armor before returning to the US following the end of their 12-month tours of duty. The XXIV Corps Commander, Lieutenant General Stilwell arrived to visit with Team Armor and D/1-9 Marines that was commanded by Captain Leonard Chapman who was the son of the Commandant of the U S. Marine Corps.[583]

Task Force Mustang and the JTGG command posts moved from their position near Khe Sanh Combat Base to LZ Tenaru. This location was created on the dominant terrain in the area that began the route A/1-77 Armor prepared to LZ Saigon.[584]

June 23:

June 23rd began with helicopters arriving to transport D/1-9 Marines to Fire Support Base Vandegrift. The entire 1st Battalion was replaced by the 3rd Battalion 9th Marines which remained with the UTAH MESA until July 7th. Team Armor completed repairs of the damaged tank and began its move toward LZ Tenaru. Team C/1-61 with 2/B/1-77 began its move to LZ Saigon from Tenaru, respectively.

Late in the afternoon, Team Armor left QL-9 and had two tanks throw tracks when they drove into B-52 bomb craters that were hidden in elephant grass. Each had to be retrieved from and placed onto level ground to repair the tracks. Team Armor established its night defensive position around the damaged tanks. Illumination was fired by the supporting artillery to assist as well as by B company's hip-pocket artillery - a 60-mm mortar acquired from the NVA in 1968 near the DMZ. The work required several hours to complete and lasted well into the darkness.[585]

June 24:

The day began early. An ambush team from 1/K/3-9 Marines identified 10 NVA at about 1:15 am and attacked them. The ambush team was about 80 yards out from the company's night positions. Subsequently, another team was attacked by an estimated two squads. This was followed at the same time by two NVA platoons attacking K/3-9's main defensive position. A Spooky gunship came on station and the fighting lasted until about 5:30 am when the NVA broke contact. K/3-9 lost three Marines and 14 wounded. Searching the area, they found 29 NVA dead, documents, small arms, an RPG, rifle grenades and other items.[586]

Team Armor departed its night defensive position for LZ Tenaru where it stopped to meet B/1-40 (105mm SP) Artillery, and the two-duster section from the 1-44 Arty (SP 40mm) . The column continued to LZ Saigon where it moved into positions. The tank platoon moved to the northern portion of the LZ where the fields of fire would be best for the main guns. Team Armor's two attached mechanized infantry platoons, 1/B/1-61 (M) and 3/C/1-61 (M), moved into positions on the west and east portions sectors, respectively. B/1-40 established its firing positions in the center of the hilltop. Captain William Starr commanded Tm C/1-61. Its positions had 1/C/1-61 and 2/C/1-61 on the east and west sectors, respectively. Team C also had 2/A/1-11 Inf attached in place of 2/B-1-77. It was transported by the Red Devil Brigade's reconnaissance platoon. Team Armor began immediately to prepare its defensive positions adding to the work started by Team C. Initially, fields of fire were cleared, concertina wire was emplaced with trip flares as well as empty drink cans filled with stones affixed to the wire. A bulldozer prepared defilade positions for the armored vehicles. Infantrymen dug fighting positions between their APCs and filled and stacked sandbags on top of the positions for overhead cover[587]

The three company commanders introduced themselves to each other when they first met and began organizing the defense. Lieutenant Colonel Hartigan had designated the senior captain to be the commander of the position. This individual was Team Armor's commander. The three understood that should the base be attacked; no ground force reinforcements could be expected. The technical (artillery and air) assets assigned to support JTGG and Task Force Hotel could be requested, but the response would not be instantaneous. The immediate and sustained response had to come from the troops occupying Saigon.

The daily routines of Teams Armor, and C/1-61(M) when they were not off of the base for other missions, and B/1-40 Artillery were improving fighting positions by increasing overhead cover, using the bulldozer to dig the vehicle defilade positions deeper, performing infantry sweeps of the perimeter area, and firing artillery defensive concentrations during the day and harassing and interdiction (H&I) fire at night. Listening posts (LPs) were sent out nightly with set times for communications checks. Between the end of the perimeter sweeps and before the after-dark placement of the LPs, the troops fired their individual weapons from the concertina wire into the low ground where NVA might be reconnoitering the US base above them. Each tank used the infrared mode of its one million candlepower Xenon searchlight mounted above the main gun on the turret periodically each hour after dark to search the sector of the perimeter it was responsible for.[588]

One creative and experienced Tm C 1/61 (M) non-commissioned officer at LZ Saigon recommended fabricating an additional antipersonnel weapon, he called fougasse. The recipe was a mixture of diesel fuel and a fuel thickener and pouring the mixture into empty 105mm artillery round containers filled with rocks. The detonators used were the model used by claymore antipersonnel mines.[589]

June 25:

Little contact with the NVA occurred on June 25th. Team C including 2/B/1-77 left LZ Saigon to search Route 926-616. The team searched east into South Vietnam until it identified its night defensive position at about 7:20 pm. About an hour before this, in addition to vehicle maintenance and missions away from the base the 3MARDIV's 3rd Reconnaissance Battalion heard vehicle engines and voices and requested an artillery strike about three miles southwest of Team C's position. Additionally, 3-9 Marines began a search and destroy mission. [590]

June 26:

What was routine, June 26th began early. Two companies of NVA attacked the entire perimeter of K/3-9 Marines' night defensive positions beginning at 3:45 am. The Marine company searched the area following the end of the battle at 6:00 am. One POW was found alive and 14 bodies were counted along with a flamethrower, one RPG with 40 rockets, several individual AK-47 and SKS Soviet-made rifles, and 250 Chinese hand grenades and documents.[591]

Team C continued its search and destroy mission in its assigned zone, and Team Armor left LZ Saigon also for Route 926-616 to begin a day-long search. Enroute, Team Armor discovered empty bunker complexes along the way as well as several destroyed Russian-made vehicles. Route 926-616 was well camouflaged. Every stream crossing had underwater fording points constructed with rocks. Handrails and guardrails made from bamboo marked the route. There was no enemy contact made and no evidence of recent activity. Team Armor reached the end of its search area and was ordered back to LZ Saigon. It left the trail and formed a temporary defensive position in an open field and then began receiving 81 mm mortar fire from an undetermined location. The soldiers closed their tank and APC hatches and returned onto the trail back to LZ Saigon.

Simultaneous with Team Armor's experience on the 26th, four of Team C's vehicles detonated mines in its zone. The first incident occurred at 2:15 pm when a bulldozer caused the explosion. Two hours later a 2/B/1-77 tank exploded that Team Armor heard in its search zone and saw the rising smoke from the site. The official report states that the tank hit a mine and there were seven US wounded. The author disputes this entry. There was one US fatality, the tank's driver, and six wounded. A Team C APC struck a mine in the same area at about 6:00 pm with no wounded and then a second 2/B/1-77 tank detonated a shaped charge at 7:00 pm also fatally wounding the driver.

The assessment of the detonations under the two tanks at the time from the author's position some distance away was thought to have been two unexploded US Air Force 500-pound bombs rigged to be electronically activated by hidden NVA soldiers. Both charges exploded under the tank drivers' positions. The three remaining tanks of 2/B/1-77 were reassigned to TF Mustang control at LZ Tenaru.[592]

The bulldozer was repairable and was recovered. The APC and two tanks were declared combat losses. The decision from Task Force Mustang and JTGG was not to attempt to tow the tanks back to LZ Saigon. They were destroyed in place. The tank drivers were Specialist 4th Class Anthony J. Marinelli and Specialist 4th Class Rafael G. Tenorio.[593]

June 27:

Early the next morning, June 27th, but much later than the usual battles that the NVA began occurred at 6:05 am at LZ Tenaru. The 407th Radio Reconnaissance Detachment (the current term would be Signals Intelligence) began detecting radio transmissions from one NVA entity to another. The 407th's challenge was to determine who was talking to whom and their locations. The analysis identified a headquarters and an attack force that was enroute to a US unit's location. .

Lieutenant Colonel Hartigan related the events that follow after Operation *UTAH MESA* ended. The NVA headquarters requested progress reports periodically, and the attack force commander stated that his unit was closing on the target. These reports and replies were exchanged several times and the 407th assessed that the attack force was lost and attempting to correct its movement in the right direction. As time went on, the 407th determined that the objective was LZ Tenaru. Instead of beginning the attack around 3 am that was the pattern that the NVA established during *UTAH MESA*, it began after first light when the NVA ought to have broken contact.

The NVA began a heavy ground attack against the LZ and the Task Force Mustang and 1-9th Marines that was also located at the LZ was at full alert and had been since Tenaru identified as the highly probable objective. The infantry, armor, and artillery defenders responded with their organic weapons. The NVA were unable to penetrate the defensive positions. After the fight ended, 27 NVA dead were found and one POW captured. Twenty AK-47 assault rifles and one SKS rifle, seven RPG-2 and two RPG-7 antitank launchers, documents, and a Soviet-made radio were found. US losses were three killed and 17 wounded.[594] The 407th reported later that radio intercepts of the NVA's reports to the unit's headquarters revealed they killed 250 US troops and destroyed six tanks.[595]

June 28:

Teams ARMOR and C/1-61 (M) used June 28th to continue improving the defensive positions and performing maintenance. A bulldozer improved the tank and APC defilade positions. Soldiers added more sandbags to their fighting positions thereby increasing the overhead protection. The infantry removed the machineguns from their APCs after dark and placed them in their fighting positions. A party from the 3MARDIV's 3rd Reconnaissance Battalion arrived at LZ Saigon with various types of electronic seismic intrusion devices (SIDs) that could be emplaced along likely routes of advance to the perimeter with an electronic readout device in the Team Armor's command post that displayed which devices were being activated. Additionally, the company's forward artillery observer placed the location of each SID in his fire plan so artillery support could respond. B/1-40 prepared its fire plans.[596]

While these activities were occurring at LZ Saigon, two contacts with the enemy occurred. First, a platoon-sized patrol from Team C confronted an NVA sniper at about 10:30 am who ran away. The unit followed him and the NVA initiated a 10-man ambush of the patrol. Second, Company L/3-9 Marines made contact at about 11:00am with an unknown size force dug into well-prepared fighting positions on high ground about three miles northeast of LZ Saigon. The Marines called for air and artillery strikes. The fighting continued for about seven hours, and the NVA still held the high ground when the fighting ended in the late afternoon. [597]

June 29:

A 1/B/1-77 Armor tank attached to Tm B 1-61(M) struck a mine about 11:00 am on June 29th. The explosion blew a roadwheel off and broke the track. There were no injuries. About two hours later, a Tm B 1-61(M) APC struck a second mine near where the tank hit the first mine. There were four US wounded in this incident and the damage to the APC resulted in it being declared a combat loss.[598]

The 3-9 Marines swept the area where its L company had engaged the NVA the day before. The Marines found a huge bunker complex that was estimated to be a regimental headquarters with 1,000 bunkers. They captured 150 Chinese grenades, 20 rifle grenades, one Russian SKS rifle with a grenade launcher adapter. 300 rounds of caliber .30 ammunition, fifty 60-mm mortar rounds, 44 RPG boosters, and 8 anti-tank mines. They did not make contact with the NVA.[599]

The next incident occurred in the evening at LZ Saigon. The SIDs began alerting that there was movement toward the hilltop at about 9:00 pm. The infantry's LPs reported voices and movement about 30 minutes later. All US troops went to full alert. Two hours after the LPs' reports, a trip flare ignited and an RPG was launched into the firebase. LZ Saigon responded. Team Armor's tanks fired the canister rounds that were in their main gun tubes and reloaded for a mad minute firing exercise, and the M88 ARV fired its machineguns into the darkness from its position. The infantry opened fire from their protected ground fighting positions. The perimeter was probed several times during the two-hour fight and the NVA's fire was heavy, but the perimeter was never breached. One infantryman was wounded fatally and five more wounded including a soldier from the B/1-40 whose wounds required an immediate medevac during the attack. A medical evacuation by helicopter in a firefight at night was not a routine request, but the TF Mustang commander demanded it and one arrived. Lieutenant Forman guided the helicopter in, loaded the soldier, and departed.[600]

The NVA withdrew at first light firing only sporadically after about 2:00 am. No enemy casualties were found when the infantry swept the perimeter at dawn; however, there were bloody bandages and blood trails found and followed with no results. Lieutenant

Colonel Hartigan arrived at LZ Saigon and told the Team Armor and Team C commanders that the best intelligence assessment was that the attack was a diversion to cover the withdrawal of the NVA force that L/3-9 Marines fought on the 28th.[601]

June 30:

The activities of the previous two days continued. M Company, 3-9 Marines reported finding the following during their search and of the regimental-size bunker complex: a dead NVA soldier who had been a victim of artillery fire, 2,000 rounds of caliber .50 ammunition, a Chinese antipersonnel device similar to a US Claymore, and an overlay that would fit a 1:25,000 scale map.[602]

The June 29-30 attack had revealed a defensive weakness. Lieutenant Forman, the B/1-77 Executive Officer, got two tank crewmen and formed a resupply team to carry more ammunition to the infantry during the fight. The quantities of ammunition flown to LZ Saigon to replenish that which had been fired indicated that fire discipline needed emphasis. The officers and NCO leadership of the three companies went among their soldiers to emphasize correcting this.[603]

Throughout the two Task Force Remagen phases and Operation *UTAH MESA*, the North Vietnamese established a pattern of attacking US Army and Marine and ARVN units when the initiative was theirs. The NVA's attacks began around 3am and ended at first light. The pattern was known and all learned from it. Meeting engagements were different.

The pattern was repeated during the night of June 30-July 1. LZ Saigon was at 50 per cent alert until 2:30 am on the 1st and then went to 100 percent. A 2/B/1-61 (M) infantryman attached to Team Armor heard movement at 3:45 am in the low ground below his fighting position in the southwest sector of the perimeter and threw a white phosphorous hand grenade that illuminated the area. He saw a North Vietnamese double over. This was followed moments later in the southeast sector by a heavy volume of automatic weapon, mortar, and RPG fire and a ground attack with hand grenades and individual weapons. By then the entire perimeter was responding with 3/B/1-77 Armor firing canister as it did the previous night. B Battery 1-40 Arty (105mm SP) fired illumination rounds and directly firing its beehive ammunition. The Saigon commander requested artillery support and an AC-47 Spooky gunship. He placed Lieutenant Robert Forman in charge of coordinating the air support. Spooky and an aircraft whose callsign was Basketball that dropped illumination flares arrived on station and orbited around the perimeter. Lieutenant Forman guided the placement of fire using a radio from a position next to the perimeter's wire.

While Spooky was approaching, ground artillery had to stop, and the ground commander's permission had to be given for Spooky to fire inside the 110-yard safety zone around the perimeter. Permission was given and Forman placed the fire up to the concertina wire.[604]

The main attack was directed up the hillside in the southwest sector between Tm C's 2/C/1-61 (M) and 2/A/1-11 Inf. The supporting attack was also uphill in the northwest sector against Tm Armor's 1/B/1-61(M) and 3/B/1-77 Armor. The NVA broke contact at about 5:15 am. It was not until dawn, when the infantry swept the perimeter that anyone knew there had been a supporting ground attack because of the ferocity of the defensive fire. The supporting attack was over almost at its outset.

There were 15 NVA bodies found in Team Armor's sector. The sweep of the main attack area found 27 more dead NVA and blood trails. Two wounded soldiers were found under some bodies, but only one survived his wounds. Equipment left by the enemy included: one flamethrower, 15 Bangalore torpedoes, four RPG-2 and -7 rocket launchers, 600 Chinese hand grenades, two machineguns, 11 AK47 assault rifles and one SKS rifle with a grenade launcher, 25 rifle grenades, rice mats to throw over the concertina wire, blocks of TNT, and a Soviet-made radio. The NVA commander moved into a bomb crater with his radio and the defenders exploded the four claymore mines they placed in the crater before the attack began. The radio had a frequency set on it and six additional frequencies written on the case.[605]

US casualties on LZ Saigon were four wounded. In addition, a motionless US soldier was seen on the ground throughout the attack in the Team Armor sector to the rear of the tanks and infantry fighting positions. When the firing subsided, a soldier left his position to move the body out of the path of any tanks or APCs needing to back away from their defilade positions. The body began moving when a second soldier touched him. He was so exhausted from the past days that he had slept through the entire June 30-July 1st action.[606]

The 9th Marine Regiment's units searched their zones on July 1st and discovered widespread bunker complexes. Company K/3-9 found 20, a dead NVA soldier and small numbers of weapons and equipment. Company M/3-9 located 83 bunkers three gas masks and two 57mm recoilless rifle carrying cases. Two K/3-9 platoons found 40 more bunkers, three dead NVA, 60- and 81-mm mortar, and machine gun ammunition, rifle grenades and RPG ammunition.[607]

July 2:

At LZ Saigon, little happened on July 2d. Team Armor and Team C/1-61 (M) swept the areas from the previous nights' attacks and buried the NVA dead using the bulldozer to dig a common grave. A Team B/1-61(M) APC hit a mine at 9:00 am, There were four wounded and the APC was unrepairable, It was a combat loss. A Soviet-made antitank mine was discovered nearby about 90 minutes later.[608]

Task Force Hotel placed the 2-9 Marines under OPCON of JTGG at about 7:30 am on the morning of 2 July. The battalion was airlifted into the vicinity of KSC and the combat base. The NVA fired 82 mm mortars onto the 2-9 Marine's position from 9:40 am to 8:15 pm. One company of 2-9 made contact with two NVA and fired on them at about 1:30pm. The NVA ran away, but the company found stores of rice, fighting holes and 10 bunkers.[609]

The 3-9th Marines continued sweeping its zone, and K/3-9 Marines reported finding 100 bunkers, 60mm and 82mm mortar ammunition and caliber .50 machinegun ammunition at 4 pm.[610]

July 3-7:

Team Armor performed maintenance including replacing tank track on the tanks at LZ Saigon. Palettes of track were airlifted where work began. Infantry patrols from Teams B/1-61(M) and Tm C/1-61 and the Second and Third Battalions of the 9th Marines continued their search and destroy missions discovering bunker complexes, finding various types and quantities, usually small of ammunition, NVA bodies who had been killed by artillery and fighting small NVA units ranging from less than five to as many as a ten. It became clear at LZ Saigon and from visits by the Lieutenant Colonel Hartigan, that the intensity of the past 19 days had diminished.[611]

Documents and POWs captured as well as *Hoi Chanhs* (defectors) reported that Task Force Mustang and the Marines had been engaging the *304th NVA Division's 24th Regiment* with its three battalions and a reinforced independent combat engineer company. The division headquarters was in the caves on the Co Roc mountains on the Laotian side of the Xe Pon River.[612]

A helicopter carrying the JTGG commander Colonel Bauman arrived at LZ Saigon on July 4th. He brought ice cream wrapped in ice inside a sleeping bag for everyone at the base could celebrate Independence Day.

The 2-9 Marines were withdrawn by helicopter from the AO to Vandegrift Combat Base beginning in the morning of July 6th. The 3-9 Marines left the next morning for Vandegrift. Team Armor, Team C, and B/1-40 Arty (105mm SP) were alerted to depart LZ Saigon on July 7th. Their objective was KSC where they would secure the intersection of QL-9 and the road to the KSCB. This was the same location that Team Armor secured on June 17th for the arrival of the 1-9 Marines' helicopters to land for the battalion to begin operating in its AO on the plain. The signal to begin the move from LZ Saigon would be a B-52 arc light strike that was scheduled to begin at 8:00 am.[613]

Eight o'clock came and nothing appeared to happen. There were no aircraft visible and no sounds of aircraft, but the Co Roc mountains exploded in black and gray smoke that stretched about a half-mile or longer. Landing Zone Saigon's defenders began their move minesweeping the entire route past Task Force Mustang's and JTGG's position at LZ Tenaru to Route 9 and on to the KSC crossroad. Two antitank mines and one antipersonnel mine were located and destroyed. B/1-40 Arty left the column at Tenaru and Teams Armor and C/1-61 completed their move at about 9:20pm on July 7th.[614]

July 8 and 9.

Task Force Mustang and JTGG leap frogged on July 8th to LZ Hawk at the top Khe Sanh plain. All of Task Force Mustang began the road march back to QTCB and LZ Sharon in three serials beginning at 6:30 am on the morning of July 9th. Team Armor was the rear guard in the last serial and passed through Ca Lu 12 hours later.

One very notable difference between the June 16th road march from Ca Lu to the Khe Sanh plain and the return trip on July 9th was that there was no flank security provided USMC infantry. The 9th Marine Regiment was the first major subordinate command of the 3MARDIV to be withdrawn from South Vietnam as were two brigades of the Army's 9th Infantry Division. The regiment had been withdrawn after being released from *UTAH MESA* first to Vandegrift Combat Base to prepare for deployment. It went from Vandegrift to Quang Tri then to Da Nang to depart for Okinawa beginning in late July.[615] Flank security to Ca Lu was provided by 101st Airmobile AH-1 Cobra gunships.

Control of the JTGG passed from Task Force Hotel to the Red Devil Brigade.[616] Team Armor was released from its attachment to 1-61 Inf (M) and B/1-77 Armor road marched to LZ Nancy where it was reunited with its parent battalion for the first time since March.

The company began a badly needed maintenance break upon arriving at LZ Nancy where it was assigned a sector of the perimeter's defense. The M88 ARV which had performed perfectly throughout UTAH MESA broke down along QL 1 outside of QTCB and had to be towed to Nancy. A second platoon tank which had a warped hull causing the failure of several engines and transmissions while it was at LZ Sharon operated without incident during *UTAH MESA*. Upon returning to Nancy, its availability for missions became sporadic again.

Operation *UTAH MESA* was the last large search and destroy operation initiated by US forces in northern I Corps. The departure of the 9th Marine Regiment reduced the remaining 3MARDIV area of responsibility. The Red Devil Brigade remained under the division's OPCON. To remain vigilant and capable of responding to NVA offensive operations throughout the area, the scale of operations was reduced from multi-battalion to single and multi-company size.[617]

Operation *IROQUOIS GROVE* June 15 - September 25

Simultaneous with *UTAH MESA* was Operation *IROQUOIS GROVE* that took place along the Street Without Joy (QL-1) from Mai Linh, Hai Lang, and Trieu Phong Districts north to Gio Linh District and west to Cam Lo District. This operation is an example of the reduced-scope missions to which the US and ARVN units remaining in Quang Tri were transitioning to. Colonel John Osteen, the Red Devil Brigade's third commander, ordered his organic maneuver battalions reinforced with 3MARDIV's Company A, 3rd Tank Battalion, and E and F Companies from Marine division's 2nd Battalion 3rd Regiment organized into combined-arms teams (that included tank-mechanized infantry, mechanized infantry-infantry, and tank-infantry that were capable of varied missions and timely responses.[618] The Brigade's Company P, 75th Rangers, the 43 Scout Dog Platoon's teams, the Rome Plows of the 59th Land Clearing Company, unit ground surveillance radars and night vision devices augmented the Red Devil's ability to locate NVA and Viet Cong entities, rocket firing positions, for rapid responses to NVA initiatives, patrolling, night ambushes, search and destroy and rice denial missions as well as early warning of enemy raids and attacks.[619] Other missions included cooperative 1-5 Inf (Mech) - 2d ARVN Regiment and RF/PF units activities in civic action and pacification operations in the populated civilian sectors demonstrating the Saigon government's continuing ability to prevent the VC from regaining control of these areas . The Red Devils also responded to regular NVA units infiltrating east and west of the former Leatherneck Square (AO ORANGE) north of QL-9.[620]

The 3MARDIV units participating in *IROQUOIS GROVE* were individual companies. The 3rd Tank Battalion attached its A Company to the operation beginning in August through September 4th. E/2-3 Marines spent August 20-29 attached to the Red Diamonds, and F/3-3 joined A Company on the 20th and remained until September 20th.[621]

The Red Devil Brigade's After-Action Report of *IROQUOIS GROVE* covers 102 days. For the first 62 days of the operation's span there was little contact made with the NVA regular and Viet Cong local force units. US and ARVN small unit operations were directed with brief daily Frag orders assigning limited missions to small units instead of the detailed major operations orders such as TF REMAGEN, *UTAH MESA*, and those that preceded them. Some Frag orders were verbal. For example, a platoon each from B/1-77 Arm and A/1-61 forming Team B/1-77 responded to a call for help from an encircled P/75th Ranger reconnaissance team west of LZ Sharon on during the night of July 21, 1969, Vietnamese Standard Time. To reach them quickly the B/1-77 commander ordered all of the vehicle headlights turned on. The rescue was successful, and all returned to LZ Sharon. Coincidentally, Vietnam is 12 hours ahead of Eastern Standard Time. Apollo 11 landed in the moon's Sea of Tranquility at 3:17 pm on July 20, 1969. Everyone remembers their locations when significant events occur[622]

Mines detonated somewhere almost daily, and rockets and mortars were fired within a five-hour window during the evening to early morning. The major enemy activity occurred in the populated areas along the Street Without Joy between Quang Tri City and the provincial boundary with Thua Thien. The VC effort was rebuilding its infrastructure in this region.[623]

Combat action became more prevalent beginning August 15 and ending 42 days later at the end of the *IROQUOIS GROVE*. The Steel Tigers' Scout Platoon killed four NVA and captured three more in AO Orange on September 24th. One of the prisoners of war stated he was from the *1st Battalion, 27th Regiment*. This NVA Regiment had infiltrated south of the DMZ after the conclusion of the follow-on operation *IDAHO CANYON* on August 15th, and it was the first indicator that the North Vietnamese had returned after the withdrawal of 3MARDIV.[624]

Operation *IDAHO CANYON*, 28 July -15 August

The 3MARDIV consisted of the 3rd and 4th USMC regiments after July as the phased withdrawal of the division from South Vietnam progressed. Both regiments' areas of responsibility had been north of QL-9 near the DMZ area during TF Remagen's phases followed by the 9[625]th Marines in the *UTAH MESA* tactical area of operations (TAOR) south of the DMZ and west along the Laotian Border prior to Operation *IDAHO CANYON*.[625] About half of the area had been known as Leatherneck Square. The 3MARDIV assigned the *IDAHO CANYON* TAORto the 3-3 Marines commanded by Colonel Wilbur Simlik.[626] The 1-5 Inf (Mech) had included it in AO ORANGE. Task Force 1st Battalion, 11th Infantry commanded by Lieutenant Colonel Walter Bickston, who replaced Lieutenant Colonel Milia as the Red Devil Brigade Operations Officer, took command of the 1-11 Infantry from Lieutenant Colonel Britton on July 3d.[627]

Operation *IDAHO CANYON* was in response to increased small NVA unit activity infiltrating across the DMZ and choosing small USMC units to attack, occasionally firing rockets into larger US bases including A-4, and emplacing mines on QL-9. It had three phases. The first phase, July 28th through August 5th, was a reconnaissance-in-force in three parallel rifle company-sized zones west from A-4 (Con Thien) and a second reconnaissance-in-force northwest of A-4 employing an infantry- tank team. Phase 2 was a seven-day search and clear operation of the same area as in the previous nine days. The planned beginning of the second phase was August 6th. A three-day final search and clear effort south of the operating area since July 28th was scheduled to start on August 13th.[628] The Steel Tigers (Team TANK), C/1-77, were the task force's reserve.

The order of battle for Task Force 1st Battalion 11th Infantry (TF 1-11 Inf) included the following:

- A/1-11 Inf:
    - One demolition team, A Company 7th Engineer Battalion (Demo Tm/A/7Engr)

- B/1-11 Inf:
- One demolition team, A Company 7th Engineer Battalion (Demo Tm/A/7Engr)
- C/1-11 Inf
    - One demolition team, A Company 7th Engineer Battalion (Demo Tm/S-7Engr)

- Team DELTA:
    - D/1-11 Inf(-):
    - Platoon/C/1-77 Armor (Plt/C/1-77 Armor)
    - Minesweep Team. A company 7th Engineer Battalion (Mnswp Tm/A/7Engr

- Team TANK: Captain Patrick Sullivan
    - C/1-77 Armor (-)

- o Plt (D/1-11 Inf)
- o (Mnswp Tm/A/7Engr

- Task Force Control:
  - o Reconnaissance Platoon, Company E/1-11 Inf)
  - o Two teams/P Company/75th Infantry (Rangers)
  - o 81 mm Mortar Section (three mortars). E/1-11 Inf
  - o Detachment (-) A/7 Engr
  - o One team/407 Radio Research Detachment
  - o One team/517 Military Intelligence (IPW)
  - o Two Scout Dog Teams. 101st Airmobile Division

- Artillery Support:
  - o B/1-40 Arty (105 SP) at A-4 Con Thien
  - o W/1-12 USMC Arty (4.2 inch mortar) at A-4
  - o C/5-4 Arty (155mm SP)
  - o 1st Provisional Battery Arty (155mm Towed) 1-12 USMC Artillery at C-2
  - o C/1-12 Arty (105mm USMC Towed) at C-2
  - o A/1-12 Arty (105mm USMC Towed) at Mai Loc Special Forces Camp

- Aviation:
  - o Army: one UH-1H Utility Helicopter or one Bell Light Observation Helicopter
  - o USMC: Ch-46 and CH 53 helicopters[629]
  - o USAF: 20th Tactical Air Support Squadron, USAF and USMC Forward Air Controllers.

The intelligence received by the Red Devil Brigade and 3MARDIV stated that three NVA Regiments had reentered South Vietnam: *27th, 246th, and 270th*. Documents and prisoners found during *IDAHO CANYON* proved that this was not the case.[630]

June 28 - 29

The mission began as planned. Task Force 1-11 (Inf) departed LZ Sharon for A-4 (Con Thien) in seven serials at 1 pm. The road marches were completed by 5:35 pm. Upon arrival the 3rd Marine Regiment assumed OPCON. Four reconnaissance teams from Team DELTA deployed east and north of the Con Thien. The Task Force command post was located at A-4. Forming a reserve and reaction force, C/1-77 Armor and Team DELTA were also based there. After dark at 8:15 pm, the three-infantry company reconnaissance-in-force phase began as planned to the southwest and northwest of the former firebase. Ten minutes later, a tank from the C/1-77 platoon attached to one of the Team DELTA reconnaissance inserts detonated a mine as it was returning to A-4. There were no injuries and only roadwheel damage to the tank.[631]

A more serious event occurred in the early afternoon of the 29th. Team DELTA departed A-4 at 9 am to reconnoiter an area northwest of A-4. An anti-personnel mine exploded in the C/1-77 Armor's motor pool at about 1:45 pm. The blast killed one Steel Tiger and wounded two others. Lieutenant Colonel Bickston ordered the engineers to place wire around the area of the explosion and then clear the area of mines. He ordered all those at A-4 to stay on well-traveled paths and roads through the base. The 3 – 3 Marine commander, Colonel Simlik, coordinating through 3MARDIV channels, informed Bickston that A-4 contained unknown minefields. Marine engineers assisted in marking them.[632]

July 30 – 31

Task Force 1-11's planned reconnaissance-in-force continued with the three infantry companies continuing southwest of A-4 and Team DELTA operated northwest of A-4. Team TANK was assigned to find a fording site across a river north of A-4.

A sighting of six NVA by one of A/1-11 Infantry at 10:10 am developed quickly into a firefight with an estimated NVA company. Team TANK was diverted from its mission to reinforce A/1-11 at 12:40 pm as was Team DELTA at 3:55 pm. While the Steel Tigers were moving toward A/1-11 Inf, the team passed seven NVA bodies and then met an NVA unit in an engagement with an NVA force of undetermined size, perhaps a platoon. Seven NVA and three US fatalities and six US wounded resulted. Team TANK linked with A/1-11 and continued the fight with the NVA company that began in late morning until the North Vietnamese withdrew. Seventeen NVA dead were counted were throughout the day, and seven AK-47 Assault rifles and three RPG-2s were captured.[633]

Another contact with an estimated two NVA companies occurred shortly before midnight with B/1-11 inf that was moving at night to a new location. It continued until dawn. A Marine C-46 medevac helicopter was hit by RPG-2 rockets and crashed at 2:55 am. The crew was rescued and the helicopter was secured by the infantry within 10 minutes. Team DELTA with its C/1-77 Armor platoon and C/1-11 Inf were ordered to reinforce Bravo company beginning at first light.

The NVA withdrew from the battle with B/1-11 Infantry at about 5:30am. Nonetheless, C/1-11 on its way to link up with B/1-11 confronted a small group of NVA at about 7:20 am. Team DELTA reached B/1-11 at 9:40 am allowing the company that had been in combat all-night to withdraw while Team DELTA swept the area.[634]

August 1-5

Colonel Simlek ordered an exclusionary zone be created 1.6 miles south of the lower limit of the DMZ in early July. Electronic detection and sensor devices were placed between within the zone along known and likely infiltration routes and used for two weeks during a 3MARDIV operation. Simlik restarted the zone on August 1st for IDAHO CANYON.[635]

Then reconnaissance-in-force continued on August 1st with A/1-11 meeting heavy fire from small arms, at least one machinegun, hand grenades, 60mm mortars at 9: 15 pm. A Spooky gunship and flareship arrived during the contact. The company continued receiving mortar fire. There were no A/1-11 casualties and one NVA soldier was reported killed. [636]

Company C/1-11 found 60 bunkers in its zone on August 2d. The bunker complex had been hit by artillery fire and air strikes previously destroying some of them. The company found four more bunkers the next day. One US M-16 rifle, four Chinese hand grenade, and three helmets were reported at the location. A C/1-77 Armor tank that was part of the platoon attached to B/1-11 detonated a mine with no injuries on August 2d. A second Steel Tiger tank that was attached to B/1-11 Inf struck a mine on August 3rd with damage to the suspension system but no casualties. The company returned to A-4 at about midnight. Finally on August 3rd, A/1-11 Inf identified a plastic antitank mine and a US Claymore antipersonnel and destroyed them where they were found. Company A 1-11 Infantry found an ammunition cache on August 4th. The company retrieved small amounts of each type and sent it to the TF 1-11 Inf CP. The remainder was destroyed where it was found. [637]

Captain Sullivan's Team TANK reacted to a *sniffer* mission on August 4th. It was assessed as significant. When the team reached the location, Sullivan reported 50 one- and two-man foxholes , and two bunkers all which contained no enemy. The 1-11's September 2nd Combat After Action Report does not specify the model sniffer that was used.[638]

Sniffers were sensing devices that US troops disliked and the NVA learned how to trick those who employed them. The XM2 was man portable. The XM3s were carried by helicopters that were trailed by helicopter gunships. XM2s were used on helicopters when XM3s were unavailable. These items detected ammonia which is an ingredient of human sweat. Sniffer models were considered second only physical observation to locating NVA hard targets such as bunkers. The infantrymen carrying the XM2 did not like the sniffer because it mad a recurring noise which disclosed night ambush positions. The NVA learned to fool the allies using the sniffers by leaving bags of urine which gave off the odor of ammonia in vegetation away from their locations.[639]

During August 5th, the last day of *IDAHO CANYON*'s Phase 1, the NVA launched 140mm rockets into A-4. The first three-to-four rounds exploded at 8:47am. There were six more attacks between 9:30 am and 7:08 pm in volleys of one to five rockets. The total of rockets that fell on A-4 was 18-21 wounding 10 Army soldiers and three Marines. US air and artillery strikes were directed at four potential firing positions.[640]

Phase II began on August 6th with repositioning Team A/1-11 and B/1-11. A major contact with the NVA occurred over the next two days when Team TANK, D/1-11 inf, and A/1-11 inf engaged two NVA companies that were later reinforced by as many as 50 more NVA. The action began when D/1-11 was ordered to initiate a ground sweep of the rocket sites identified earlier in the operation. They were located on terrain named *Rocket Ridge* about one kilometer (0.62 miles) south of the exclusion zone. Initially, Colonel Simlik refused permission to use ground forces so close to the zone where he only authorized air and artillery strikes. He gave TF 1-11 permission to move D/1-11 into the area where it encountered the two enemy units fighting from well- prepared bunker positions at about noon on August 7th. Air and artillery support were requested as D/1-11 withdrew from the bunker area.[641]

An hour later, Lieutenant Colonel Bickston ordered Captains Sullivan and Boozer to move Team TANK and A/1-11. Relieve the pressure on D/1-11. Sullivan moved to a position about three football fields from D/1-11 could place effective direct fire on the NVA while A/1-11 attacked along a route that covered them from fire from across the DMZ . Following the withdrawal of the NVA, after they had been caught in the open. The infantry companies swept the area and remained in the area overnight. The Steel Tigers returned to A-4. The three companies returned to the same area on August 8th after reports of additional rocket attacks. They found blood trails, destroyed bunkers, hand grenades and rocket launchers aimed at C-2.[642]

August 9-13

The remaining five Phase II days of *IDAHO CANYON* produced little enemy contact and discovery of bunker complexes that had been used in the recent past. A Team A/1-11 Inf platoon, two of the four reconnaissance teams and a USMC sensor team were fired on by two NVA on August 9th. Five more were engaged later in the day, and Team C/1-11 Inf located a long-empty 40-bunker complex. A tank from C/1-77 and another from the platoon attached to Team A/1-11 Inf struck mines with only damage to the suspension systems on August 10th. Team ALPHA discovered a box of 12.7mm (Caliber .50) heavy machinegun ammunition and its firing position. A search by Team DELTA on August 11 revealed 12 140mm rocket firing positions, four new bunkers, a trail, and communications wire extending to the top of a nearby ridge. Two NVA defectors surrendered to TF 1-11 and were taken by helicopter where they were fed and debriefed. [643]Team TANK left A-4 on August 11th to reinforce Ranger Team 17 that had engaged three NVA soldiers on August 12th. A Team DELTA ambushed the rear of a column of 25-30 NVA moving north on August 13th. The NVA withdrew to the south. Two other events occurred that day. First was the release of TF 1-11 Inf from OPCON of the 3-3 Marines at 7:30 am. The Task Force returned to the control of its parent unit: The Red Devil Brigade. Second, Task Force 1-61 Inf (Mech) and A/4-12 Cav arrived to prepare for a mission to begin the next morning. Phase II was extended an extra day.[644]

Phase III August 14-15

Phase III began at 6:45 am on August 14th. Task Force 1-11 Inf's A, B, and D companies joined with TF 1-61 (Mech) companies, and A/4-12 Cav, C/1-11 Inf, and TF 1-61 Inf Mech search and clear mission south of A-4 without meeting any NVA. Operation *IDAHO CANYON* ended on the 15th, and TF 1-11 Inf returned to LZ Sharon by 5 pm.[645]

The Third Regiment, 3MARDIV was the second major command to taken out of action in preparation for leaving South Vietnam at the end of September. Units moved to Dong Ha and then deployed to the United States. The Fourth Regiment, 3MARDIV assumed responsibility for the Third's area of operations in *IDAHO CANYON* at the end of September 1969. And the Red Devil Brigade's area of responsibility began returning to

Cam Lo along QL-9 and the key C-3 Bridge connecting the East-West highway with the roads north past C-3, C-2, C-2 Bridge and to A-4.[646]

The east to west boundaries between 1-5 Inf (Mech), 3- and 4-3 Marines, and the 1st ARVN Division's 2nd Regiment (2-1 ARVN) prior to IDAHO CANYON included the following regions:

- 1-5 Inf (Mech): the coastal area south from Dong Ha to the Quang Tri-Thua Thien boundary
- 4-3 Marines: VIRGINIA RIDGE, IDAHO and ARLINGTON CANYONS, GEOGIA TAR, and UTAH MESA.
- 2-1 ARVN: C-2 along QL-1 south to Dong Ha and Quang Tri, and southwest to Mai Loc and Base Areas 101.[647]

The 4-3 Marines shifted east when the 3-3 Marines left Vietnam. Next the 4-3 Marines began its initial withdrawal from Quang Tri in early October 1969. The 1-4 Marines ended combat operations on October 5th. The 2-4 Marines ended operations on October 22nd. The Fourth Battalion boarded trucks that took them to the Quang Tri airbase from which they flew to Da Nang and then they boarded ships for the four-day trip to Okinawa.[648] The Red Diamond Brigade took control of QTCB, and the former firebases north of Cam Lo. TAORs VIRGINA RIDGE AND IDAHO CANYON were renamed AO Orange. The 101st Airmobile Division reorganized its area of responsibility as did the 1st ARVN Division. The Marines closed LZ Vandegrift and the 2d ARVN' s 2d Battalion (2/2-1 ARVN) took usable items to rebuild Camp Carroll.[649]

Operation *FULTON SQUARE* 22 October 1969 - 18 January 1970

The North Vietnamese were not idle during the period when US forces reduced their presence and expanded the roles of ARVN's best units. Intelligence indicated that the NVA were moving their units north of the DMZ. The intelligence was supported by the reduced level of NVA attacks during the fall months of 1969, especially November and December compared with spring and summer. Charles Smith states there were 30 percent fewer NVA initiated contacts. For example, The 2-4 and 3-4 Marines conducted the three-month Operation *ARLINGTON CANYON* in the TAOR adjacent to the western boundary of IDAHO CANYON. The results were 23 NVA killed and eight weapons captured. [650]

The stimulus for Operation *FULTON SQUARE* was the reemergence of the NVA's 7th Front with its headquarters, the 808th and 814th infantry battalions, the 10th and 11th sapper battalions and the 34th Rocket Battalion. Located in Base Area 101 since 1968, Its missions continued collecting and transporting rice and other food stuffs, and occasional attempts to interdict QL-9. Also, elements of the NVA 5th Front's 27th, 31st, and 270th regiments were identified in the central DMZ area. Operation *IROQUOIS GROVE* reports gave weight to the estimate that the NVA were reconnoitering new US and ARVN boundaries for infiltration and food transport routes, identifying targets, and establishing 5th and 7th Front contact for future action.[651]

The Steel Tigers' first order under its parent Brigade was to be the controlling headquarters for Operation *FULTON SQUARE*. It began on October 22, 1969 and terminated on January 18, 1970. The task organization was varied. Initially, C/1-77 and B/1-61 Inf (M) were the combat maneuver units until October 31st when the 1-61 Inf (Mech) and 1-11 Inf exchanged responsibility for AO Orange on November 1st. A/1-11 Infantry company joined TF 1-77 Arm on October 31st, and a platoon from A/4-12 Cav replaced B/1-61 Inf (M) on the same day. Table 7-1 displays the order of battle in detail. The Brigade assumed control of the US Army's Rome Plow 59th Land Clearing Company (LCC), 18th Engineer Brigade, which had been located at QTCB since early 1969 when 3MARDIV departed.

Table 6.2 displays the varying task organizations for the Steel Tigers' control of Fulton Square.

Date	Unit	Unit	Unit	Unit	Unit	Unit	
Oct 22-31 Oct	C/1-77 Arm	B/1-61 Inf (M)					
Oct 31-Nov 1	C/1-77 Arm	3/A/4-12 Cav	B/1-11 Inf				
Nov 1-16 Nov	C/1-77 Arm	A/4-12 Cav	B/1-11 Inf				
Nov 16-Nov 28	C/1-77 Arm	A/4-12 Cav	C/1-11 Inf				
Nov 28-Dec 1	A/1-77 Arm	A/4-12 Cav	C/1-11 Inf				
Dec 1-Dec 8	C/1-77 Arm	A/4-12 Cav	A/1-61 Inf (M)	B/1-11 Inf			
Dec 8-Dec 13	C/1-77 Arm	A/4-12 Cav	A/1-61 Inf (M)	B/1-11 Inf	C/3-5 Cav	59 LCC	
Dec 13-Dec 22	C/1-77 Arm	A/4-12 Cav	C/1-61 Inf (M)	B/1-11 Inf	C/3-5 Cav	59 LCC	
Dec 22-Dec 26	C/1-77 Arm	A/4-12 Cav	C/1-61 Inf (M)	C/1-11 Inf	A/3-5 Cav	59 LCC	

Table 6-2 Unit Assignments during Operation Fulton Square
Source: Adapted from Combat After Action Report - Fulton Square, Headquarters 1st Battalion 77th Armor APO San Francisco 96477, n.d, p.1.

The 1-77 Armor's 4.2-inch mortar platoon, and the 5 – 4 Art (155mm SP) from its battery locations at LZ Sharon, Sandy, and C-2 supported the 1-77 with direct fire support. These batteries changed positions to QTCB, Dong Ha Combat Base, and FSB Fuller during the operation. General fire support came from the units at the locations below:

- C/2-94 Arty 8-inch SP, LZ Nancy
- A/6-33 Arty 105mm, A-4
- C/6-33 Arty 105mm, FSB Fuller
- A/8-4 Arty 8-inch SP, Camp Carroll
- B/8-4 Arty 175mm SP, C1 and then C-2
- C/8-4 Arty 8-inch SP, A-4
- 5th Guns Marine Arty, 8-inch SP, A2
- 5th Guns Marine Arty 175mm SP, Camp Carroll.

The 1-5 Inf (Mech)'s Forward Air Control (FAC) Detachment provided US Air Force air support. The time required before an immediate air strike arrived on target was 30-50 minutes.[652] Bombing missions directed by radar (Ground-Directed Bombing) were used at night and during poor visibility and bad weather.[653]

Task Force 1-77's missions included the physical security of LZ Nancy, Firebase Sandy, the Cua Viet Naval Installation, and sharing responsibility for QTCB as well as the populated villages and towns. Missions coordinated with 2 ARVN Regiment and Regional and Popular Force (RF/PF) units included rice denial, using ambushes, search and clear, and pacification tactics. Civil affairs and pacification activities included treating more than 6,000 civilians, evacuating adults and children needing hospital care, and distributing soap and school kits as well as building a bridge. The Steel Tigers also were responsible for the physical security of Fire Support Bases (FSB) C-2 and A-4 when its units were conducting operations in AO Orange.[654]

North Vietnamese and Viet Cong activity in TF 1-77's AO was sporadic. First contact was made by Hai Lang District's 148th RF Company on October 25th when it encountered 30 VC The RF unit killed one enemy guerilla and capture one AK 47. Ten days later, A/4-12 Cav caught a Vietnamese civilian making a map of the unit's night defensive position in Gio Linh District. The next night either 10 mortars or RPG-2-fired B-40 rockets were directed at Hai Lang District headquarters. NVA or Viet Cong-emplaced mines sunk a US Navy tanker and patrol boat. The following contacts were made with the enemy from October 22 to December 31, 1969:

- Mines were detonated by A/4-12 Cav (2); A/1-61 inf (M) (APC 1); C/1-61 M(1); C-1-77 Armor (2); bulldozers (2), and C/1-61 Inf (M) (5). Only the APC had to be declared a combat loss. There were no casualties.
- Mortar rounds were fired at A/1-61 (M) (5); C/1-61 Inf (M) (8), C/1-11 Inf (7).
- 122mm rockets were fired at C-2 (18).[655]

Contact with the NVA occurred in AO Orange regularly, but they were minor engagements primarily after October. The B/1-77 Armor was attached to 1-11 Inf during late summer into fall 1969. Task Force 1-11 had been operating throughout the AO from Cam Lo to north of A-4. In October Team B/1-77 reinforced an ambushed 1-11 Inf company when Team B, itself was ambushed by another NVA unit as it was returning from the first ambush.

Specialist 4 Duane (Redd) Carr was the driver of company commander Captain John Moore' s B-66 tank. Also riding on the tank was the TF 1-11 commander Lieutenant Colonel Bickston. Redd Carr became the B-66 driver after Specialist 4 Joe Davis who had deployed with the company in July 1968 completed his Vietnam tour. Carr was wounded on the right side of his head but was able to keep his tank moving clear of the ambush's kill zone as he was losing his sight. He was awarded the Bronze Star Medal with the V device for his heroic effort in combat against the NVA. Redd regained his vision after treatment on the hospital ship off the Quang Tri coast that was followed by further care in Japan and the United States. [656]

Staff Sergeant Donald Desmarais one of B/1-77's tank commanders was fatally wounded on the day Operation FULTON SQUARE began, October 22, 1969. He was one of the most respected noncommissioned officers in the company. He began his tour in Vietnam as the company commander's gunner on B-66. Prior to the completion of his required 12-month assignment to Vietnam, he received the Army's highest award for heroism but not against the enemy in combat. He rescued a fellow Steel Tiger from a burning M48A3. Desmarais extended his tour in Vietnam for an additional six months so he could be discharged and return home to Massachusetts.[657]

The 1-61 Inf (M) replaced TF 1-11 Inf on November 1st because of the heavy contact. A/1-77 replaced B/1-77 in November.[658] The 1-61 Inf (M) became Task Force 1-61 Inf(M) with the following organization:

- Headquarters and Headquarters Company 1-61 Inf(M)
- A/1-61 Inf(M)

- B/1-61 Inf(M)
- C/1-61 Inf(M)
- D/1-61 Inf(M)
- A/1-77 Armor
- D/1-11 Inf
- 2/A/ 7th Eng
- Demolition Teams 4 and 11 3/A/7thn Eng
- Prisoner of War Interrogation Section , 517 Military Intelligence Detachment
- Teams 1, 2,3,4,and 5, Section A/43rd Scout Dog Platoon

The following units directly supported TF 1-61 Inf (M)

- 5 – 4 Arty (SP) 155mm
- 1 (Duster)/Hqs Plt/8-4 Arty
- Det/407 Rad Res Group
- Det/298 Sig Co
- Teams 1,2,3,4, 5, 6, 7, and 8 Minesweep and Demolition/A/7th Eng
- Contact Teams/D/75 Spt Bn
- Teams Blue and Green, Attack Helicopter Support Company, 101st Airmobile Division[659]

TF 1-61 Inf(M), away from the population centers encompassed in Operation *FULTON SQUARE*, performed search and destroy, security, and reconnaissance in force missions within AO ORANGE. Its most significant engagement began during the early morning of November 11, 1969 when a platoon of the *27th NVA Regiment* probed the perimeter of D/1-11's night defensive position. The probe was a night reconnaissance patrol and not a determined attack. The infantry company began its pursuit of the NVA unit at first light (Beginning Morning Nautical Twilight or BMNT), and by the time D/1-11 Inf located the platoon, it had reunited with its parent company in a strong defensive position in a bunker complex about 3.7 miles south of the DMZ.[660] Two TF 1-61 Inf (M) companies moved to support D/1-11 Inf. Reinforcing the Delta Company was C/1-61 Inf (M), and B/1-61Inf (M) attacked the NVA company's flank. The attack defeated the enemy in that location.

The next engagement occurred on November 12th when the NVA began firing at 1/C/1-61 Inf (M) that was searching a draw in the area of the previous day's fighting. The NVA hit a Medevac helicopter with an RPG-7 rocket causing it to crash. The infantry platoon attempted to rescue the helicopter's crew and began receiving enemy fire surrounding their location. Almost simultaneously, an NVA unit began firing at 2/C/1-61 Inf (M) from fighting positions in more well-constructed bunkers in another draw not far from the 1st Platoon. The TF 1-61's Scout Platoon and D/1-11 went to the 2d Platoon's assistance when the TF Commander, Lieutenant Colonel John Swaren assessed that the battalion was meeting a major NVA force. Despite the best efforts of a combined arms mechanized infantry battalion supported by artillery and tactical air support, the NVA remained in their positions at the end of daylight.[661]

During this portion of the five-day battle, Captain William Starr, commander of C/1-61 who had been at LZ Saigon in Operation *UTAH MESA* with Tm B/1-77 during June and July, was severely wounded when he shielded a hand grenade from those around him while trying to dispose of it. He lost his right arm and later received the Distinguished Service Cross.[662] Captain Stanley Blunt, commander of D/1-11 Inf led a seven-man patrol of volunteers to free the 2/C/1-61 that remained embattled in their position. They infiltrated through the enemy complex about three-quarters of a mile to the platoon and brought them back into friendly lines. Every man in the platoon had been wounded at least once. Blunt also received the Distinguished Service Cross.[663]

The next NVA attack was in its final preparatory stage on November 13th at about 1:00am when A/1-61 Inf (M) with its mortar platoon and those of B and C companies heard movement outside of its defensive positions. Antitank rocket fire (RPG-7) and mortar fire signaled the start of the assault by an estimated NVA combat engineer battalion (Sapper) battalion. Lieutenant Kevin McGrath, the artillery forward observer assigned to A/1-61,[664] took command when the Captain Robert Gallagher, the company commander was killed. Captain David Ellis commander of A/1-77 Armor brought his tanks to the infantry's position by dawn, broke up the attack, and assumed control of the location by 6:15 am.

The post-battle assessment was that TF 1-61 destroyed two battalions of the NVA's *27th Regiment* rendering it combat ineffective. The Task Force, including the Steel Tigers of A/1-77 Armor, received the Presidential Unit Citation.[665]

Other contacts with the NVA reported during November and December 1969 are displayed in Table 6-3 below:

Date	Location	Unit	Description	Result
Nov 5	Vic. Cua Viet Naval Base North Bank Cua Viet (CV) River 1.2 miles from South China Sea	A/4-12 Cav	Apprehended Vietnamese drawing map of unit's night defensive position	Transported to Gio Linh District Hqs
Nov 6	Hai Lang District Hqs	Gov't Vietnam (GVN)	10 RPG-2 or 60mm mortar rounds. Small arms fire returned by RF defenders; unconfirmed results.	1 RF KIA and 2 RF WIA
Nov 13	Cua Viet River near CV Naval Base	USN tanker	Struck two water mines	Tanker sunk
Nov 14	Cua Viet River near CV Naval Base	USN patrol boat	Discovered and detonated U/I mine	
Nov 16	Cua Viet River near CV Naval Base	USN patrol boat	Struck mine	Patrol boat sank
Nov 25	Dune area north bank CV River 0.3 mile west of coastline	A/4-12 Cav	Tank hit mine	1 WIA; tank combat loss
Dec 4	AO Orange, 3.75 mi northwest Cam Lo	A/1-61	Received 2 rounds 82 mm mortar fire	Requested gunships; 0 casualties
Dec 5	Cam Lo Village	B/1-11 Inf	Truck received automatic weapons fire	0 casualties; reported to village officials
Dec 11	2.4 miles SW of southern DMZ border north of A-4	A/4-12 Cav	Tank struck mine	0 casualties and minor damage
Dec 11	3.5 miles S of DMZ southern border between A-4 and C-2	A/1-61 Inf (M)	Received 3 rounds 82 mm mortar fire landed outside of perimeter	0 casualties and minor damage
Dec 12	Vic Mutter's Ridge west of A-4 and C-2	A/1-61 Inf (M)	APC struck mine	0 casualties; vehicle combat loss
Dec 13	North of A-4 2 mi south of southern DMZ line	C/1-77 Armor	Tank struck mine	0 casualties and minor damage
Dec 14	AO ORANGE	FSB C-2	One 122mm rocket landed outside of perimeter	0 casualties and no damage
Dec 15	Vic Mutter's Ridge	A/4-12 Cav	1 RPG hit APC, and received 15 rounds of 82mm and 60mm mortar rounds	1 KIA in APC; no casualties in mortar attack

Table 6.3 Enemy Contacts in Leatherneck Square November 11-13, 1969
Source: Data adapted from Operational Report Lesson Learned, Headquarters, 1ˢᵗ Tank Battalion, 77ᵗʰ Armor for Period Ending 31 January 1970. RCS CS FOR-65, Headquarters 1ˢᵗ Tank Battalion, 77ᵗʰ Armor. APO San Francisco 96477 , 1 February 1970 pp, 1,2 , National Archives and Records Administration (NARA), 8601 Adelphi Road, College Park MD 20740, December 2019

Lieutenant Colonel Thomas Miller turned the Steel Tiger's over to Lieutenant Colonel Niven J. Baird on December 16, 1969.

The Steel Tigers' first full year of combat in Vietnam disproved General Westmoreland's initial reluctance to use armor and mechanized units in the country because of the terrain. Although armored and armored cavalry units were in Vietnam before the Red Devil Brigade arrived in the summer of 1968, the 1ˢᵗ Battalion 77ᵗʰ Armor proved that it could operate and provide all classes including food, fuel, petroleum and lubricants and other fluids, ammunition of all types and calibers, repair and replacement parts including major end items such as engines, transmissions, final drives, and track without direct ground lines of communications over long distances by air.

Chapter 7: Vietnam 1970 -1971

Introduction

The North and South Vietnamese communists began 1968 with 195,000 soldiers of which 85,000 were killed or disabled during the initial weeks of the Khe Sanh Combat Base (KSCB) siege that began on January 21st and the Tet offensive that was launched 10-days later. The estimate of NVA losses increased by another 204,000 by December 31, 1968.[666] Looked at differently, the North Vietnamese and South Vietnamese communists lost 94,000 more soldiers by the end of 1968 than they had available in January when the offensives began.

President Johnson's national political goal was not to defeat North Vietnam and replace it with a democratic form of government. It was to force Ho Chi Minh to the negotiating table. The Military strategy was to do this through a war of attrition. General Westmoreland assessed the South Vietnamese as poorly led, trained, and equipped. He used US military forces with their superior ground, air, and naval weapons systems to inflict irreplaceable losses of combat troops on the Vietnamese communists. The Government of Vietnam (GVN) forces were dependent on US air, artillery, and naval support when they confronted the enemy. GVN units were equipped with similar but older or obsolete systems.

Westmoreland appeared successful. The United States and North Vietnam agreed to begin peace discussions in May 1968. The North Vietnamese dragged the talks out. President Nixon followed President Johnson in January 1969 promising to end US involvement in Vietnam. Delay followed delay for five years, The final peace accords were not signed until January 27, 1973.

Lieutenant General Melvin Zais, the new US XXIV Corps Commander and formerly the commander of the 101s Airborne Division, visited the Steel Tigers at LZ Nancy during August 1969 shortly after his reassignment from the 101st. He introduced himself to the officers and senior NCOs of the 1-77 Armor.

One of his comments was that US progress in northern I Corps had advanced from the surprise attacks of Tet 1968 to the current situation 18-months later when the sighting and engagement of three NVA together was a significant reportable contact at his headquarters following the successes of the April – July Task Force Remagen-Operation *UTAH MESA* in Quang Tri's Khe Sanh area of operations, other missions north of QL-9 toward the DMZ,3MARDIV initiatives in its areas of responsibility, and the 101st Airborne Division's 3rd Brigade with three battalions and two 1st ARVN Division battalions drive into Thua Thien province's A Shau Valley in May. This action was marked by the battle for Ap Bia Mountain, (Hill 937) nicknamed Hamburger Hill. [667]

The withdrawal of US forces from the war in northern Quang Tri Province, described in the previous chapter began in mid-summer 1969 following the June 8th meeting between Presidents Nixon and Thieu at Midway Island. The first units selected were from the most secure military South Vietnamese military regions: the Army's 9th Infantry Division in the south and 3MARDIV in the north. Quang Tri Province's 1st ARVN Division with General Truong in command remained one of the best units in the South Vietnamese Army. Both US divisions departed incrementally by year's end.

At the same time the US began planning for its systematic withdrawal of troops, there was intelligence that NVA replacements were journeying south along the Ho Chi Minh Trail and had begun reconstituting their units in the Cambodian and Laotian safe areas prior to deploying some back across the borders into South Vietnam base areas.[668] The Steel Tigers began their second full year in Vietnam adjusting to their expanded area of responsibility now that 3MARDIV redeployed to Okinawa, Japan, and the United States during October and November 1969 in Operation KEYSTONE CARDINAL. There were three major differences between the Red Devils' first 18 months in South Vietnam and January 1,1970 through August 1971. First, responsibility for the defense of Quang Tri Province contracted. The province's defense was to be shared with the five-battalion 2nd ARVN Regiment, 1st ARVN Division (2-1 ARVN) commanded by Colonel Vu Van Giai who also had a Vietnamese marine brigade assigned to him in addition to his 2d Regiment. Together, his force formed the 1st ARVN Division Forward with its headquarters at Dong Ha. Giai rotated his battalions among the fire bases beginning at A2 in the East to Camp Carroll in the west to keep the NVA off balance and his own troops at peak proficiency. His plan was to prevent the soldiers from settling into a defensive posture. Lieutenant Colonel Tran Ngoc Hue assumed command of the regiment's 2nd Battalion in July 1970. Hue was one of the ARVN heroes in the battles for Hue during Tet 1968 and highly respected by the US advisors who collaborated with him.[669]

Another hero of Tet 1968 was Lieutenant Colonel Pham Van Dinh. Dinh established himself as a combat leader earlier and General Truong assigned him to command the 200-man ready reaction force to reinforce any unit in the Division in 1965. This unit was named the Black Panther (Hac Bao) Company.[670] Truong later assigned Dinh to be the executive officer of the 1ˢᵗ ARVN's 54ᵗʰ Infantry Regiment in late spring 1970 working primarily with the 101ˢᵗ Airborne along the border of Thua Thien and Quang Tri provinces. He led an attack on a communist battalion that had moved into the My Chanh village area on the east side of QL-1 across from LZ Nancy -the pre-Vietnam drawdown Steel Tigers' headquarters.[671]

The experienced Hue with his 54ᵗʰ Regiment and Dinh with his 2d Battalion were present at the 1971 Operation LAM SON 719, where they continued sustaining the excellent battlefield reputation of the 1ˢᵗ ARVN Division.[672]

The second difference was that conscription remained in effect in the US, and soldiers were sent to Vietnam to replace those who were returning to the US after turning the war over to the Vietnamese and their US advisors. Numerous sources present instances of indiscipline including refusing to follow orders, drug use, and junior enlisted soldiers attacking officers and senior NCOs using hand grenades among other weapons, and the corrective actions that commanders and senior non-commissioned officers took to restore order. It is enough to state here that the Red Devil Brigade was not immune to these problems.

The third change was a force multiplier. The 1-5 Inf (Mech) gained direct Army air support when it gained OPCON of Troop C, 3ʳᵈ Squadron, 17ᵗʰ Air Cavalry in mid-1970. The Brigade went to South Vietnam in 1968 with an aviation section of four UH-1H multipurpose and four OH-6A light observation helicopters.

Fewer US and ARVN units in northern I Corps meant yielding the western portions of Quang Tri and Thua Thien Provinces to the returning Viet Cong and NVA; however, reconnaissance-by-force and search and clear missions were ordered when intelligence indicated that the communists were concentrating units in locations prior to initiating significant combat actions. Daily operations played cat-and-mouse with the enemy. Some sources state that the Hanoi did not want to interfere with the withdrawal of US forces. Others posit that the goal of NVA and Viet Cong raids was to demonstrate to the South Vietnamese that the Saigon government could not protect them and to inflict US casualties to increase opposition to the war in the United States.

Lewis Sorely presents evidence indicating two conclusions: first, the politico-military infrastructure of the COSVN)was not destroyed during Tet 1968. It was stated in Chapter 6 that COSVN was organized into two entities: political (Revolutionary Party), and military (People's Liberation Armed Forces of South Vietnam (PLAF) aka Viet Cong. Although

COSVN was controlled by Hanoi, Viet Cong units with their own chains of command fought alongside northern communists. Viet Cong units deployed in the field and those of the NVA both suffered heavy losses during Tet and subsequent offensives.[673]

Second, that the communists were adjusting to their recurring defeats, and assessed that their efforts had failed. Sorely recounts that General Abrams's chief of intelligence, Major General William Potts concluded that the US defeat of the communists was indisputable to the communists. Corroborating the MACV analysis was the 199th Infantry Brigade's October 1969 capture of a lesson plan about the July 1969 41-page COSVN Resolution 9. The document was an analysis of the post-Tet 1968 US victories along with US strategies employed, strengths, and weaknesses. Later, a subsequent prisoner corroborated the document. This individual had attended a study session about how to disseminate its contents to Viet Cong units. The new communist goal was to stretch out the war by large units revering back to small units that employed guerrilla warfare and terrorism as they did before Tet 1968. This would reduce communist casualties and still influence US public opinion against continuing the fight.[674]

Operations During 1970

Operation *GREENE RIVER* January 19 – July 31

Operation *GREENE RIVER* was not a single mission for the Steel Tigers. It was the name given to the half-year period within which Red Devil Brigade units conducted a variety of missions of short duration with specific task organizations including ARVN and Regional and territorial units. Missions included rocket suppression, reconnaissance-in-force, search and clear, restoring lines of communications in Quang Tri's western region, installation security (existing sites and reopening those abandoned), and infrastructure security (roads, fords, bridges), and interdicting the flow of supplies and combat units along infiltration routes to and from western base areas into eastern villages and towns. Operation *GREENE RIVER* had begun before January 19th.[675]

Shortly after the beginning of *GREENE RIVER* in mid-January, the 3-5 Armored Cavalry Squadron and A/4-12 Cavalry replaced their M48A3 tanks with the 16-ton M-551 Sheridan Armored Reconnaissance/Airborne Assault Vehicle (M-551 Sheridan). This was a light tank with a main gun capable of firing a 152mm conventional ammunition and a Shillelagh antitank missile that was guided by the gunner. It also contained a 7.62mm coaxial machinegun inside the turret, a caliber .50 machinegun mounted on top for the tank commander. Each cavalry troop trained with their new vehicles for one week including live firing. The troops began using their M-551 Sheridans on combat mission in early March.[676]

Each of the Red Devil's battalions operated throughout Quang Tri Province. The 1 – 11 Infantry initially performed its missions in Hai Lang District along QL 1 west to FSB Fuller which was northeast of the Rockpile along QL-9 and halfway north of the highway toward the DMZ. Task Force 1/61 Inf (M) operated east and west from the C-2 and A-4 (Con Thien) fire support bases. Task Force 3-5 Cavalry was responsible for the area south of QL-9 from Dong Ha and including Mai Loc, and Cam Lo. The Squadron also supported a joint US and ARVN near the former 3MARDIV bases between Langley and Tun Tavern and the 14th Engineers reopening of reopening Route 558 from Mai Loc to FSB Holcomb.[677]

Task Force 1-77 Armor (TF 1-77) was located in Leatherneck Square (AO GOLD) with its headquarters at the C-2 Fire Support Base and securing it and the A-4 (Con Thien) Fire Support Base at the beginning of *GREENE RIVER*. It had been executing search and clear, and reconnaissance-in-force missions north of the Cua Viet River. One tank company provided security for the Cua Viet Naval Installation and this mission lasted until July 9th. The other Steel Tiger units went first to QTCB and then to Hai Lang District Headquarters during January through April 14th. The TF's US infantry company's platoons joined with a South Vietnamese RF company, PF platoon, and Civilian Irregular Defense Group (CIDG) units to conduct joint operations in Hai Lang District following a joint training period. These operations included MEDCAPS. [678] The Steel Tigers began returning to QTCB from Hai Lang on April 15th and closing there on the 19th. One tank company was assigned Sector E of the installation's defensive perimeter. In addition to continuing its responsibility for AOs Gold and Black, and the Navy's Cua Viet installation, TF 1-77 added AO BLUE to its portfolio. This AO was framed by QL 1 in the east, QL 9 in the north, the Quang Tri River in the south and Mai Loc in the west.[679]

The Steel Tigers launched a joint operation during May 29-June 4 with nine PF platoons and nine RF companies between Cua Viet and Wunder Beach along Route 555, the coastal road. [680] The final phase of TF 1-77's participation in *GREENE RIVER* occurred when it secured the reestablishment of a fire support base at Vandegrift Combat Base and reopened Route 556 through the Ba Long Valley searching and clearing the route and performing a reconnaissance-in-force. [681]

Tables 7.1 through 7.3 below summarize details of the operation.

Unit	Commander	Unit	Commander	Unit	Commander
1st Bn, 77th Armor	LTC Niven Baird then LTC John McNamara	A/1-11 Inf	CPT William McDonald	B/1-61 Inf (M)	CPT Adolph Borysko
HHC/1-77 Armor	CPT Gerald Dunklin	B/1-11 Inf	CPT Roger Iacovoni then CPT Curtis Hedener		
A/1-77 Armor	CPT Eugene Rorie, Jr				
B/1-77 Armor	CPT Peter Manza	D/1-11	CPT Stanley Blunt then CPT Joseph Wortham		
C/1-77 Armor	CPT Timothy O'Neil then CPT Henry Grego				
D/1-77 Armor	CPT Orvel Stiles then Captain Donald L. McClary				

Table 7.1. *GREENE RIVER* Maneuver Organization USARV
Source: Adapted from Combat After Action Report – Operation GREENE River, Headquarters, 1st Bn, 77th Armor, APO San Francisco 96477, National Archives and Records Administration (NARA), 8601 Adelphi Road, College Park MD 20740, pp 1-2.

Table 7.2 GREENE RIVER	District Chief/Commander			
Hai Lang District	CPT Tinh-A-Nhi			
3/2/2ARVN	Unknown			
101 RF Co	1st Lt Phan-Hien	151 RF Co		1st Lt Luv Trong-Tat
121 RF Co	1st Lt Le-Dinh-Mung	174 RF Co		2nd Lt Huynh-Van-Nam
124 RF Co	Unknown	915 RFB		

Table 7.2 *GREENE RIVER* Maneuver Organization ARVN and Regional Force
Source: Adapted from Combat After Action Report – Operation *GREENE RIVER*, Headquarters, 1st Bn, 77th Armor, APO San Francisco 96477, National Archives and Records Administration (NARA), 8601 Adelphi Road, College Park MD 20740, pp 1-2.

Direct Fire Support US				
A/5-4 Arty, 155mm SP	QTCB	FSB Pedro	LZ Nancy	
B/5-4 Arty, 155mm SP	DHCB	FSB Pedro	FSB Holcomb	
C/5-4 Arty, 155mm SP	FSB C-2	FSB Vandergrift	FSB C-2	
4.2 in Mortar Plt/HHC/1-77 Armor	QTCB	Cua Viet Naval Support Activity	FSB Vandergrift	Benh Dao Bridge

General Fire Support US		
A/2-94 Arty 8-in (SP)	LZ Barbara	
B/2-94 Arty 8-in (SP)	Camp Carroll	
A/8-4 Arty 175mm (SP)	Camp Carroll	
B/8-4 Arty 175mm (SP)	FSB C-2	
General Fire Support ARVN		
A/62 Arty 105mm Towed	Camp Carroll	
B/62 Arty 105mm Towed	FSB Fuller	
C/62 Arty 105mm Towed	FSB Sarge	
B/48 Arty155mm Towed	Camp Carroll	
C/8-4 Arty 8-in (SP)	FSB A-4	

Table 7.3 *GREENE RIVER* Direct and General Fire Support
Source: Adapted from Combat After Action Report – Operation *GREENE RIVER*, Headquarters, 1st Bn, 77th Armor, APO San Francisco 96477, National Archives and Records Administration (NARA), 8601 Adelphi Road, College Park MD 20740, pp 1-2.

The cumulative totals of the engagements during period of Operation *GREENE RIVER* were 37 friendlies killed in action and 320 wounded. NVA and VC killed in action were 106. Twenty-four individual and nine crew-served weapons were captured.[682]

The effort to promote civilian support of the South Vietnamese Government was the civil affairs effort. These included MEDCAPS and dental civic action projects (DENTCAP) where field medical sites were placed in villages and physicians, dentists, and enlisted medical assistants treated local villagers. Other projects were undertaken also. School furniture, medical dispensary, school, and well construction were parts of the GREENE RIVER period. MEDCAPS treated 1800 South Vietnamese monthly.[683]

There was one example of an atypical NVA thrust during Operation GREENE RIVER but not part of the operation. More than 150 NVA attacked the Khe Gio Bridge successfully in a three-hour battle on March 12th. Security for the bridge was the mission of the two M-41A1 Duster section from C and one searchlight from G Batteries of the 1-44 Air Defense Artillery (ADA) Battalion that was based at QTCB about 20 miles east, and a 40-man company from Lieutenant Colonel Hue's 2/2 ARVN who were based at Camp Carroll that was two miles away. There were 14 Americans present including the US Army assistant advisor to the 2/2 ARVN. The NVA destroyed both dusters. Once the dusters were out of action, the US troops escaped to Camp Carroll in a truck.[684]

Table 7.4 summarizes the reportable contacts with the NVA during the first half of 1970.

Date	Location	Unit	Description	Result
May 4	FSB Fuller	D/1-11 Inf	Received 32 120mm mortar rounds with 11 inside perimeter. Counter-battery fired	No US casualties
May 10	On roadmarch along Hwy 9 between FSB Fuller and Khe Gio Bridge	D/1-11 Inf	Received intermittent sniper small arms and 120mm mortar fires. UH-1H medevac helicopter crashed into D/1-11 column	Helicopter pilots and crew KIA; two D/1-11 Inf KIA
May 1-31	AO ORANGE	1-61Inf (M)	Experienced increase in mining incidents. Mined areas covered by RPGs; RPG fire used to force US tanks and APCs into the minefields	Light US and NVA casualties
May 28	AO ORANGE	A/1-77 ARM attached to TF 1-61 Inf (M)	Contacted NVA squad	Five NVA KIA; 5 US WIA
Jun-Jul	AO ORANGE	One platoon (plt) A/1-77 Armor One plt, C/1-61 Inf (M) and one plt	Mine incidents, attacks by fire, small NVA VC contacts	
Jun29		One platoon (plt) A/1-77 Armor One plt, C/1-61 Inf (M) and one plt	NVA Platoon attacked two US plts	Arty, gunships, and flare ship called for support. KIA 3 US and 2 NVA; 3 US WIA
Jul 15	Hwy 9	B/1-77 ARM	Convoy escort QTCB to CB Vandegrift received small arms and 3 RPG fire	

Table 7.4 Steel Tiger Contacts with NVA through July 31, 1970
Source: Adapted from Operational Report – Lessons Learned. 1st Inf Bde, 5th Inf Div (Mech) for period ending 31 July 1970, HQ, 1st Infantry Brigade, 5th Infantry Division (Mech), Camp Red Devil, APO San Francisco 96477, 12 Aug, pp. 2,3.

Operation *WOLFE MOUNTAIN* July 22, 1970 – January 31, 1971

Operation *WOLFE MOUNTAIN* was the name of the umbrella code name for Red Devil Brigade battalion's activities during the second half of 1970. It included a subset of five missions: Operation JUMP THRU, July 30, 1970, to September 24,1970; Operation SLIDE LEFT, July 24 to December 2, 1970; Operation JEFFERSON GLENN December 12-15, two unnamed artillery raids January 18-20, and January 29, 1971; and quarterly training for selected elements of 1-77 Armor and 1-61 Inf (M) for 38 days beginning December 20, 1970.[685]

Operation *JUMP THRU* was conducted in AO BLUE. Its boundaries included QL-1 in the east; the Quang Tri River (Song Thach Han) in the south; Mai Loc in the west; and QL-9 in the north. The Steel Tigers conducted included rocket suppression, reconnaissance-in-force, base security, night ambushes and combined operations with ARVN and Regional and Popular Force[686]

Operation *SLIDE LEFT*, September 24-December 2, occurred took place in AO WHITE. It included Huong Hoa District and focused on the Mai Loc village which was about two kilometers west from Cam Lo on QL 9 and six kilometers south of the QL 9-Route 558 intersection. The Steel Tigers performed the same variety of operations with South Vietnamese units as JUMP THRU: search and clear, reconnaissance in force, security, night ambushes, combined operations, and sweeping Route 558 for mines.[687]

Operation *JEFFERSON GLENN* was the last codenamed operation conducted by the 101st Airborne Division during its presence in South Vietnam. The units participating in *JEFFERSON GLEN* were the 101st Airborne Division, 1st Brigade, 5th Infantry Division (M),and the 1st ARVN Division. *JEFFERSON GLENN* began on September 5, 1970, and ended on October 8, 1971, when the 101st redeployed to the United States. Its purpose was to provide security for Hue and Da Nang from rocket attacks in the mountains overlooking the cities.[688] The 3rd Brigade, 101st Airborne Division (Airmobile) operationally controlled Task Force 1-77 Armor that was commanded by Lieutenant Colonel Richard M. Meyer.

The Steel Tigers' role in Operation *JEFFERSON GLENN* occurred during the winter monsoon season. The weather hindered tank movement; however lighter weight M-113 APCs were not impacted. It was a combined arms mission to search and clear the area northwest of Camp Evans in Thua Thien Province beginning on December 12th and concluding on December 15th. Task Force 1-77 Armor searched eight of nine planned objectives for NVA, bunker complexes, base camps, caches of ammunition, weapons, food, other supplies, and booby traps. Also, the units searched for infiltration routes from the base areas in the west into the populated areas near QL-1.[689]

Table 7.5 summarizes the details of the Steel Tigers' organization in Operation *JEFFERSON GLENN*

TF HQ	Team A	Tm B	TF Reserve	TF Trains	Artillery Fire Spt	Aviation Spt
TF CP	A/1-77	B/1-77	2/A/4-12 Cav	Mint Sec (-) /1-77 Arm	A/5-4 Arty 155mm (SP) (DS)	B/158 Aslt Helicopter
4.2-inch Mortar Sec	Security Plt/1-5 Inf (M)	Scout Sec/1-77	D/1-506 Inf	Spt Plt (-)/1-77 Armor	B/2-319 Arty (Reinf)	C/158 Aslt Helicopter
Hq Tank Sec	Mine Dog Tm, 101st	Mine Sweep and Dem teams, A/7-Engr AVLB, A/7Engr		Med Plt (-) /1-77 Arm	C/2-319 Arty (Reinf)	3rd Bde, 101st Abn Div
Flame Sec/1-61 Inf (M)	2 Sct Dog Tms, 101st			Commo Sec (-)/1-77 Armor	A/2-11 Arty	Aviation Sec
White Tm (101st)	Mine Sweep and Demo Tms, A/7 Engr					ASHC
UH- 1H C&C (101st)	CEV, A/7 Engr					
	1 AVLB/1-77 Armor					

Table 7.5. Task Force 1-77 Armor Task Organization: *JEFFERSON GLENN*
Source: Adapted from Task Organization, Combat Operations After Action Report, Operation *JEFFERSON GLENN* 12 December -15 December 1970, Headquarters, 1st Battalion, 77th Armor, APO San Francisco, 96477, 19 December, p.1, National Archives and Records Administration (NARA), 8601 Adelphi Road, College Park MD 20740, December 2019.

Task Force 1-77 was a combined arms task force that included not only Red Devil Brigade units, but also airmobile infantry and helicopter support from the 101st Airborne. Teams A and B searched their assigned sectors on December 12 and 13. The task force completed searching eight of its nine assigned objectives. Suspected enemy positions were subjected to indirect artillery fire. Howitzers fired 845 rounds of 155mm ammunition and 222 rounds of 105mm ammunition. The M48A3 tanks of Teams A and B shot 417 main tank gun rounds of high explosive, cannister, and beehive. The M-551 Sheridans fired an unreported number of their 152mm main gun ammunition, and the A/7 Engr's M778 Combat Engineer Vehicle (CEV) fired two of its 165mm shaped charges. Additionally, vehicular-mounted machineguns were used. Targets were identified by the ground units and those reported by aerial reconnaissance. There were occasions when canister and beehive were used to break through dense vegetation.[690]

There were no US casualties during *JEFFERSON GLENN*, and the body of one NVA soldier who was killed by artillery earlier was found in a shallow grave. Eight bunkers were discovered and two had been destroyed already by artillery. The task force destroyed the remaining six. Task Force 1-77 prepared to return to QTCB in the afternoon of December 15th. Team A secured the withdrawal route from the AO at a chokepoint where an AVLB had been emplaced. Team B relieved Team A and continued securing the exit route until all units had passed it and the AVLB was retrieved. Team A, the lead unit for the road march, crossed the start point on QL-1 at 3:20 pm for home station.[691]

The first of the two artillery raid support missions, January 18-20, 1971, occurred in the vicinity of Fire Support Base Vandegrift. The Steel Tigers provided security for the QL-9 route from QTCB to Vandegrift, searched for supply caches and fortified sites, identified and cleared booby traps, and located infiltration routes. The January 29th artillery raid support mission was to secure the same route to Ca Lu and the artillery units within Ca Lu.[692]

Quarterly Training for the maneuver companies and scout platoons of the Steel Tigers and 1-61(M) and the Brigade Security Platoon was conducted during the December 20, 1970-January 27, 1971. period. This included tank gunnery training.[693]

Operations During 1971

Introduction

Operation *WOLFE MOUNTAIN* ended at the end of January 1971; however, preparations began for a bold new approach during 1971 following *WOLFE MOUNTAIN* that evolved from the combination of national polices, military strategies, operational art, and battlefield tactics that began in the White House and Hanoi. In response to the politics of growing American public discontent over continuing the war in Vietnam, senior US policymakers in Washington initiated discussions with MACV about crossing into the communist safe zones in Cambodia and Laos to capture and destroy supplies, equipment, and ammunition. US military commanders had understood the need to eliminate the enemy's capabilities to wage war since US troops were introduced into Vietnam. The leadership in Hanoi developed a system for moving and securing the materiel and men necessary to begin large scale combat assaults. The policy level adoption of this course of action developed momentum as did the senior North Vietnamese-Viet Cong leaderships' determination to protect what had been resupplied since Tet 1968.

The first attack into a safe area was the April-July 1970 into Cambodia led by four ARVN Corps (29,000 troops) beginning April 29th and joined by the US 1st Cavalry Division, 25th Infantry Division, and the 11 Armored Cavalry Regiment on May 1st (19,300 troops). US troops were withdrawn by June 30th and the South Vietnamese departed by July 22d.[694] Although the incursion was successful. the thrust into Cambodian to attack communist sanctuaries sparked widespread demonstrations in the United States. Even more apparent was the lack of progress of the peace talks in Paris.

By the late 1970-early 1971 period, the ground truth of the extent and complexity of communist safe areas in Laos had been known for two years. The 3MARDIV assessed intelligence from all human and technical sources available and concluded that the communists were actively rebuilding their forces and repairing and restocking their infrastructure along the Ho Chi Minh Trail that followed the border with Laos. One location where there was a significant level of activity was detected and protected by troops with their individual weapons and their air defense gun systems was in Base Area 611 that straddled the international border. Men, vehicles, and equipment were moved from Laos along Route 922(Laos)-548 (Vietnam) through the Da Krong valley into Quang Tri's Base Area 101 and to the A Shau Valley route toward Base Area 114 west of Hue in early 1969.[695]

The 3MARDIV commander at the time, Major General Davis, requested and received approval for an operation to disrupt future communist plans in the Da Krong area. He selected the 9th Marine Regiment to search and clear. Code named Operation Dewey Canyon, preparations began in mid-January 1969 to reestablish the US presence in Quang Tri areas that would secure the Marines' flanks and rear. The move into the Da Krong started on February 11th. Charles Smith's history of the Marine Corps in I Corps during 1969 stated that the communist resistance to the 9th Marine Regiment's presence was determined and the fighting was hard.[696] February 18 -22 witnessed the most intensive period of the fighting on the Vietnamese side of the border. As the Marines pressed closer to the Laotian border, observers reported that the communist forces were withdrawing heavy artillery and wheeled and tracked vehicles into Laos. The rules of engagement prohibited US ground troops crossing the international border unless it was for self-defense. Although a plan to cross the border was formulated and sent up the XXIV Corps and Marine chains of command and over to COMUSMACV, General Abrams, events overtook the decision-making process. The result was a two-platoon night ambush into

Laos on the night of February 20-21, 1969. The ambush was in position by 1:00 am and destroyed a convoy of eight trucks that had been travelling with their lights on at 2:30 am. The platoons were back in South Vietnam with no casualties before dawn. Abrams approved the original plan on February 24th.[697]

The difference between 1970 and 1971 was the rapid deterioration in the US domestic support for the war and the US Congressional response. First, there were the anti-war student rallies at Kent State University in Kent Ohio when Ohio National Guard soldiers killed four and wounded nine students on May 4, 1970. Second, there was the Cooper-Church Amendment attached to the Foreign Military Sales Act of 1971 that would end funding for US forces operating in Cambodia and Laos after June 1970. This cutoff of funding for US support of the South Vietnamese outside of their country passed the US Congress on January 5, 1971. Third, Intelligence reached MACV in Fall 1970 and COSVN and North Vietnam were planning a spring 1971 offensive in I Corps with the objective of retaking Hue and Quang Tri now that 200,000 US troops had left the country already and more would be leaving. Fourth, The US Chairman of the Joint Chiefs of Staff, Admiral Thomas Moorer sent General Abrams a message proposing three operations: Laos, Cambodia again, and covert operations in North Vietnam, and that President Thieu had to approve one of them.[698]

Lewis Sorely using a North Vietnamese history of the period states that their support units stationed the length of the Ho Chi Minh Trail had enough supplies to support 50,000 - 60,000 troops for four-to-five months by January 1971. He added that the North Vietnamese and COSVN had detected preparations for a major US-RVN operation in I Corps but did not have enough information on whether it would be land or sea-launched.[699]

Operation *DEWEY CANYON II* and *LAM SON 719*, January 29 – April 8

The test of whether the Government of Vietnam (GVN) armed forces would be capable of conducting a major combat operation against Hanoi-controlled forces without a US troop and US advisory presence on the ground was about to be put into motion at the policymaking, strategic, operational art, and tactical levels. Laos was chosen for the location and the route would follow QL-9. It would be led by Lieutenant General Hoang Xuan Lam who was the commander of I ARVN Corps. The First Armored Brigade (ARVN) equipped with US-made M-41 Walker Bulldog gasoline-powered light tanks with 76-mm main guns and reinforced with two airborne infantry brigades would lead the attack. The First Infantry Division (ARVN) with additional ARVN units was to move through to the Base Area 604 objectives. The Laotian town of Tchepone was the major objective.[700]

The code name for the cross-border thrust was *LAM SON 719*. There are three excellent sources describing this very significant operation: Lewis Sorley's *A Better War* (1999), Keith William Nolan's *Into Laos* (1986), and Andrew Wiest's *Vietnam's Forgotten Army* ((2008). Combined, these books tell the story of *LAM SON 719* in great detail from the four levels of analysis described above national policy, military strategy, operational art, and tactical. For the purposes of this study, Lieutenant Colonel Richard M. Meyer's "The Road to Laos," published in the March-April 1972 *Armor* Magazine will be the fourth source. Meyer commanded the Steel Tigers during *LAM SON 719*.[701]

Planning for the spoiling attack into Laos began in earnest in December 1970 with cables between the White House, and Department of Defense in Washington, Admiral McCain Commander, US Forces Pacific in Honolulu, and a December 7th meeting with President Thieu, Ambassador Bunker, and General Abrams in Saigon where an outline of the three-option plan was discussed. Sorley states that Thieu thought the best choice for the Laotian thrust was a move along QL-9 along into the logistics area marked by the town of Tchepone as the principal objective.[702] Visits to General Abrams by Brigadier General Alexander Haig who was the military assistant to National Security Staff of Henry Kissinger and Secretary of Defense, Melvin Laird in December and early January 1971 respectively, and meetings with the GVN head of the Joint General Staff, General Cao Van Vien, cemented the choice of *LAM SON 719*.[703]

The commander of US XXIV Corps, Lieutenant General James Sutherland, who was the equivalent of the GVN's Lieutenant General Lam, and Lam were ordered by General Abrams to begin planning on January 7, 1971, and to submit the plan to Abrams and Vien not later than January 16th. Sutherland ordered the commander of the Red Devil Brigade, Brigadier General John G. Hill, Jr. to Phu Bai later on the 7th where Sutherland briefed him on the operation's concept. Hill's brigade would lead *LAM SON 719* in its first phase that was code named *DEWEY CANYON II*. This was for the US forces only. No US troops would enter Laos during the *LAM SON 719* portion. [704] One reason for this was it was the only US unit remaining in the country with M48A3 tanks. He was given four missions: 1) attack from QTCB on QL 1 and then QL-9 to the Laotian border; 2) secure QL-9 as the main line of communications (LOC) and protect the engineers who would improve the highway; 3) build a temporary pioneer road to Khe Sanh to be an alternative LOC in case the NVA severed QL 9 successfully; and 4) secure Ca Lu, Khe Sanh, and Lang Vei, and patrol the QL-9 route to prevent a North Vietnamese counterattack that would interdict the support GVN's phase of the mission.[705]

The 101st Airborne Division's missions were also essential to the success of the entire operation. The included 1) command, control, and maintenance support for all aviation units in *LAM SON 719*; 2) assume control of the 1ˢᵗ ARVN Infantry Division's AO in Quang Tri and Thua Thien when it left for the operation; 3) Attach the units designated for operational control by the Red Devils; 4) Reinforce security of QL-9 from Dong Ha to Vandegrift; and 5) provide helicopter support for all US and ARVN units on both sides of the international border.[706]

Phase II of *LAM SON 719* was planned to be a swift ARVN attack into Laos led by the 1ˢᵗ ARVN Armored Brigade and two airborne battalions. The first day's objective was the town of A Loui (aka Ban Dongthat was about 20 miles inside Laos and halfway to Tchepone. Phase III was to be the ARVN drive south into Base Area 604 and destroying stockpiles of enemy supplies and equipment, and then returning into Vietnam along Route 922-548 and moving north onto the A Shau Valley route back toward Hue.[707]

Figure 7.1 displays the route and major landmarks of Task Force Remagen and Joint Task Group Guadalcanal operations on the Khe Sanh plateau in 1969 and Operations *DEWEY CANYON II* and *LAM SON 719* in 1971.

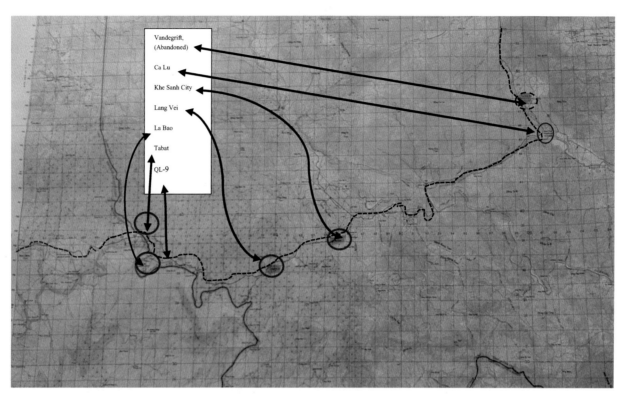

Figure 7.1 Operation Dewey Canyon II and Lam Son 719 into Laos
Source: Map Courtesy of Lawrence Wills, Graphics by Author

DEWEY CANYON II was not a repetition of the 1969 TF Remagen and Operation *UTAH MESA* operations when gravel narrow strip of QL-9, barely wide enough for the widths of the M48A3 tank (12 ft) and M-88 VTR (11.25 ft) to travel and make sharp turns had to be reopened and repaired for tracked vehicles to travel between Ca Lu and up to the Khe Sanh plateau and then perform the assigned missions following the spring-summer 1969 Task Force Remagen and Operation *UTAH MESA* journeys to the plateau . All resupply was conducted by air then. *LAM SON 719* would require wheeled vehicles and a reestablishment of the KSCB so that aircraft could use its airfield in support of the ARVN penetration into Laos. For this reason, a second road to Khe Sanh plateau and to the combat base had to be constructed from scratch across the mountainous terrain generally west from the Rockpile area and turning south to the KSCB once on the plateau.

The Red Devil Brigade with the Steel Tigers leading moved west under the ruse of conducting an artillery raid. This plan had two parts. First was to establish the artillery raid's firebase at Ca Lu. Second was occupying defensive positions to secure the portion of QL-9 serving as the MSR from Camp Carroll to the Ca Lu area up to the point where the highway turned into the narrow gravel road to the plateau. One of the cavalry troops occupied a defensive position near this transitional point. One tank company with the battalion's scout platoon defensive position on high ground from which it could secure the Ca Lu firebase. [708]

Table 7.6 below displays the 1-5 Inf Bde (Mech) Initial Task Organization with the Steel Tigers' organization in bold.

1st Bde. 5th Inf (M) Brig Gen John Hill	TF 1-77; Lt Col Richard Meyer	TF 1-61 Inf(M) Lt Col Arnold Stallman	TF 1-11 Inf; Lt Col Raymond Farrar	TF 3-5 Cav; Lt Col Robert Osborn	TF 3-187; Lt Col Bryan Sutton	TF 4/3, Lt Col Albert Coast	1/1 Cav, Lt. Col. Sheldon Burnett (WIA)and then Lt. Col. Gene Breeding Effective Feb 4	5/4 Arty Bn-Grp; Lt Cols Bergerson to Feb 5 and Ridgway from Feb 5
HHC Bde	1-77 Armor (-B Co)	1/61 Inf (M) (-2 Co)	1-11 Inf	3-5 Cav (-2 Trp)	3/187	4/3 Inf (-)	1/1 Cav (-Air Cav Trp)	5/4 Arty (155mm SP)
75th Spt Bn	A, 1-61 (Inf M)	B/1-77 Armor	Trp/3-5 Cav (OPCON on O)	A/7 Engr (-)	Sqd, 14 Engr	3 Sct Dogs		8/4 Arty three btry (155mm How T). 2/94 Arty (175mm SP) (-)
C/3-17 Cav	C, 1-61 (Inf M)	A/4-12 Cav	Sqd +/A-7 Engr	2 Mine Dogs	4 Sct Dogs	Trp/3-5 Cav (On O)		A/1-44 (SP) ADA (eight M42A1 Dusters)
F/8 Cav	Tm A Trp 3-5 Cav; released 1/31	Co 4-3 Inf		TF Plt 1-11 Inf (On O)	TF Trp/3-5 Cav			
P/75 Rangers	C Trp/3-5 Cav; released 1/31	Btry/1-82 Arty (155 T)		Plt 1-11 Inf	Trp/3-5 Cav			
298 Sig Co	Co + 14 Engr (DS)	Sqd A/7 Engr		Engr Element A/7 Engr	Co+ 14 Engr Bn			
407 RRD	2 Mine Dogs	2 Mine Dogs			2 Mine Dogs			
Plt, A/7Engr	B/5/4 Arty	2 Sct Dogs						
43 Sct Dog Plt (-)								
86 Chem Det								
Regional Force Co	1 Co							
Regional Force Company	! Co (Released o/a 5 Feb							

Table 7.6 Initial Red Devil Brigade Organization Operation *DEWEY CANYON II* and *LAM SON 719*
Source: Adapted from Annex A, (Task Organization) to OPORD 2-71, 1st Bde, 5th Inf Div (M) Quang Tri RVN 261200 Jan 71, TASK ORGANIZATION (D-DAY). National Archives and Records Administration (NARA), 8601 Adelphi Road, College Park MD 20740, p. A-1. December 2019., Nolan, Into Laos, op.cit, pp.51-52, and Meyer, "The Road to Laos," op.cit., p.19.

The dominant terrain feature in Ca Lu area is Thon Khe Tri. It is a 790-foot-high mountain with sheer cliffs above the Cam Lo River that could only be reached by helicopter. It was 16 miles west of Dong Ha and 10 miles south of the DMZ's southern boundary and one mile from QL-9. It was better known to US troops as The Rockpile It served as an observation post to detect communist infiltration. The flat land around the mountain had been an artillery base with 8-inch howitzers and 175-mm gun batteries during the post-Tet 1968 counteroffensive. During the 1968 Red Devil Brigade advanced party's May-June information gathering visit to PCV at Phu Bai, the team flew to Camp Carroll for briefings. This was followed by an aerial orientation along QL -9 to the CA Lu-Fire Support Base Vandegrift complex and included circling around The Rockpile.[709]

Securing the Ca Lu firebase by patrolling The Rockpile area was the mission of the 3-5 Cavalry's second troop which reconnoitered to the southwest from defensive positions. The second 1-77 tank company that had an attached mechanized infantry platoon from one of the two 1-61 (M) Infantry companies under the OPCON of the TF 1-77 patrolled north and northeast of the Rockpile. One of the two 1-61 Inf (M) mechanized infantry companies, each with an attached B/1-77 tank platoon from operated west and northwest of The Rockpile while the second secured the northern approach.[710]

Operation *DEWEY CANYON II* began at 4 am on January 29th. The Steel Tigers departed QTCB and travelled along QL-9 in radio silence until they passed Camp Carroll. The first tank in the task force reached Ca Lu at about 5:30 am. The Ca Lu firebase was in action by that evening.[711]

Task Force 1-77 began opening the final narrow leg of the QL-9 to the Khe Sanh plateau at about 1:00 am on January 30th.

A Troop, 3d Squadron 5th Armored Cavalry (A/3-5 Cav) commanded by Captain Thomas Stewart moved with half of the vehicle crews dismounted. Several troopers securing the scout dog and mine clearing teams led the way on point followed by one M-551 Sheridan using its infrared searchlight searching for any enemy, one M-106 4.2-inch mortar track prepared to fire illumination rounds, and a single bulldozer. The troop's command group was next in the road march. Half of the normal crews of the tracked vehicles provided infantry support for the Troop. The M-551 Sheridans and M-106 tracked vehicles threw tracks and the bulldozer had to turn its headlights on to function.[712]

The remainder of the 3-5 Cav's column moving along QL-9 included the Troop A/3-5 Cav's vehicles with its two-man-crewed Sheridans and M-106 mortar carriers, and the driver-only M-113 ACAVs, the 59th Land Clearing Company's bulldozers two 14th Engineer Battalion companies, and units from the 18th Engineer Brigade with their bridging and site preparation equipment including that needed for setting AVLBs, constructing culverts, M4T6 dry span bridges to cross rivers that were too wide for the 60 foot AVLBs to be used. The 1st Squadron 1st Cavalry, 23rd Infantry Division (1-1 Cav). Six dry span bridges and five AVLBs were in position ready for use by 11:30 am on January 31st. Tracked vehicles could move up to the Khe Sanh plateau and move between KSCB to Lang Vei, and the Laotian border.[713]

Once QL-9 had been reopened, both Stewart's A Troop and the second 3-5 troop were released back to their parent unit to build and then secure the second road to the Khe Sanh plateau through the 3-5 Cav's AO. Work began on January 30th and reached Khe Sanh on February 8th. Initially, the road was named the Pioneer Road. It was renamed Red Devil Road following improvements necessary to allow wheeled vehicles to drive on it. It began near The Rockpile at FSB Elliott and went across terrain nicknamed the Punchbowl (Figure 8-a).[714]

Three infantry battalions were prepared to move into the AO after the conclusion of TF 1-77's initial effort. The Red Devil's 1-11 Infantry commanded by Lieutenant Colonel Raymond E. Farrar was located at QTCB except for A Company that was in the field, 3rd Battalion 187th Infantry (3-187 Inf), 101st Airborne Division located at Camp Evans, and the 4th Battalion 3rd Infantry, 23rd Infantry Division (4-3 Inf) that was based in Quang Ngai Province were alerted about Operation *DEWEY CANYON II* on January 29th. Task Force 1-11 air assaulted into KSCB in 45 UH-1 Huey helicopters. Task Force 4-3 Inf combat assaulted into its AO which was north of QL-9, east of the Laotian border, and west of FSB Fuller below the southern boundary of the DMZ. Task Force 3-187 began on the Khe Sanh Plateau east of KSCB and the terminus of the Red Devil Road. Its southern boundary adjoined TF 3-5 Cav.[715]

The fourth infantry battalion in *DEWEY CANYON II* was TF 1-61 Inf (M). This battalion sent its A and C companies to TF 1-77. The unit's mission was to operate in the eastern-most part patrolling an AO bordered by the DMZ-Con Thien (A-4)-Cam Lo-Dong Ha along QL-9. The battalion's headquarters was C-2.[716]

All of the initial objectives of *DEWEY CANYON II* were completed by the night of February 1st. The maneuver battalions (three infantry, one armor, one mechanized infantry, and two armored cavalry squadrons) and the combat support battalions (three engineer and three artillery) were on the Khe Sanh plateau area of operations with no combat injuries.

Task Force 1-77 Armor began its MSR security mission in its sector as did the other battalions in their AOs. Meyer assigned each his of team commanders to keep two roads open: QL-9 and the Pioneer Road (Red Devil Drive) and their surrounding areas under continuous and overlapping observation within their sectors. They were to use multiple methods including geographic positions on dominant terrain and visual including day and night, patrolling, and ambushes; electronic observation employing TVS-4 night observation devices, AN/PPS-5 ground surveillance radars during periods of reduced visibility; and seismic intrusion devices.[717] The other maneuver units pushed beyond KCSB, and the destroyed Khe Sanh town along QL-9 to Lang Vei and the Laotian border where they initiated diversionary movements south toward the A Shau Valley and north to the DMZ. Meyer states that the Steel Tiger teams conducted independent missions coordinating with each other and supporting missions of adjacent battalion task forces.[718]

No combat fatalities were suffered during the move to the Khe Sanh plateau as stated above. Although deception and ruses were employed, it was the first indication to the COSVN and Hanoi where the South Vietnamese and Americans might attack. They reacted slowly but began engaging the Steel Tigers first near the Rockpile and later on the plateau.

Once QL-9 was open to the Laotian border with US forces in place, the ARVN invasion force moved into position near the QL-9 crossing point into Laos. It consisted of the 1st Armored Brigade ARVN, 1st Ranger Group ARVN, two infantry regiments of the 1st Infantry Division ARVN, two engineer battalions ARVN, the Airborne Division ARVN, and the 258th Marine Brigade, Republic of Vietnam Marine Division. Eleven B-52 strikes early in the morning of February 8th announced the beginning of Operation *LAM SON 719*. Airstrikes and artillery preparation fire followed. The 1st Armored Brigade's 2d Troop, 17th Armored Squadron led the South Vietnamese into Laos on QL-9 toward Tchepone.[719] Lewis Sorely states that Madame Binh a COSVN central committee member and one of the signatories of the 1973 Paris Peace Accords sent a cable to sympathizers in the US to "…mobilize peace forces in your country. Check U.S. dangerous ventures Indochina."[720]

Throughout DEWEY CANYON II, each day's operation by the Steel Tigers emphasized maintaining a 2–3-mile safe zone from QL-9 which was the maximum range of the Soviet-made 82-mm mortar depending on the terrain. The types of team operations performed were artillery raids, mounted and dismounted reconnaissance missions, airmobile assaults, and joint missions with other teams. During February and March, contacts were usually with small NVA or Viet Cong groups that were attempting to establish ambush sites along QL-9. Meyer recounts he moved the tank company and battalion's scout platoon that were securing the artillery at Ca Lu to another position southwest of the Rockpile so it could operate with one of the 1-61 (M) teams. [721]

On one occasion early in February, this resulted in confronting heavy communist resistance near the Steel Tigers' western boundary with the 4-3 Inf. The intensity of this engagement required the commitment of the 4-3 Inf to the eastern portion of its AO. The 4-3 Inf encountered a determined enemy defense of its area as well. Meyer stated that the 4-3 Inf uncovered NVA camps and caches of food, weapons, and ammunition. General Hill exchanged the 4-3 Infantry with the 3/187 Inf after two weeks of heavy fighting. The resistance continued unabated. Hill next moved the 3-5 Cav back to the east and ordered the two infantry battalions to attack supported by the massing of the Red Devil's artillery on the targets. The Steel Tigers were the blocking force. This was the first major battle to defend the QL-9 MSR according to Meyer, and it ended in early March. The result was forcing the communist units engaged during the battle to pull back further from QL-9 from where they began resisting US forces.[722]

Meyer describes why the communist attempts to close the MSR failed. One reason was the early detection by the observation tools used by Steel Tigers, noted earlier. He attributes the second reason for the success of keeping QL-9 open was the close coordination between the 1-77's operations center and the transportation battalion moving the supplies based on reports from its gun trucks escorting the convoys. Once the enemy initiated an ambush, the cavalry, mechanized infantry, or tank team closest to the location was ordered to respond. Artillery fire was placed on any escape routes that were inaccessible to the ground unit team, and that team would perform a detailed search and clear of the ambush site and the area surrounding it. Meyer stated that this tactic nearly always located the enemy entity that was hiding from the American sweep and captured their weapons and explosives also.[723]

The Steel Tigers were placed under the OPCON of the 3d Brigade, 101st Airborne Division early in March. Task Force 1-77 Armor released operational control of one infantry and one RF company and withdrew to Ca Lu. MSR security became the responsibility of two 101st infantry battalions. The maneuver elements of Colonel Meyer's task force were now the 1-77 scout platoon, B/1-77 Arm, C/1-77 Arm, B/1-61 (M) Inf and one cavalry troop, and it returned to Ca Lu.[724]

Lieutenant General Lam's decision to withdraw the 1st Armored Brigade ARVN was made on the night of March 18th. The Brigade began its 20-kilometer journey back into Vietnam from A Loui, Laos the next morning along QL-9 toward the La Bao crossing point at the Xe-pon River.[725] The brigade was ambushed shortly after departing along QL-9 slowing its progress eastward.

Until March 19-20, the North Vietnamese had been attacking US forces regularly but not in force in the vicinity of La Bao and the nearby uninhabited village of Ta Bat which was on the north side of QL-9. The latter was CP of the Red Devils' 1-11 Inf and two battalions of XXIV Corps artillery: 8-4 Arty 175mm (SP) guns and 2-94 Arty 8-inch (SP) howitzers. Also present was A/1-44 Air Def Arty (ADA) Bn (SP) with eight M42A1 40mm AA Guns (SP) (Dusters) to provide perimeter security. The 1-11 Inf was responsible for securing QL 9 from the La Bao entry point. The artillery had arrived on February 9[th.] The 1-1 Cav was responsible for the portion of QL-9 east from the 1-11.[726]

Communist troops increased the intensity and the number of troops committed to their goal closing QL-9 during March 19-20 period as the armored brigade was approaching La Bao. The communists even crossed into South Vietnam to attack 1-1 Cav and 1-11 Inf defenders on two axes at the boundary between the two units who had been securing QL-9 after which they withdrew back into their Laotian safe areas. These cross-border penetrations along QL-9 disabled several APCs, Sheridans, and a helicopter The 1-11 Inf was preparing to be withdrawn by helicopter and the two artillery battalions were ordered to move east into new positions east of Lang Vei. General Hill sent three Long Range Reconnaissance Patrol (LRRP) teams into the 1-11's AO with the mission of pinpointing the origins of the indirect mortar and rocket attacks as well as snipers' sites on March 20th. Also, he gave the 3-187th infantry commander a warning order to combat assault into the area and ordered the commander of the 1-1 Cav to send a troop to the 1-1's sector to rescue the LRRPs.[727]

The 8-4 Arty175mm (SP) left the La Bao-Ta Bat area for the Lang Vei area unopposed. It was followed by B/2-94 Arty 8-inch (SP) and A/2-94 Arty 8-inch (SP) batteries which came under heavy enemy attack. The last battery, C/2-94 8-inch (SP) Arty, and the A/1-44 ADA Dusters could not leave plus they had not been resupplied for three days because of the ferocity of the combat.[728]

The Steel Tigers received a new mission in response to the developments of March 20th at La Bao-Ta Bat: first, reopen QL-9 and keep it open until the 1[st]Armored Brigade ARVN was back in South Vietnam. Second, provide security for the withdrawal of the two trapped batteries to their new Lang Vei positions. Third, recover all equipment that was not assessed as combat losses.[729] The Steel Tigers left Ca Lu on the March 21st with orders to stop at Lang Vei where the Deputy Brigade Commander Colonel James Townes was located. Meyer placed his CP there, and it was in this vicinity that the battalion's scout platoon encountered a 1-1 Cav troop. The scouts remained to assist the cavalry, and the rest of the task force continued moving west with C/1-77 Armor leading followed by B/1-77 and A/1-61 (M). The first tank encountered poorly aimed RPG fire at one location at a bend in the Xe-pon River and again at the next bend. The tanks moved through the ambush returning fire.[730] The column met a second troop of the 1-1 Cav and one 1-11 Infantry company. The second C/1-77 Armor tank in the column drove into a B-52 bomb crater hidden by elephant grass in the attempt to bypass a damaged APC and helicopter along QL-9. The enemy began firing RPG and small-arms fire with some rockets and rounds striking the C/1-77 Armor's command APC wounding several inside the vehicle who required medical evacuation. Mortar and 122-mm rocket fire followed the RPG attack. B/1-77 Armor, the second tank company in the column remained until the C Company tank was retrieved and the medevacs completed. The rest of the column continued on QL-9 encountering combinations of RPG and small arms fire and linked up with a second 1-11 Infantry company and the first of the retrograding 2-94 artillery batteries. C/1-77 reached Ta Bat at the 1-11 Infantry's command post (CP) position where the third rifle company was located. While the tanks maneuvered into position around the CP, 122-mm artillery fire fell into the position's perimeter.[731]

The action at La Bao-Ta Bat included the following missions for the Steel Tigers: first, providing security for the withdrawal of the 1-11 CP and third infantry company by helicopters, and transferring the 1-11's ground equipment to the 1-77 for retrograde to Khe Sanh. The second mission was assigned to B/1-77 for two its tank platoons to escort the two trapped artillery batteries and the Dusters to their new positions east of Lang Vei. The remaining B/1-77 tank platoon escorted a 1-61 (M) Infantry platoon to the 1-11's former position and now the C/1-77's thus forming the combined arms Team C/1-77 at La Bao-Ta Bat. The two B/1-77 Armor platoons returned west from the Lang Vei area to be placed under the OPCON of A/1-61 (M) making it the Steel Tiger's Team A. By nightfall on March 21st, TF 1-77 Armor stretched from the Laotian border to positions east of Lang Vei. March 22-23 were spent recovering several ACAVs, Sheridans, three M48A3s with mine damage, and two 175mm and two 8-inch howitzers while also clearing the south side of QL-9 with Team B's infantry and tank fire supported by artillery and airstrikes.[732]

The 1st Armored Brigade ARVN column's vehicles began fording the Xe-pon River on the 23rd and the brigade's vehicles began crossing the La Bao bridge on QL-9 in the early morning hours on March 24th.[733] Once the South Vietnamese had moved through the Steel Tigers' sector, Meyer ordered Team C to positions west of Lang Vei and Team B east of TF 1-77's CP. Over following days, the 1-1 Cav and 1-11 units were released to their parent organizations. Meyer received two 5-4 Arty 155mm SP) batteries to keep QL-9 open for recovering US equipment. The 1-11 Inf replaced the Steel Tigers at Lang Vei and combined with TF 1-77 to the rear of the infantry and 3-5 Cav which was a north of KSCB, were the covering force during the close out of the Lam Son 719 support base. The Steel Tigers and two 3-5 Cav troops covered the final withdrawal of US and ARVN elements from the plateau. The Steel Tigers moved next to Ca Lu and came under the OPCON of the 3d Brigade, 101st Airborne where it performed the covering force mission as Ca Lu's forward support activity for *LAM SON 719* was closed. The Steel Tigers returned to QTCB on April 9th. It was the last unit to depart Operation *LAM SON* 719.[734]

Operation *MONTANA MUSTANG*, April 8 – July 1

Operation *MONTANA MUSTANG* began immediately following *LAM SON* 719. The communists continued moving troops from Laos into western South Vietnam and attacked US and ARVN firebases across Quang Tri Province. Operating in small teams using individual weapons, RPGs, and antitank mines. Sensors and other detection devices signaled the increasing activity.

The Steel Tigers were ordered to initiate search and clear, reconnaissance, security, and pacification operations with GVN and RF units in AO GREEN which was in the Mai Loc area to the west and north. The capability to maximize the utility of tracked vehicles was impacted by heavy rains and high winds.[735]

Figure 7.2 displays the Mai Loc location of AO GREEN operations. Table 7.7 presents the Task Force 1-77 Armor organization.

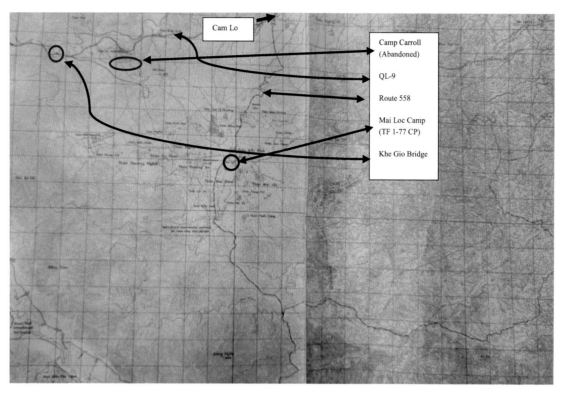

Figure 7.2 Mai Loc Area with TF 1-77 CP
Source: Map Courtesy of Lawrence Wills, Graphics by Author

TF 1-77 Armor	A/1-77	B/1-77	C/1-77	Company 1-11 Inf	B/5/4 Arty 155mm (SP)
HHC 1-77	Co Hqs			Co Hqs	
Hqs Tank Sect	Supply			1st Inf Platoon	
Scout Plt	Communications			2nd Inf Platoon	
Mortar Plt	Maintenance			3rd Inf Platoon	
Ground Surv	Medical			Weapons Platoon	
Sniper Team	1st Tank Platoon				
	2nd Tank Platoon				
	3rd Tank Platoon				

Table 7.7 Task Force 1-77 Armor Organization for Mai Loc Operations
Source: Adapted from After Action Report ,Operation MONTANA MUSTANG, 8 April 1971 to 1 July 1971, Department of the Army, 1st Battalion, 77th Armor, APO SF 96477, 4 July 1971, National Archives and Records Administration (NARA), 8601 Adelphi Road, College Park MD 20740, pp 1-2, December 2019.

Dismounted patrols, search and clear sweeps and frequent moving night defensive positions out of QTCB were standard for the first month of MONTANA MUSTANG. Beginning May 2d, The Steel Tigers moved to the abandoned Mai Loc Special Forces Camp where a CIDG had been located and established a task force command post and began joint US-RF operations within conjunction with the Huong Hoa District Commander's intelligence. The scouts and tank companies performed reconnaissance missions. The attached 1-11 Infantry company was assigned missions in areas where communist activity had occurred in the past generally running east of Mai Loc between the northern boundary of AO GREEN near the Route 558 Intersection with QL-9 about one mile west of Cam Lo. The infantry was transported on tracked vehicles while the tank units including the TF 1-77's headquarters tank section and the scout platoon kept the road open and secured engineers who had moved into the AO to improve the route to facilitate ARVN and Vietnamese Marine units' movement through the area to their assigned AOs.

MONTANA MUSTANG ended for the Steel Tigers on June 28th. The mission in AO GREEN was assumed by 3-5 Cav and the 1-77 returned to QTCB.[736]

Operation *KEYSTONE ORIOLE (BRAVO)*: Standdown, June 12-31 August

The Red Devil Brigade was informed on June 12th that it had been designated a KEYSTONE ORIOLE BRAVO unit and would depart South Vietnam on August 31st. The Brigade formed a Redeployment Planning Group to begin phasing units for standdown beginning July 1st and return the brigade's colors to Fort Carson for inactivation. Only A/4-12 Cav would remain active, and it would be reassigned to XXIV Corps.[737]

The Brigade's personnel plan was for the Steel Tigers to turn over its MONTANA MUSTANG mission on June 25th to the Vietnamese 147th Marine Brigade. The 1-77 Armor departed its FSB Mai Loc for QTCB, and the 147th moved in the same day. The 2d Infantry Regiment, 1st Infantry Division ARVN assumed control of Con Thien (A-4) and C-2 while the 101st Airborne replaced the 1-11 Infantry at FSB Anne on July 8, 10, and 11, respectively. [738]

Upon arrival at QTCB, the Steel Tigers assumed responsibility for one designated sector of the base's bunker through July 13th, the battalion also began an intense maintenance effort in preparation for moving its share of the Brigade's 975 tracked and wheeled vehicles more than 100 miles south to the KEYSTONE turn-in center at Da Nang.[739]

The Brigade staff sections had the responsibility for the following functions:

- Personnel and Administration: reassigning personnel, concluding the activities of the Brigade's Chaplain, Provost Marshal, Finance, records disposition, transferring and closing non-appropriated funds.
- Intelligence: disposing of classified material and transferring electronic intelligence gathering equipment to the 1st ARVN Infantry Division.
- Logistics: moving all TO&E equipment and personnel from QTCB to Da Nang, turning in bulk supplies, and providing personnel with billets and food.
- Civic action and Psychological Operations: completing, concluding, and transferring projects and programs.
- Communications and Electronics: phasing the turn-in of communications equipment while maintaining essential communications during the redeployment period.
- Final roll-up Force: conduct final audits of property books, funds, mess accounts, and clearance of facilities[740]

The decision was made to use the brigade's replacement depot at QTCB as the final outprocessing site. Those whose Vietnam tours were ending, or whose tours were cut short, or in excess of the brigade's personnel requirements would depart QTCB. Those whose tours were not ending would be housed and fed at the replacement depot until ordered to report to their new units.[741]

Redeploying individuals to new assignments out of South Vietnam as the method for reducing troop strength vs sending units back out of the country was a source of major disagreement between General Abrams in Saigon and General Westmoreland who was now the Army's Chief of Staff according to Lewis Sorley before the force reduction occurred in South Vietnam in 1969 ; Abrams wanted to maintain unit cohesion by retaining experienced personnel. Westmoreland thought it only fair to send the personnel home who had been in Vietnam the longest. Westmoreland rejected Abrams' proposal.[742]

The Red Devil Brigade created a Redeployment Planning Group (RPG) that created a four-phase plan about 30 days before the official notification that it was to enter the standdown process: Phase 1 – initial planning: Phase 2 – notification of standdown and detailed planning; Phase 3 – implementation; and Phase 4 – roll-up. The RPG established a Redeployment Control Center (RCC) to centralize the complex management tasks that had to be performed and report daily to the Brigade Commander, Brigadier General Harold H. Dunwoody, and his staff. Also, it was a central point for the battalions and separate companies to turn in reports and receive answers to questions.[743]

The Steel Tigers began the standdown process on July 1st. The RPG's plan called for an awards ceremony to be conducted individually by each battalion and separate company on Day 3 of the unit's standdown period. The Steel Tigers' ceremony was July 3rd. The deadline for reaching zero strength was July 21st. July 6-15, 1971, was set as the turn-in period for equipment and supplies less PC&S items at the 92d Composite Battalion (aka Keystone Composite Service Battalion) (KCSBn) in Da Nang.[744]

The reassignment of personnel was the top priority. Those being reassigned in the US or discharged from active duty were first in line. Those being reassigned to other units in South Vietnam were retained to assist in duties requiring more than short periods. The next deadline was meeting the turn-in window at Da Nang. The deadline rate was reduced as much as possible considering that C/1-77 returned from TF 1/61(M) on July 2d and had two of its tanks damaged by mines on the July 1st.[745]

To facilitate the movement of wheeled and tracked vehicles to Da Nang, wheeled vehicles would be driven in convoys south on QL-1 led by each company's officers. The first wheeled convoy left on July 5th and two other convoys were scheduled for July 9th and 11th. Company commanders took their tracked vehicles to the formerly US Navy-controlled Tan My Naval Support Activity northeast of Hue and loaded onto naval landing craft for shipment to Da Nang. The schedule was one company daily beginning with B/1-77 on July

4th with an arrival date in Da Nang on the 5th.[746] The order of march for the other companies was A/1-77, D/1-77, C/1-77 with vehicles from HHC/ 1-77 mixed among the convoys.[747]

The Steel Tigers' experience during the implementation phase was that the turn in was divided between Quang Tri and Da Nang's KCSBn. The battalion commander remained at QTCB to manage the departures of soldiers and the convoys as well turning in the PC&S equipment, and the executive officer supervised the arrival of equipment and vehicles, the process of turning all into the KCSBn, and the return of the personnel to Quang Tri.

Table 7-8 displays the baseline task organization at the beginning of the drawdown.

!st Bde 5th Inf Div (M) Control	TF 1-77 Armor (-)	
	1-77 Armor	A/4-12 Cav (Atch)
5-4 Arty		
75th Spt Bn		
D/3-5 Air Cav	TF 1-11 Inf (-)	
A/7 Engr	TF 3-5 Cav (-)	
P/75 Ranger	TF 1-61 Inf (M)	
43 Sct Dog Plt		1-61 Inf (M)
Det 2/7 PSYOPS Bn		B/3-5 Cav
86th Chem Det		C/1-77 Arm
407 RRD		
517 MID		
Bde Sec Plt		
Bde Avn Sect		
Avn Spt Pkg, 101 Abne		
Bde TACP (USAF		

Table 7.8 Operation *KEYSTONE ORIOLE (BRAVO)*: June 25, 1971
Adapted from Appendix I (Task Organization) to ANNEX D (Operations), 1st Bde, 5th Inf Div (M) After Action Report KEYSTONE ORIOLE (BRAVO) National Archives and Records Administration (NARA), 8601 Adelphi Road, College Park MD 20740, p. A-1. December 2019., p.56.

The US Army Support Command, Da Nang was the location where units processed their equipment and supplies according to whether they had been identified for redeployment or inactivation. Technical assistance would be provided by the Support Command's Keystone Composite Service Battalion (KCSBn).[748]

The KCSBn's processing sites are listed below:

• Multiple Item Processing Point (MIPP): this location received small arms, crew-served weapons, communications and electronics, and comparable categories of equipment.
• Single Item Processing Point (SIPP): this location received rolling stock including tracked and wheeled vehicles, engineer, artillery, and similar items.

Post, camp, and station (PC&S) property would be turned in near the location of the unit standing down instead of being moved to Da Nang. The mission of the KCSBn personnel was to overwatch and inspect the items being turned in and assist the standdown unit's personnel by training them to perform simple assembly line tasks at the MIPP and move equipment at the SIPP. The KCSbn was also responsible for housing, feeding, and coordinating transportation for the personnel of the unit standing down.[749]

The 1-77 Armor experienced challenges at Da Nang. Among them were two typhoons during a three-day period that delayed track vehicle arrival and processing at the SIPP for A, D, and C companies and one of the wheeled convoys. There was confusion at the MIPP about turning in serial-numbered items, and the distances from the troop billets to the MIPP (7 miles) and SIPP (8 miles). Four trucks could not be turned in because they had to be used to transport Steel Tigers between their work sites and housing. There was also a problem with returning those in the convoys from Da Nang to Quang Tri to meet their reassignment dates. The solution was to transport the soldiers by CH-47 helicopters instead of using regularly scheduled USAF flights between the two locations.[750] There were other personnel departure issues including but not limited to weather delays, double checking records for completeness.[751]

The colors of the 1st Brigade 5th Infantry Division (Mechanized) were returned to Fort Carson on August 22, 1971, at which time the Brigade was deactivated.

Chapter 8: Conclusions, 77th Armor 1940-1992

Introduction

The 77th Armor was one entity within the nation's uniformed services demonstrating to its allies in western Europe, Asia, and elsewhere that they could trust the United States to keep its word to safeguard them against threats to their security. The Steel Tigers were born when the country stepped onto the international stage and supplanted the United Kingdom as the guarantor of military power projection in the post-World War II world. Although this study identifies the five Steel Tiger battalions active during the Cold War years, its detail is limited to the first battalion. Originating in 1940 as the 753rd Tank Battalion and redesignated the 77th Medium Tank Battalion in the Far East during the occupation of Japan. The evolution continued to the present.

The one common feature, except for the three years when it served in South Vietnam, was that it was an independent tank battalion which supported one infantry division in two categories. First, it was one of the instruments used by the United States to demonstrate its influence as an international actor among the community of nations. The Steel Tigers put faces on the Americans who combined all of the economic, social, political and historical elements of the American culture to the citizens of the nations where they served.

The second feature was that the Steel Tigers were among the specialists in the application of military force beginning as a small regular Army force reinforced by the citizen-soldiers of the Army Reserve and Army National Guard. This model evolved into a large standing conscript Army also reinforced by citizen-soldiers for the nation's worldwide responsibilities. It became a regular Army of volunteers comprised of active duty members and voluntary citizen-soldiers who could be activated and their units integrated into the force structure's operational planning immediately whether in the previous division structure where the division was the lowest self-contained tactical unit. The US Army Regimental System adopted in 1981 transitioned into the Army's force structure as the Brigade Combat Team in 2006 which is the smallest deployable self-contained tactical organization. Originally, the Heavy Brigade Combat Team of 87 Abrams Tanks and 152 Bradley Infantry Fighting Vehicles ((IFV) included three Combined Arms Battalions each with two tank companies and two mechanized infantry companies and additional combat (armored cavalry, artillery, and combat engineers) and combat service support (signal, medical, military intelligence as well as other units.[752]

Today, the 1st Battalion 77th Armor is the one active Steel Tiger unit in the Army. It is part of the 4th Brigade Combat Team, 1st Armored Division. It transitioned in 2016 to a combined arms battalion (armor) with two tank companies comprised of three tank platoons with four M1A2 Abrams tanks each and one mechanized infantry company with three platoons of four M2A3 Bradley Infantry Fighting Vehicles each. The tank company headquarters has two Abrams tanks and the infantry company headquarters has two Bradleys. Each company headquarters includes wheeled and tracked support vehicles.[753]

The Armored Brigade Combat Team established the goal set by US armored forces in World War I: an integrated tank-infantry organization that evolved into an entity that worked and trained together on a daily basis so commanders and soldiers of various branches knew each other's personnel and equipment strengths, weaknesses, and capabilities, and how to harness them into a team to accomplish their assigned missions.

Levels of Analysis:

This study examines how the Steel Tigers got to the locations where they became part of the faces of US policy when joining in combat. Five levels of analysis were created. They used the metaphor of a funnel. Looking through the funnel from the top's widest diameter, the resulting "funnel vision" included national security policy and strategy formulated in Washington by the nation's senior decisionmakers first. Second, the combination swirls downward blending into military strategy both in Washington and to the theater of operations. Third, operational art is added to the blend as it continues downward, and adds the tactics employed near the bottom. Individual soldiers ingest the final mixture at the lowest level of analysis – the "field-ration" which is where they interact with their immediate chain of command for missions and support and apply their skills and training to daily requirements ordered from the higher levels of the funnel. These levels were included in each of the Steel Tigers' gates from their 1941 establishment to the present. The field-ration level is the location at which the Steel Tigers operated and every other tactical unit regardless of military service. The funnel's levels establish the boundaries for the field-ration level to work within.

World War II
National Security Policy and Strategy

The country was neutral but planned for war from 1939 through December 11, 1941. Japan attacked Pearl Harbor on December 7th and Germany declared war four days later. Unconditional Surrender of western allies' enemies was announced by President Roosevelt and Prime Minister Churchill at the January 14-24 1943 Casablanca Conference. Stalin did not attend because the outcome of the Battle for Stalingrad remained in doubt. One reason was for this policy was to avoid repeating the post-World War I myth that Germany was defeated from within and not militarily. A second reason was to reassure Stalin that no separate peace would be negotiated with Germany that would leave the Russians to fight the remainder of the war alone.

The first US military offensive operation was chosen by President Roosevelt and Prime Minister Churchill in July 1942. The target, codenamed Operation TORCH, was North Africa. TORCH was objected to by the US Army Chief of Staff and the Commander-in-Chief, United States Fleet. Roosevelt remained adamant and ordered his military advisors that TORCH was the top priority and that it take place as soon as possible.

The objective was to drive the Germans out of North Africa and to restore French forces to the allies' side. Under the terms of the 1940 French surrender, the new French state nominally governed France and its colonies in North Africa and elsewhere from the south-central resort town of Vichy. The reality was that the Germans controlled all of northern and coastal France.

Military Strategy:

There was no independent Department of Defense or Joint Chiefs of Staff in World War II. There was a Department of War (Army) whose senior civilian was the Secretary of War, and the Secretary of the Navy led the Department of the Navy. The closet position to the wartime joint chiefs of staff chairman was Admiral William Leahy who retired from active service in 1939. He was a personal friend of President Roosevelt, and he recalled Leahy to serve in senior civilian roles. He put his uniform on again in 1942 to be Roosevelt's interface with the active duty leaders of the uniformed services. General Marshall was the Army Chief of Staff and Admiral Harold Stark was named Chief of Naval Operations a month before Germany attacked Poland. He was followed in 1942 by Admiral Ernest King who was the Commander-in-Chief, United States Fleet and Chief of Naval

Operations. Army General Henry "Hap" Arnold became the first commander of the Army Air Forces in 1942.

The Committee of the Combined Chiefs of Staff was a consultative group reporting to their respective heads of state. The US members were Army Generals Marshall, Arnold, and Major General John Deane who was the Chief of US Military Mission in Moscow, and Admirals Leahy and King. British members included Vice Admiral Louis Mountbatten, Sir Dudley Pound, Sir Alan Brooke, Sir Charles Portal, Sir John Dill, Lieutenant General Sir Hastings Ismay, Brigadier Harold Redman, and Commander R.D. Coleridge.

Marshall assigned then Lieutenant General Eisenhower as the Supreme Commander, Allied Expeditionary Force Europe (SHAEF), and General MacArthur was named Commander, US Army Forces in the Far East. Operation TORCH began in November 1942. Initially, the US military strategy was to be landings on the west coast of Morocco. The British argued for landings on the Mediterranean coast. Eisenhower compromised with landings on both coasts as far east as Algiers. Eisenhower's headquarters was in Gibraltar.

These individuals not only responded to the civilian policymakers' decisions, but also coordinated that the transport and supplies would be in place to support those fighting the battles.

Operational Art:

Major Generals George Patton and Lloyd Fredendall commanded the Western and Mediterranean landings in Operation TORCH and the subsequent operations in North Africa. The plan was for US forces to move east with the British 8th Army under Lieutenant General Bernard Montgomery attacking from the west enveloping Field Marshal Erwin Rommel in Tunisia. Hitler ordered Rommel to return to Germany The Germans and Italians surrendered on May 13th. Action in North Africa tested the US Army at its first major battle against the Germans at the February 1943 battle of the Kasserine Pass under Fredendall in which it retreated. The second test came at El Guettar in March 1943 after Patton replaced Fredendall as the II Corps commander, and revamped discipline and training.

Lieutenant General Patton commanded the US troops in Sicily beginning on July 10, 1943 who were members of Seventh US Army As part of Operation HUSKY. His immediate subordinate commander was Lieutenant General Omar Bradley who commanded US II Corps. The major tactical commands included the 1st Infantry Division, 9th Infantry Division, the 45th Infantry Division to which the 753rdTank Battalion was assigned, 2nd Armored Division, and the 82nd Airborne Division.

Operation AVALANCHE was the US landings in Italy that began near Salerno, Italy on September 9, 1943. Lieutenant General Mark Clark was the commander of the US Fifth Army. His force included US VI Corps whose commander was Ernest Dawley and British 10th Corps. The major US tactical units were 36th Infantry and the 45th Infantry Divisions.

Operation ANVIL renamed Operation DRAGOON two weeks before it commenced was the landing of allied forces in Southern France's Mediterranean coast. It began on August 15, 1944. The US Seventh Army was commanded by Lieutenant General Alexander Patch. US VI Corps commanded by Major General Lucian Truscott. His subordinate major tactical commands included the 3rd Infantry, 36th Infantry, and 45th Infantry Divisions. The Steel Tigers were one of three independent tank battalions supporting the VI Corps infantry divisions. The units were part of the allied drive through the Vosges mountains into the Alsace Lorraine and finally across Germany and into Austria until the May 7th surrender.

Tactics:

The battles across North Africa, Sicily, Italy, Southern France, and Germany were symmetrical. The opponents fought to seize and hold objectives with divisions, regiments, battalions, companies and platoons. Mechanization to achieve the asset of mobility to put a force at decisive locations was employed. Observing maps from the many operations, there were boundaries between units, lines of departure, routes and avenues of advance, lines of defense incorporating the terrain, barrier plans including minefields. The graphics of phase lines and checkpoints to track movement on the battlefield are present whether in the attack conducting an offensive operation, including the movement to contact, contact, attack, exploitation, and pursuit, or defensive operations, and other operations.

Table 8-1 is a sample of World War II Army Field Manuals about tanks and tactics

Armored Force Field Manual: Tactics and Technique	Armored Force Field Manual: Tank Gunnery	Assault Gun Section and Platoon
Armored Force Field Manual: Tank Gunnery	Combat Practice Firing Armored Force Unit Combat Practice Firing	Armored Force Field Manual: 81MM Mortar Squad and Platoon
Armored Force Field Manual: Tactics and Technique	Armored Force Field Manual: Employment of Armored Units Reconnaissance Platoon and Company	Armored Force Field Manual: The Armored Battalion, Light and Medium
Armored Force Field Manual: Tank Platoon	Armored Force Field Manual: Reconnaissance Battalion	Armored Force Field Manual: Armored Force Drill

Table 8.1 World War II Field Manuals
Source: Adapted from World War II Military Field Manuals,, John S. McCain POW CIA-Defense Department Documents, retrieved from World War II Military Field Manuals (paperlessarchives.com) December 6, 2023.

Field Ration Level

The US Army Armor School was established at Fort Knox, Kentucky in 1940. Officer tactical training emphasized combat against the linear warfare of World War II and the Warsaw Pact. The first year of the Korean War in which the objective was to gain and hold ground and force the enemy to withdraw. The Armor School as well as other Army training centers presented enlisted soldier training following basic training learning the skill sets necessary for graduates qualified to perform in their Military Occupational Specialties (MOS) regardless of the unit types to which they would be assigned.

Those who served in uniform during WW II knew that they would remain on active duty until the Axis powers surrendered. Table 3.1 displayed that there were 8,266,373 soldiers on active duty in 1945. Following the victory, the Army wanted to go home. Three years later, the 1948 manpower strength of the Army was 550,030.

Demobilization contained three thresholds before those on active duty would be discharged: establishing return priorities for veterans; assembling the assets and then implementing the transport schedules; and moving them from the debarkation points to designated separation centers to process them from active duty to civilian status. Planning began in 1943. The first veterans began returning to the US in June 1945 after the May 7th German surrender.

The tool used to identify priorities for returning troops was named the Adjusted Service Rating Score (ASRS). Points were to be awarded for the following: each month in the Army, each month serving overseas; each campaign; each medal for merit or valor; each Purple Heart awarded for being wounded; and each dependent child (limited to three). To be at the top of the priority list a veteran had to have a minimum of 85 or more points. The ASRS was the official name of the plan. It was nicknamed "the points system." The points system ended in 1946 following veterans' formal and informal complaints as well as demonstrations protesting that their return to the US was taking too much time. ASRS was replaced by discharging soldiers once they completed two years of service.[754]

Four categories of units were established in which the European veterans were placed. Those with low points were in the first category and would remain as occupation forces. The second category was comprised of the units that would deploy to the Pacific or return to the US to become part of the Army reserve. Category three units would be reorganized and placed into either the first or second category. The fourth category contained units of veterans who had their 85 or more points.[755]

The second threshold was transportation back to the US. Operation FLYING CARPET was a massive sea and airlift effort that included all classes of Naval surface vessels, hospital ships and commercial ocean liners. Army and Navy air transport units were part of the operation. FLYING CARPET included round trips from Europe bringing home US military, servicemen's' foreign born wives, and seriously wounded, The return trips repatriated German and Italian prisoners of war (POWs) from confinement in the US. The same occurred in the Pacific following Japan's surrender. Another FLYING CARPET task was moving occupation forces to their assignments.[756]

The final threshold was moving veterans to separation centers for discharge.

Korean War
National Security Policy and Strategy

Events on the Korean peninsula had two major surprises for President Truman and the senior US national policymakers between 1945 and June 1950. The first occurred in August

1945. Originally, the United States was to accept the Japanese surrender in Korea and repatriate its troops back to Japan. The Soviet Union declared war against Japan two days after the first atomic bomb dropped on Hiroshima on August 6th. Stalin ordered the Soviet Far East Command to move forces into Korea and the southern Sakhalin and Kuril Islands that had been ceded to Japan following the 1905 Russo-Japanese War. Soviet ground forces reached Pyongyang on August 11th. The initial national political policy problem was where to get the Soviets to stop and to agree to a division of the Korean peninsula between the two governments for disarming and returning the Japanese troops to their homeland. Truman and Stalin agreed that the 38th parallel would divide North and South Korea and that once separate governments were established, the occupation troops would leave the Koreas. This occurred in 1948.

The second surprise came on June 25, 1950 when North Korea invaded South Korea. US policymakers took the North Korean invasion to the United Nations Security Council where the US asked for an international response to drive the North back into its own boundaries. The Security Council approved the motion to react and formed an alliance of 21 nations named the United Nations Command. Its commander was General Douglas MacArthur who was also the Supreme Commander of Allied Powers(SCAP) and Far East (FE) Command.

The National Security Act of 1947 established the US Air Force, changed the name of the Department of War to the Department of the Army and placed all of the military services into a Department of Defense. Its head was a civilian Secretary of Defense (SECDEF) who was also a member of the President's Cabinet. The first SECDEF was James Forrestal who assumed his new office in 1947 and was succeeded by Louis Johnson in 1949. Johnson served until September 1950. President Truman asked Johnson to resign given the June's North Korean attack into South Korea, and then asked General Marshall, who accepted Truman's request, to move from serving as Secretary of State to becoming the third SECDEF with the caveat that he would serve one year in the position. Marshall retired in September 1951.

President Truman and his civilian and military advisors with the concurrence of the United Nations agreed to negotiate an end to the war in June 1951 as UN forces advanced above the 38th Parallel and reached the outskirts of Pyongyang and the transportation-communications hub within the area bounded by Chorwon (Choerwon), Kumwha (Gimhwa-eup).and Pyongyang better known as the Iron Triangle.

Military Strategy:

Retired General of the Army Omar Bradley was the 1st Chairman of the Joint Chiefs of Staff. General Joseph Lawton Collins followed Bradley as Chief of Staff of the Army. General Douglas MacArthur was the SCAP and FE Commander. General Matthew B Ridgway succeeded MacArthur.

Operational Art:

General MacArthur inserted himself into this category until spring 1951. Lieutenant General Walton Walker assumed command of Eighth US Army during the occupation of Japan in 1948. When war broke out in Korea, his focus changed to organizing South Korea's defense by trading space for time. Walker led the delay south to the Pusan perimeter. He died in a vehicle accident in December 1950 and was replaced by Lieutenant General Matthew B. Ridgway shortly thereafter. MacArthur removed himself from the Operational Art category upon Ridgway's arrival.

MacArthur conceived, designed, and orchestrated the end run around the North Koreans when he ordered the US Xth Corps with its 7th Infantry and 1st Marine divisions to conduct amphibious landings at Inchon which was close to Seoul. He gave command of the Corps to his chief of staff Major General Edward Almond and kept him in both positions. Xth Corps regained Seoul and then attacked while Eighth Army broke out of Pusan and attacked north. The two commands linked up and then began attacking north across the 38th parallel toward China. MacArthur ordered the move to envelop the enemy in Korea at the border with China-the Yalu River and to force North Korea's surrender and regime change.

The Chinese entered the war launching a surprise counteroffensive in November that forced UN forces to withdraw south again to Pusan which they reached by the end of 1950. General Ridgway met in Japan with Generals MacArthur, and the Army Chief of Staff, J Lawton Collins and the Air Force Chief of Staff, Hoyt Vandenburg in January 1951 to discuss the role of the United States in South Korea. Ridgway, Collins, and Vandenburg met again on January 15th at Ridgway's headquarters in Pusan where the decision was made to attack the Chinese and North Koreans because Ridgway believed the enemy had expended itself. The US Eighth Army had three Corps (I, IX, and X) within which there were seven other Army divisions and the 1st Marine Division in addition to the 7th Infantry, and three Army regimental combat teams. Fourteen UN members sent combat troops to fight the Chinese and North Koreans.

Ridgway ordered his commanders to counterattack the North with his Koreans and Chinese and threatened Pyongyang and the other two cities comprising the Iron Triangle by late spring 1951. Ridgway succeeded MacArthur after President Truman replaced him for insubordination in April 1951. He was promoted to General. The new Eighth Army and UN forces commander was Lieutenant General James Van Fleet Van Fleet was promoted to General in 1951 also. Some corps and division commanders also moved to new assignments between January and June 1951.

Tactics:

The Korean War was symmetrical in that the opponents fought for objectives using tactics very similar to those in WWII. It was not fought for unconditional surrender after the Chinese counterattack in November 1950. Ridgway gave his orders to the corps commanders who gave their orders to the division commanders. The assigned missions to the commanders of the brigades and battalions who turned their orders into missions for the companies, platoons and squads. Control measures were the same also as in WWII so that units operated in their assigned zones. They attacked, defended, and reconnoitered as they had been trained and adapted to the terrain and weather in Korea.

Field Ration Level:

The draft ended formally in 1947. Conscription did not begin again until 1948 in response to the actions by the Soviet Union in Eastern Europe that began the Cold War, Congress approved President Truman's request to reinstate the draft. The Selective Service Act of 1948 required all young men, 18 and older to register for the draft. Those who fought in WWII did not have to register. Men under between 18 and 25 were eligible to be drafted to serve a five-year commitment. They could serve 21 months on active duty and the remainder in the reserves. The demands of the Korean War increased the term of service. The Universal Military Training and Service Act of 1951 increase the active duty requirement to 24 months and extended the total active and reserve obligation to eight years . Extensions were granted for those attending college or post-secondary school training programs.[757]

A soldier's term of service in Korea took place within the required active duty period which included training prior to being sent to Korea. The type of war was linear for the first year as the North Korean and Chinese forces battled those of the United Nations on the Korean peninsula. The type of war changed to one of limited objectives once the civilian leadership of the United Nations, China, and the Soviet Union agreed to end the fighting.

Field-Ration-level soldiers performed their assigned duties throughout the peace negotiating period from early June 1951 to July 27, 1953. They patrolled. They fought famous battles for terrain including Old Baldy and Pork Chop Hill only to give them back to the North Koreans.

Old Baldy was a series of five battles between June 26, 1952 and March 36 1953 to seize 12 Chinese outposts being used to observe US forces. Hill 266, Outpost 11, was Old Baldy. Hill 255 was Outpost 10 and was Pork Chop Hill. The first battle for Old Baldy was initiated by an infantry squad and later reinforced by elements of the rest of the company. This first battle began as a US squad against two Chinese squads. Hill 255 involved infantry combat between two US and two Chinese platoons

The later battles for Hill 255 now formally named Pork Chop Hill in US Army history took place during the April-June 1953 period. They involved the 7th Infantry Division's 31st Infantry Regiment, the unit supported by the Steel Tigers until December 1951. It began on April 16th when a US infantry 15-man ambush site was established at the base of the hill and was attacked by approximately two Chinese platoons at 11 pm. Two Chinese companies reached defending forces' perimeter undetected. Counterattacks were initiated and the Chinese withdrew on April 18th. Subsequent heavy fighting occurred into June when the armistice went into effect with Pork Chop Hill being placed within the Demilitarized Zone.

The negotiations began to end the fighting in Korea began on June 26, 1951. They dragged out until the armistice was signed on July 27, 1953. The North Koreans supported by the Chinese argued everything about getting down to business including the height of the national flags on the stands of the conference table at Panmunjom.[758]

President Eisenhower promised to end the war in Korea during his campaign for the presidency. He used diplomacy and military strong arming to achieve the armistice. Richard Nixon did the same thing when he ran for president in 1968. President Johnson and his advisors and the North Vietnamese began seeking an end to the Vietnam War in March 1968, but it took until June 1973 before the Paris Peace Accords were signed. The North Vietnamese used the same tactic as the North Koreans and the Chinese – delay progress. Nixon broke the deadlock when he connected Vietnam with opening relations with China in 1972 which reduced tensions with the Soviet Union.[759]

The Korean War has been called the Forgotten War because it was sandwiched between World War II and Vietnam. Carmelo Milia, the future Steel Tiger commander in Vietnam stated in a letter that he believed the fighting was harder in Korea. Joseph D. Offut, the A/1-77 First Sergeant, told his company commander, Jerry Brown, how he had been captured by the Chinese but he escaped back to friendly lines. The author met two Korean War veterans at a Local Walmart. One had been in the 7th Infantry Division. He had been wounded and evacuated before the November 1950 Chinese counteroffensive that stopped the UN drive to the Yalu River. The second veteran served during 1952-1953 period. Among his expletives, he stated one of the things that had stuck in his mind was why no one told the enemy they could stop shooting during the negotiations. Each veteran represented soldiers who served during that conflict because they were expected to serve whether draftee or volunteer regardless of rank.

Vietnam War
National Security Policy and Strategy:

US involvement in Southeast Asia began during President Eisenhower's term in 1954 and ended in 1973 when the last US combat troops were withdrawn. There were about 5,000 Americans remaining in Vietnam in 1975 when the South Vietnamese government collapsed during Gerald Ford's presidency.

President Eisenhower and his national strategy team including Secretary of State John Foster Dulles followed by Christian Herter; Secretaries of Defense, businessmen Charles Wilson, Neil McElroy and Thomas Gates; and his National Security Advisor, Robert Cutler believed that Vietnam's division into a communist north and democratic south at the 17th Parallel in the 1954 Geneva Accords was wrong given the communist movements elsewhere in the region. No one wanted another military confrontation in Asia so soon after the Korean War; however, the President authorized sending military assistance including to South Vietnam.

President Kennedy ordered US Army Special Forces and advisors to South Vietnam in 1961 and more were sent throughout his presidency. His national security team included Secretary of State, Dean Rusk; Secretary of Defense Robert McNamara; Allen Dulles, Director of the Central Intelligence Agency, and McGeorge Bundy the National Security Advisor.

President Johnson sent US Marines to Danang to protect the air base there and the Army's 173rd Airborne Brigade in 1965 to protect the Bien Hoa air base complex near

Saigon. Johnson's national security team included Secretary of State Dean Rusk; Secretaries of Defense Robert McNamara and Clark Clifford; National Security Advisors McGeorge Bundy and economist and political theorist Walt Rostow; and CIA Directors John McCone, Vice Admiral William Raborn, and Richard Helms. Johnson was averse to the possible entry of the Chinese into the Vietnam War and having another Korea on his plate. He authorized bombing across the 17th Parallel (along the Ben Hai River) but no attacks by ground forces. His goal was to convince the North Vietnamese that its government could not accept the costs in casualties and infrastructure destruction.

President Johnson did not achieve his goal. Ho Chi Minh and his counselors accepted the high casualty numbers and continued their goal of wearing down US resolve to remain in Vietnam. Meanwhile talks began in Paris to negotiate an end to the conflict.

President Nixon's security and national strategy team included: Secretaries of State William Rogers and Henry Kissinger; Secretaries of Defense Melvin Laird, Elliot Richardson, and James Schlesinger; CIA Directors Richard Helms; and National Security Advisor Henry Kissinger. President Ford's team following Nixon's resignation and through the April 1975 fall of Saigon was Secretary of State Henry Kissinger; Secretaries of Defense James Schlesinger and Donald Rumsfeld; National Security Advisor Henry Kissinger; CIA Director, Richard Helms, James Schlesinger, and William Colby. Nixon campaigned for the presidency stating that he had a plan to end the war. Hanoi continued its tactic until Nixon's opening of a US-Chinese dialogue led to pressure applied by China and the Soviet Union on Hanoi to end the fighting.

There was another feature of the Vietnam War that was different from earlier wars: tension in the US caused by the combination of Legislative Branch oversight and Executive Branch objectives as President Nixon applied pressure on Hanoi to negotiate an agreement that would allow US combat forces to leave South Vietnam. Senators John Sherman Cooper and Frank Church amended the Foreign Military Sales Act of 1971 that ended funding for US combat troops and advisors to operate outside of South Vietnam. in Hanoi's safe havens in located in Cambodia where the US and South Vietnamese operated during the April-July 1970 period and in Laos beginning in February1971. The Cooper-Church Amendment did not pass the US Senate and House of Representatives until January 1971.

The US entry into Vietnam from Eisenhower through Ford was a limited one and consistent: to allow its citizens the freedom to choose their government and not to have it imposed on them. It was not to oust the communists in the north. It was to preserve the opportunity for the South Vietnamese government to solidify its position as a nation capable of defeating subversive movements and open aggression. Eisenhower pledged $1 billion in economic and military assistance. The purpose of this aid was not to do the fighting for the South Vietnamese.[760]

The Red Devil Brigade's, including the Steel Tigers, final major mission in South Vietnam was LAM SON in 1971. This operation fell under an amendment to US Congress' 1970 defense appropriations act forbidding US ground troops to enter Laos. The ARVN had to prosecute the LAM SON 719 without advisors to communicate the required support to U.S. air, artillery and logistics organizations.

Military Strategy:

During the US military's presence in South Vietnam, there were six chairmen of the Joint Chiefs of Staff between 1954 and 1976, and 10 Chiefs of Staff of the US Army beginning with General Ridgway in 1954 and ending with General Frederick Weyand who served in the office from 1974 to 1976. They transmitted the national civilian leadership's instructions and desires to first the Military Assistance Advisory Group (MAAG), Vietnam This organization, authorized by President Truman in 1950 was named MAAG Indochina and commanded by an Army brigadier general while the French controlled Vietnam. Once the French left in 1955, it was renamed MAAG, Vietnam and commanded by either lieutenant or major generals. The MAAG became part of the US Military Assistance Command, Vietnam (MACV) in 1964 following the substantial increase in US presence and responsibilities, and the arrival of US combat troops began in March 1965.[761]

Operational Art:

General Paul D Harmon was the first Commander US Military Command (COMUSMACV) served from 1962 until June 1964.[762] He was followed by General William Westmoreland between 1964 and 1968. General Creighton Abrams, Westmoreland's deputy, took command in June 1968 and turned MAACV over to General Weyand in 1972-1973 when MACV stood down and turned its mission over to the US Military Attaché in Saigon until South Vietnam surrendered in 1975.

Westmoreland used US ground forces to fight the communists. He assessed the GVN to be unable combat the communists, There were 23,000 advisors in South Vietnam at the end of 1964.The arrival of the 1st Brigade 5th Infantry Division (M) in July 1968 raised the total to more than 549,000. General Abrams changed to focus from US forces fighting in place of the South Vietnamese to demonstrating to the civilian population in the provinces that the Saigon government could secure them in the hamlets, villages and towns while the Americans remained in the background and took the fight to the communists in the unpopulated countryside without requesting more US troops.

Tactics:

The 1st Battalion, 77th Armor fought as a combined arms task force generally with one tank company supporting an infantry battalion and an attached mechanized infantry company that was reinforced occasionally with an infantry company from July 1968 through August 1971. The battalion's task organization depended on the missions it was assigned and the terrain. Operations included night ambushes, route reconnaissance, search and clear, and artillery raids. Cordons by brigade units and village searches by Government of Vietnam (GVN) units were common in populated areas.

The Steel Tigers initiated Red Devil Brigade-directed combat missions and supported 3MARDIV units in areas void of civilians. Under Abrams, the effort was on joint operations with GVN units to deny enemy access to populated portions of the province. Cordons and searches, civic action projects various scale depending what the villages needed to be done, and medical and dental care were delivered to villages. US forces were in the background in many cases and were observed by the locals to be with South Vietnamese community and district leaders when necessary.

The Steel Tigers operated throughout South Vietnam's northernmost province: Quang Tri. The province was bordered by the Demilitarized Zone across the north, Thua Thien Province at its border with Quang Tri in the south, the Laotian border in the west, and the South China Sea in the east.

When the 1-77 arrived, it shared Quang Tri Province with the following combat units: 1st Air Cavalry Division, 3MARDIV, the First Infantry Division (ARVN), and the 9th Infantry Division's 3rd Squadron, 5th Armored Cavalry. Other Army units were non-divisional artillery, engineers, and other combat support and service support units. The 101st Airborne (Airmobile) Division and 3rd Brigade 82d Airborne were directly south in Thua Thien Province.

North Vietnamese and COSVN South Vietnamese communist regular units fought in battalion, and regimental strength when surprised. When they initiated attacks, surprise was the tactic of choice. Offensive actions began in darkness and usually after midnight.

The enemy withdrew just before first light in the mornings when US ground units could expect USAF and Army air support to arrive.

The North Vietnamese reaction to the ARVN's LAM SON 719 thrust into Laos was that they were able to apply larger numbers of troop units from inside the Laotian safe haven than they had been able to infiltrate into South Vietnam. Combined US air and artillery support accounted for large NVA losses of men and equipment. Various sources from the military strategy, operational art, and tactical levels concluded negative and positive assessments on LAM SON 719; but it was indisputable that this 1971 mission was the first time the GVN had conducted a major ground force operation on its own.

Field Ration Level:

The popular assessment by many veterans of the 1971 *DEWEY CANYON II-LAM SON 719* operation including members of the Steel Tigers was that it was a debacle. Detailed studies of the battle were that it went well for the South Vietnamese army's first time out of the gate without their units' US advisory teams given the impact of the month-old Cooper-Church Amendment. Differences of opinion existed at each level of analysis. The best that can be said is that where a veteran stood on the success or failure of this operation depends on where that individual served in it.

The draft was in effect when the Steel Tigers were at Fort Carson, deployed to South Vietnam and were deactivated in 1971. The Fort Knox Armor School's officer tactical training emphasized combat against the Warsaw Pact, and the linear warfare of World War II and the first year of the Korean War in which the objective was to gain and hold ground and force the enemy to withdraw. Enlisted training stressed learning the skill sets necessary for becoming qualified to perform in the Military Occupational Specialties (MOS) at the training centers designated for the required skills regardless of where graduates might be assigned.

In addition to the armor training, officers and enlisted at the Field-Ration level brought their individual skills from their officer basic courses and their enlisted basic followed by advanced individual training at the appropriate training schools to their units: the 1-77, 2-77, 3-77, 4-77, and 5-77. For example, the battalion signal officer trained at Fort Monmouth, New Jersey while the enlisted signal specialists learned their skills at Fort Gordon Georgia, and the medics did the same at Fort Sam Houston Texas after basic training. Each Steel Tiger battalion was led by commissioned and non-commissioned officers who were experienced professionals, and others who were serving their obligated service. All had responsibilities commensurate with their ranks. Enlisted soldiers who were not in leadership roles also had those who volunteered and those who had been drafted performing in their MOS's. Officers and enlisted were sent to the 2-77 Armor, 3-77 Armor, 4-77 Armor, and 5-77 Armor as individual replacements.

Those newly assigned to the 1-77 Armor at Fort Carson combined this diverse group. trained as a unit. and then deployed as a unit. The term of service in Vietnam was 12 months, Once in South Vietnam, some members were sent to other units in return for replacements whose end-of-tour departure dates varied. On the one hand, this prevented an entire Red Devil battalion from departing South Vietnam at the same time. On the other hand, the camaraderie and experience gained from soldiers working together that developed beginning in March 1968 ended.

Once in South Vietnam, the 1-77 Armor continued limited objective warfare. At the top of the funnel was national strategy that was designed to force North Vietnam's leadership to negotiate a peace agreement through punishing them with unacceptable casualties was unsuccessful. Punishing the enemy's ground force bases in South Vietnam but not crossing north of the 17th Parallel that divided North and South Vietnam and being forbidden to cross the Laotian and Cambodian borders which were safe havens did not lead to negotiations. President Nixon succeeded President Johnson at the national policymaking level and initiated some changes. Military-strategic, and operational art levels were consistent with the national strategies of the two presidents.

The Field-Ration level focused on performing in their skill sets in the limited objectives framework they entered. The Red Devil Brigade deployed from Fort Carson into Quang Tri Province that had become more stable following the US responses to the January 1968 Tet and the 1969 Khe Sanh offensives. The Brigade adapted to new tactical demands placed on it. They were assigned areas of operations and worked freely within them to deplete any enemy opposition in uninhabited portions. Restraint was required to protect noncombatant civilians in populated towns and villages.

The Steel Tigers, 1-61 Inf (M), and the 1-11 Inf task forces operating within their respective populated and unpopulated areas did not occupy the objectives they cleared. They moved to their next missions. The withdrawal of US forces stationed in Quang Tri Province accelerated the number and scope of the challenges the Red Devils faced until August 1971 when they withdrew. Fewer units were responsible for larger areas of operations. The enemy reconstituted their previously decimated units and infiltrated them back into South Vietnam from their cross-border safe havens filling the vacuums with increasing impunity.

Battalion Administration

Guy Holmes was the Steel Tigers' Personnel Noncommissioned Officer; He was serving his third 12-month tour in South Vietnam. He was assigned to the 1-77 Armor for this tour. Although he was a member of a combat organization, his assignment did not require him to fight the enemy. Nevertheless, he experienced stressful situations. He had to interact with the brigade's graves registration unit. Also, there was always the probability of a non-combat injury. One example was the incident where he and a younger soldier tried to fix the battalion's flagpole. The flagpole bent and snapped as the soldier shinnied toward the top causing him to fall and break both ankles. The one hostile event occurred when was driving on QL-1 south from LZ Nancy to XXIV Corps headquarters at Phu Bai with a jeep and a trailer to pick up various supplies. On his return trip towing a full trailer, a guerilla hidden in a civilian bus full of passengers opened fire at Holmes and his driver. Holmes told his driver to accelerate without losing the trailer while he stood up in the jeep with his weapon. Holmes did not return fire. When they arrived at LZ Nancy, the driver requested to be reassigned back to his tank company. Holmes did not want to endanger a replacement, so he stated he drove his jeep alone after that incident.[763]

Tank Platoon Warfare

Kevin Dunne was the driver of Tank A-34 which was the A/1-77 third platoon sergeant's tank. The original platoon sergeant who had deployed with the battalion from Fort Carson, Merton Texeira, rotated back to the US and was replaced by a new platoon sergeant during the time after A/1-77 replaced C/1-77 operating on the Khe Sanh Plateau when the 1-61 Inf (M) assumed control of Task Force Remagen on April 11th. Task Force Remagen's final mission was to occupy defensive positions beginning April 24th, perform maintenance, and then depart the Plateau for LZs Sharon and Nancy on the 26th. The 3rd platoon and two 1st platoon tanks were assigned to reinforce an ARVN battalion located in the vicinity of the abandoned KSCB.

The North Vietnamese attacked the ARVN position with about a battalion at 3:30 am beginning with a mortar attack followed by an infantry and engineer attach using satchel charges, RPGs hand grenades, small arms, and a flame thrower. The NVA penetrated the perimeter. Dunne recalled that the new platoon sergeant panicked, disconnected his control helmet and sat on the turret floor. The three-man crew already short the tank gunner was reduced to two with Dunne and the loader firing A-34's machineguns and beehive main gun ammunition. His platoon leader called on the radio stating he and his crew were about to abandon Tank A-31. Another tank commander replied that the lieutenant could not do that and that crew remained fighting their vehicle. The attackers withdrew at about 6:00 am when daylight occurred.[764] The retrograde operation that was to begin on the 26th was delayed until the 28th. The rest of A/1-77 Armor was attacked early that morning and the movement off from Khe Sanh was delayed again. It began on the 29th.

B/1-77 Armor was the Steel Tiger company identified for Operation UTAH MESA that was subordinate again to the 1-61 Inf(M). Movement to the plateau began in mid-June. Company B's 1st Platoon was part of Team B attached to B/1-61 Inf (M). An attack of the same intensity as experienced by A/1-77 Armor's 3d platoon on April 25th occurred early in the morning of June 18th. Once again, the enemy numbering about 100, broke through Team B/1-61's perimeter, and then withdrew at daylight when they became vulnerable to US air support. The tankers fired all of their beehive ammunition and began using their High Explosive Antitank ammunition against enemy infantry and sappers (combat engineers) who were carrying satchel charges.

Tank Battalion Maintenance

Maintenance is a full time undertaking especially in units with tracked vehicles. Task Force Remagen and Operation UTAH MESA demanded special mention because all maintenance had to be done with materials located at the forward support base at Ca Lu next to the Vandegrift Combat Base airfield. Transport to the Plateau had to be by air. Rations, ammunition, fuel, water, medical, major end items, and repair parts to keep vehicles operational, and the soldiers supported with their needs.

There was one occasion when the B/1-77 maintenance section assisted in the recovery of a 17-ton USMC Sikorsky CH-53E Super Stallion heavy lift helicopter. The aircraft was forced to land near LZ Sharon on a Sunday afternoon. There were neither any injuries nor enemy action involved.

The company sent a tank platoon to secure the helicopter and crew while they called for assistance from their unit at Da Nang. The weight of the downed helicopter was too great for a second Sea Stallion to lift intact using an external sling because its capacity was 6.5 tons. The scaffold and winch that was designed to be used in a hangar that the Marines sent could not be used in the field. Recovery of the aircraft meant reducing the aircraft's weight by removing the two engines and transmission. The plan was to load these items into a second CH-53E and then rig the fuselage for external transport using a sling on the second helicopter for the 115 mile trip back to Da Nang.

The Steel Tigers called for its maintenance section to assist. Figure 8.1 shows the maintenance section using its M-88 VTR with the 22-ton lifting capacity of its a-frame winch and boom removing the transmission from the CH-53. The two engines lightening the fuselage's weight had been removed earlier. The VTR had been designed to lift tank engines, transmissions, turrets, and other equipment including pallets of tank track and vehicles in a field environment. The entire operation consumed several hours, but this was because of the distance to the Marines' base. The helicopter, crew, engines and transmission were evacuated to Da Nang finally, and the Steel Tigers returned to LZ Sharon where the maintenance section painted a CH-53E helicopter silhouette on the side of the VTR along with individual tanks recovered since July 1968 for all to see.

Figure 8.1 Steel Tigers Assist Retrieval of USMC CH-53E Super Stallion
Source: Photo Courtesy of Robert Forman

Medical Specialists

Each Steel Tiger tank company was assigned one medic per platoon and one in the company headquarters section who rode in a M-113 A1 Armored Personnel Carrier with caliber.50 machine gun at the vehicle commander's hatch and a Red Cross painted on a large white square on the sides. Medics were often decorated for valor their caring for wounded soldiers. Dedicated to their specialty, they also suffered casualties. Two medics in one of the Steel Tiger companies, Jimmy Dolvin and Harold Stump, were killed in action. Stump was a conscientious objector who did not carry a weapon. Instead, he always had his bible.[765]

Artillery Support

Artillery officers and enlisted soldiers are trained at the Field Artillery School located at Fort Sill Oklahoma. Each Steel Tiger tank company was authorized an artillery officer in the role of the forward observer (FO) a reconnaissance noncommissioned officer and a radiotelephone operator. The three were authorized a jeep, but the officer normally rode on the 2d tank in the company headquarters tank section so he could interact with the company commander. The FO planned artillery fire missions and requested fire support in the field. An artillery coordinating officer was located in a battalion's tactical operations center who coordinated all artillery support in the battalion's area of operation. These individuals were attached to the maneuver battalions but were assigned to the 5th Battalion, 4th Artillery 155mm Self Propelled which was the Red Devil Brigade's direct support field artillery battalion.[766]

Those who operate at the field-ration level apply their skill sets as those who served before them within the boundaries established by the upper levels of the funnel. In addition to the 77th Armor's experiences in South Vietnam, this study presented the similarities and differences between the experiences of France's 1,017-man volunteer battalion who fought with the 2d US Infantry Division from November 1950 through October 1953 during the Korean War and then in Vietnam's Central Highlands between January and July 1954 when the fighting ended against what Ho Chi Minh named the first Indochina War. Examples since and before are easily found in histories of warfare.

This story of the Steel Tiger Regiment since its creation ends at the end of the Cold War. It continues into the years since with its deployments to Bosnia, Kosovo, Iraq, Afghanistan, and elsewhere.

About the Author

Donald L Cummings served in the 1ˢᵗ Battalion 77ᵗʰ Armor in 1968 when it deployed to South Vietnam. He was the battalion's intelligence officer and then a tank company commander. He served overseas in the 1ˢᵗ Battalion 72ⁿᵈ Armor, 2ⁿᵈ Infantry Division in South Korea and 3ʳᵈ Brigade, 1ˢᵗ Armored Division in West Germany. Assignments in the United States included company command at Fort Leonard Wood, Missouri, membership on an interagency team where he coauthored the methodology that led to the production of the US Intelligence Community's first coordinated study of the Warsaw Pact's current and projected combat arms force structure. Cummings served as a senior analyst in the Defense Intelligence Agency's Africa Branch where he was responsible for seven former French and Portuguese colonies and later for Ethiopia. He joined a major defense contractor as a senior analyst and program manager. He was an adjunct faculty member in George Mason University's Department of Public Affairs where he presented an upper division course in Latin American government and politics and a lower division comparative politics survey course. He later joined the doctoral program at National American University's Henley-Putnam School of Strategic Studies. Cummings holds an MA and PhD in Political Science from the University of California, Santa Barbara and a BA from The Virginia Military Institute. He is a graduate of the US Army Command and General Staff College.

Index

Endnotes

Preface

[1] Title 50-War Appendix, Selective Training and Service Act of 1940, Act, Sept. 16, 1940, 3:08 pm, E.S.T., Ch 720, 54 STAT 885, Article 302, Page 269

[2] Ray Cline, The United States in World War II, The War Department, Washington Command Post, Center of Military History, United States Army, Washington, DC, 1990, pp. 29-30.

[3] Thomas C. Schelling, Foreword, in Roberta Wohlstetter, *Pearl Harbor: Warning and Decision,* Stanford, California, Stanford University Press, 1962, pp vii-ix., and Henry Kissinger, *Leadership: Six Studies in World Strategy,* New York, Penguin Press, 2022, pp. xv-

[4] Henry Kissinger, *Leadership: Six Studies in World Strategy,* New York, Penguin Press, 2022, p. xvi

[5] Arthur Conan Doyle, A Study in Scarlet, First published I 1887, Copyright 2020 Classica Libris. Kindle locations 145,154, and 163 of 1834.

[6] Samuel Huntington, *The Soldier and the State: The Theory and Politics of Civil-Military Relations*, New York, Vintage Books, 1957, pp. 2, 7-18.

[7] National Security Strategy (United States) Retrieved from https://en.wikipedia.org/wiki/National_Security_Strategy_%28United_States%2 and National Security Strategy (defense.gov)September 2, 2022

[8] AcqNotes,: Program Management Tool for Aerospace, PPBE National Defense Strategy, Retrieved from www.bing.com/search?q=us+definition+military+strategy&cvid=9ae2712f35424170892f8ef2c52b91e8&aqs=edge. 0.69i59i450l8...8.921911j0j4&FORM=ANAB01&PC=U531, September 2, 2022

[9] National Military Strategy (United States) Retrieved from National Military Strategy (United States) - Wikipedia September 2, 2022.

[10] William P. Baxter, *Soviet AirLand Battle Tactics*, Novato, CA Presidio Press, 1986, pp 27-28, and Lt Col Wilson C. Blythe, A History of Operational. Art, *Military Review*, November-December 2018, pp. 37-49. Retrieved from English Military Review November-December 2018 Blythe (army.mil)

[11] M.S. Ridgway, The Korean War,: Issues and Policies, pp 370-371 as quoted in Billy C. Mossman, The United States Army In the Korean War: Ebb and Flow, November 1950-July 1951, Center of Military History, United States Army, Washington, DC 8 September 1988, p.229, retrieved from UNITED STATES ARMY IN THE KOREAN WAR: EBB AND FLOW, NOVEMBER 1950-JULY 1951

[12] Excerpts from Secretary Powell's Response to George Carey, Archive, US Department of State, World Economic Forum, Davos, Switzerland, January 26, 2003 retrieved from U.S. Department of State: Excerpts From Secretary Powell's Response to George Carey

Chapter 1

[13] Forrest Pogue, George C. Marshall: Organizer of Victory:1943-1945, New York , Viking Press, 1973

[14] Little Willie, Wikipedia, retrieved from Little Willie - Wikipedia August 29, 2022.

[15] Tank Mk I (Big Willie/Centipede/Mother: Medium/Heavy Tank 1916, retrieved from Tank Mk I (Big Willie / Centipede / Mother) (militaryfactory.com)

[16] John Keegan, *The First World War*, New York, Vintage Books, 1998, p. 298

[17] Discover Battle of Cambrai 1917: Facts & History | CWGC, and https://en.wikipedia.org/wiki/Battle_of_Cambrai_(1917), retrieved August 27, 2022

[18] Schneider CA 1 schneider tank WW I - Search (bing.com), Retreived August 29, 2022

[19] Saint-Chamond (tank) Retrieved from https://en.wikipedia.org/wiki/Saint-Chamond_(tank)#The_Saint-Chamond August 29, 2022

[20] The Renault FT-17 light tank, Renault FT - Wikipedia, and Renault FT - Tank Encyclopedia (tanks-encyclopedia.com) retrieved August 29, 2022

[21] German A7V Heavy Tank, A7V - Wikipedia Retrieved August 29, 2022

[22] Tanks of the United States, Tanks of the United States - Wikipedia, August 29, 2022

[23] Martin Blumenson, *The Patton Papers 1885-1940*, Boston, Houghton Mifflin Company, 1972, pp.421-423, 430, 434.

[24] German A7V, op.cit., August 30. 2022

[25] Martin Blumenson, *The Patton Papers 1885-1940,* op.cit. pp.583-586.

[26] Ibid. 596

[27] US Military Manpower 1789-1997, Big Book of Warfare and Other Stuff. Retrieved from U.S. Military Manpower - 1789 to 1997 (alternatewars.com) September 2, 2022.

[28] Kent Roberts Greenfield, Robert R. Palmer, and Bell I Wiley, *The Army Ground Forces, op.cit.* p.57.

[29] Martin Blumenson, *The Patton Papers 1885-1940,* op.cit., p. 446

[30] Ernst Volckheim retrieved from Ernst Volckheim – Wikipedia, September 5, 2022

[31] Kent Roberts Greenfield, Robert R. Palmer, and Bell I Wiley, *The United States Army in World War II, The Army Ground Forces: The Organization of Ground Combat Troops*, Washington, D.C., Center of Military History, 1987, pp. 1-2.

[32] Marshall and the Benning Revolution, The George C. Marshall Foundation, January 2015, retrieved from https: www.marshall foundation.org. October 23, 2022, and Infantry School: An Almost Complete Revamping of the Instruction and Technique, The George C. Marshall Foundation, November 12, 2020, retrieved from https: www.marshall foundation.org

[33] George C. Marshall, retrieved from en.m.wikipedia.org

[34] Troy. H. Middleton, retrieved from en.m.wikipedia.org, October 19, 2022., and Garland, Albert N and Smyth, Howard McGaw with Blumenson, Martin, *Sicily and the Surrender of Italy: United States Army in World War II: The Mediterranean Theater of Operations*. Washington, DC, Center of Military History,, 1993. Retrieved from Sicily and the Surrender of Italy (army.mil) October 31, 2022, p, 95.

[35] Bill Mauldin-A Legend Passes On-45th Infantry Division, http://www.45th division.org, October 23, 2020

[36] William S. Key, retrieved from en.m.wikipedia.org, October 19, 2022.

[37] History of the 753rd Tank Battalion (M), Headquarters, 753rd Tank Battalion (M) U.S. Army, APO New York, N.Y. 700, June 17, 1943, p. 1. Retrieved from History of the 753rd Tank Battalion. - World War II Operational Documents - Ike Skelton Combined Arms Research Library (CARL) Digital Library (oclc.org) August 30, 2022.

Chapter 2

[38] http://www.753rdtankbattalion.com/index3.html

[39] Military.com Unit Pages, 753rd Tank Battalion, Stand to it Stoutly, Retrieved from http://www.military.com/HomePage/UnitPageFullText/1%2C13476%2C733011%2C00.html

[40] Colonel Anthony F. Daskevitch II (15 March 2008), *Insights in modularity: 753rd Tank Battalion in World War II*, Carlisle, PA, US Army War College, pp. 5-6 retrieved from https://apps.dtic.mil/dtic/tr/fulltext/u2/a478430.pdf

[41] *Ibid.*, p.7.

[42] *Ibid.,* p.8.

[43] Garland, Albert N and Smyth, Howard McGaw with Blumenson, Martin, *Sicily and the Surrender of Italy: United States Army in World War II: The Mediterranean Theater of Operations*. Washington, DC, Center of Military History,, 1993. Retrieved from Sicily and the Surrender of Italy (army.mil) October 31, 2022, pp 3-12.

[44] *Ibid.*, pp.32-43

[45] *Ibid.*, p. 50,51 and 267,268.

[46] *Ibid.*, pp 283-284.

[47] Daskevitch, *Insights in modularity,*op.cit.,p.7 and Camp Patrick Henry, Camp Patrick Henry | Military Wiki | Fandom and Camp Patrick Henry - Wikipedia

[48] *Ibid.,*

[49] Ibid. and <u>45th Infantry Division (United States) - Wikipedia</u>

[50]USS Ancon (AGC-4) <u>USS Ancon (AGC-4) - Wikipedia</u>

[51] Hampton Roads Port of Embarkation 45h Infantry Division retrieved from <u>45th infantry division embarkation port - Search (bing.com)</u> October 5, 2020.

[52]USS Ancon (AGC-4) <u>USS Ancon (AGC-4) - Wikipedia</u> op.cit.

[53] Daskevitch, *Insights in modularity,*op.cit.,p.7

16. <u>Ibid.</u>, p., 7

[54] Retrieved from the hall of valor project, *The Military Times* https://valor.militarytimes.com/hero/67182

[55] Daskevitch *Insights in modularity*, op.cit. p. 7-8.

[56] Albert N. Garland and Howard McGaw Smyth Assisted by Martin Blumenson, The United States Army in World War II, The Mediterranean Theater of Operations, Sicily and the Surrender of Italy, Center of Military History United States Army Washington, DC, 1993, pp.95,98. Retrieved from <u>Sicily and the Surrender of Italy (army.mil)</u> October 7, 2022

[57] Leo V. Bishop, Lieutenant Colonel, GSC, AC ofS.G2; Frank J. Glasgow, Major, GSC, AC of S G1 and George A Fisher, Major, Staff Judge Advocate, *The Fighting Forty-Fifth: The Combat Report of an Infantry Division, Unit History Part 1,* page 25.

[58] Ibid., pp 41 and 44.

[59] Historical Record of the 191st Infantry Battalion. Page1 retrieved from <u>p4013coll8_5185.pdf</u>

[60] Garland, Albert N and Smyth, Howard McGaw with Blumenson, Martin, "Appendix A, Composition of U.S. Forces on D-Day, July 10, 1943," *Sicily and the Surrender of Italy: United States Army in World War II: The Mediterranean Theater of Operations*. Washington, DC, Center of Military History,, 1993.<u>pp. 64, 81-82</u>

[61] Ibid., and Daskevitch op.cit. pp. 8-9.

[62] Ibid., pp 200-201.

[63] Germans issued orders to evacuate all German air units and consolidate Ibid., pp 283-4

[63] Albert N. Garland and Howard McGaw Smyth Sicily and the Surrender of Italy 1993 op.cit. . Retrieved from <u>Sicily and the Surrender of Italy (army.mil)</u> October 31, 2022, p, 63, 76, 80

[64] <u>Ibid.,</u> pp. 48,51,75.

[65] *Ibid.* pp 406-410.

[66] *Ibid.*, pp508 and 515

[67] Ibid. pp 442.

[68] Daskevitch *Insights in modularity*, op.cit p. 11.

[69] *Ibid.*, p. 12-14.

[70] *Ibid.*, p. 13-16.

[71] *Ibid.*, p. 16.

[72] Martin Blumenson, *Salerno to Cassino. United States Army in World War II: The Mediterranean Theater of Operations*, Center of Military History, United States Army, Washington, DC 1993, p. 271, retrieved from <u>Salerno To Cassino (army.mil), p. 226-7, 262</u>

[73] Center of Military History (1990), *Fifth Army at the winter line (15 November – 15 January 1944)*, CMH Pub 100-9, retrieved from <u>https://history.army.mil/html/books/100/100-9/CMH_Pub_100-9.pdf</u>. P 2-16. 04.28.2018

[74] *Ibid.*, p. 18, 05.01.2018.

[75] Center of Military History (1990), *Fifth Army at the winter line (15 November – 15 January 1944)*, CMH Pub 100-9, retrieved from <u>https://history.army.mil/html/books/100/100-9/CMH_Pub_100-9.pdf</u>. P 4-8. 04.30.2018

[76] Martin Blumenson, *Salerno to Cassino*. <u>op.cit</u>. p. 271, retrieved from <u>Salerno To Cassino (army.mil)</u>.

[77] Daskevitch *Insights in modularity*, op.cit. p. 17-20. O5.01.2018

[78] Center of Military History (1990), *Fifth Army at the winter line (15 November – 15 January 1944)*, p.67, 05.01.2018

[79] Daskevitch *Insights in modularity*, op.cit p. 17-22. 05.02.2018

[80] Ibid., pp. 21-22. 05.02.2018.

[81] Ibid., pp. 22-23, pp 05.02.2018.

[82] *Ibid.*, p.24, 05.02.2018.

[83] Martin Blumenson, *Salerno to Cassino.* op.cit. p. 271, and 358-357, retrieved from <u>Salerno To Cassino (army.mil)</u>.

[84] Ibid., pp. 368-371 and The Italian Campaign, Page 4, Cassino, *New Zealand History*, retrieved from <u>Cassino – The Italian Campaign | NZHistory, New Zealand history online</u> June 7, 2023

[85] Daskevitch *Insights in modularity*, op.cit p. 17-22. 05.02.2018

[86] *Ibid.*, p.26., 05.02.2018

[87] Ibid., p.26 05.02.2018

[88] Harry Yeide, Steel victory: the heroic story of American independent tank battalions at war in Europe, Presidio Press, 2003, p. 117.

[89] Center of Military History,(CMH Pub 72-31), p.6, retrieved from <u>https://history.army.mil/brochures/sfrance/sfrance.htm</u> , 05.30.2018

[90] Harry Yeide, *Steel victory*, *op.cit.* p. 117.

[91] Center of Military History, (CMH Pub 72-31), retrieved from <u>https://history.army.mil/brochures/sfrance.htm</u>, P.7, 06.25.2018

[92] *Ibid.,* P.14, 05.30.2018

[93] *Ibid.,* P.17, 05.30.2018

[94] Daskevitch *Insights in modularity*, op.cit p. 28.

[95] Center of Military History, (CMH Pub 72-3) *op.cit., p. 16,17*

[96] Michael J. Volpe, (2007) Task force Butler: a case study in the employment of an adhoc unit in combat operations, during Operation Dragoon, 1-30 August 1944 (Masters thesis) retrieved from <u>http://www.dtic.mil/dtic/tr/fulltext/u2/a475573.pdf</u> p. 10. 05.30.2018

[97] Jeffrey J. Clarke and Robert Ross Smith (1993) *United States Army, The European Theater of Operations: Riviera to the Rhine* retrieved from <u>https://history.army.mil/html/books/007/7-10-1/CMH_Pub_7-10-1.pdf</u>, p. 145-7 05.31.2018.

[98] *Ibid.*, p. 148-154.

[99] Daskevitch *Insights in modularity*, op.cit p. 28.

[100] Clarke and Smith (1993), *op.cit.* p. 223.

[101] *Ibid.*, p. 231-3.

[102] *Ibid.*, p. 392.

[103] *Ibid.*, p. 392.

[104] Daskevitch *Insights in modularity*, op.cit p. 29.

[105] French Moments retrieved from <u>https://frenchmoments.eu/vosges/</u> 06.13.2018

[106] Clarke and Smith (1993), *op.cit*, p. 313.

[107] *Ibid.*, p. 315.

[108] Lost Battalion (Europe, World War II retrieved from <u>https://en.wikipedia.org/wiki/Lost_Battalion_(Europe,_World_War_II)</u> October 15, 2022

[109] *Ibid.*

[110] Clarke and Smith (1993), *op.cit*, p. 343-345

[111] *Ibid.*, p. 392.

[112] *Ibid.*, p. 404.

[113] *Ibid.*, p. 455-459.

[114] *Ibid.*, p. 464.

[115] *Ibid.*, p. 488.

[116] *Ibid.*, p. 493.

[117] *Ibid.*, p. 495.

[118] *Ibid.*, p. 495-7.

[119] *Ibid.*, p. 500.

[120] Daskevitch *Insights in modularity*, op.cit p. 29-30.

[121] Clarke and Smith (1993), *op.cit*, p. 513.

[122] Company A, 753rd Tank Battalion, Company Narrative for January 1945, 6 Februray 1945, pp 1-3, in 753rd Tank Battalion, 8735 TB 10/c in 753rd Tank Battalion. - World War II Operational Documents - Ike Skelton Combined Arms Research Library (CARL) Digital Library (oclc.org) pages 23-25.
[123] Ibid., p.3.
[124] Ibid., pp3,4.
[125] Charles McDonald (1993), The last offensive, The United States Army in World War II, European Theater of operations, center of military history, Washington, DC CMH Pub_7-9-1.pdf, p.254-5 retrieved from https://history.army.mil/html/books/007/7-9-1/CMH_Pub_7-9-1.pdf 06.16.2018
[126] Daskevitch Insights in modularity, op.cit p. 30.
[127] Charles McDonald (1993), The last offensive, The United States Army in World War II, European Theater of operations, center of military history, Washington, DC CMH Pub_7-9-1.pdf, p.254-5 retrieved from https://history.army.mil/html/books/007/7-9-1/CMH_Pub_7-9-1.pdf 06.16.2018
[128] Daskevitch Insights in modularity, op.cit p. 30.
[129] Ibid., p. 30.
[130] Ibid., p. 31.

[131] John E. Dahlquist, Headquarters, 36th Infantry Division, Office of the Commanding General, "Departure of the 753rd Tank Battalion," memorandum for Commanding Officer, 753rd Tank Battalion, 11 June 1945. Document from the personal papers of the author's father, Anthony F. Daskevitch, wartime member of the 753rd Tank Battalion as quoted in Daskevitch Insights in modularity, op.cit p. 51.

Chapter 3

[132] George F. Kennan, The Sources of Soviet Conduct, Foreign Affairs: An American Quarterly Review, Volume 25, Number 4, July 1947, ((New York: Council of Foreign Relations) pp. 566-611.

[133] Donald A. Carter, Forging the Shield: The U.S. Army in Europe, 1951-1962, CMH Publication 45-3-1 (Washington, D.C.: Center of Military History) 2015, pp. 7-9.

[134] Max Hastings, Vietnam: An Epic Tragedy, 1945-1975, New York: Harper Perennial, 2018, pp. 79, 85, 92, and Bernard B. Fall, The Street Without Joy: The French Debacle in Indochina, Stackpole Books, 1961 and republished 1994, Stackpole Military History Series, pp 249-264, 267, 281, 282,and 287.
[135] China Contributed Substantially to Vietnam War Victory, Claims Scholar, Interview with Qiang Zhai and Tim Dilorio, Wilson Center Cold War International History Project, January 1, 2001, retreived from China Contributed Substantially to Vietnam War Victory, Claims Scholar | Wilson Center, February 17, 2023.
[136] Henry Kissinger, Charles De Gaulle: The Strategy of Will, Leadership: Six Studies in World Strategy, New York, Penguin Press, 2022, p 91.
[137] Carter,op.cit, p.6.

[138] Carter, Ibid., p.5.

[139] Forest C. Pogue, George C. Marshall 3, Organizer of Victory (New York: Viking Press) p.585.

[140] Carter, op.cit. p358.

[141] Carter, Ibid., pp. 358- 359.

[142] Carter, Ibid. , P.407.

[143] Carter, Ibid., pp. 407, 409.

[144] Carter, Ibid., pp. 411-413.

[145] Carter, Ibid., pp 415-419.

[146] Carter, Ibid., pp. 415, 420.

[147] Carter,. Ibid 18-28, 161

[148] Carter, Ibid., pp. 19-21

[149] Carter Ibid., pp. 9-28

[150] Samuel P. Huntington, The Soldier and the State: The Theory and Politics of Civil-Military Relations (New York: Vintage Books) 1957, pp 428-455.

[151] John B Wilson, Maneuver and Firepower: the Evolution of Divisions and Separate Brigades, CMH Publication 60-14-1, Washington, D.C. Center of Military History, The Army Lineage Series, 1997, pp 225-6, 256.

[152] Ibid., p. 266-269.
[153] Ibid. pp 270-283.

[154] Ibid. pp 293.

[155] Ibid., p.307.
[156] Ibid. pp 293, 296-297, 299, 325.

[157] Ibid., p. 306.

[158] Wilson, op.cit., pp. 310, 323-325.
[159] Wilson, Ibid. p.328, 329, 336
[160] Annual Historical Supplement for Calendar Year 1967, Department of the Army, Headquarters, 1st Battalion 77th Armor, Fort Carson Colorado 80913, National Archives and Records Administration (NARA), College Park, MD , December 2019, pp 1-3.
[161] Ibid., pp 3-5.
[162] Paul J Scheips, The Role of Federal Military Forces in Domestic Disorders 1945-1992, Center of Military History, CMH Pub 30-20-1, (Washington, DC) p. 6..
[163] Ibid., pp. 4-7.
[164] Ibid., pp 141-176
[165] Ibid., pp. 142-143
[166] Ibid.,p 224-226
[167] Personal experience. The author was the battalion intelligence officer for the 1st Battalion 77th Armor, 1st Brigade, 5th Infantry Division (Mechanized) at the time of the Martin Luther King assassination and subsequent riots. His office controlled the Garden Plot packets.
[168] Ibid., p.273.
[169] Ibid.,p 289-313.
[170] Ibid., p. 297, 313.
[171] Wilson, op.cit. p. 379.

[172] James D. Cockcroft, Latin America: History, Politics and U.S. Policy, Second Edition, Chicago: Nelson-Hall Publishers, 1996, pp 570-1.

[173] Ibid., pp. 267-268.

[174] Wilson, op.cit. p. 356,

[175] Wilson, op.cit. p.. 353

[176] Ibid., pp 353-355, 383.

[177] Ibid., p.364.

[178] Ibid., p. 389.

[179] Ibid., p. 389.

[180] Ibid., p. 390.

[181] Ibid., p 383.

[182] William P. Baxter, Soviet AirLand Battle Tactics, Novato, CA, Presidio Press 1986, pp. 4-5.

[183] Ibid., p. 6

[184] Ibid., 16.

[185] Wilson, op.cit , p. 384-389.

[186] Goldwater–Nichols Department of Defense Reorganization Act of October 4, 1986 Pub.L. 99–433

[187] Wilson, op.cit. p. 384.

[188] Aumiller, op.cit. pp. 131-2.

[189] Carl R. Johnson, email, July 29, 2019

[190] Wilson, op.cit. p. 344

[191] Ibid., p. 364.

[192] Ibid., p. 422.

[193] Ibid., p 422 and *5th Infantry Division (United States) retrieved from* Wikipedia, https://en.wikipedia.org/wiki/5th_Infantry_Division_(United_States) Feb.26.2021

[194] Wilson, op.cit. p. 355,

[195] Stanley Izyk, Letter to author undated.

[196] Aumiller, op.cit. pp 131.

[197] Retrieved from 4th US Infantry Division 1989 - 4th Infantry Division (United States) - Wikipedia https://en.wikipedia.org/wiki/4th_Infantry_Division_(United States)#/media/File:4th_US_Infantry_Division_1989.png

[198] Wilson, op.cit., Table 37, pp. 404-405 and Table 38 p.406.

[199] Wilson, op.cit. p.422

[200] Ibid., Table 39, p. 407

[201] Ibid., p 422.

[202] Ibid., p. 386; Timothy S. Aumiller, United States Army: Infantry, Armor/Cavalry, Artillery Battalions, 1957-2011, (Takoma Park, MD: Tiger Lily Publications) March 19, 2008, pp 131-132; and USAREUR Units & Kasernes 1945-1989, 8th Infantry Division (Mech), Retrieved from http://www.usarmygermany.com/Sont.htm?http&&&www.usarmygermany.com/units/8th%20inf%20div/usareur_8th%20inf%20div.htm

[203] Aumiller, op.cit. pp 131-132, and John Moss personal email to Carmen Milia and forwarded to cwin@affirmative.net and mrushforth@verizon.net , January 13, 2009.

[204] Wilson, op.cit. p.422.

[205] Wilson, Ibid., pp 312; Table 25, p 313; and 340-341; Aumiller, op.cit. pp 131-132; and Organization 1963 to 1995, 157th Infantry Brigade. Retrieved from <en.m.wikipedia.org>.

Chapter 4

[206] Arthur W. Connor, The Armor debacle in Korea, 1950: implications for today, *Parameters*, U.S.Army War College, Carlisle, PA , 1992, p.66, Retrieved from https://apps.dtic.mil/dtic/tr/fulltext/u2/a528176.pdf

[207] Ronald D Offutt, One tank, 31 boxes of Cal.50, and 11 men: an analysis of the Armor-Infantry Team in Korea, June 1950-July 1952, unpublished thesis for Masterod Military Arts and Science, US Army Command and General Staff College, Ft. Leavenworth, Kansas, 1989, p. 33, Retrieved from www.dtic.mil/dtic/tr/fulltext/u2/a212041.pdf 09272018

[208] Hoffman, George F,(2000 September-October), Tanks and the Korean War: a case study in unpreparedness, Armor, Ft Benning, GA: September -October 2000, p 9, retrieved from www.benning.army.mil/armor/eARMOR/content/issues/2000/SEP_OCT/ArmorSeptemberOctober%202000web.pdf 07142018

[209] Connor, op.cit. pp.67-8.

[210] Chapter 1, *Korea: A case history of a pawn,* US Army Center for Military History, p.7 retrieved from https://history.army.mil/books/PD-C-01.HTM

[211] Ibid., pp 8-9.

[212] James F Schnabel, The United States Army in the Korean War: policy and direction: the first year, 1992, pp. 4-11, retrieved from https://history.army.mil/html/books/020/20-1/CMH_Pub_20-1.pd,

[213] Ibid., p. 13-16.

[214] Ibid., p. 17.

[215] Reports of General MacArthur, MacArthur in Japan: The occupation: military phase, Volume 1 supplement, Center for Military History, CMH Pub 13-4, 1994, pp. 4-11. retrieved from https://history.army.mil/books/wwii/MacArthur%20Reports/MacArthur%20V1%20Sup/ch1.htm, 08202018

[216] Major General Paul Mueller, Occupation of Japan-A Progress Report, August 27, 2007, NEEED PG NOs retrieved from https://www.army.mil/article/4613/occupied_japan_a_progress_report 08.01.2018

[217] Lieutenant Colonel Michael F. Trivet, MacArthur's Occupation of Japan: Lessons on Counterinsurgency, Warfare History Network Dec 1, 2016, retrieved from warfarehistorynetwork.com/daily/wwii/macarthurs-occupation-of-japan-lessons-of-counterinsurgency/ 09142018.

[218] Ibid.

[219] Chapter 9.pdf pp. 1-3, retrieved from www.31stinfantry.org/wp-content/uploads/2014/01/Chapter-9.pdf, 08.17.2018

and [219] Nothing was found in the research about the occupation of Hokkaido except that the 7th Infantry Division engaged in military training. The troops were allowed to go into Sapporo and neighboring towns where order was maintained by the US military police. Occupation missions of the division were not found.

[220] Chapter 9.pdf, pp. 4-14.

[221] Department of the Army Field Manual 17-33, Tank Battalion, September 1949, pp. 286-7, retrieved from https://archive.org/details/FM17-331951, 08.15.2018

[222] Ibid. p. 290.

[223] SEE KOREANWAR PROJECT S1/G1 31st RCT PERSONNEL AND EQUIPMENT STATUS REPORTS SEP-DEC 1950

[224] SEE KOREANWAR PROJECT S4/G4 31st RCT EQUIPMENT STATUS REPORTS SEP-DEC 1950

[225] Connor, op.cit. pp.68.

[226] William J Webb, The Korean War: The Outbreak 27 June – 15 September, Center for Military History, cmh pub 19-6, updated 23 June 2011 p. 8 Retrieved from https://history.army.mil/brochures/KWOutbreak/outbreak.htm#intro1) 09.17.2018

[227] William J Webb, op.cit. pp. 7-8

[228]Korean War Project 7ID-007558,Narrative Summary, Inclusive, War Diary, Seventh Infantry Division, 1 September to 30 September, p. 1.

[229] Ronald D Offutt, One tank, 31 boxes of Cal.50, and 11 men: an analysis of the Armor-Infantry Team in Korea, June 1950-July 1952, unpublished thesis for Master of Military Arts and Science, US Army Command and General Staff College, Ft. Leavenworth, Kansas, 1989, p.68, Retrieved from www.dtic.mil/dtic/tr/fulltext/u2/a212041.pdf 09272018. NOTE: Arthur O'Connor states that Lieutenant Samuel R. Fowler and his men were assigned to the Japan-based 1st Cavalry Division and then formed the into the 8064th Heavy Tank Platoon (Provisional) in order to get a tank presence into Korea to combat the North Korean T-34 Russian-made tanks, Arthur W. Connor, The Armor debacle in Korea, 1950: op.cit. pp 70,71, and Murray Williamson, ed., printed a response to Connor's paper from Alvin Clouse who was a member of Fowler's platoon and stated that they were members of the 77th Tank Battalion in Transformation Concepts for National Security in the 21st Century Brief Facts Strategic Studies Institute Papers, Carlisle, PA, September 2002, retrieved from www.koreanwar educator.org/topics/brief/p_strategic_studies_institute.htm, November 3, 2019.

[230] Offut, op.cit, p, 68-69., and Murray Williamson, Ibid.

[231] Russell A. Gugeler, Combat Actions in Korea, Center of Military History, United States Army, Washington DC, 1987, Retrieved from https://history.army.mil/html/books/030/30-2/CMH_Pub_30-2.pdf, 09272018. and Hardy, Capt. Harry B., Horne, Capt. Kibby M., Koch, Capt. Kenneth W., 1st Lt. Matteson, Jack F., & Thompson, Capt. Milton R., Employment of Armor in Korea: The First Year, Volume 1, A Research Report Prepared at the Armored School, Fort Knox, KY, May 1952, retrieved fromhttps://mcoepublic.blob.core.usgovcloudapi.net/library/Armorpapers/ASTUP/A-F/Committee%2011%20Employment%20of%20Armor%20in%20Korea_vol_1.pdf

[232] Hardy, Capt. Harry B., Horne, Capt. Kibby M., Koch, Capt. Kenneth W., 1st Lt. Matteson, Jack F., & Thompson, Capt. Milton R., Employment of Armor in Korea: The First Year, Volume 1, A Research Report Prepared at the Armored School, Fort Knox, KY, May 1952, retrieved fromhttps://mcoepublic.blob.core.usgovcloudapi.net/library/Armorpapers/ASTUP/A-F/Committee%2011%20Employment%20of%20Armor%20in%20Korea_vol_1.pdf

[233] KATUSA Training Academy, Wightman NCO Academy, history, retrieved fromhttps://8tharmy.korea.army.mil/ncoa/kta.asp March 1, 2019

[234] (Korean War Project 7id-000640 Headquarters , 31st Infantry Regiment, APO 7, Narrative Report for the Period 1 September 1950 to 30 September 1950 dated 30 October 1950). Retrieved from www.koreanwar2.org/kwp2/jpac/7id_31st_inf_sep_to_dec_1950_box_3179.pdf, and Korean War Project 7ID-000645, War Diary and Historical Report. Hqs 31st Inf Regt, for Period 6 Sep through 9 Sep 1950, dated 13 September 1950 Retrieved from https://www.koreanwar2.org/kwp2/jpac/7id_31st_inf_sep_to_dec_1950_box_3179.pdf, 09.27.2018

[235] George E. Goebel Korea, The Trap The winter of 1950-51,Steel Tigers, 77th Armor Association, On the Road: Individual Stories of Traveling to the unit or front, 1941-2005, Retrieved from www.steeltigers.org/cgi-bin/history/journal.cgi?folder=journal&next=2, February 23, 2019, and Borske, Michael, Entry 15930, Pics of Unit in Camp Chitose, April 13, 2001, Korean War project, retrieved from https://www.koreanwar.org/html/units/77tnk.htm

[236] Association of Graduates, Robert E. Drake, 1944 Retrieved from https://www.westpointaog.org/memorial-article?id=819884c0-080f-485e-ac5e-ab30ff0af020 May 31. 2019 and Robert E. Drake, "The Infantry Regiment's Tank Company," Armor Magazine, September-October 1951, Retrieved from https://www.benning.army.mil/Armor/eARMOR/content/issues/1951/SEP_OCT/1951SeptemberOctober.pdf

[237] George E. Goebel Korea, The Trap The Winter of 1950-51, Steel Tigers, 77th Armor Association, On the Road: Individual Stories of Traveling to the Unit or Front, 1941-2005, Retrieved from www.steeltigers.org/cgi-bin/history/journal.cgi?folder=journal&next=2, February 23, 2019.

[238] Korean War Project 7ID-000644 War Diary and Historical Report, 31st Infantry Regiment for Sept 6-Sept 9, 1950 dated September 13, 1950 Retrieved from https://www.koreanwar2.org/kwp2/jpac/7id_31st_inf_sep_to_dec_1950_box_3179.pdf and Korean War Project 7ID-000696, Training Memorandum Number 24, Headquarters 31st Infantry Aboard Assault Ship Butner, 9 September 1950).Retrieved from:https://www.koreanwar2.org/kwp2/jpac/7id_31st_inf_sep_to_dec_1950_box_3179.pdf, 07.03. 2019

[239] Korean War Project 7ID-000648 , War Diary and Historical Report, 31st Infantry Regiment for Sept 17-Sept 23, 1950 dated September 24, 1950 Retrieved from https://www.koreanwar2.org/kwp2/jpac/7id_31st_inf_sep_to_dec_1950_box_3179.pdf, 09.27. 2018

[240] Roy E. Appleman, South to the Naktong, North to the Yalu: The United States Army in the Korean War (June-November 1950), Washington, DC, Center of Military History, 1992, p. 493, 498, and 503, Retrieved from https://history.army.mil/books/korea/20-2-1/toc.htm

[241] Ibid., p. 491.

[242] Ibid., pp. 520-523.

[243] Ibid., pp. 520-523.

[244] Fort Beavers Korea, 73rd Armor History, from the 1967 Fort Beavers Yearbook , Courtesy of Jess R. Lopez, Retrieved from the fortbeavers.tripod.com/id43.html, and Global Security.org, Military, 3rd Battalion 73rd Armor Regiment undated, Retrieved from https://www.globalsecurity.org/military/agency/army/3-73ar.htm July 15,2019, and A brief History of the 756th Tank Battalion, retrieved from History – 756tankbn.com , July 15, 2019

[245] 27th Infantry, Regiment United States, Wikipedia, Retrieved from https://en.wikipedia.org/wiki/27th_Infantry_Regiment_(United_States), July 15, 2019

[246] Distinguishing A-77 and A-73 in the 31st Infantry's original sources was difficult initially; however,A-77 is listed as the 31ST tnk co (tank company) or 31st Hvy Tnk Co (Heavy Tank Company) in unit operations orders and The A-73 Tank Company is referred to with its official designation.
Capt. Harry B. Hardy, Capt. Harry B., Capt. Kibbey M Horne, Capt. Kenneth W Koch, 1st Lt. Jack F Matteson, & Capt. Milton R Thompson, Employment of Armor in Korea: The First Year, Volume 1, A Research Report Prepared at the Armored School, Fort Knox, KY, May 1952, retrieved from https://mcoepublic.blob.core.usgovcloudapi.net/library/Armorpapers/ASTUP/A-F/Committee%2011%20Employment%20of%20Armor%20in%20Korea_vol_1.pdf

[247] Ibid.

[248] Korean War Project 7ID-000648 Narrative Summary, Inclusive, War Diary, Seventh Infantry Division, 17 September to 23 September, 1950, p.1-3, Retrieved from https://www.koreanwar2.org/kwp2/jpac/7id_31st_inf_sep_to_dec_1950_box_3179.pdf, Korean War Project 7ID 000640-643, Headquarters, 31st Infantry Regiment, APO 7, narrative report for the period 1 September 1950 to 30 September 1950 dated 30 October 1950).

[249] Korean War Project 7ID 000641, Headquarters, 31st Infantry Regiment, APO 7, narrative report for the period 1 September 1950 to 30 September 1950 dated 30 October 1950) and Korean War Project 7ID-000646 War Diary and Historical Report. Hqs 31st Inf Regt, for Period 10 Sep through 16 Sep 1950, dated 19 September 1950 Retrieved from https://www.koreanwar2.org/kwp2/jpac/7id_31st_inf_sep_to_dec_1950_box_3179.pdf, 09.27.2018

[250] Korean War Project 7ID-000646 War Diary and Historical Report. Hqs 31st Inf Regt, for Period 10 Sep through 16 Sep 1950, dated 19 September 1950 Retrieved from https://www.koreanwar2.org/kwp2/jpac/7id_31st_inf_sep_to_dec_1950_box_3179.pdf, 09.27.2018

[251] Korean War Project 7ID-000641-643, Headquarters , 31st Infantry Regiment, APO 7, Narrative Report for the Period 1 September 1950 to 30 September 1950 dated 30 October 1950, p2) and Korean War Project 7ID-000648 War Diary and Historical Report, 31st Infantry Regiment for Sept 17-Sept 23, 1950 dated September 24, 1950.

[252] Korean War Project 7ID-000651-654, War Diary and Historical Report, 31st Infantry Regiment for Sept 24-Sept 30, 1950 dated October 3, 1950. Retrieved from
https://www.koreanwar2.org/kwp2/jpac/7id_31st_inf_sep_to_dec_1950_box_3179.pdf, 09.27. 201

[253] Korean War Project 7ID-000669 Reference: Op Order No 9 , HQ RCT 31, 250600 Sep 50) Retrieved from
https://www.koreanwar2.org/kwp2/jpac/7id_31st_inf_sep_to_dec_1950_box_3179.pdf, 09.27. 2018 and Korean War Project 7ID-00066**x**Op Order No 10 , HQ RCT 31, 242200 Sep 50 (25.1-25.2) Note: Operations Order No 9 erroneously date 242200 Sept 50 and should have read 241000 Sep 50. Retrieved from
https://www.koreanwar2.org/kwp2/jpac/7id_31st_inf_sep_to_dec_1950_box_3179.pdf, 09.27. 2018

[254] The Korean War Project 7ID-000672, Periodic Operations Report No. 13, RCT 31 (25.1-25.2) 252200 Sep30, and 7ID-000685,686, 687, 688, and 689 26 Sep Periodic Operations Report Number 16, RCT 31 (25.1-25.2) 271000Sep50, Retrieved from
https://www.koreanwar2.org/kwp2/jpac/7id_31st_inf_sep_to_dec_1950_box_3179.pdf, 09.27. 2018

[255] The Korean War Project 7ID-000641,642, and 643 War Diary and Historical Report, 31st Infantry Regiment for September 1-September 30, 1950 dated October 30, 1950). Retrieved from
https://www.koreanwar2.org/kwp2/jpac/7id_31st_inf_sep_to_dec_1950_box_3179.pdf, 09.27. 2018.

[256] The Korean War Project 7ID-000693, Con't Unit Report, 31st Infantry 291800I Sep 50,
https://www.koreanwar2.org/kwp2/jpac/7id_31st_inf_sep_to_dec_1950_box_3179.pdf, 09.27. 2018.

[257] Korean War Project 7ID-000709 2 October 1950, Retrieved from
https://www.koreanwar2.org/kwp2/jpac/7id_31st_inf_sep_to_dec_1950_box_3179.pdf, 09.27.2018

[258] Korean War Project 7ID-000715 from Korean War Project 7ID-000711-716, Operations Order No 12, Oct RCT 31, 021200 Oct 50 Retrieved from
https://www.koreanwar2.org/kwp2/jpac/7id_31st_inf_sep_to_dec_1950_box_3179.pdf
09.27.2018

[259] Korean War Project 7ID-000732 Op O 13 31st RC RCT 040800 Oct 50, and Korean War Project 7ID-000722, 5 October 1950, Retrieved from
https://www.koreanwar2.org/kwp2/jpac/7id_31st_inf_sep_to_dec_1950_box_3179.pdf
09082019. The Operations order 13 directs the 31st RCT tank company to move to Pusan with the 77th Tank Battalion. This is a typographical error. The only tank battalion identified in 7th Division orders and reports through October 1950 is the 73rd tank battalion. I changed the unit designation. The 73rd was part of Task Force Whirlaway that was the first 7th Division unit that was planned to land at Wonson following the 1st Marine Division, and there is no 77th Tank Battalion identified in the Korean War during 1950.

[260] Korean War Project 7ID-000724, 7 October, Retrieved from
https://www.koreanwar2.org/kwp2/jpac/7id_31st_inf_sep_to_dec_1950_box_3179.pdf
09.27.2018

[261] Korean War Project 7ID-000736 War Diary for Period 8 Oct to 15 Oct 1950 dated 30 October 1950 Retrieved from https://www.koreanwar2.org/kwp2/jpac/7id_31st_inf_sep_to_dec_1950_box_3179.pdf
09.27.2018.

[262] Korean War Project 7ID-000722, 5 October 1950; 723, 6 October 1950; 724, 7 October 1950; and Korean War Project 7ID-000725, Op O 100, 9 Oct 1950, and Korean War Project 7ID-000736,738, and 739), Retrieved from https://www.koreanwar2.org/kwp2/jpac/7id_31st_inf_sep_to_dec_1950_box_3179.pdf

09.27.2018, and Korean War Project 7ID-000732, 733, 734, Op O 13, 040600 Oct 50 Retrieved from: https://www.koreanwar2.org/kwp2/jpac/7id_31st_inf_sep_to_dec_1950_box_3179.pdf 09.27.2018,

[263] Korean War Project 7ID-000743-746, Op Order 16, RCT 31,171400 Oct1950 and Korean War Project 7ID-000753, Annex 5 to Op O #16 Debarkation and Order of Movement from Port Area, Retrieved from https://www.koreanwar2.org/kwp2/jpac/7id_31st_inf_sep_to_dec_1950_box_3179.pdf 09.07.2019

[264] Korean War Project 7ID-000754, Op Order 17, RCT 31, 220900Oct50 Pusan, Retrieved from https://www.koreanwar2.org/kwp2/jpac/7id_31st_inf_sep_to_dec_1950_box_3179.pdf 09.27.2018,

[265] Roy E Appleman, East of Chosin: Entrapment and Breakout in Korea, 1950, College Station TX, Texas A&M Press, 1987, p.5-8,and Korean War Project 7ID-000754, Op Order 17, RCT 31, 220900Oct50, Retrieved from https://www.koreanwar2.org/kwp2/jpac/7id_31st_inf_sep_to_dec_1950_box_3179.pdf 09.27.2018,

[266] Roy E Appleman, East of Chosin, op.cit., p.8.

[267] Roy E. Appleman, South to the Naktong, North to the Yalu, op.cit., pp.633-637, Retrieved from: https://history.army.mil/books/korea/20-2-1/sn38.htm July 15, 2019

[268] Korean War Project 7ID-000811, War Diary for 16 November 1950, Hqs 31st RCT, 16 November 1950, retrieved from https://www.koreanwar2.org/kwp2/jpac/7id_31st_inf_sep_to_dec_1950_box_3179.pdf 09.06.2019,

[269] Korean War Project 7ID-6300 and -6301, War Diary, 7th Infantry Division , 0001-2400 07Nov 1950 Retrieved from https://www.koreanwar2.org/kwp2/jpac/7id_war_diary_nov_1950_box_3174.pdf, 09.08.2019.

[270] Roy E. Appleman, South to the Naktong, North to the Yalu, op.cit., pp.732

[271] Roy E Appleman, East of Chosin, op.cit., p.8,10. and Map 4, p. 25

[272] Korean War Project, &-ID000774, Appendix 1 to Annex 3 (Intelligence) Operations Order 17,27 October 1950,retrieved from https://www.koreanwar2.org/kwp2/jpac/7id_31st_inf_sep_to_dec_1950_box_3179.pdf, and Roy E. Appleman, East of Chosin, op.cit., p.

[273] Korean War Project, 7ID-000774, Appendix 1 to Annex 3 (Intel) to Opn O 17, Brief of Climate and Weather in the 7th Division Area of Operations, 27 October 1950 Retrieved from https://www.koreanwar2.org/kwp2/jpac/7id_31st_inf_sep_to_dec_1950_box_3179.pdf

[274] Korean War Project, 7ID-000774, Ibid.

[275] Roy E. Appleman, East of Chosin, op.cit., p. 5, 13-14, 22, and Martin Russ, Breakout The Chosin Reservoir Campaign, Korea 1950, New York, Penguin Books, 1999, ,Map: Area of Operations 1st Marine Division October-December 1950, two pages unnumbered between pages 16 and 17.

[276] CMH 20-2-1 Chapter 38, X Corps Advances to the Yalu, Center for Military History, p. 732, and Korean War Project 7ID-000769 and 770, Daily Diary for the Week Ending 5 November 1950 (Essentially Narrative) op.cit. , Retrieved from https://www.koreanwar2.org/kwp2/jpac/7id_31st_inf_sep_to_dec_1950_box_3179.pdf, 09.06.2019

[277] Korean War Project 7ID-000770, Daily Diary for Week Ending 5 November 1950 (Essentially Narrative), Hq 31st RCT, 7 Nov 1950. Retrieved from https://www.koreanwar2.org/kwp2/jpac/7id_31st_inf_sep_to_dec_1950_box_3179.pdf 09.06.2019

[278] Korean War Project 7ID-000767, War Diary of the 31st Infantry Regiment, 7th infantry Division, Operations in Korea from 1 Nov 1950 – 30 November 1950, undated; Korean War Project 7ID – 000769,770, and 773, Daily Diary for Week 5 ending 5 Nov 1950 Essentially Narrative Hqs RCT 31, dtd 7 Nov 1950.

[279] Roy E. Appleman, South to the Naktong, North to the Yalu, op.cit., pp.739-741, Retrieved from: https://history.army.mil/books/korea/20-2-1/sn38.htm July 15, 2019.

[280] Glenn C. Cowart, Miracle In Korea: The Evacuation of X Corps from the Hungnam Beachhead. Columbia: University of South Carolina Press, 1992. ISBN 0-87249-829-8, .Retrieved from: https://en.wikipedia.org/wiki/3rd_Infantry_Division_(United_States)#cite_note-13) July 15, 2019, and Gordon L. Rottman, Korean War Order of Battle, Greenwood Publishing Group, Incorporated, December 2002 ISBN 978-0-275-97835-8 Retrieved from: 12) July 15, 2019, and Roy E. Appleman, Ibid., pp.739-741

[281] Korean War Project 7ID000785, RCT 31 090100Nov50 Periodic Operations Report # 16, 072400 Nov 50 - 082400Nov), (Korean War Project 7ID–000786, 787, and 788, S3 Journal 9 Nov 50) retrieved from https://www.koreanwar2.org/kwp2/jpac/7id_31st_inf_sep_to_dec_1950_box_3179.pdf 09.06.2019

[282] Korean War Project 7ID-000789 Intelligence, Hqs, RCT 31, 9 Nov 50, Retrieved from https://www.koreanwar2.org/kwp2/jpac/7id_31st_inf_sep_to_dec_1950_box_3179.pdf,

[283] Korean War Project 7ID–000791, S3 Journal 31 RCT 07Nov50, Retrieved from https://www.koreanwar2.org/kwp2/jpac/7id_31st_inf_sep_to_dec_1950_box_3179.pdf,

[284] Richard W. Stewart, CMH Pub 19-8, The Korean War: The Chinese Intervention, 3 November -24 November 1950, Washiington, DC, US Army Center for Military History pp. 6-9, Retrieved from: https://history.army.mil/brochures/kw-chinter/chinter.htm 09.09.2019

[285] Roy E. Appleman, East of Chosin, op.cit., pp. 3-5.

[286] Ibid., pp. 7-8.

[287] Korean War Project 7ID – 000782 RCT 31, Unit Report 23, 161800Nov 50 to 171800Nov 50.

[288] Roy E. Appleman, East of Chosin, op.cit., p.10.

[289] Footnote Korean War Project 7-ID 005164, 7inf Div

[290] FOOTNOTE KWP 7ID-002634 and Appleman, East of Chosin, p.18, Map 4, p.25

[291] Roy E. Appleman, East of Chosin, op.cit., p.10.

[292] Roy E. Appelman,. The US Army in the Korean War, South to the Naktong, North to the Yalu ((June-November 1950), Center of Military History, United States Army, 1961, CMH Pub 10-2-1, , pp. 736-738.

[293] Donald Chisholm, Escape by Sea: the Hungnam Redeployment, Washington, DC, Institute for National Strategic Studies, National Defense University, 2001, p.54-56, Retrieved from https://apps.dtic.mil/dtic/tr/fulltext/u2/a524800.pdf

[294] Martin Russ, Breakout: The Chosin Reservoir Campaign, Korea 1950, New York: Penguin Books, 1999.

[295] Roy E. Appleman, East of Chosin, op.cit. pp 3-397.

[296] National Archives and Records Administration, 8601 Adelphi Road, College Park, Maryland 20740

[297] Captain Robert E. Drake Statement, KWP 7ID-001185 and KWP 7ID-001186, Korean War Project: Tank Company, 31st Infantry Regiment, Operations Report 25 November-11 December 1950, 12 December 1950 Retrieved From Box 3179 10.19.2019 Appleman, East of Chosin, Ibid. pp 12-19.

[298] Appleman, Ibid., p.163.

[299] Appleman, Ibid., p.40.

[300] Appleman, Ibid., pp.28, 42, and . Map 6, p.60.

[301] Captain George A. Rasula Statement, KWP 7ID-001175-1178 Korean War Project: Summary of Operations in the Chosin Reservoir Area 25 November-11 December 1950, 12 December 1950 Retrieved From Box 3179 10.19.2019 and Appleman , Ibid., p. 86.

[302] Appleman, Ibid., pp. 65, 79.

[303] Drake Statement, KWP 7ID-001185 and KWP 7ID-001186, Korean War Project: Tank Company, 31st Infantry Regiment, op.cit., and Appleman East of Chosin Ibid., p 108-118.

[304] Drake Statement, Ibid., and Appleman Ibid., p.112-114.

[305] Appleman, Ibid. p.115.

[306] Appleman, Ibid., pp.118-19, 305-307.

[307] Appleman, Ibid., p130-33.

[308] Appleman, Ibid., pp. 145-47, 152

[310] Appleman, Ibid. pp.180-181.

[311] Drake Statement, KWP 7ID-001185 and KWP 7ID-001186, Korean War Project: Tank Company, 31st Infantry Regiment, Op.cit. and Appleman, Ibid., pp.157-59.

[312] See KWP 7-ID-005167, 5168, 5169, and 5170, After Action Report of the 7th Infantry Division From 21 November to 20 December 1950, From Hyesanjin to Hungnam Outloading, Retrieved from https://www.koreanwar2.org/kwp2/jpac/7id_cmd_rptsop_orders_nov-dec_1950_box_3173.pdf January 11, 2020.

[313] Drake report Drake Statement, KWP 7ID-001185 and KWP 7ID-001186, Korean War Project: Tank Company, 31st Infantry Regiment, Op.cit; Appleman, East of Chosin op.cit. pp. 186-87; and Korean War Project 7ID-005187,After Action Report of the 7th Infantry Division From 21 November to 20 December 1950, op.cit.,

[314] Appleman East of Chosin op.cit , pp.176,188, 208

[315] Appleman, Ibid., pp. 213-15.

[316] Appleman, Ibid., pp. 275-77,and Lt Col Anderson Statement, 31st Infantry, KWP 7ID-001179, Retrieved from https://www.koreanwar2.org/kwp2/jpac/7id_31st_inf_sep_to_dec_1950_box_3179.pdf, 10.24.2019

[317] Chisholm, Escape by Sea, op.cit. pp.54-60

[318] 7ID-006189, 006190 Command Report 1 December -31 December 1950, Headquarters 73rd Heavy Tank Battalion to Commanding General 7th Infantry Division, ATTN G3 Historian, 10 January 1951. Retrieved from https://www.koreanwar2.org/kwp2/jpac/7id_medical_tk%20bn_1950_box_3185.pdf December 11, 2019.

[319] Drake Statement, KWP 7ID-001185 and KWP 7ID-001186, Korean War Project: Tank Company, 31st Infantry Regiment, Op.cit

[320] Drake Statement, Ibid.,

[321] KWP 7ID-0006190, Command Report 1 December-31 December 1950, Headquarters 73rd Heavy Tank op.cit.

[322] Command Report 7th Infantry Division, Operations in Korea, From 1 December 1950 to 31 December 1950. Daily Chronological Summary for December 1950, KWP 7ID-005285, 7ID-005289, KWP 7ID-005315, KWP 7ID-005320-5324. Retrieved from https://www.koreanwar2.org/kwp2/jpac/7id_cmd_rptsop_orders_nov-dec_1950_box_3173.pdf 11 December 2019 and Korean War Project 7ID- 001236 Command Report for 11-12 December 1950 Inclusive, Hqs 31st RCT 11 December 1950 retrieved from https://www.koreanwar2.org/kwp2/jpac/7id_31st_inf_sep_to_dec_1950_box_3179.pdf, 12.December,2019.

[323] FOOTNOTE: KWP 7ID-005170 https://www.koreanwar2.org/kwp2/jpac/7id_.pd and KWP 7ID-1238 Periodic Report Operation Report No 8, RCT 31 12 Dec 50 Retrieved from https://www.koreanwar2.org/kwp2/jpac/7id_31st_inf_sep_to_dec_1950_box_3179.pd

[324] KWP7ID-001200 Command Report for 5 December 1950, Hqs 31 RCT 052400 Dec 50 Retrieved from https://www.koreanwar2.org/kwp2/jpac/7id_31st_inf_sep_to_dec_1950_box_3179.pd. 10 December 2019.

[325] KWP 7ID-001208 and -001209, 7th Infantry Division Op Order 31, 6 December 1950, Retrieved from https://www.koreanwar2.org/kwp2/jpac/7id_31st_inf_sep_to_dec_1950_box_3179.pd, 10 December 2019

[326] Drake Statement, KWP 7ID-001185 and KWP 7ID-001186, Korean War Project: Tank Company, 31st Infantry Regiment, Op.cit. and KWP 7ID-001237, S-3 Journal. 11 Dec 50, RCT 31 11 Dec 50, and KWP 7ID-001238 Periodic Report Opn No 8 Period 111800 Dec to 121800Dec 50, RCT 31 12 Dec 50, Retrieved from https://www.koreanwar2.org/kwp2/jpac/7id_31st_inf_sep_to_dec_1950_box_3179.pd, 10 December 2019.
Korean War Project 7ID- 001218 Embarkation Order 3-50, 7th Infantry Division 101900 retrieved from https://www.koreanwar2.org/kwp2/jpac/7id_31st_inf_sep_to_dec_1950_box_3179.pd, 10 December 2019.

[327] Korean War Project 7ID- 001218 Embarkation Order 3-50, 7th Infantry Division 101900 retrieved from https://www.koreanwar2.org/kwp2/jpac/7id_31st_inf_sep_to_dec_1950_box_3179.pd, 10 December 2019.

[328] KWP 7ID-001239, Command Report for 13-14 December, 31st RCT 14 Dec 50, retrieved fromhttps://www.koreanwar2.org/kwp2/jpac/7id_31st_inf_sep_to_dec_1950_box_3179.pd, 10 December 2019.

[329] KWP 7ID-001255, Command Report 17-19 December 1950 Inclusive, 31st RCT 17 Dec 50, and KWP 7ID-001268 and 001269, Periodic operations Report No. 1, Period 201800 to 211800 Dec 50, RCT 31, 211800 Dec 50, retrieved from https://www.koreanwar2.org/kwp2/jpac/7id_31st_inf_sep_to_dec_1950_box_3179.pd, 10 December 2019.

[330] KWP 7ID-001314 Extract, Training Memorandum 29, 30 December 1950. retrieved from https://www.koreanwar2.org/kwp2/jpac/7id_31st_inf_sep_to_dec_1950_box_3179.pd, 10 December 2019.

[331] KWP 7ID-001282, Command Report for 23 December 1950, RCT 31, 23 Dec 50, and KWP 7ID-001280 Training Memorandum Number 28, 22 Dec 50, and KWP 7ID-001267, 31st RCT Command Report for 21 December 1950, RCT 31 21 Dec 50, and KWP, 7ID-001313 Periodic Operation Report Number 9 for the period 301800 to 311800December 1950, 31st RCT, 31 Dec 50, retrieved from https://www.koreanwar2.org/kwp2/jpac/7id_31st_inf_sep_to_dec_1950_box_3179.pd, 10 December 2019.

[332] Billy, C. Mossman, Ebb and Flow: November 1950-July 1951, United States Army in the Korean War, Center of Military History, United States Army, Washington, DC 1990, Retrieved from https://history.army.mil/books/korea/ebb/fm.htm, p. 178.

[333] Korean War Campaigns, US Army Center for Military History, Retrieved from https://history.army.mil/html/reference/army_flag/kw.html, and Billy, C. Mossman, Ebb and Flow: Ibid., p. 178 and Map 15 on p 181, 183, 188, 211 and Map 16 on p.216, retrieved from https://history.army.mil/books/korea/ebb/fm.htm

[334] Billy, C. Mossman, Ebb and Flow: Ibid., p. 234 retrieved from https://history.army.mil/books/korea/ebb/fm.htm

[335] Korea, French Battalion of the United Nations Organisation (Korean War) Retrieved from French Battalion (Korean War) - Wikipedia, 05242021

[336] Billy, C. Mossman, Ebb and Flow: Ibid., Retrieved from https://history.army.mil/books/korea/ebb/fm.htm, p. 178, 180-185 and Map 15 on p 181.

[337] Billy, C. Mossman, <u>Ibid</u>., Retrieved from https://history.army.mil/books/korea/ebb/fm.htm, pp. 234-237.

[338] Billy, C. Mossman, <u>Ibid</u>., Retrieved from https://history.army.mil/books/korea/ebb/fm.htm, pp186,187.

[339] Billy, C. Mossman, <u>Ibid</u>., Retrieved from. 192,194, 196, 198

[340] Billy, C. Mossman, <u>Ibid</u>., Retrieved from https://history.army.mil/books/korea/ebb/fm.htm,p pp.217, 218 Map 17 on pp. 219-221.

[341] Command Report for Period of 1-31 January 1951(Inclusive), Hqs RCT 32' United States Army32nd Infantry Command Reports for January , February and March 1951, Maneuver Center of Excellence (MCoE) Libraries, Hqs Donovan Research Library, Armor Research Library, Fort Benning Georgia Retrieved from https://www.koreanwar2.org/kwp2/ftbenning/ds16_i15.pdf 11.18.2019 and Billy, C. Mossman, Ibid., Retrieved from https://history.army.mil/books/korea/ebb/fm.htm, p. 217, retrieved from https://history.army.mil/books/korea/ebb/ch17.htm, Nov 7, 2019.

[342] Billy, C. Mossman, Ibid., Retrieved from https://history.army.mil/books/korea/ebb/fm.htm, pp. 283-301 retrieved from https://history.army.mil/books/korea/ebb/ch17.htm, March 28, 2020.

[343] Billy, C. Mossman, Ibid., Retrieved from https://history.army.mil/books/korea/ebb/fm.htm, p. 295. retrieved from https://history.army.mil/books/korea/ebb/ch17.htm, Nov 7, 2019.

[344] Billy, C. Mossman, Ibid., Retrieved from https://history.army.mil/books/korea/**ebb**/fm.htm, p.296-301- retrieved from https://history.army.mil/books/korea/ebb/ch17.htm, Nov 7, 2019.

[345] Billy, C. Mossman, Ibid., Retrieved from https://history.army.mil/books/korea/ebb/fm.htm, p.301-303 and Map 25 on p 304. retrieved from https://history.army.mil/books/korea/ebb/ch17.htm, Nov 7, 2019.

[346] Billy Mossman, Ibid., Retrieved from https://history.army.mil/books/korea/ebb/fm.htm, pp.307-308. retrieved from https://history.army.mil/books/korea/ebb/ch17.htm, Nov 7, 2019

[347] Billy, C. Mossman, Ibid., Retrieved from https://history.army.mil/books/korea/ebb/fm.htm, p.309. retrieved from https://history.army.mil/books/korea/ebb/ch17.htm, Nov 7, 2019

[348] Billy, C. Mossman, Ibid., Retrieved from https://history.army.mil/books/korea/ebb/fm.htm, p.310. retrieved from https://history.army.mil/books/korea/ebb/ch17.htm, Nov 7, 2019

[349] Billy, C. Mossman, Ibid., p 312 Retrieved from https://history.army.mil/books/korea/ebb/fm.htm,Nov 7, 2019

[350] Billy, C. Mossman, Ibid., p.312, 316-318 and Map 26 and 27 on pp. 317 and 319, Retrieved from https://history.army.mil/books/korea/ebb/fm.htm, respectively. retrieved from https://history.army.mil/books/korea/ebb/ch16.htm, Nov 7, 2019.

[351] Billy, C. Mossman, Ibid., p.314, retrieved from https://history.army.mil/books/korea/ebb/ch16.htm, Retrieved from https://history.army.mil/books/korea/ebb/fm.htm, Nov 7, 2019

[352] Billy, C. Mossman, Ibid., pp.324-328, retrieved from https://history.army.mil/books/korea/ebb/ch17.htm, Retrieved from https://history.army.mil/books/korea/ebb/fm.htm, Nov 7, 2019.

[353] Billy, C. Mossman, Ibid., p.328, retrieved from https://history.army.mil/books/korea/ebb/ch17.htm, Retrieved from https://history.army.mil/books/korea/ebb/fm.htm, Nov 7, 2019.

[354] Billy, C. Mossman, Ibid., p.335, retrieved from https://history.army.mil/books/korea/ebb/ch18.htm, Retrieved from https://history.army.mil/books/korea/ebb/fm.htm, Nov 7, 2019.

[355] Billy, C. Mossman, Ibid., p.341-347, retrieved from https://history.army.mil/books/korea/ebb/ch18.htm, Retrieved from https://history.army.mil/books/korea/ebb/fm.htm, March 10, 2020 and John J. Miller, Jr., Owen J. Carroll, Major US Army, and Margaret F. Tackley, United States Army Center for Military History, Korea: 1951-1953, CMH Pub 21-2, Center for Military History, Department of the Army, Washington D.C. 1997, p. 20 Map 3, and p. 23, Retrieved from https://history.army.mil/html/books/021/21-2/CMH_Pub_21-2.pdf, April 3, 2020.

[356] Billy, C. Mossman, Ibid., p.347, retrieved from https://history.army.mil/books/korea/ebb/ch18.htm, Retrieved from https://history.army.mil/books/korea/ebb/fm.htm, March 10, 2020, and Miller, Jr., Carroll, and Tackley, Ibid. Korea: 1951-1953, pp. 24-26, Retrieved from https://history.army.mil/html/books/021/21-2/CMH_Pub_21-2.pdf, April 3, 2020.

[357] Billy, C. Mossman, Ibid., p.348-9, retrieved from https://history.army.mil/books/korea/ebb/ch18.htm, Retrieved from https://history.army.mil/books/korea/ebb/fm.htm, March 10, 2020.

[358] Billy, C. Mossman, Ibid., p.349-351, retrieved from https://history.army.mil/books/korea/ebb/ch18.htm, Retrieved from https://history.army.mil/books/korea/ebb/fm.htm, March 10, 2020.

[359] Miller, Jr., Carroll, and Tackley, Ibid. Korea: 1951-1953, p. Map 3, p.20, and p. 25, Retrieved from https://history.army.mil/html/books/021/21-2/CMH_Pub_21-2.pdf, April 3, 2020

[360] Billy, C. Mossman, Ibid., p.362-364, retrieved from https://history.army.mil/books/korea/ebb/ch19.htm, Retrieved from https://history.army.mil/books/korea/ebb/fm.htm, March 10, 2020.

[361] Miller, Jr., Carroll, and Tackley, Ibid. Korea: 1951-1953, p. 24-26, Retrieved from https://history.army.mil/html/books/021/21-2/CMH_Pub_21-2.pdf, April 3, 2020, p.25

[362] Miller, Jr., Carroll, and Margaret F. Tackley, Korea: 1951-1953, Ibid, p. 26, Retrieved from https://history.army.mil/html/books/021/21-2/CMH_Pub_21-2.pdf, April 3, 2020

[363] Miller, Jr., Carroll, and Tackley, Ibid. Korea: 1951-1953, p. 103, Retrieved from https://history.army.mil/html/books/021/21-2/CMH_Pub_21-2.pdf, April 3, 2020

[364] Miller, Jr., Carroll, and Tackley, Ibid. Korea: 1951-1953, p. 104-5, Retrieved from https://history.army.mil/html/books/021/21-2/CMH_Pub_21-2.pdf, April 3, 2020

[365] Miller, Jr., Carroll, and Tackley, Ibid. Korea: 1951-1953, p. 104-5, Retrieved from https://history.army.mil/html/books/021/21-2/CMH_Pub_21-2.pdf, April 3, 2020

[366] Miller, Jr., Carroll, and Tackley, Ibid. Korea: 1951-1953, p. 105-7, Retrieved from https://history.army.mil/html/books/021/21-2/CMH_Pub_21-2.pdf, April 3, 2020

[367] Miller, Jr., Carroll, and Tackley, Ibid. Korea: 1951-1953, p. 106-7, Retrieved from https://history.army.mil/html/books/021/21-2/CMH_Pub_21-2.pdf, April 3, 2020

[368] Billy, C. Mossman, op.cit., pp. 491 and Map 37, p.471, retrieved from https://history.army.mil/books/korea/ebb/ch27.htm, April 10, 2020

[369] Billy, C. Mossman, op.cit., pp. 491-2 and Map 37, p.471, retrieved from https://history.army.mil/books/korea/ebb/ch27.htm, April 10, 2020

[370] Billy, C. Mossman, op.cit.., ., p 499, 500, and 502, retrieved from https://history.army.mil/books/korea/ebb/ch27.htm, April 10, 2020. And Maneuver Center of Excellence (MCoE) Libraries, Hq Donovan Research Library, Armor Research Library, Fort Benning, Georgia, Headquarters 31st Infantry Regiment Command Report for the Month of June 1951, Headquarters 31st Infantry 20 July, 1951, Part 1, retrieved from https://koreanwar2.org/kwp2/ftbenning/ds15_i14.pdf, 11 April 2020

[371] Miller, Jr., Carroll, and Tackley, Ibid. Korea: 1951-1953, p. 105 Retrieved from https://history.army.mil/html/books/021/21-2/CMH_Pub_21-2.pdf, April 10, 2020.

[372] Billy, C. Mossman, ibid., pp. 484-86 and Map 37, p.471, retrieved from https://history.army.mil/books/korea/ebb/ch26.htm, April 10, 2020 and pp. 491- 494, https://history.army.mil/books/korea/ebb/ch27.htm, April 10, 2020

[373] Miller, Jr., Carroll, and Tackley, op.cit.. Korea: 1951-1953, p. 111 Retrieved from https://history.army.mil/html/books/021/21-2/CMH_Pub_21-2.pdf, April 22, 2020

[374] Billy, C. Mossman Ibid.., p 490, retrieved from https://history.army.mil/books/korea/ebb/ch27.htm, April 10, 2020.

[375] Billy, C. Mossman, Ibid.., p 490, retrieved from https://history.army.mil/books/korea/ebb/ch27.htm, April 10, 2020.

[376] Billy, C. Mossman Ibid., p 497-500, retrieved from https://history.army.mil/books/korea/ebb/ch27.htm, April 22, 2020.

[377] Billy, C. Mossman Ibid., pp494-496, retrieved from https://history.army.mil/books/korea/ebb/ch27.htm, April 10, 2020.

[378] Billy, C. Mossman Ibid., pp 490, retrieved from https://history.army.mil/books/korea/ebb/ch27.htm, April 10, 2020.

[379] Billy, C. Mossman, Ibid., pp. 502 - 3, retrieved from https://history.army.mil/books/korea/ebb/ch27.htm, April 10, 2020.

[380] Miller, Jr., Carroll, and Tackley, Ibid. Korea: 1951-1953, p. 283-4 Retrieved from https://history.army.mil/html/books/021/21-2/CMH_Pub_21-2.pdf, April 10, 2020.

[381] Billy, C. Mossman, Ibid., p 504-506, retrieved from https://history.army.mil/books/korea/ebb/ch27.htm, April 10, 2020.

[382] James F Schnabel, Policy and Direction: The First Year, United States Army in the Korean War, Center of Military History, United States Army, Washington, DC, 1992 p. 405, Retrieved from

https://history.army.mil/html/books/020/20-1/CMH_Pub_20-1.pdf

[383] Billy, C. Mossman, Ibid., Map 17, p.218 retrieved from https://history.army.mil/books/korea/ebb/ch27.htm, April 10, 2020.

[384] Maneuver Center of Excellence (MCoE) Libraries, Hq Donovan Research Library, Armor Research Library, Fort Benning, Georgia, 32nd Infantry Regiment Command Report for the Period 1-31 January (Inclusive) , Hqs 32 RCT 1951, for January 12, retrieved from https://koreanwar2.org/kwp2/ftbenning/ds16_i15.pdf, 11 April 2020

[385] Maneuver Center of Excellence (MCoE) Libraries, Hq Donovan Research Library, Armor Research Library, Fort Benning, Georgia, Command Report for the 31st Infantry Regiment for the Period 1-31 March 1951(Inclusive) , Hqs 31st Infantry, 10 April 1951, pp. 1-2; Inclosure 4, Supporting Documents for March 4, 1951, Periodic Operations Report No 71, 031800 to 041800 March 4 RCT 31 04 Mar; Inclosure 5, Supporting Documents for March 5, 1951, Periodic Operations Report No 72, 041800 to 051800 March 4 RCT 31 05 Mar; Inclosure 6, Supporting Documents for March 6, 1951, Periodic Operations Report No 73, 051800 to 061800 March 6 RCT 31 06 Mar; and Inclosure 7, Supporting Documents for March 7, 1951, Periodic Operations Report No 74, 061800 to 071800 March 7 RCT 31 07 Mar 51;   https://koreanwar2.org/kwp2/ftbenning/ds72_i201.pdf, April 14, 2020.

[386] Maneuver Center of Excellence (MCoE) Libraries, Hq Donovan Research Library, Armor Research Library, Fort Benning, Georgia, Command Report for the 31st Infantry Regiment for the Period 1-31 March 1951(Inclusive) , Hqs 31st Infantry, 10 April 1951, p 9, 10, https://koreanwar2.org/kwp2/ftbenning/ds72_i201.pdf, April 14, 2020 and Miller, Jr., Carroll, and Tackley, op.cit. Korea: 1951-1953, p. 25 Retrieved from https://history.army.mil/html/books/021/21-2/CMH_Pub_21-2.pdf, April 10, 2020.

[387] Maneuver Center of Excellence (MCoE) Libraries, Hq Donovan Research Library, Armor Research Library, Fort Benning, Georgia, Command Report for the 31st Infantry Regiment for the Month of June 1951 , Headquarters 31st Infantry, 20 July 1951, Part 1, June 5, 1951 and June 23, 1951, retrieved from https://koreanwar2.org/kwp2/ftbenning/ds15_i14.pdf April 14, 2020

[388] Headquarters 31st Infantry Regiment Command Report with Supporting Documents for July 1951 dated August 1951, p 1-2, Retrieved from https://koreanwar2.org/kwp2/ftbenning/ds73_i201.pdf ,May 2, 2020
[389] Headquarters 31st Infantry Regiment Command Report with Supporting Documents for August 1951, dated September 1951, p 1-3. Retrieved from https://koreanwar2.org/kwp2/ftbenning/ds73_i201.pdf ,May 2, 20.

[390] Headquarters 31st Infantry Regiment Command Report with Supporting Documents for September 1951, dated 1 October 1951, p 1-3. Retrieved from https://koreanwar2.org/kwp2/ftbenning/ds73_i201.pdf ,May 2, 2020.

[391] Headquarters 31st Infantry Regiment Command Report with Supporting Documents for September 1951, dated 1 October 1951, p 1-3, and Periodic Operations Report 261, 091801 Sep -101800 Sep 51, and Periodic Operations report 262, 101801 Sep-111800 Sep 51 Retrieved from https://koreanwar2.org/kwp2/ftbenning/ds73_i201.pdf , May 2, 2020.

[392] Headquarters 31st Infantry Regiment Command Report with Supporting Documents for October 1951, dated 1 November 1951, p 1-2 Retrieved from https://koreanwar2.org/kwp2/ftbenning/ds73_i201.pdf ,May 2, 2020.

[393] Lineage and Honors Information, Center of Military History, Department of the Army, retrieved from https://history.army.mil/html/forcestruc/lineages/branches/armor-cav/077ar.htm May 2, 2020

[394] Lineage and Honors 5th Squadron, 73 Cavalry (Airborne Thunder), Center of Military History, Department of the Army Retrieved from https://history.army.mil/html/forcestruc/lineages/branches/armor-cav/073cvrg005sq.htm, May 2, 2020.

[395] Personal discussions with Colonel Pickarts in Vietnam and at 77th Armor unit reunions.

[396] Personal and periodic correspondence with Colonel Milia.

[397] Wikipedia: The Free Encyclopedia, Raymond G. Davis, Retrieved from https://en.wikipedia.org/wiki/Raymond_G_Davis , May 3, 2020.

[398] Personal discussion with Jerry Brown, former A/1-77 Co commander, May 18, 2020; Martin Funeral Home, Dignity Memorial, Joe D. Offutt Obituary, October 9, 2016 Retrieved from https://dignitymemorial.com/obituaries/el-paso-tx/joe-offutt712080 and KWP 7ID-006779; and Op Order 26, 7th Inf Div, 26 Nov50 Retrieved from https://www.koreanwar2.org/kwp2/jpac/7id_war_diary_nov_1950_box_3174.pdf May 3.2020

[399] Mossberg, Ebb and Flow, op.cit. pp 51-2 Retrieved from https://history.army.mil/books/korea/ebb/fm.htm, and Appleman South to Naktong and North to Yalu, op.cit. pp. 10-11.

[400] Mossberg, Ebb and Flow, Ibid., pp. 53-55, https://history.army.mil/books/korea/ebb/fm.htm

[401] Mossberg, Ibid., pp.53-5, Retrieved from https://history.army.mil/books/korea/ebb/fm.htm, and Appleman South to Naktong and North to Yalu, op.cit., pp. 11-12

Mossberg Ibid., pp.53-5 and Appleman South to Naktong and North to Yalu, op.cit., pp. 11-12 Retrieved from,

[402] Mossberg, Ebb and Flow Ibid. , pp 90-92 Retrieved from https://history.army.mil/books/korea/ebb/fm.htm, and Appleman, East of Chosin, op.cit., 52-56.

[403] Mossberg, Ebb and Flow Ibid., p. 54, Retrieved from https://history.army.mil/books/korea/ebb/fm.htm,

[404] Paragraph 287b, The tank battalion attached to an infantry regiment, and Paragraph 287d One tank company with each infantry regiment, US Department of the Army, *Field Manual 17-33, Tank Battalion*, September 1949, pp. 299-301 Retrieved from https://archive.org/stream/FM17-331951#page/n315/mode/2up/search/Part+IV

[405] Richard K. Kolb, Korea's Invisible Veterans' Return to an Ambivalent America, Reprinted from the November 1997 issue of VFW Magazine retrieved from <www.koreanwar-educator.org/topics/vfw/p_koreas_invisible_veterans.htm>

[406] Captain Robert C McCaleb, Facts, Not Prejudice," Armor Magazine, January-February 1951, p.3, FOOTNOTE retrieved from https://www.benning.army.mil/Armor/eARMOR/content/issues/1951/JAN_FEB/1951JanuaryFebruary.pdf

[407] Colonel William P. Withers, Report from Korea, Armor Magazine, March-April 1951, p.22, FOOTNOTE retrieved from https://www.benning.army.mil/Armor/eARMOR/content/issues/1951/MAR_APR/1951MarchApril.pdf

[408] Robert E. Drake, The Infantry Regiment's Tank Company, Armor Magazine, September—October 1951, pp. 14, FOOTNOTE retrieved from
https://www.benning.army.mil/Armor/eARMOR/content/issues/1951/SEP_OCT/1951SeptemberOctober.pdf
[409] Ibid., pp14-17, Retrieved from
https://www.benning.army.mil/Armor/eARMOR/content/issues/1951/SEP_OCT/1951SeptemberOctober.pdf
[410] First Lt Robert S Brown, Sum and Substance, Armor Magazine, May-June 1951, pp. 26-27, FOOTNOTE retrieved from https://www.benning.army.mil/Armor/eARMOR/content/issues/1951/MAY_JUN/1951MayJune.pdf

Chapter 5

[411] Stanley Karnow, Vietnam: A History, (New York, Penguin Books) 1991, pp 109-110.
[412] Bernard B. Fall, The Street Without Joy: The French Debacle in Indochina, Stackpole Books, 1961 and republished 1994, Stackpole Military History Series., p 38.
[413] Ibid., p. 40.
[414] Ibid., p.41 and p.26: *Viet Minh* is the Vietnamese language abbreviation for League for the Revolution and Independence of Vietnam. *Viet Cong* is a pejorative abbreviation for *Viet Nam Cong San* used in South Vietnam for Vietnamese Communists.
[415] Karnow, Vietnam op.cit., p.152.
[416] Ibid., pp147-148.
[417] Fall, The Street, op. cit., p. 42.
[418] Andrew Wiest, Vietnam's Forgotten Army: Heroism and Betrayal in the ARVN, New York: New York University Press, 2008, pp. 11-13.
[419] Ibid., p.124
[420] Fall, The Street, op.cit., p. 413.
[421] Korea, French Battalion of the United Nations Organisation (Korean War) Retrieved from French Battalion (Korean War) - Wikipedia, 05242021, and Bernard B. Fall, Chapter 9 End of a Task Force, The Street op.cit., pp. 227-229; 263-264; and 283-289.
[422] The New York Times Reports that General William C. Westmoreland, has requested 206,000 Additional Troops, March 10, 1968, retrieved from https://Timeline Details, vietnamwar50th.com July 12, 2021.
[423] Graham A. Cosmas, MACV: The Joint Command in the Years of Withdrawal, 1968-1973, Washington, DC Center Of Military History, 2006, pp.105-6.
[424] Presidential Speeches Lyndon B Johnson Presidency, October 31, 1968: Remarks on the Cessation of Bombing of North Vietnam, UVA Miller Center. October 31, 1968: Remarks on the Cessation of Bombing of North Vietnam | Miller Center,retrieved from https://the-presidency/presidential-speeches/october-31-1968-remarks-cessation - of-bombing-north-Vietnam, September 6, 2021.
[425] Neil T. Howell, Letter to author, October 30,2017
[426] Movement Orders Number 9, Department of the Army, Headquarters 5th Infantry Division (Mechanized) and Fort Carson, Fort Carson, Colorado 80913, 1 May 1968, p.2, and Vietnam-Society of the Fifth Division , retrieved from http://www.societyofthefifthdvision.com April 29, 2021, paragraphs 1 and 2.
[427] Letter, Col Carmelo P. Milia, 2018 to author read on October 18, 2021
[428] Terry Foster, Provisional Corps Vietnam, U.S. Army Military History Institute, February 21, 2012, retrieved from https://www.army.mil.article/73555/provisional_corps_vietnam, May 4, 2021
[429] Robert Forman, Fort Carson. Colorado: Alert for Vietnam, unpublished diary,1967-1973, pp.15-19
[430] Movement Orders Number 9, op.cit. p.1.
[431] Ibid., pp. 16-19.
[432] Date in Country (DIC), Company Roster, HHC 1st Bn 77th Armor, 1st Inf Bde, 5th Inf Div(M) APO San Francisco 96477, 7 August 1968.
[433] Ibid., pp. 22-3.
[434] Personal recollections of the author who was the Armor representative on the team
[435] Bernard B. Fall, The Street Without Joy: The French Debacle in Indochina, Stackpole Books, 1961 and republished 1994, Stackpole Military History Series.

[436] Ibid., Chapter 7, pp.179-182

[437] Lewis Sorely, "Adaptation and Impact: Mounted Combat in Vietnam," in George F. Hofman and Donn A. Starry, eds., Camp Colt to Desert Storm: The History of U.S. Armored Forces, The University Press of Kentucky, 1999, pp. 344, 347, 349-50.

[438] Sorley, Adaptation and Impact, op.cit. pp. 347, 349-50.

[439] Personal recollections of the author who was the Armor representative on the team.

[440] Personal recollections of the author who was the Armor representative on the team.

[441] Personal recollections of the author who was the Armor representative on the team.

[442] M60 Tank, retrieved from https://en.m.wikipedia.org, May 6, 2021.

[443] Battle Tanks, 1956-USA Medium Tank M48A2C Patton, retrieved from http:// battletanks.com, May 6, 2021

[444] Robert Forman, Fort Carson. Colorado: Initial Work-up for Deployment, unpublished diary,1967-1973, p. 20.

[445] Date in Country (DIC), Company Roster, op.cit., 7 August 1968, and Annex H (PCS for Main Party) to MO 9, Hq 5th Inf Div (Mech) and Ft Carson, 1 May 1968.

[446] Personnel recollections of the author and Forman, op.cit, Vietnam, pp1-4.

[447] Wilson, op.cit., pp. 332-3.

[448] Activities in Republic of Vietnam, History of the 1st Tank Battalion 77th Armor, undated, National Archives and Records Administration, (NARA), College Park, MD, December 2019.

[449] USA M48 Patton Medium Tank, Gary's Combat Vehicle Reference retrieved from https://www.inetres.com,

[450] Email between author and Joseph Davis B/1-77 Armor, Driver, Tank B-66, July 5, 2021.

[451] Wilson, op.cit., p. 330.

[452] Andrew Wiest, Vietnam's Forgotten Army, op.cit. p. 13.

[453] Map Overlay, Operations Order 14-68 Headquarters 1st Brigade, 5th Infantry Division,

[454] Multiple sources: Leatherneck Square, The McNamara Line, Vietnam's Demiltarized Zone all retrieved from en.m.wikipedia.org, from creative commons, creativecommons.org, June 9 and 10, 2021

[455] Prelude, Operation Kentucky, retrieved from https://Operation Kentucky - Wikipedia, January 31, 2022.

[456] Ibid., June 9-10, 2021.

[457] Operations Order 2-68, Headquarters, 1-77 Armor, YD 139615, 261400H Aug 1968, YD 9, p 1. 77th Armor Association, from Archival Research International 1539 Foxhall Road, NW, Washington, DC,

[458] Email from Everett Nagel to author, August 5, 2021; Email from Kevin Dunne to Author July 28, 2021; Award of the Bronze Star Medal, General Orders Number 859, Department of the Army, Headquarters XXIV Corps, July 2, 1968.

[459] Ibid.

[460] Email Leonard G. Renoux to Robert Rushforth, June 18, 2002, and Operations Order 2-68, Ibid., pp1-4 , 77th Armor Association, from Archival Research International 1539 Foxhall Road, NW, Washington, DC, and Frag Order 5 to OPORD 2-68 Headquarters, 1-77 Armor, YD 139615, 311700H Aug1968, YD 9, p 1. 77th Armor Association, from Archival Research International 1539 Foxhall Road, NW, Washington, DC, p.1, and

[461] Operations Order 2-68, Ibid., pp1-4 , 77th Armor Association, from Archival Research International 1539 Foxhall Road, NW, Washington, DC, and Frag Order 5 to OPORD 2-68 Headquarters, 1-77 Armor, YD 139615, 311700H Aug1968, YD 9, p 1. 77th Armor Association, from Archival Research International 1539 Foxhall Road, NW, Washington, DC, p.1.

[462] Ibid.

[463] Personal recollections of the author

[464] Ibid.

[465] E-mail from C. Warren Trainor to Robert Rushforth, Oral History, April 11, 2003.

[466] Email from John M. Pickarts to Robert Rushforth, May 17, 2002, 77th Armor Archives.

[467] Multiple Sources: Email Leonard G. Renoux to Robert Rushforth, June 18, 2002, Email from John M. Pickarts to Robert Rushforth, May 17, 2002, and Combat Operations After Action Report, Department of the Army, 1st Battalion, 77th Armor, APO San Francisco 96477.1 Nov 1968, National Archives and Records Administration (NARA), College Park, MD, December 2019.

[468] Pickarts email to Robert Rushforth, May 17, 2002, 77th Armor Archives, op.cit.

[469] Ibid.

[470] Ibid.

[471] Combat Operations After Action Report, Department of the Army, 1st Battalion, 77th Armor, APO San Francisco 96477.1 Nov 1968, National Archives and Records Administration (NARA), College Park, MD, December 2019.

[472] Letter Robert Forman to Robert Rushforth, an account of Operation Sullivan, November 28, 2001.

[473] Ibid., and Combat Operations After Action Report, Department of the Army, 1st Battalion, 77th Armor, APO San Francisco 96477.1 Nov 1968, NARA, College Park, MD, December 2019.

[474] Multiple Sources: Email Leonard G. Renoux to Robert Rushforth, June 18, 2002, Email from John M. Pickarts to Robert Rushforth, May 17, 2002, and Combat Operations After Action Report, Department of the Army, 1st Battalion, 77th Armor, APO San Francisco 96477.1 Nov 1968, National Archives and Records Administration (NARA), College Park, MD, December 2019.

[475] Email, Jim Davis to Robert Rushforth May 24, 2002.

[476] Multiple Sources: Email Leonard G. Renoux to Robert Rushforth, June 18, 2002, Email from John M. Pickarts to Robert Rushforth, May 17, 2002, and Combat Operations After Action Report, Department of the Army, 1st Battalion, 77th Armor, APO San Francisco 96477.1 Nov 1968, National Archives and Records Administration (NARA), College Park, MD, December 2019.

[477] Ibid.,

[478] Ibid.,

[479] Ibid.,

[480] Ibid.

[481] Email C. Warren Trainor to Robert Rushforth April 11, 2003.

[482] Multiple Sources: Email Leonard G. Renoux to Robert Rushforth, June 18, 2002, Email from John M. Pickarts to Robert Rushforth, May 17, 2002, and Combat Operations After Action Report, Department of the Army, 1st Battalion, 77th Armor, APO San Francisco 96477.1 Nov 1968, National Archives and Records Administration (NARA), College Park, MD, December 2019

[483] Letter Robert Forman to Robert Rushforth, an account of Operation Sullivan, November 28, 2001 and Combat Operations After Action Report, Department of the Army, 1st Battalion, 77th Armor, APO San Francisco 96477.1 Nov 1968, National Archives and Records Administration (NARA), College Park, MD, December 2019, and Letter, John MJ. Pickarts to Robert Rushforth, After Thoughts on Operation Sullivan, 26 May 2002.

[484] Combat Operations After Action Report, Department of the Army, 1st Battalion, 77th Armor, APO San Francisco 96477.1 Nov 1968, National Archives and Records Administration (NARA), College Park, MD, December 2019, and Letter, John MJ. Pickarts to Robert Rushforth, After Thoughts on Operation Sullivan, 26 May 2002.

[485] Combat Operations After Action Report, Department of the Army, Headquarters, 1st Battalion (Mech) 61st Infantry, APO San Francisco 96477, 16 November 1968, National Archives and Records Administration (NARA), College Park, MD, December 2019.

[486] Ibid.

[487] Ibid.

[488] Ibid.

[489] Ibid.

[490] Ibid

[491] Ibid

[492] Ibid

[493] Ibid

[494] Discussion between Arthur McGowan and the author in January 1969.

[495] Combat Operations After Action Report, Department of the Army, Headquarters, 1st Battalion (Mech) 61st Infantry, APO San Francisco 96477, 16 November 1968, op.cit.

[496] Ibid.

[497] Ibid.

[498] Ibid.

[499] Discussion between Arthur McGowan and the author in January 1969.

[500] Robert Forman, Vietnam, unpublished diary,1967-1973, p. 13-14.

[501] Guy A. Holmes, 1-77 Battalion Personnel Staff NCO email to the author July 15, 2021.

[502] Robert Forman, Vietnam, unpublished diary,1967-1973, p. 13-14. Letter, John M. Pickarts to Robert Rushforth, After Thoughts on Operation Sullivan, op.cit., and personal recollections of the author.

[503] Letter, John M. Pickarts to Robert Rushforth, After Thoughts on Operation Sullivan, op.cit

[504] Lewis Sorely, A Better War: The Unexamined Victories and Final Tragedy of America's Last Years in Vietnam, (New York, A Harvest Book, Harcourt, Inc) 1999, 123-125.

[505] Con Thien, Military retrieved from https://military.wikia.org?wiki/Con _Thien#, and Charles Smith, US Marines in Vietnam, High Mobility and Standdown 1969, History and Museum Division, Headquarters, U.S. Marine Corps, Washington D.C. 1988,p. 10-13, Retrieved from https://www.marines.mil/portals/1/Publications/U.S.%20Marines%20in%20Vietnam_High%20Mobility%20and%2 0Standown%201969%20%20PCN%2019000310300.pdf

[506] Our Lady of La Vang: the Catholic Side of Vietnam, retrieved from Our Lady of La Vang: The Catholic Side of Vietnam - Catholicism.org

[507] Colonel (ret) Richard Benson recollection to the author July 16, 2021 at Gettysburg 77th Armor Reunion.

[508] Ibid.,

[509] Ibid.

[510] OPORD 11-68, 1-77 Armor, 291800H Nov 68 77th Armor Association Archive.

[511] Email Richard Benson Revision response to author, August 8, 2021

[512] Ibid.

Chapter 6

[513] Charles R. Smith, US Marines in Vietnam: High Mobility and Standdown, 1969, History and Museums Division, Headquarters, US Marine Corps, Washington, D.C. 1988, p.7

[514] Lewis Sorely, A Better War: The Unexamined Victories and the Final Tragedy of America's Last Years in Vietnam, (New York: A Harvest Book, Harcourt, Inc.), 1999, p. 127.

[515] Keith William Nolan, Into Laos: The Story of Dewey Canyon II/Lam Son 719 Vietnam 1971, Novato, CA Presidio Press, pp 12-13.

[516] Ibid., p.7

[517] Andrew Wiest Vietnam's Forgotten Army: Heroism and Betrayal in the ARVN, New York, New York Univ Press, 2008 p. 182

[518] After Action Report-Operation Napoleon Saline II &AO Marshall Mountain, 1 November 1968-28 February 1969, HQ, 1st Infantry Brigade, 5th Infantry Brigade (Mech), APO San Francisco 96477, 8 April 1969 pp. 1-3. National Archives and Records Administration (NARA), 8601 Adelphi Road, College Park MD 20740, December 2019

[519] Smith, Us Marines 1969, op.cit., p.15.

[520] Ibid., p.2

[521] Ibid., p.15

[522] Ibid., p.4

[523] Ibid., p.4

[524] Ibid., p. 5

[525] Ibid., p. 9

[526] After Action Report, Napoleon Saline II, op.cit., p. 8

[527] Combat After Action Report Fulton Square, Headquarters 1st Battalion 77th Armor APO San Francisco 96477, n.d, p.2. and Vietnam Land Clearing History, retrieved from http://www.59thlandclearing.org 01012022.

[528] *Author, notes.*

[529] *Smith, Us Marines 1969, op.cit., pp.60-61.*

530 *Ibid., pp.60-61.*

531 Ibid., pp. 32, 40, and 65.

532 Ibid., p. 41.

533 Ibid., p.52.

534 Ibid., p.52-53.

535 Carmelo P Milia, "Task Force to Khe Sanh". *Armor*, Vol.79, no 3, May-June 1970 p. 42, retrieved from 1970Jan-Jun.pdf (usgovcloudapi.net), October 7, 2021, and letter to author 14 October 2021

536 Operational Report, Lessons Learned, Headquarters, 1st Infantry Brigade, 5th Infantry Division, April 1969, ACDA (M).(3 Sep 69),OACSFOR, FOR/OT-UT-692327, 30 May 69 , Department of the Army, Office of the Adjutant General, Washington, DC, 18 September 1969, p.7.

537Milia, Armor Task Force, op.cit., pp 42-43.

538 M546 APERS-T 105-mm, Military Analysis Network retrieved from man.fas.org October 27, 2021

539 M48A3 Patton (Late Model) Specifications, retrieved from Patton Tanks in Vietnam mikesresearch.com October 27, 2021.

540 Milia, Armor Task Force, op.cit., pp 42-43, and Frag Order 1 to OPORD 3-69, TF Remagen (1-77 Armor) 181920H March 1969

541 Milia, Armor Task Force, op.cit, p.,43 and 45

542 Ibid., p.43 and 45..

543 Ibid., p.43 and 45.

544 Ibid., p.44.

545 Ibid., p.46.

546 Milia letter to author 14 October 2021, op.cit., and Operational Report, Lessons Learned, 18 September 1969, op.cit. p. 11, NARA, December 2019

547 Ibid.

548 Milia, Armor Task Force, op.cit, p.,46, and Operational Report, Lessons Learned, 18 September 1969, op.cit. p.12.

549 Milia, Armor Task Force, op.cit, p.,43 and 45.

550 Milia letter to author 14 October 2021, op.cit., Milia, Armor Task Force, op.cit, p.,46, and Operational Report, Lessons Learned, 18 September 1969, op.cit. p. 10-11, NARA December 2019.

551 Operational Report, Lessons Learned, 18 September 1969, op. cit., p11

552 Ibid., p.11., and letter from Carmelo P. Milia, 2018 and read October 18, 2021, phone discussion with Jerry Brown on October 16, 2021, and Operational Report, Lessons Learned, 18 September 1969, op. cit., p12

553 Smith, Us Marines 1969, op.cit., pp.62-63.

554 Phone discussion with Jerry Brown on October 16, 2021, and Operational Report, Lessons Learned, 18 September 1969, op. cit., p12

555 Operational Report, Lessons Learned, 18 September 1969, op. cit., p13.

556 Ibid. p.13.

557 Ibid. p.13.

558 Combat Operations After-Action Report, Operation Massachusetts Bay, 23 April-15 June 1969, HQ 1st Infantry Brigade, 5th Infantry Division (Mech), APO San Francisco 96477, 21 August 1969, p. 3, NARA, December 2019.

559 Combat After Action Report, Massachusetts Bay, Headquarters 1st Battalion 77th Armor, APO San Francisco 96477, 1 July 1969, p.1, NARA, December 2019.

560 Ibid., p.1

561 Ibid., p.2

562 Library of Congress, Manuscript/Mixed Material Unidentified Element, 812th Regiment, Suspected 324 B Division. retrieved from https://loc.gov 4 Oct 2021

563 Smith, Us Marines 1969, op.cit., p.58.

564 Combat After Action Report, Massachusetts Bay, 1st Bn 77th Armor op.cit., p.2

565 Ibid., p.2.

566 Ibid., p.2

567 Ibid., pp. 3-4.

[568] Ibid., pp. 2-4.

[569] Joint Task Group Guadalcanal After Action Report-Operation Utah Mesa, 12 June 1969-9 July 1969, HQ 1st Infantry Brigade, 5th Infantry Division (Mech) APO San Francisco 96477, 29 August 1969 p 3, NARA December 2019, and Charles R. Smith, US Marines in Vietnam: High Mobility and Standdown, 1969, op.cit, p. 71.

[570] Joint Task Group Guadalcanal After Action Report-Operation Utah Mesa, 12 June 1969-9 July 1969, op.cit., pp 2-4.

[571] Charles R. Smith, US Marines in Vietnam: High Mobility and Standdown, 1969, op.cit, pp 71, 73.

[572] Joint Task Group Guadalcanal After Action Report-Operation Utah Mesa, 12 June 1969-9 July 1969 op.cit., pp1,2

[573] Ibid. p. 5.

[574] Ibid., pp 1-3.

[575] Ibid, pp. 6-7, and Robert Forman, Vietnam, Operation Utah Mesa, unpublished diary, 1967-1973, p. 62.

[576] Ibid, p.7

[577] Ibid., p 7 and author's notes, and Robert Forman, Vietnam, Operation Utah Mesa op.cit., p. 62.

[578] Joint Task Group Guadalcanal After Action Report-Operation Utah Mesa, 12 June-9 July 1969, op.cit. pp 6-7

[579] Ibid., p. 7.

[580] 'Spooky" Gunship Operations in the Vietnam War, HISTORYNET, retrieved from historynet.com November 12, 2021.

[581] Charles R. Smith, US Marines in Vietnam: High Mobility and Standdown, 1969, op.cit, p. 147 and author's notes..

[582] Joint Task Group Guadalcanal After Action Report-Operation Utah Mesa, 12 June-9 July 1969, op.cit. p. 7, NARA December 2019; author's notes; and Robert Forman, Vietnam, Operation Utah Mesa, op.cit., p. 50-51.

[583] Charles R. Smith, US Marines in Vietnam: High Mobility and Standdown, 1969, op.cit, p. 67 and author's notes.

[584] Joint Task Group Guadalcanal After Action Report-Operation Utah Mesa, 12 June-9 July 1969, op.cit. p. 8.

[585] Ibid., p.8

[586] Ibid., p.8 and Charles R. Smith, US Marines in Vietnam: High Mobility and Standdown, 1969, op.cit, pp 71-72.

[587] Donald Cummings, "Mobile Combat Base: A School Solution," Armor, vol 79, No. 5, September -October 1970, p.8.

[588] Cummings, "Mobile Combat Base: A School Solution," op.cit., p. 8.

[589] Ibid., pp. 7-8.

[590] Joint Task Group Guadalcanal After Action Report-Operation Utah Mesa, 12 June-9 July 1969, op.cit. p. 8.

[591] Ibid., p.8.

[592] Ibid., p. 9 and the author's notes.

[593] Ibid., p. 9 and the author's notes.

[594] Ibid., p. 9, Charles R. Smith, US Marines in Vietnam: High Mobility and Standdown, 1969, op.cit, p. 72. and author's discussion with Lieutenant Colonel Hartigan.

[595] Joint Task Group Guadalcanal After Action Report-Operation Utah Mesa, 12 June-9 July 1969, op.cit. p. 4.

[596] Cummings, "Mobile Combat Base: A School Solution," op.cit. pp.7-9.

[597] Joint Task Group Guadalcanal After Action Report-Operation Utah Mesa, 12 June-9 July 1969, op.cit. p. 9.

[598] Ibid., p 9.

[599] Ibid., p.9.

[600] Robert Forman, Vietnam, Operation Utah Mesa, op.cit., p. 66.

[601] Cummings, "Mobile Combat Base: A School Solution," op.cit., p 9, and Joint Task Group Guadalcanal After Action Report-Operation Utah Mesa, 12 June-9 July 1969, op.cit. pp. 9-10.

[602] Joint Task Group Guadalcanal After Action Report-Operation Utah Mesa, 12 June-9 July 1969, op.cit. p. 10.

[603] Cummings, "Mobile Combat Base: A School Solution," op.cit., p 9.

[604] Ibid., pp .9-10, and Robert Forman, Vietnam, LZ Saigon unpublished diary,1967-1973, p. 57-69.

[605] Joint Task Group Guadalcanal After Action Report-Operation Utah Mesa, 12 June-9 July 1969, op.cit. p. 10, and

[605] Cummings, "Mobile Combat Base: A School Solution," op.cit., p 9., and Forman, Operation Utah Mesa, LS Saigon, Vietnam, op.cit., pp 65-68

[606] Ibid., pp. 9-10, and Joint Task Group Guadalcanal After Action Report-Operation Utah Mesa, 12 June-9 July 1969, op.cit. p. 10.

[607] Joint Task Group Guadalcanal After Action Report-Operation Utah Mesa, 12 June-9 July 1969, op.cit. p. 10.

[608] Ibid., p.10.

[609] Ibid., p,10.

[610] Ibid., p.10.

[611] Ibid., p. 11.

[612] Ibid., p.4

[613] Ibid., p.12.

[614] Ibid., p.12. and author's notes.

[615] Charles R. Smith, US Marines in Vietnam: High Mobility and Standdown, 1969, op.cit, p. 67

[616] Joint Task Group Guadalcanal After Action Report-Operation Utah Mesa, 12 June-9 July 1969, op.cit. p. 12.. and author's notes

[617] Charles R. Smith, US Marines in Vietnam: High Mobility and Standdown, 1969, op.cit, p.132

[618] Combat Operation Report-Operation Iroquois Grove, 15 June-25 September 1969, HQ 1st Brigade, 5th Infantry Division (Mech), APO San Francisco 96477, 15 December 1969, pp. 1 and 2, NARA December 2019.
****

[619] Ibid., pp2,3, and 5.

[620] Ibid., p. 6.

[621] Ibid., p.2

[622] Author's notes.

[623] Combat Operation Report-Operation Iroquois Grove, 15 June-25 September 1969.op.cit, pp.4-6.

[624] Ibid., p.4.

[625] *Charles R*. Smith, US Marines in Vietnam: High Mobility and Standdown, 1969, op.cit,. pp.58, and 65.

[626] Ibid., p.138.

[627] Combat Operation Report-Operation Iroquois Grove, 15 June-25 September 1969, HQ 1st Brigade, 5th Infantry Division (Mech), APO San Francisco 96477, 15 December 1969, p. 1.

[628] Task Force 1-11 Combat After Action Report (Operation IDAHO CANYON), 1st Battalion, 11th Infantry, APO San Francisco 96477, 2 September 1969, pp 1,2, and 5, NARA December 2019, and Charles R. Smith, US Marines in Vietnam: High Mobility and Standdown, 1969, op.cit, p.131.

[629] Ibid. pp. 1-2, and Combat After Action Report -Operation IDAHO CANYON 28 July-15 August 1969, HQ, 1st Infantry Brigade, 5th Infantry Division (Mech), APA San Francisco 96477, 18 October 1969, pp. 2-3, NARA December 2019.

[630] Task Force 1-11 Combat After Action Report (Operation IDAHO CANYON, op.cit., p.3

[631] Ibid., pp. 5-6.

[632] Ibid., pp. 6

[633] Ibid., pp. 6

[634] Ibid., pp. 6

[635] Ibid., p.5, and Charles R. Smith, US Marines in Vietnam: High Mobility and Standdown, 1969, op.cit, p.139-140.

[636] Ibid., p.8

[637] Ibid., p.8.

[638] Ibid., p.8.

[639] Operation Snoopy: the Chemical Corps ' "people sniffer", The Free Library by Farlex, retrieved , December 15, 2021.

[640] Task Force 1-11 Combat After Action Report (Operation IDAHO CANYON, op.cit., p.8

[641] Ibid., p.10, and Charles R. Smith, US Marines in Vietnam: High Mobility and Standdown, 1969, op.cit,, p.142.

[642] Ibid., p.10.

[643] Ibid., p.10, 12.

[644] Ibid., p.10, 12

[645] Ibid., p.12.

[646] Smith, Us Marines 1969, op.cit., p.164

[647] Ibid., p.144 and 151.

[648] . Ibid., pp. 164, 166, and 167.

[649] Ibid., p.165.

[650] Ibid., p. 163-164.

651 Combat After Action Report Operation Fulton Square, Headquarters, 1st Battalion 77th Armor, APO San Francisco 96477, n.d., pp. 2-3., NARA December 2019.

652 Ibid., p.2.

653 Combat Skyspot, Military, ground-directed bombing, retrieved from https://military-history.fandom.com/wiki/Combat_Skyspot, 01012022

654 Combat After Action Report Operation Fulton Square, op.cit., p.3., and 8.

655 Ibid., pp. 3-4.

656 Vietnam- Mid Years July 1969-March 1972, retrieved from www.one-six-one.com/161index/htm, VIETNAM Mid Years Cont. (fifthinfantrydivision.com), and DUANE (REDD) CARR (fifthinfantrydivision.com), January 20, 2022

657 Author's notes, January 20, 2022.

658 www.one-six-one.com/, VIETNAM Mid Years Cont. (fifthinfantrydivision.com), January 20, 2022

659 Ibid., and Recommendation for Award of the Presidential Unit Citation, Headquarters, 1st Infantry Brigade, 5th Infantry Division (Mechanized), Camp Red Devil, APO San Francisco 96477, n.d., p.2., NARA December 2019.

660 Recommendation for PUC, 1st Brigade, 5th Infantry Div (M), pp.1-2.

661 Ibid., p.2.

662 Ibid., p.2.

663 www.one-six-one.com/, VIETNAM Mid Years Cont. (fifthinfantrydivision.com), op.cit. January 21, 2022

664 Recommendation for PUC, 1st Brigade, 5th Infantry Div (M), pp. 2-3, and www.one-six-one.com/, VIETNAM Mid Years Cont. (fifthinfantrydivision.com), op.cit. January 21, 2022.

665 Presidential Unit Citation, Award of the Presidential Unit Citation by the President of the United States of America to the following unit of the Armed Forces of the United States is confirmed in accordance with Paragraph 194, AR 672-5-1, The 1st Battalion (Mechanized) 61st Infantry, 1st Brigade , 5th Infantry Division (Mechanized) and assigned and attached units, Enclosure 6, n.d., NARA December 2019.

Chapter 7

666 Lewis Sorely, A Better War: The Unexamined Victories and Final Tragedy of America's Last Years in Vietnam, New York, A Harvest Book, Harcourt, Inc. 1999, pp 93,94.

667 Author's notes.

668 Sorely, A Better War op.cit., p.94.

669 Andrew Wiest, Vietnam's Forgotten Army: Heroism and Betrayal in the ARVN, New York: New York University Press., 2008, pp 182-185.

670 Ibid., pp. 50-51.

671 Ibid., p 190-192.

672 Ibid., pp. 202, 213.

673 Sorely, A Better War, op.cit., pp.154-155.

674 Ibid., pp.154-157.

675 Combat After Action Report – Operation Greene River, Headquarters, 1st Bn, 77th Armor, APO San Francisco 96477, National Archives and Records Administration (NARA), 8601 Adelphi Road, College Park MD 20740, and Operational Report – Lessons Learned, 1st Brigade, 5th Infantry Division, Period Ending 31 July 1970 (U), Department of the Army, Office of the Adjutant General, Washington D.C., 20130, retrieved A9R1xys16n_19chob7_5s4.tmp (ttu.edu),February 2, 2022, p.1

676 Operational Report – Lessons Learned, 1st Brigade, 5th Infantry Division, Period Ending 31 July 1970 (U), Department of the Army, Office of the Adjutant General, Washington D.C., 20130, retrieved A9R1xys16n_19chob7_5s4.tmp (ttu.edu),February 2, 2022,p. 5, and M551 Sheridan - Wikipedia, retrieved July 14, 2022.

677 Ibid., pp 1,2.

678 Ibid., p.7.

679 After Action Report (Wolfe Mountain) for the period 22 July70 to 31 January 1971, Headquarters 1st Battalion 77th Armor APO San Francisco 96477, 28 February 1972, National Archives and Records Administration (NARA), 8601 Adelphi Road, College Park MD 20740, p.1

680 Combat After Action Report – Operation Greene River, Headquarters, 1st Bn, 77th Armor, APO San Francisco 96477, National Archives and Records Administration (NARA), 8601 Adelphi Road, College Park MD 20740, December 2019. pp3,4

681 Combat After Action Report – Operation Greene River, Headquarters, 1st Bn, 77th Armor, APO San Francisco 96477, National Archives and Records Administration (NARA), 8601 Adelphi Road, College Park MD 20740, pp3-4

682 Operational Report – Lessons Learned, 1st Brigade, 5th Infantry Division, op.cit., p3.

683 Operational Report – Lessons Learned, 1st Brigade, 5th Infantry Division, op.cit., p5.

684 Don Wittenberger The Battle at Khe Gio Bridge: Location Coordinates: 164656N, 1999 retrieved from The Battle at The Khe Gio Bridge! (angelfire.com) March 18, 2022.

685 Ibid., pp 1,2.

686 After Action Report (WOLFE MOUNTAIN), op.cit., p.1

687 Ibid., p.1

688 Combat Operations After Action Report, Operation JEFFERSON GLENN, 12 December 1970-15 December 1970, Headquarters 1st Battalion 77th Armor, APO San Francisco 96477, 19 December 1970, National Archives and Records Administration (NARA), 8601 Adelphi Road, College Park MD 20740, December 2019, and Operation Jefferson Glen. From Wikipedia, Operation Jefferson Glenn - Wikipedia, March 28,2022.

689 After Action Report (WOLFE MOUNTAIN), for period 22 July 70 – 30 Jan 71, Headquarters, 1st Battalion 77th Armor, APO San Francisco 96477, 28 February 1971, National Archives and Records Administration (NARA), 8601 Adelphi Road, College Park MD 20740, pp 1-2. December 2019.

690 After Action Report, Operation JEFFERSON GLEN, op.cit, p. 3

691 After Action Report, Operation JEFFERSON GLEN, op.cit, pp 1-4.

692 After Action Report (WOLFE MOUNTAIN), for period 22 July 70 – 30 Jan 71, op.cit., p. 2

693 Ibid., p.2

694 Sorely, A Better War, op.cit., pp.202-204.

695 Charles R. Smith, U.S. Marines in Vietnam, High Mobility and Standdown, 1969, (Washington, D.C.: History and Museums Di vision, Headquarters United States Marine Corps, 1988, pp 27-28.

696 Ibid., 29-38

697 Ibid., pp 41-45.

698 Sorely, A Better War, op.cit., pp 228-237.

699 Ibid., p. 242

700 Ibid., pp 244-245

701 Lewis Sorely, A Better War: The Unexamined Victories and Final Tragedy of America's Last Years in Vietnam, New York, A Harvest Book, Harcourt, Inc. 1999; Andrew Wiest, Vietnam's Forgotten Army: Heroism and Betrayal in the ARVN, New York: New York University Press., 2008; Keith William Nolan, Into Laos: The Story of Dewey Canyon II/Lam Son 719, Vietnam 1971, Novato, CA, Presidion Press, 1986; and Lieutenant Colonel Richard M. Meyer, "The Road to Laos," Armor Volume 81, No. 2, March-April 1972, pp 18-26.

702 Lewis Sorely, A Better War, op.cit., p. 234.

703 Ibid., pp. 236-237.

704 Wiest, Vietnam's Forgotten Army, op.cit., p. 201

705 Nolan, Into Laos, op.cit., pp 30-31.

706 Ibid. p.31.

707 Wiest, Vietnam's Forgotten Army, op.cit., p. 201

708 Meyer, "The Road to Laos", op.cit., pp. 19-20

709 Author's notes 1968.

710 Meyer, "The Road to Laos", op.cit., pp. 19-20.

711 Ibid., p. 19

712 Nolan, Into Laos, op.cit., pp. 65-66.

713 Ibid., p.66, 79.

[714] Meyer, "The Road to Laos", op.cit., p.21. and Item d. Engineer, Combat Operations After-Action Report Lam Son 719, 29 January to 7 April 1971, Headquarters 1st Brigade 5th Infantry Division (Mech), Camp Red Devil, APO San Francisco 96477, retrieved from Lam Son 719 (societyofthefifthdivision.com)

[715] Myer, The Road to Laos, p.21, and Nolan, Into Laos, op.cit. pp.56, 59-61,63.

[716] Nolan, Into Laos, op.cit., p.211

[717] Myer, Ibid., p.21 and Item d Engineer, Combat Operations After-Action Report Lam Son 719, 29 January to 7 April 1971, op.cit.

[718] Myer, Ibid., p 21.

[719] Wiest, Vietnam's Forgotten Army, op.cit., pp.204-204.

[720] Sorley, A Better War, op.cit, pp. 245-246.

[721] Myer, op.cit., pp. 21-22

[722] Ibid., p. 22

[723] Ibid., p.22.

[724] Ibid., p 22-23.and Nolan Into Laos, op.cit. p 302

[725] Nolan Into Laos, op.cit. p 295

[726] Ibid., p 289-90. and Meyer, The Road to Laos, p.22.

[727] Ibid., p 296-298, Meyer, The Road to Laos, p.22.

[728] Meyer Ibid., pp. 22-23.

[729] Ibid., p. 23.

[730] Ibid., p. 23.

[731] Ibid., pp.23-24

[732] Ibid., p. 24

[733] Nolan Into Laos, op.cit., p. 316.

[734] Meyer op.cit., p.25, and Nolan, Ibid., p. 354.

[735] After Action Report, Operation Montana Mustang, 8 April 1972 to July 1, 1971, Department of the Army, 1st Battalion 77th Armor, APO SF 96477, 4 July 1971, p.1, retrieved from National Archives and Records Administration (NARA), 8601 Adelphi Road, College Park MD 20740, December 19, 2019.

[736] Ibid., p. 2.

[737] After Action Report KEYSTONE ORIOLE (BRAVO), HQ, 1st Infantry Brigade, 5th Infantry Division (Mech), Camp Red Devil, APO San Francisco 96477, 19 August 1971, p.1, retrieved from National Archives and Records Administration (NARA), 8601 Adelphi Road, College Park MD 20740, December 19, 2019.

[738] Ibid., pp.4-5

[739] Ibid., pp. 2, 55

[740] Ibid., pp. 2-4.

[741] Ibid., p.14.

[742] Sorely, A Better War, op.cit. p. 129.

[743] After Action Report KEYSTONE ORIOLE (BRAVO), op.cit., p. 5

[744] ANNEX M (After Action Report- 1st Bn 77th Armor) to 1st infantry Brigade, 5th Infantry Division (M) After Action Report KEYSTONE ORIOLE (BRAVO), July 20, 1971, op.cit., p. 112.

[745] Ibid., p. 113.

[746] Ibid., p. 113

[747] Ibid., p. 114.

[748] Keystone Oriole Alfa, Headquarters US Army Support Command, Da Nang, Office of the Commanding General, APO San Francisco 96349, 17 June 1971, p. 1, retrieved from National Archives and Records Administration (NARA), 8601 Adelphi Road, College Park MD 20740, December 19, 2019.

[749] Ibid., p 2.

[750] ANNEX M (After Action Report- 1st Bn 77th Armor), op.cit, p. 114.

[751] Ibid., 115.

Chapter 8

[752] Brigade Combat Team, Wikipedia, retrieved from en.m.wikipedia.org February 2.2023

[753] FM 3-96 Brigade Combat Team, Washington, DC, Headquarters, Department of the Army, 19 January 2021, pp 1-15 and 1-16, and 3rd Armored Brigade Combat Team, 1st Armored Division, retrieved from https://en.m.wikipedia.com February 2. 2023.

[754] WWII Points-Adjusted Service Rating Score (ASRS), WWII Dog Tags, World War II Notched Dog Tags, Retrieved from WWII Dogtags, WW2 Points - Adjusted Service Rating Score (ASRS) (wwiidogtags.com) January 10, 2023.

[755] Ibid.

[756] Operation Magic Carpet, Wikipedia, The Free Encyclopedia, retrieved from Operation Magic Carpet - Wikipedia January 11, 2023.

[757] Selective Service System, 1948 to 1969, Wikipedia retrieved from en.m.wikipedia.org 02.11.2023.

[758] Author visited Panmunjom and received this information during the US briefing by a member of the United Nations Command Security Battalion stationed in the Joint Security Area, during a tour in 1966.

[759] Henry Kissinger, Leadership: Six Studies in World Strategy, New York: Penguin Press, 2022, pp 132 and 141.

[760] Lieutenant Colonel James F Slaton, USAF, Intervention in Vietnam: President Eisenhower's Foreign Policy, Air War College ADA 328884, Air University: Maxwell Air Force Base, Alabama 1995, pp 33-34. , Retrieved https://www.airuniversity.af.edu/AWC> February 14, 2023

[761] U.S. Military Advisory Effort in Vietnam: Military Assistance Advisory Group, Vietnam, 1950-1964, Archives Unbound, retrieved from <http://gdc.gale.com/archivesunbound/ March 1, 2023.

[762] Paul D Harkins, Vietnam, retrieved from en.m.wikipedia, March 1, 2023

[763] Guy Holmes, email to author July 3, 2021.

[764] Kevin Dunne, Recollections, email to author July 28,2021

[765] Kevin Zak, Pillroller, In Memoriam, unpublished memoirs, 11-12.

[766] William Rosevear, Notes Written in Vietnam, 1968-1969, unpublished

Made in the USA
Las Vegas, NV
14 October 2024